The Moral of the Story

APPLICATIONS OF POLITICAL THEORY

Series Editors: Harvey Mansfield, Harvard University, and Daniel J. Mahoney, Assumption College

This series encourages analysis of the applications of political theory to various domains of thought and action. Such analysis will include works on political thought and literature, statesmanship, American political thought, and contemporary political theory. The editors also anticipate and welcome examinations of the place of religion in public life and commentary on classic works of political philosophy.

The Moral of the Story

Literature and Public Ethics

Edited by
Henry T. Edmondson III

LEXINGTON BOOKS
Lanham • Boulder • New York • Oxford

LEXINGTON BOOKS

Published in the United States of America
by Lexington Books
4720 Boston Way, Lanham, Maryland 20706

12 Hid's Copse Road
Cumnor Hill, Oxford OX2 9JJ, England

British Library Cataloguing in Publication Information Available

Library of Congress Cataloging-in-Publication Data

The Moral of the story : literature and public ethics / edited by Henry T. Edmondson III.
    p. cm. — (Applications of political theory)
    Includes bibliographical references and index.
    ISBN 0-7391-0148-X (alk. paper)—ISBN 0-7391-0149-8 (pbk. : alk. paper)
    1. Literature and morals. 2. Politics and literature. 3. Literature, Modern—History
and criticism. I. Edmondson, Henry T., 1955- II. Series.

PN49 .M66 2000
809'.93353—dc21   00-036225

Printed in the United States of America

⊖™ The paper used in this publication meets the minimum requirements of American
National Standard for Information Sciences—Permanence of Paper for Printed Library
Materials, ANSI/NISO Z39.48–1992.

To my father who taught me excellence
To my mother who taught me goodness
To my wife who taught me love
To my children who teach me life

Contents

Acknowledgments

Above all, I'm grateful to my wife, Dorothy Marie, my very own saint, for her infinite patience and goodness. I must acknowledge Miss Naomi Williams, my junior high school English teacher, and Gene Miller, at the University of Georgia, who, many years later in my doctoral program, picked up where she left off. I'm appreciative also of my chairman, Mike Digby. A better departmental chair can't be found. A special thanks to Sam Spangler for his proofreading; Amy Watson for her help with the index and copyright permissions; and, especially to Dave Steele, the businessman-would-be-professor who reads and writes better than some Ph.D.s I know.

Thanks to the good folks at Lexington Press, in particular Serena Leigh and Stephen Driver for their professional, friendly, and encouraging manner. Most of all, a sincere thank-you to all of those who have contributed to this volume; and, especially to Peter Lawler, Bob Schaefer, Greg Johnson, and Peter Kalkavage for their service above and beyond the call of duty in offering astute comments on my chapter and the introduction. A special nod goes to Peter Kalkavage for his help on Dante. For those who admire the title, I must (reluctantly) ascribe credit to Greg Johnson for the first half thereof.

Finally, I look with admiration to Flannery O'Connor, the witty, devout, and brilliant muse of letters whose memory and inspiration wafts through the camellias, azaleas, magnolias, pecans, and Corinthian columns of Georgia College & State University.

Milledgeville, Ga., January, 2000

Chapter 1

Introduction: Literature and Public Ethics

Henry T. Edmondson III

> There was a time when the average reader read a novel
> simply for the moral he could get out of it,
> and however naïve that may have been,
> it was a good deal less naïve
> than some of the more limited objectives he now has.
> —Flannery O'Connor

The *Moral of the Story* is written to aid the teacher, student, and interested layman in returning to a use of literature for the ethical principles good books illuminate and for the moral formation they provide. These original essays are compiled for those engaged in the habit of a lifetime of learning who seek to get the most from reading the "classics." Although recent decades have seen a rebirth of interest in moral philosophy—or ethics as it is usually called—contemporary approaches to the subject often neglect the time honored role of literary classics in making us better human beings. Modern approaches to ethics are sometimes detached from the everyday demand for persistently strong character, an instinctive sense of justice, and a reliable habit of practical wisdom. The liberal arts, advocates claim, not only make us more knowledgeable and intelligent, but better, since good books stretch the imagination and stir the emotions while informing the intellect. For this reason, those who teach, study and strive to live ethical lives, whether it be in the spheres of the public service, business, medicine, or the home, are rediscovering the usefulness of serious reading for moral and intellectual formation and for the encouragement and support of right living. The humanities teach us to use our leisure, enable "us to see ourselves in perspective, to become more enlightened citizens, and to think more deeply about important issues in our lives."[1]

Although this text is more concerned with public ethics than private, this emphasis does not proceed from a belief in a fictitious dichotomy between public and private morality. Many of the policy concerns found here reach far into private life, and most importantly, the attention given to personal integrity is equally applicable to—indeed inseparable from—private virtue.

Public Life and the "Whole Soul of Man"

Regarding his grandson's education, Thomas Jefferson wrote to his daughter, Martha, "It would be time lost for him to attend professors of ethics" because ethical conduct "may be as well acquired in the closet as from living lectures."[2] Jefferson wrote to his nephew Peter Carr that it "lost time to attend lectures" on moral philosophy. Our creator, Jefferson continues, would have been "a pitiful bungler" if moral conduct was an intellectual calculation, because the great proportion of the population has not the capacity or training for discursive reasoning.[3] After discouraging study in moral philosophy, he told his nephew to "read good books because they will encourage as well as direct your feelings."[4]

Jefferson's view is similar to the principles of moral development explained by Aristotle in his discussion of literary tragedies. Aristotle explains that when tragic stories are presented in artful form, the spectator experiences intense fear or pity at the demise of the protagonist. If the plot of the drama is constructed well, the cause of the protagonist's downfall is due to some character defect in an otherwise decent human being, rather than the consequence of an extraordinarily corrupt personality. This defect is ordinary enough that the spectator can personally identify with this degree of vice. For example, Oedipus's inordinate curiosity is a fault to which many might admit. The active identification of the spectator with the actor, compounded by the intense pity or fear he experiences while watching the play, will motivate the spectator to improve his own conduct.[5] Those in the audience participate in the presentation of the drama sufficiently to benefit personally from the moral lesson involved. From this discussion and others, Aristotle shows how moral formation is promoted by creative dramatic and musical presentations.[6] A more contemporary observer, J. Patrick Dobel, notes, "Art matters in education. Good art possesses the power to engage emotions, stretch moral imagination, and influence judgment."[7] Coleridge explains "The poet . . . brings the whole soul of man into activity."[8]

Aristotle had in mind the tragedies of Euripides including his portrayal of the tragically flawed leader, Agamemnon. With each successive turn of events, the pitiful weaknesses in Agamemnon's character are exposed. Although he is not a malicious person, he cannot overcome the moral weakness that renders him indecisive and confused when confronted with the demands of public command. Several opportunities pass by the passive king until the macabre denouement of the story. In a condemnation as relevant for leaders today as it was for those living in the fourth century, B.C., Menelaus tells Agamemnon, "One day you plan one thing, another day, another, / Tomorrow you will shift again."[9]

In an increasingly complex and cybernetic world, the metaphorical quality of literature is needed to discern a "kafkaesque" situation, resist a "faustian bargain," or avoid a "quixotic" scheme. As one observer explains, "Thinking metaphorically, in addition to thinking literally, may help us to become more aware of choices, to pay attention to the essence and potential of things rather than to be blinded and inhibited by the categories assigned to them. Metaphors may help us take inductive leaps toward more creative solutions to public policy problems."[10]

Government and public administration students will find that lodging, for a brief time, in Franz Kafka's *Castle*, is advantageous for two reasons: First, it will prepare them for the inexpugnable absurdity that they must face in the public service. Second, it will motivate them to reform what may be reformed, while helping them to recognize what may not.[11] Law students will find the courtroom experience of Kafka's *Trial* equally beneficial. The classic captures the "lunatic logic of the bureaucracy" characteristic of "our professions, litigations, visas, fiscalities." Bureaucracy, at its worst, can wound its citizens just as it "thrust the knife deep into [K.'s] heart and turned it there twice."[12]

Joseph Conrad's work is replete with insights for public life; and, following Coleridge's axiom, Conrad artfully presents them to the reader so as to involve the "whole" person. In the space of one page in *Lord Jim*, he dispenses advice in several different areas of public concern. For the busy (and frequently misguided) job of sex education or drug abuse prevention in public schools, he notes, "as long as there is any life before one, a jolly good fright now and then is a salutary discipline."[13] The criminologist or sentencing judge might take note of Conrad's remark, only a few lines away, "The real significance of crime is in its being a breach of faith with the community of mankind."[14]

Those involved in the fight against global terrorism, from the FBI to London's Scotland Yard to Interpol, would be better equipped for their work—they would be wiser and more imaginative—by reading and discussing Conrad's *The Secret Agent*. This perspicacious and visionary book offers not simply a psychological profile of the terrorist, but an equally important philosophical profile. Through the thought of Chief Inspector Heat, Conrad explains that the anarchist lives in an entirely different world from the more conventional criminal. The thief operates by dishonest but relatively mundane incentives, incentives that do not greatly differ from the desire for self-gain that the rest of us share. He simply conducts his business a few steps outside of approved boundaries. The terrorist, by contrast, is an entirely, almost unfathomable aberration. Conrad's terrorist Michaelis explains,

> "I have always dreamed," he mouthed fiercely, "of a band of men absolute in their resolve to discard all scruples in the choice of means, strong enough frankly to give themselves the name of destroyers. . . . No pity for anything on earth, including themselves, and death enlisted for good and all in the service of humanity—that's what I would have liked to see." [15]

In Conrad's powerful and moving *Nostromo* the author explodes the human pretentiousness that would dispatch life's mysteries and complexities by audaciously wielding political solutions. At one point in the story, when Charles Gould, the cold master of the San Tomé, mine is said to be "calmness personified . . . extremely sure of himself," the peculiar but perceptive Dr. Monygham wryly observes, "If that's all he is sure of, then he is sure of nothing. . . . It is the last thing a man ought to be sure of."[16] Yet Conrad does not endorse hopelessness—he condemns hubris. When the skeptic Decoud is stranded on the isle of

Great Isabel, alone with his stolen silver, the solitude exposes his philosophical emptiness and he cannot tolerate his "great unbroken solitude of waiting without faith." He finds he is not "fit to grapple" even with himself "singlehandedly" and his conditions expose his "state of soul in which the affections of irony and skepticism have no place."[17]

Those who (sometimes overzealously) craft regulatory policy might paste above their computer monitor Conrad's warning in *The Shadow-Line* that, "The atmosphere of officialdom would kill anything that breathes the air of human endeavour, would extinguish hope and fear alike in the supremacy of paper and ink." The book could then be passed along to all those in the growing industry of managing juvenile delinquency so that they might better understand "that twilight region between youth and maturity." Among the many lessons that the young captain learns in his first command, as he struggles to cross the "shadow-line" into adulthood, is "[a]ll roads are long that lead towards one's heart's desire."[18]

It is one thing to claim to have answers; it is more difficult to articulate vital questions. The medium of literature conveys concepts in such a way that the imagination, by its "synthetic and magical power"[19] plays a supportive role to the understanding; thus, the artist, as no other, is able to speak to the "sense of mystery surrounding our lives."[20] Conrad explains, "My task . . . is, by the power of the written word, to make you hear, to make you feel—it is, before all, to make you see." In so doing, Conrad hopes to impart "that glimpse of truth for which you have forgotten to ask."[21]

"Reality" and Consolation

A frequent emphasis in contemporary ethics is the imperative to acquaint students with the "real world." Although the world is understood by its imitation, it may be perceived better by its distortion. Goya's "Dark Period" paintings, most of which hang in Madrid's Prado Museum, record the nineteenth-century French invasion of Spain. Through his gloomy colors and his smeared and distorted figures with ghoulish expressions, he captured the physical, social, and psychological horror of that war far better than a photographer possibly could. Flannery O'Connor's distorted literary characters are a key to her mastery as a moral teacher. She notes, "Today many readers and critics have set up for the novel a kind of orthodoxy. They demand a realism of fact which may, in the end, limit rather than broaden the novel's scope."[22] She explains that "the realism of each novelist will depend on his view of the ultimate reaches of reality."[23]

> Such a writer will be interested in what we don't understand rather than in what we do. He will be interested in possibility rather than probability. He will be interested in characters who are forced out to meet evil and grace and who act on a trust beyond themselves—whether they know very clearly what it is they act upon or not.[24]

O'Connor asserts that "a literature which mirrors society would be no fit guide for it. . . . The novelist must be characterized not by his function but by his vision and we must remember that his vision has to be transmitted and that the limitations and blind spots of his audience will very definitely affect the way he is able to show what he sees."[25] Ironically, fiction may be "truer to reality" than other methods of moral formation,[26] just as Mark Twain's *Pudd'nhead Wilson* may have more to teach about the social psychology of racism than does the Equal Employment Opportunity Commission in Washington, D.C.[27]

Indeed, those who struggle with the messy business of life need something more than a mirror of the same to sustain them. Good books enjoy a noble reputation of providing comfort and consolation to those who struggle with moral complexity and the disillusionment of unfulfilled ideals. From the sixth to the seventeenth centuries the *Consolation of Philosophy*, by Ancius Manlius Severinus Boethius, was in the hands of almost every educated person. Boethius, born in 470 A.D., was a Roman, skilled in mathematics, linguistics, and public administration. He served under the rule of Theodoric, the Ostrogothic king, who later ruled the Roman Empire. In time, Boethius fell from favor and was unjustly accused of treason. He was incarcerated and found himself awaiting probable torture and execution. In such a state, he wrote his most famous work where he records that in the wretched despair of prison, he enjoyed the comfort of a visitor whose name was "Philosophy." Boethius recounts,

> While I was pondering thus in silence, and using my pen to set down so tearful a complaint, there appeared standing over my head a woman's form, whose countenance was full of majesty, whose eyes shone as with fire and in power of insight surpassed the eyes of men, whose colour was full of life, whose strength was yet intact though she was so full of years that none would every think that she was subject to such age as ours.[28]

Philosophical consolation may as easily come, not in the guise of Boethius' ethereal visitor, but in the form of a novel, play, or poem. A public leader who sees things as they should be but may not enjoy the support of like-minded colleagues experiences a kind of Churchillian or Lincoln-like loneliness. Although Abraham Lincoln did not spend much time reading fiction, he delighted in Shakespeare, sometimes memorizing long passages, especially in his early informal education under the guidance of William Scott's *Lessons in Elocution*. His favorite line from *Macbeth* was King Claudius' tardy lament over Hamlet's father, "O, my offence is rank, it smells to heaven." He owned and frequently read the Bard in Springfield, later enjoying the privilege of live performances after taking office in Washington. According to David Herbert Donald,

> In February and March 1864, at one of the most dangerous periods of the civil War, he took time off from his duties to see the great tragedian Edwin Booth perform in *Richard III, Julius Caesar, The Merchant of Venice*, and *Hamlet.* . . . The great tragedies, with their stories of linked ambition and guilt, especially appealed to him. He also seemed to have enjoyed *King Lear*. As an often lonely leader, he found it easy to identify with Shakespeare's heroes; he could sympathize with their fears and understand their anxieties.[29]

Stephen Oates reports that after Lincoln's wife Mary and the boys were asleep and "while waiting for sleep to come, he would read his worn copy of Shakespeare's tragedies, turning again and again to *Hamlet* and *Macbeth.*" He also found comfort in the poetry of Burns, Whittier, and Holmes. He would "recite half aloud those sad and pathetic stanzas he knew by heart and loved so well. 'Green be the graves where her martyrs are lying! Shroudless and tombless they sunk to their rest.'"[30]

Theodore Roosevelt, both when he left the presidency in 1908 in favor of Taft, and again when he pursued it once more in 1911, checked his motives by reference to Dante. On both occasions, he had to assure himself that he could not be identified with the Italian poet's *il gran refiuto*.[31] Roosevelt once wrote that Dante "illustrated fundamental truths . . . by examples drawn alike from human nature as he saw it around him and from human nature as he read of it."[32] After Roosevelt's second term of office, he departed for a "scientific" and hunting expedition to Africa. When he set sail in March 1909, his luggage included specially bound copies of the Bible, Shakespeare, Homer (in Greek), and "the novels of Cooper, Scott, Dickens, Thackeray, and Mark Twain." He also, took, in addition to Dante (in Italian), *Don Quixote*, Goethe's *Faust*, Milton's *Paradise Lost* and Lewis Carroll's *Alice in Wonderland*.[33] Apparently, Roosevelt found that *Alice in Wonderland* articulated realities of public life in an inimitable and gratifying way. Alice's bewilderment in Wonderland appeals to the sensible person confronted with the absurdity of the public world, especially a world made illogical and irrational by those who abuse language. A better metaphor for politics—whether totalitarian or democratic—has never been written. In *Through the Looking-Glass*, the hapless Alice confronts the misuse of language as a means of grasping and maintaining power. The association between linguistic abuse and political power is made explicit in Alice's conversation with Humpty Dumpty who reveals,

> "When *I* use a word," Humpty Dumpty said, in rather a scornful tone, "it means just what I choose it to mean—neither more nor less."
> "The question is," said Alice, "whether you *can* make words mean so many different things."
> "The question is," said Humpty Dumpty, "which is to be master—that's all."[34]

Literature is relevant to public life, not because it endorses one position over another; but because it offers a plumb line by which imperfectly conceived political doctrines are measured. It helps us to distinguish the conventional but defective application of important ideas from those true ideas themselves—such as justice, loyalty, equality, and dignity, and as with Alice, truth and sincerity. Coleridge explains, "No man was ever yet a great poet, without being at the same time a profound philosopher."[35] Literature, like philosophy, reminds us that in public life, while the meritorious are ignored, the undeserving are rewarded. C.S. Forester's WWI General, because of his lack of military imagination and strategic creativity, led thousands of British soldiers to their death in France. After the disastrous defeat, an injured General Curzon was carried by lorry and "when they reached the hospital he was crying out loud, a mere shattered fragment of a man despite his crossed sword and baton and crown, and his red tabs and his silly sword."[36] This most maddening of all public injustices, the inappropriate bestowal of high office and benefits, is addressed by Conrad in the short story "Typhoon." Captain MacWhirr tries to substitute with books the vacuum that should have been filled with the instinctive practical wisdom of leadership. By sheer luck, his ship survives the South China Sea hurricane, but young Mr. Jukes, the chief mate, accurately assesses the ship's leader when he notes, "'I think that he got out of it very well for such a stupid man.'"[37]

The Text

Each of the following seventeen original essays is based upon a notable work of literature, or in a few cases, several works by the same author. They include poetry, short stories, drama, and novels. The literature in this collection represents seven hundred years of thought-provoking writing, from the thirteenth century to the twentieth. The nationalities represented are American, English, Italian, Spanish, Nigerian, French, and Russian. Each chapter is written in a "narrative" style, in which the author of the chapter follows the text of the literature under consideration in order to best illuminate its meaning and elucidate the philosophy that it conveys. In this way, the reader can obtain a sense of the classic work itself, although of course, the full appreciation of any story is accessible only by a careful, if guided, reading of the text. The epigraph under each chapter title, usually taken from the text of the book, play, or poetry itself, represents the thesis of the chapter or at least highlights an idea germane to the study.

Although the range of the text is wide and its contents diverse, several important themes recur throughout these chapters. One of these is the importance of self-knowledge, both for the leader and the citizen, for the king and the commoner. Self-knowledge, as several authors explain it, is both a disposition and an activity that leads to moral improvement. Another theme is that of moral and intellectual virtue as the definition of the ethical person. Intellectual virtue, such as wisdom and prudence, enables one to recognize and apply important principles; moral virtue supplies the habits of fortitude and self-control, for example, to conduct one's personal affairs according to what is just and true.

The chief intellectual virtue, prudence, points to another salient theme in these chapters. This theme has to do with the limits of democratic governance. Several of these writers recognize not only the benefits, but also the dangers and inadequacies of the modern democratic regime. As Alan Levine demonstrates in chapter seven, the Nigerian novelist Chinua Achebe teaches that although the idealist demands immediate change, the more prudent realist recognizes that the world must be taken at "its own pace." Although democracy brings its own particular hazards, democratic government is not immune from those universal and timeless foibles of human nature, even though a democracy is preferable to tyranny and certainly more possible than a benevolent monarchy. These essays teach that living together requires different virtues of those who lead and those who are led. All citizens should cultivate the diligence, tenacity, toughness, and self-control necessary for a good life. Outstanding individuals, on the other hand, are recognized by their magnanimity or "greatness of soul." Magnanimity grants one the depth and vision to accomplish great things while furnishing the capacity to suffer those tribulations particular to leadership.

Following this introduction, James Seaton, in chapter two, uses Henry James' novel, *The Princess Casamassima*, to show that those who are inflamed by revolutionary ideals and drawn to the opportunity for radical change cannot escape the influence and limitations of their personal—and sometimes petty— motives. This chapter explores James' wisdom regarding the limits of equality and the importance of preserving existing culture, especially when there is nothing with which to replace it. As Seaton explains, this novel also demonstrates the wide spectrum of philosophical profiles drawn to anarchy or revolution, profiles that range from sincere idealism to stark nihilism. In this sense, *The Princess Casamassima* is reminiscent of Dostoevsky's *The Brothers Karamazov* and Joseph Conrad's *Under Western Eyes* and *The Secret Agent*.

Peter Kalkavage's essay on Dante in chapter three demonstrates how easily we ignore and escape personal responsibility for the consequences of our passion. He uses Francesca's rationalization of her adultery to demonstrate that private passion has unavoidable public consequences. Although, as Kalkavage explains, Francesca's and Paolo's transgression begins with their erotic obsession, their misappropriation of romantic love must not obscure Dante's teaching on love's power to ennoble our lives and to transform us into something better.

Peter Lawler, in chapter four, employs the late Walker Percy as a foil against the late Carl Sagan by exposing the pretensions of Sagan's self-made philosophical world, a world constructed out of a defective understanding of human nature and a deficiency of self-knowledge. Such pretensions are quite germane to public policy given that renowned scientists like Sagan carry great influence in American and international science policy. At the time of this writing, policy on space exploration and development is badly in need of a clear view of the universe that can only come through the lens of sound philosophy.

The essay on Shakespeare's *Henry V* in chapter five builds upon the traditional interpretation of Shakespeare's portrait of statesmanship by emphasizing Henry's aptitude for self-examination as a means to moral leadership. The essay then draws implications for contemporary leaders who wish to imitate Henry's example. Shakespeare's king teaches that an ethical "examination of conscience" must take advantage of life's solemn moments; and, such ethical introspection must ultimately rest on an attitude of piety whereby the leader recognizes that he is ultimately responsible to something or someone for his moral choices. The leader who successfully examines his own soul is likely to be more persuasive if not inspiring in his public rhetoric.

Pádraig Ó Gormaile's chapter six speaks to this same theme of self-knowledge by combining a French novelist and a French philosopher: Ó Gormaile illuminates François Rabelais' fiction with Blaise Pascal's *Les Pensées* to argue that leaders must recognize their moral inadequacy through quiet reflection. If they do not, they are prone to engage in all sorts of (sometimes dangerous) frivolity as a distraction from their spiritual poverty.

In chapter seven, Alan Levine, in a thorough review of Chinua Achebe's first two novels *Things Fall Apart* and *No Longer at Ease*, extracts Achebe's teaching on the gradual nature of social change and the illusions of ungrounded idealism. Achebe, a Nigerian, explains through his writing that the culture, history, political structure—and human beings—of a country render it impervious to simplistic manipulation and reform. Achebe—and Levine—should be required reading, not only for those intervening to reform the troubled African continent, but also for those attempting to create stability and restoration out of the chaos and wreckage of former Soviet-bloc countries.

Juan José Sendín Vinagre, in chapter eight, takes one of Cervantes' delightful short stories, *Rinconete and Cortadillo*, and illuminates Cervantes' incisive insight into human nature as the sixteenth century Spanish literary genius displayed it in a witty story about juvenile delinquents. Cervantes teaches that those who appear to pursue unfettered liberty may actually be seeking accountability, a sense of community, and the fulfillment of an intrinsic longing for adventure. In this chapter, Sendín also provides a helpful overview of Cervantes' *Exemplary Stories*, the collection in which *Rinconete and Cortadillo* appears. In so doing, he offers a summary of the political and literary milieu in which Cervantes wrote, whose charming tales often give the reader a "peek" at the colorful life of Cervantes himself.

Gregory R. Johnson, in chapter nine, reviews several of Jane Austen's classics to elucidate the important quality of magnanimity or "greatness of soul." He convincingly shows that this quality is a salient virtue of several of Austen's characters; he further suggests that Austen herself possessed this most important trait. By using Aristotle to explain the concept of magnanimity and Austen, writing over two millennia later, to illustrate it, Johnson demonstrates the timeless relevance of this trait of excellence and character.

Pyotr Stolypin, a forgotten statesman of the Russian Revolution, is the focus of Daniel J. Mahoney's chapter ten on Aleksandr Solzhenitsyn's historical novel about the Russian Revolution, *August 1914*. The chapter is an important study in Stolypin's "prudent statesmanship." Had Stolypin survived, modern history might be fundamentally different; unfortunately, he became a tragic martyr of the Marxist revolution. His memory survives, however, as a model of the statesmanlike wisdom that leaders must possess to guide a nation during a crisis.

J. Patrick Dobel, in chapter eleven, uses Dostoevsky's story of "The Grand Inquisitor" to demonstrate in a fascinating and imaginative way how all those with the responsibility to lead are tempted to misuse the resources by which they must govern. This abuse of power occurs when leaders, in the interest of governing more efficiently, grow impatient with their obligation to respect the freedom and dignity of those they lead. Dostoevsky teaches that the temptation to abuse is inescapable and leaders of good will must adapt to the tension inherent in this paradox of rule. Dobel explains that the Grand Inquisitor's concepts of "miracle, mystery, and authority" are the three temptations that Christ suffered from the Devil in the desert. These temptations to abuse one's advantage as a leader are the very tools that leaders of modern industrialized nations must wield—but not abuse—in democratic governance.

Paul Peterson's discussion in chapter twelve of Sinclair Lewis' *It Can't Happen Here* also addresses the theme of tyranny. In this case, the protagonist is the petty Shad Lerue who, given a measure of unmerited power, wields it in an opportunity to vent his resentment over his previously low—but appropriate—social status. Peterson concludes by harmonizing the insight of writers as diverse as Aristotle and C.S. Lewis to elucidate the timeless propensity for people to resent excellence in others when they themselves do not possess it.

Joseph Conrad's important short story, "The Secret Sharer," is explained by Michael Platt in chapter thirteen. Platt's essay is about the young captain of a ship faced with a dilemma in which doing what is ordinarily right would produce a solution fundamentally unjust. This chapter deals with the very important and intriguing issue of a conflict between an otherwise competent code of maritime justice that inadvertently conflicts with the more fundamental principles of natural law. After reading the story for himself, the reader will find that Platt adopts a pleasant "storytelling" style in this chapter as he uses Conrad to explain the interplay—and conflict—between the concepts of "natural right" and "conventional right."

James Seaton returns in chapter fourteen to explain how Willa Cather in *O Pioneers!* is the quiet muse of imperfect but noble middle-class morals—the fortitude, resilience, and contentment exemplified by turn-of-the-century mid-Western life. As Seaton points out, Cather's novel is no morality tale: instead, it is a poignant recital of the chronicle of flawed people who succeed, fail, and encounter tragedy in their pursuit of a decent life.

In chapter fifteen, Judith Lee Kissell explicates Robert Penn Warren's prize-winning *Brother to Dragons*, and by means of her explication, offers a different kind of commentary on our common ethic. She uses Warren to discuss the important concept of "complicity" and to ask whether rugged individualism has been purchased at the price of social responsibility and community. Warren's poem is a dramatic account of Thomas Jefferson's hypothetical response to a tragic historical event in his family that shakes the philosophical foundation of his Enlightment ideals. As Kissell suggests, Warren, by means of his artfully presented conception of complicity, throws down a challenge to conventional opinions about public policy issues, ranging from social welfare reform to international humanitarian intervention.

In one more perspective on civic virtue in chapter sixteen, Will Morrisey uses Jean Dutourd's novel, *The Springtime of Life*, to explain the generic "manliness" required of any citizenry if they are to perpetuate their life together. *The Springtime of Life* is, like Cervantes' *Don Quixote*, a book about books: it demonstrates the way in which literature both reflects and influences national character. Morrisey concludes by echoing Johnson's discussion in chapter nine in a concise teaching on magnanimity and leadership. The eighteenth-century conception of "manliness," as likely found in women as men, refers to the tough, courageous and tenacious adherence to essential personal and civic principles.

Robert M. Schaefer, in chapter seventeen, employs the American novelist Mark Twain to offer a teaching on statesmanship. Schaefer explains how Twain's *A Connecticut Yankee in King Arthur's Court* teaches that "Yankee" ingenuity, representing the Western faith in unlimited progress, must be tempered by an appreciation for the persistence of religion, codes of behavior and prejudice. When customs and institutions have provided a people with personal meaning and social stability, such forces may prove impossible to dislodge despite the promise of general betterment. Schaefer demonstrates that Twain, in this ambitious novel, is not only a humorist and novelist, but also a political philosopher.

Finally, in chapter eighteen, Gregory R. Johnson writes again, this time on Flannery O'Connor's inspiring short story, "Revelation." Johnson uses O'Connor's writing to address the conflict in the modern world between pagan and Christian ethics. This essay speaks to every Christian charged to be "in the world but not of it" and offers a middle ground for public activity between self-limiting religious extremism and equally intolerant soulless secular materialism. Although O'Connor, often in irritation, rebuked laymen and academics alike who spun arcane interpretations of her symbolism, she undoubtedly would have approved of Johnson's keen insight.

The Moral of the Story is compiled for all those who feel that the wealth of literature has been strip-mined by revisionists, deconstructionists, or anyone else who is unwilling or incapable of submitting themselves to the authority of great thinkers and writers. In pursuing a praiseworthy life, it is wise to avoid innovations in ethical theory that treat traditional philosophy and literature with disdain. It is better to imitate the attitude of the French essayist Montaigne who confessed, "I welcome truth . . . in whoseoever hand I find it; I surrender to it cheerfully, welcoming it with my vanquished arms as soon as I see it approaching from afar."[38] For all those wishing to do so, this volume is written to assist in "the moral discovery which should be the object of every tale."[39] Such an approach to moral improvement admittedly requires imagination, creativity, and energy. But, as the Chorus in *Iphigenia* observes, "Oh, a mighty quest is the hunting out of virtue."[40]

Notes

1. John M. Ellis, *Literature Lost: Social Agendas and the Corruption of the Humanities* (New Haven: Yale University Press, 1997), 3.

2. Roy J. Honeywell, *The Educational Views of Thomas Jefferson* (Cambridge: Harvard University Press, 1931), 125

3. Letter to Peter Carr, Paris, August 10, 1787.

4. Letter to Peter Carr, Paris, August 10, 1787.

5. Aristotle, *The Poetics*, James Hutton, trans. (New York: W.W. Norton & Company, 1982), 1452b12-1454b,18. The title of Aristotle's work is derived from the Greek verb, *poéo*, meaning "to do" or "to make"; hence, the description "poet" is often used as a general term for all those in the fine and liberal arts. The term "artist" also often carries the same general meaning. The reader will find such to be the case in *The Moral of the Story*.

6. For example, in the *Politics* Aristotle provides a discussion of moral character and music that runs parallel to this explication of dramatic presentations. *The Politics*, Carnes Lord, trans. (Chicago: The University of Chicago Press, 1984), 1339all-1342b33.

7. Patrick Dobel, "The Moral Realities of Public Life: Some Insights of Fiction," *American Review of Public Administration*, 22 (June 1992): 127.

8. *The Collected Works of Samuel Taylor Coleridge, Biographia Literaria, Vol. II*, Kathleen Coburn, ed. (London: Princeton University Press, 1983), 14, 15.

9. There are several useful translations, among which is the one used here: *Iphigenia in Aulis*, Charles R. Walker, trans. in *The Complete Greek Tragedies: Volume VII*, David Greene and Richard Lattimore, eds. (New York: A Mentor Book, 1958), 128. Because Euripides' play was meant for live performance, simply reading the text is not sufficient for the full impact of the story. English subtitles notwithstanding, Michael Cacoyannis' 1977 adaptation of Euripides tragedy is an artistic and powerful screenplay. Viewing this videocassette is an emotional experience, perhaps similar to that which the Greeks would have experienced several millennia ago. In one memorable scene, Iphigenia, on her knees, pleads with her father for her life. Terrifying, also, is the Greek army that, upon learning of the prophet's oracle, demands as with one voice the sacrifice of the general's daughter.

10. Fred A. Kramer, "Using the Classics to Expand Public Administrative Thought: An Exhortatory Note," *American Review of Public Administration* 2 (December 1992): 301-306.

11. Franz Kafka, *The Castle* (New York: The Modern Library, 1969); *The Trial* (New York: The Modern Library, 1974).

12. Franz Kafka, *The Trial* (New York: Schocken Books, 1937), vii, 229. The most clever essay submitted to me on this book was written by graduate student Capt. Ron Heath, who was then the Reactor Officer of the U.S.S. *Carl Vinson*. His paper cleverly imitated Kafka's strange style: "H. approached this assignment as he had any other." Not all students, though, appreciate this approach. Another student of differing caliber concluded his review in exasperation: "I would not recommend this book to any of my friends. It is for classroom use, and classroom use only."

13. Joseph Conrad, *Lord Jim*, Cedric Watts and Robert Hampson, eds. (London: Penguin Books, 1986), 158.

14. Conrad, *Lord Jim*, 158.

15. Joseph Conrad, *The Secret Agent: A Simple Tale* (New York: Penguin Books, 1983), 50.

16. Joseph Conrad, *Nostromo* (New York: Penguin Books, 1990), 269.

17. Conrad, *Nostromo*, 413.

18. Joseph Conrad, *The Shadow-Line* (Oxford: Oxford University Press, 1985), 26, 29, 44.

19. *The Collected Works of Samuel Taylor Coleridge, Biographia Literaria, Vol. II*, 16.

20. Joseph Conrad, "Preface," in *The Nigger of the "Narcissus,"* Robert Kimbrough, ed. (New York: W.W. Norton & Company, 1979), 146.

21. Conrad, "Preface," 147.

22. Flannery O'Connor, "Some Aspects of the Grotesque in Southern Fiction," in *Flannery O'Connor: Collected Works* (New York: The Library of America, 1988), 814.

23. O'Connor, "Some Aspects of the Grotesque," 815.

24. O'Connor, "Some Aspects of the Grotesque," 816.

25. O'Connor, "Some Aspects of the Grotesque," 819.

26. Dobel, "Moral Realities," 128.

27. Mark Twain, *The Tragedy of Pudd'nhead Wilson and those Extraordinary Twins* (Ware, Hertfordshire: Wordsworth American Library, 1996).

28. Boethius, *The Consolation of Philosophy*, W.V. Cooper, trans. (London: J. M. Dent and Company, 1902), 2. *http://ccat.sas.upenn.edu/jod/boethius/boetrans.html.*

29. David Herbert Donald, *Lincoln* (New York: Touchstone, 1995), 569.

30. Stephen B. Oates, *With Malice Toward None.* (New York: Harper and Row, 1977), 269.

31. H.W. Brands, *T.R.: The Last Romantic* (New York: Basic Books, 1997), 628, 705. "Il gran refiuto" is found at *Inferno 3, line 60* and is translated by Sinclair as "the great refusal." The reference is to Pope Celestine V, who became pope at the age of eighty and abdicated five months later in favor of the evil Boniface VIII who had manipulated him into the decision. Dante relegates Celestine to share eternity with the "Neutrals," among whom are included the angels who, in the Rebellion, were neither for God nor for Satan but were "for themselves." (*The Divine Comedy*, translated, with a commentary, by Charles S. Singleton, Bollingen Series LXXX, [Princeton: Princeton University Press, 1970-76], *Inferno* 3.60, pp. 47 ff.)

32. "Dante and the Bovery," in *Theodore Roosevelt: An American Mind, Selected Writings*, Mario R. DiNunzio, ed. (New York: Penguin Books, 1994), 351.

33. *TR, The Story of Theodore Roosevelt*, prod. and dir. David Grubin, 240 min., David Grubin Productions, Inc., 1996, videocassette. Joseph L. Gardner, *Departing Glory: Theodore Roosevelt as ex-President* (New York: Charles Scribner's Sons, 1973), 112. "'In consequence,' he later wrote, 'the books were stained with blood, sweat, gun-oil, dust, and ashes'" (112).

34. Lewis Carroll, *Alice in Wonderland*, 2nd edition. Authoritative texts *of Alice's Adventures in Wonderland, Through the Looking-Glass, The Hunting of the Snark.* Donald J. Gray, ed. (New York & London: W.W. Norton & Company, 1992), 163.

35. *The Collected Works of Samuel Taylor Coleridge, Biographia Literaria, Vol. II*, 25-6.

36. C.S. Forester, *The General* (Baltimore, Md.: The Nautical & Aviation Publishing Company of America, 1982, c. 1936, 1947), 263. This is Forester's scathing critique of British military leadership in WWI. Forester reports in the foreword to the 1947 edition that the book was being read "in the very highest circles. . . . The *Fürher* himself had read it and was recommending it to his friends; among the Christmas presents which he gave away in 1938 were several specially bound copies"(xi).

37. Joseph Conrad, "Typhoon," in *Typhoon and Other Tales* (Oxford: Oxford University Press, 1998), 102.

38. Michel de Montaigne, "On the Art of Conversation," in *The Complete Essays*, M.A. Screech, trans. (London: Penguin Books, 1987), 1047.

39. Joseph Conrad, *Under Western Eyes*, (London: Penguin Books, 1996), 49.

40. Euripides, *Iphigenia in Aulis* in *The Complete Greek Tragedies: Volume VII.* David Grene and Richard Lattimore, eds. (New York: The Modern Library, 1958), 139.

Chapter 2

Henry James' *The Princess Casamassima*: Revolution and the Preservation of Culture

James Seaton

> *"The old ferocious selfishnesses must come down.*
> *They won't come down gracefully, so they must be smashed."*
> —The Princess Casamassima

The Value of Literature

The belief that literature can be a source of insight about human affairs goes back at least to Aristotle's declaration in his *Poetics* that "poetry is something more philosophical and more worthy of serious attention than history; for while poetry is concerned with universal truths, history treats of particular facts." The universal truths Aristotle has in mind are not truths about the natural world but rather insights into "the kinds of thing a certain type of person will probably or necessarily say or do in a given situation."[1] In *The Princess Casamassima* Henry James fulfills Aristotle's claim by dramatizing the sort of responses that certain kinds of people are likely to make when confronted with the inequities of modern society. James goes further than Aristotle's formulation anticipates by offering an implicit judgment about at least one possible response. The political question posed by *The Princess Casamassima* is whether a revolution committed to "a thorough-going system of equality" but likely to destroy the art and high culture nurtured and preserved by civilization would benefit humanity.[2] James' response is "no," but much of the authority of the novel derives from the reader's sense that this answer is not offered without acknowledging much that points in a contrary direction.

In *The Liberal Imagination* Lionel Trilling credited *The Princess Casamassima* with both "a brilliantly precise representation of social actuality" and with something even more important, a "moral realism" that, Trilling argued, "yields a kind of social and political knowledge which is hard to come by."[3] Recently, however, deconstructionists like Paul de Man have rejected the notion that literature "is a reliable source of information about anything but its own language,"[4] while criticism informed by one or another of the currents of postmodernist cultural studies often seems willing to grant political or social significance to the novel only in order to demonstrate the extent to which the awareness of the critic surpasses that of the novelist. Mark Seltzer, for example, believes that the political significance of *The Princess Casamassima* resides in a parallel that James himself refused to see between "the techniques of the novel and the social technologies of power."[5] *The Princess Casamassima* tells him nothing new but simply confirms what he already has learned from Foucault: power relations are fundamental, and all other ties are epiphenomena. Mike Fischer emphasizes "[t]he text's marked inability to resolve the tensions implicit in the questions about power and authority that it raises." The "true lesson" of the novel, in his view, owes nothing to any special insight of James but is, according to Fischer "the lesson of every reading and writing . . . that no book can be permanently bound."[6] Eileen Sypher sees *The Princess Casamassima* as little more than a failed "attempt to contain the disruptive forces of anarchism and sexuality."[7] Wendy Graham asserts that the novel's ostensible emphasis on political issues is merely "a screen for the underlying theme of sexual subversion."[8] For her, *The Princess Casamassima* is little more than "an elaborate sexual fantasy."[9] It will serve as "an excellent text for contemporary gay and gender studies" because it exemplifies "the convergence of late nineteenth-century discourses on sexuality, race, and class."[10] Graham seems to intend a kind of praise when she writes that Henry James' portrait of Hyacinth Robinson "succeeds in . . . rendering the abject homosexual as a kind of nineteenth-century poster-child for same sex love,"[11] but it is difficult to imagine James taking any comfort in such approval.

Henry James himself felt the need to respond to those in his own time who wanted the novelist to "renounce the pretension of attempting really to represent life." This James understandably refused to do, since he believed that "the only reason for the existence of a novel is that it does attempt to represent life."[12] In writing *The Princess Casamassima* James audaciously claimed the ability to write about aspects of life and types of individuals with which he had no first-hand acquaintance. Recognizing that his knowledge of "revolutionary politics of a hole-and-corner sort" might be challenged, James admitted that his direct experience of such matters was slight but added that the novelistic imagination has the capacity to extrapolate greatly from a small store of factual knowledge:

> [I]f you haven't, for fiction, the root of the matter in you, haven't the sense of life and the penetrating imagination, you are a fool in the very presence of the revealed and assured; but that if you *are* so armed you are not really helpless, not without your resource, even before mysteries abysmal.[13]

Taking James at his word, one must consider the possibility that novels like *The Princess Casamassima* may indeed have something to tell us about politics and human life and especially about the dilemma that occurs when one attempts to balance the claims of art and high culture against the demand for human equality.

Revolutionary Aspirations

The Princess Casamassima accepts as a given the main charge of the revolutionaries. Although their ideology is vague, they seem to share a set of beliefs that might be summarized as follows: the wealth of the rich is based on the misery of the poor. The wealthy are engaged in a conspiracy to keep the good things of the world for themselves and to prevent the poor from getting them. The rich, therefore, are one and all morally responsible for the suffering of the poor. No punishment, therefore, could be more than the rich deserve. And in the world of *The Princess Casamassima* such views seem plausible enough. Society seems to be divided between a few rich and many poor and likely to stay that way in the absence of a revolution.

Nobody in the novel makes an intelligent case for existing society. The available arguments are ignored: no one argues that capitalism will prove in the end to be beneficial to the many as well as to the few; nobody suggests that industrial and technological developments are raising living standards for all; no defender of either liberalism or democracy makes the case that nineteenth-century England had made great advances toward both and was likely to continue doing so. The explicit affirmations of the goodness of the existing society offered in the novel are unpersuasive on their face. The strongest declaration of the rightness of things as they are is Captain Godfrey Sholto's admission to Hyacinth that

> I believe those that are on top of the heap are better than those that are under it, that they mean to stay here, and that if they are not a pack of poltroons they will. (345)

The Captain's affirmation is, however, undermined by his own shallowness, convincingly noted by both Madame Grandoni and the Princess. Prince Casamassima's belief that "It is the will of God" that "there is misery everywhere" is vitiated by the novelist's unwillingness to grant the notion of "God" any imaginative vitality; the Prince's statement that "the true faith" at least "helps suffering to be borne" may be true enough—he confides that it has been "a support" to him personally, and the reader is given no reason to doubt the Prince on this point (512)—but in this novel, where religious belief does not appear as an active force in anybody's life, it seems irrelevant to the main question.

If the reader of *The Princess Casamassima* nevertheless concludes the novel with little enthusiasm for a revolution that would institute the new regime of equality, it is in part because James' presentation of the revolutionaries themselves—especially Eustace Poupin, the Princess Casamassima, and Paul Muniment—brings out not only their good faith and sincerity but also the insurmountable limitations of their vision. Those limitations are brought home by the reflections of Anastasius Vetch, a friend and mentor of the protagonist Hyacinth Robinson and a character whose decency and good judgment is amply demonstrated throughout the novel. As Mr. Vetch moves from his earlier radicalism to a final rejection of all revolutionary schemes, the reader is induced to share his skepticism, especially because it is clear that Mr. Vetch's ideas are not tainted by the prejudices for or against the aristocracy or the "people" that affect so many of the other characters. The judgment of the

novel is finally conveyed, most eloquently and convincingly, through the medita-
tions of its protagonist, Hyacinth Robinson, whose move from enthusiastic commitment to eventual disillusion with the revolutionary cause is presented as a
journey from naivete to wisdom. James convinces us that Hyacinth's change of
views proceeds not from any diminished feeling for the poor but rather from the
larger, fuller view of the world and human life that he attains after his trip through
Europe, to Paris and Venice.[14]

The revolution that is the central political theme of *The Princess Casamassima*
is described by Eustace Poupin, the erstwhile Communard, as "the revindication,
the rehabilitation, the rectification." Its coming is for him "the day of justice," the
time of "the reintegration of the despoiled and disinherited" (122). What the
"rectification" will involve is never explained in detail, but its enthusiasts assume
that it will both punish the oppressors and institute a new regime of absolute
equality. Hyacinth Robinson believes that its success will result in "a thorough-
going system of equality" (282), but even in his early enthusiasm he cannot help but
worry that individuals like his friend Mr. Vetch might be attacked on the "day of the
great revenge" (124). It is none too clear, despite his poverty, that Anastasius Vetch
is a member of "the people,"—the mass of the downtrodden and oppressed—and
as Poupin has explained to Hyacinth, "in the day of the great revenge it would only
be the people who should be saved." (124) Anastasius Vetch's description of
Poupin toward the end of the novel is convincing:

> He's a very old friend of mine, and he's an honest man, considering everything.
> But he is always conspiring, and corresponding, and pulling strings that make a
> tinkle which he takes for the death-knell of society. He has nothing in life to com-
> plain of, and he drives a roaring trade. But he wants folks to be equal, heaven help
> him . . . He isn't serious, though he thinks that he's the only human being who
> never trifles; and his machinations, which I believe are for the most part very in-
> nocent, are a matter of habit and tradition with him. (467)

James' portrait of Eustace Poupin and his unmarried spouse demonstrates convincingly that individuals who themselves are not bloodthirsty may take great
delight in bloodthirsty slogans—and in doing so encourage others to commit violent
acts that they themselves would never carry out.

The Princess Casamassima repeatedly characterizes the wealthy as moral monsters. The upper classes, she informs Hyacinth early in their acquaintance, are
characterized by "selfishness," "corruption," "iniquity," "cruelty," and "imbecility"
(250). The present English aristocracy reminds her of the "old regime" before the
French Revolution; the former is dominated by "rottenness and extravagance" and
is "bristling with every iniquity and every abuse" found in the latter. Or perhaps, she
reflects, the contemporary upper class more closely resembles "Roman society in
its decadence," when it was "gouty, apoplectic, depraved, gorged and clogged with
wealth and spoils" (312-3). Late in the novel, knowing that Hyacinth no longer
shares her zeal, she tells him "the old ferocious selfishnesses *must* come down. They
won't come down gracefully, so they must be smashed" (574)! The Princess is no
strategist, but her language seems to justify in advance any violence of the revolu-

tionaries against the wealthy. Since those in power refuse to change their ways, the bloodshed of the revolution will be their "responsibility," it will be "on *their* head" (574).

Perhaps Hyacinth gives the former Christina Light too much credit when he tells Millicent Henning that the Princess is motivated by "the great question of material misery; she wants to do something to make that misery less" (530). It is Lady Aurora for whom the alleviation of suffering seems to be truly important. When the Princess tells Lady Aurora that she is "one of those who believe that a great social cataclysm is destined to take place, and that it can't make things worse than they are already" (432-3), her language suggests that her primary interest is in the "cataclysm" itself and only secondarily in whatever social good might come of it. Although the Princess takes it upon herself to give away money to the poor, Hyacinth is aware that this sort of charity, so at odds with the "principles of economical science" that the Princess professes to understand, is "after all, more addressed to relieving herself than to relieving others" (476). When the Princess tells Lady Aurora that she has gotten rid of her "tapestry and old china" as a tribute to those "thousands and tens of thousands" who "haven't bread to put in their mouths" (412), she seems motivated more by the desire to strike a pose than humanitarian sympathy, and not merely because, as Hyacinth notices that "though the lady in question could dispense with old china and tapestry, she could not dispense with a pair of immaculate gloves, which fitted her like a charm" (412-3). Later the same day, when Hyacinth asks the Princess what the revolution will do about "an embarrassing type" like the "big, hard red woman" behind the bar they are visiting, no humanitarian scruples prevent her from replying in an "off-hand" way, "Oh, drown her in a barrel of beer" (419)! The revolution seems important to the Princess largely because of its promised destruction of the traditions and perhaps the people that have left her feeling "humiliated, outraged, tortured" (250); its putative reduction of poverty fails to excite her imagination.

Paul Muniment, unlike the Princess and unlike the other revolutionaries, seems to have given a good deal of thought to the sort of society that is to emerge after the great rectification. Having heard that Hoffendahl has spent "twelve years in a Prussian prison," a fellow radical, a shoemaker, asserts that "the main part of the job" is "to smash that sort of shop altogether" (287). This sentiment is in keeping with the sort of radical anarchism embraced by many of those who have turned to assassination as a political device, and thus it is understandable that the shoemaker expects the other would-be conspirators to agree. And indeed Schinkel does agree, adding only that Hoffendahl's term in prison will prove useful, since "They will smash best, those who have been inside" (287). Muniment, however, thinks otherwise. He is apparently no anarchist, since he expects the rectification to mean not the end of the sort of coercive state power exemplified in prisons but rather its expansion:

"Ah, no; no smashing, no smashing," Muniment went on. "We want to keep them standing, and even to build a few more; but the difference will be that we shall put the correct sort in." (288)

The regime that Paul Muniment anticipates will not only imprison more people, it will execute many more. Muniment does not hope for the abolition of capital punishment—a goal of many reformers and radicals—but instead looks forward to "extending it much further" (206). While in the society before the rectification "those who habitually lied or got drunk" typically suffer no legal penalty at all, in the society Muniment envisions they will be executed (206). Muniment apparently desires a society in which refractory human material will be disciplined into obedience, a government in which equality will mean the subjection of the many to a powerful few. There will be no more rich and poor, but only rulers and ruled. Although Muniment does not often betray the depth of his feelings, his warning to the Princess about the absoluteness of the rectifiers' commitment reveals the religious intensity of his own dedication: "But you ought to remember that, in the line you have chosen, our affections, our natural ties, our timidities, our shrinkings . . . All those things are as nothing, and must never weigh a feather beside our service" (503). Muniment seems to be contemptuous of ordinary human nature; he warns the Princess that those seeking revolution must be able to set aside their own human feelings. He is working with single-minded devotion toward the goal of a society in which the weaknesses endemic to human beings are regulated, controlled and finally extirpated. If human beings themselves must be extirpated as well, that does not deter him.

Personal Limitations

Eustace Poupin, Paul Muniment and the Princess Casamassima are all individuals impossible to sum up in a phrase. It is a mark of James' mastery and not his limitation that the reader's understanding of each is never complete; they retain the mystery and complexity of independent characters. We are able, nevertheless, to see that the commitment of each to the great "rectification" springs from something more than solicitude for suffering humanity, though James is careful not to deprive them of that emotion.

Like Lady Aurora, Anastasius Vetch shares the rectifiers' desire for social change but not their embrace of violence. At the end of the First Book, Mr. Vetch assures Hyacinth that he is indeed "a radical" but "not an exterminator." Mr. Vetch anticipates the disdain his views would arouse among Hyacinth's new friends by wryly admitting that his radicalism is "of the old-fashioned, constitutional, milk-and-water, jog-trot sort" (173). His ultimate renunciation of even this sort of radicalism has nothing to do with complacency or any diminution of human feeling. The reader learns about his change of views shortly after Hyacinth compares Mr. Vetch's "humble, continuous, single-minded practice of daily duties" in looking after Pinnie in her final illness with the Princess and her set, who, Hyacinth thinks to himself, "fidgeted from one selfish sensation to another and couldn't even live in the same place for three months together." The "invincible fidelity" (361) displayed by Mr. Vetch seems to mark a difference more important than any difference of mere opinions. And if Mr. Vetch no longer believes in the "idea of great changes" (367), he is all the more determined to assist and protect Hyacinth; having safeguarded Pinnie's "little hoard," (372), he refuses to take the money Hyacinth owes him so that Hyacinth will have a chance to "see the world" and discover that "society, even as it is, has some good points" (374).

In this dramatic context, Mr. Vetch's rejection of his old "idea of great changes" (367) seems to express not cynicism or apathy but rather hard-won insight. No change of government or society, he has come to feel, could extirpate the "passions and jealousies and superstitions and stupidities" (367) of human beings, and the attempt to do so would inevitably "make a bigger mess than the actual muddle of human affairs" (366). Significantly, these conclusions do not lead Mr. Vetch to give up on political change; indeed, it was his former belief in some grand "social solution" (366) that had caused him to dismiss elections and political parties. Now, however, he was "even . . . taking an interest in current politics" (366). If Mr. Vetch's point of view can be described by the narrator as "having accepted this world," (367), the implication is not that he has grown complacent but that he is not willing to exchange the chances for happiness of actual human beings in the world as it is for the new world that the rectifiers believe will come into being after the cataclysm in which the enemies of the people will have paid for their crimes. "'Why,'" Mr. Vetch asks the Princess Casamassima, "'are some human beings the people, and the people only, and others not?'" It is an acute question, one that has troubled Hyacinth Robinson in regard to Mr. Vetch in particular, but one that the Princess does not seem to consider worth an answer (462).

Although Mr. Vetch is finally unable to save Hyacinth Robinson from becoming a "catspaw" in the "abominable brotherhood" (467), the money he provides does allow Hyacinth to travel to Europe, to Paris and to Venice, and the trip does convince Hyacinth, as Mr. Vetch had hoped, that "society, even as it is, has some good points" (374). This awareness is not purchased at the cost of any loss of sensitivity toward the lot of the poor. Hyacinth writes the Princess from Venice that "the clearest result of extending one's horizon" as he has done is an increased sense "that want and toil and suffering are the constant lot of the immense majority of the human race" (396). If Hyacinth now deprecates any upheaval that would destroy the art and high culture of the past, it is not because he thinks art more important than human beings, but because he has come to feel that the great achievements of civilization are not mere decorative luxuries but ameliorate life for all, not just for the rich. In his Venice letter Hyacinth associates "the monuments and treasures of art . . . the conquests of learning and taste" not with the pleasures of the few but with "the general fabric of civilisation." He does not oppose art to life but instead argues that the great art of the past, preserved in "the great palaces and properties" makes "the world . . . less impracticable and life more tolerable" (396). The prosaic adjectives—"impracticable," "tolerable"—suggest that Hyacinth values great art not because it brings intense but exclusive delight to a few connoisseurs but because its influence ameliorates and enriches the lives of the many, even those who never enter a gallery or a museum. He himself, with only a few pounds, has been able to experience "the fascination of great cities, the charm of travel and discovery, the generosity of admiration" (393). Against this "generosity of admiration" Hyacinth is now able to recognize and reject the "kind of invidious jealousy which is at the bottom of the idea of a redistribution" (397). The fundamental impulse behind the dreams of rectification, including his own, has not been humanitarian love but instead a mean "intolerance of positions and fortunes that are higher and brighter than one's own" (397). Despite his reawakened "sense of everything that might hold one to the world, of the sweetness of not dying" (393), Hyacinth writes that what he fears is not so much the thought of his own death "while I am yet young" but the possibility that he would die without having purged "that odious stain upon my soul" (397).

Contemporary Egalitarianism

Henry James' *The Princess Casamassima* retains its political relevance for Americans today, although no sizable political parties in the United States seem interested in instituting the "thorough-going system of equality" favored by Paul Muniment and Eustace Poupin. The continuing authority of James' insights into the sources of the revolutionary aspiration to absolute equality vindicate his faith in the power of "the sense of life and the penetrating imagination" to reveal central truths about human beings, truths that have remained remarkably constant from ancient Greece to the present, despite vast social, cultural and technological changes. In his *Politics* Aristotle observed that the chief grievance of revolutionaries is "inequality," since "those who are bent on equality start a revolution if they believe that they, having less, are yet the equals of those who have more."[15] The "rectification" Diedrich Hoffendahl's plans would not, at first glance, seem to have much to do with contemporary movements such as environmentalism, gay liberation, animal rights or feminism. A second look, however, raises the suspicion that these movements are fueled by a common impulse, one shared by Muniment, Poupin, Schinkel and the mysterious Hoffendahl: the drive to establish absolute equality between human beings. At the close of the twentieth century Aaron Wildavsky finds "radical egalitarianism," not Marxism or nationalism or anything else, at the root of the most powerful contemporary social movements in the United States:

> It is all radical egalitarianism, and it is nothing but radical egalitarianism. There is nothing else to it. There is nothing underneath it! There is nothing on top of it! There is nothing crouching behind it! There is nothing to the left or right of it![16]

To suggest that *The Princess Casamassima* is relevant to conte.nporary politics is not to say that today's political radicals or progressives are analogous to the "rectifiers" of the novel. The case for environmentalism, gay liberation, feminism and animal rights is unaffected by a reading of *The Princess Casamassima*, except insofar as the appeal of such causes depends on the attractions of the ideal of absolute equality.[17] And even if it were the case, as Wildavsky believes, that the rectifiers' ideal of absolute equality is shared by contemporary radicals, there would be no justification for using the novel's ultimate rejection of revolution to condemn the specific reforms such groups advocate. The great "rectification" aside, the novel takes no stand on any specific reforms or economic systems; it neither advocates nor condemns capitalism, socialism or any mixed economy, though it is true that the novel's critique of the ideal of absolute equality seems to vitiate one of the strongest rhetorical weapons of advocates of socialism and communism over capitalism.[18]

A reading of *The Princess Casamassima* prompts caution about revolutionary zeal without, however, endorsing society as it is. Perhaps we would do better to aim not at some definitive solution, some "great rectification," but rather at the more modest goal of making "the world . . . less impracticable and life more tolerable" (396) in the words of Hyacinth's Venice letter. Perhaps, the novel encourages one to think, there is something dangerous about ideals so grandiose that they seem to excuse any means that might be necessary to attain them. We should not be eager to destroy "things with which the aspirations and the tears have been mixed" (396) until we are confident that what will replace them is truly something better. Hyacinth's suspicion that absolute equality will result in nothing more wonderful than "a similar *nuance* of asininity" seems "very clever" (444) even to Paul Muniment; a century of experience with revolutionaries willing to forgo equality before the law in search of absolute equality reveals the ease with which seemingly lofty ideals can become pretexts for mass murder.

When is violence on behalf of social change justified? *The Princess Casamassima* provides no answers, but it does raise some cautions. The rhetoric of egalitarianism, Wildavsky points out, makes it easy "to moralize . . . political differences so that the opinions of opponents are not merely considered mistaken but denounced as depraved."[19] And if one's adversaries are not merely wrong but evil, then the use of force against them becomes not only justifiable but praiseworthy. Since the self-discipline necessary to control violent urges is burdensome, the attraction of violence that not only can be justified but also proves one's moral superiority is always strong. Wildavsky cites Tracy Chapman's "Talkin' Bout a Revolution" ("Poor people gonna rise up/And get their share/ Poor people gonna rise up/And take what's theirs") and Public Enemy's "Fight the Power" ("What've we got to say/ Power to the People, no delay/ To make everybody see/ In order to fight the powers to [sic] be").[20] Such lyrics suggest that the violence expected to attend the future rectification remains as seductive for some today as it was for the Princess Casamassima. The novel that bears her name, however, leads one to doubt that it is ever possible to neatly divide the world into the guilty and the innocent, oppressors and oppressed, the class that deserves violent retribution and the class on whose behalf it will be meted out.

The desire to achieve equality between human beings seems to derive its strength both from an admirable willingness to recognize the full humanity of others and from a contemptible unwillingness to tolerate—let alone enjoy—the good fortune of others. How is one to distinguish between idealism motivated by a compassion that leaves room for what Hyacinth calls "the generosity of admiration" (393) and the sort of zeal fueled by "invidious jealousy" (397)? The problem is all the more difficult because the same parties, causes and even individuals inspired by the former may also be energized by the latter. Even though one may hope that the age of totalitarian "rectifications" is over, it remains important to understand as fully as possible the complicated ways in which the desire to relieve suffering and uphold justice can be intertwined with a willingness to assassinate and even exterminate. The works of sociologists, psychologists and philosophers provide some assistance in this task, but it may be that the insights offered by novels like *The Princess Casamassima* are not only conveyed more powerfully but also plumb greater depths.

Notes

1. Aristotle, *On the Art of Poetry (The Poetics)*, trans. T. S. Dorsch, *Classical Literary Criticism: Aristotle, Horace, Longinus* (New York: Penguin, 1965), 43-4.

2. Henry James, *The Princess Casamassima*, ed. Derek Brewer (New York: Penguin, 1977), 282. All parenthetical references refer to this text.

3. Lionel Trilling, "*The Princess Casamassima*," in *The Liberal Imagination: Essays on Literature and Society* (New York: Harcourt Brace Jovanovich, 1979), 71, 85.

4. Paul de Man, "The Resistance to Theory," in *The Resistance to Theory* (Minneapolis: University of Minnesota Press, 1986), 11.

5. Mark Seltzer, *Henry James: The Art of Power* (Ithaca: Cornell University Press, 1984), 57.

6. Mike Fischer, "The Jamesian Revolution in *The Princess Casamassima*: A Lesson in Bookbinding," *The Henry James Review* 9, 2 (Spring, 1988): 102.

7. Eileen Sypher, "Anarchism and Gender: James' *The Princess Casamassima* and Conrad's *The Secret Agent*," *The Henry James Review* 9, 1 (Winter 1988): 1.

8. Wendy Graham, "Henry James' Subterranean Blues: A Rereading of *The Princess Casamassima*," *Modern Fiction Studies* 40, 1 (Spring 1994): 53.

9. Graham, "Henry James' Subterranean Blues," 68.

10. Graham, "Henry James' Subterranean Blues," 96-97.

11. Graham, "Henry James' Subterranean Blues," 78.

12. Henry James, *Literary Criticism, Essays on Literature*, "The Art of Fiction" (New York: Literary Classics of the United States, 1984), 45.

13. Henry James, "Preface to the New York Edition of 1909," *The Princess Casamassima*, ed. Derek Brewer (New York: Penguin, 1977), 44, 48.

14. I share Martha Nussbaum's view that "we can count on Hyacinth Robinson not only as our storyteller, but also, in some sense, as a fine moral touchstone and guide" (*Love's Knowledge: Essays on Philosophy and Literature* [New York: Oxford University Press, 1990], 199). Against those who argue that the narrator's occasionally belittling references to Hyacinth indicate that the reader should not accept Hyacinth's final judgments as those of James himself, Margaret Scanlan observes that "[c]ondescending references to Hyacinth's size . . . are offset by many other references to his sensitivity, his instinctive good manners, and his nobility of spirit. She rightly observes that

Hyacinth's views of culture seem inseparable from James'. . . . Unlike most latter-day proponents of the Great Tradition, James and Hyacinth thoroughly recognize that such art is produced in concrete historical circumstances by people who have to deal with practical matters. Moreover, they also anticipate Walter Benjamin's argument that there is "no document of civilization which is not at the same time a document of barbarism." ("Terrorism and the Realistic Novel: Henry James and *The Princess Casamassima*," *Texas Studies in Language and Literature* 34:3 [Fall 1992]: 385, 392.)

For another view, see Warren Johnson's argument that not Hyacinth but the Princess Casamassima ultimately emerges as the closest representative of James' own views about the relation of art and life:

> The princess shows how, when one is offered a choice between life and art, one can choose art and get life in an imagining of experience—the dream of possibilities, the discovery of limitations—and the memory of an illusion of freedom. ("Hyacinth Robinson or The Princess Casamassima?" *Texas Studies in Language and Literature* 28, 3 [Fall 1986]: 321.)

The debate about which character speaks for the author assumes that the author is an authoritative voice who has something meaningful to tell us about human life. This debate is meaningless, of course, for those postmodernist critics who deny, first, that the concept of the author is meaningful and, second, that any work of fiction has the ability to point to truths about the world outside the text.

   15. Aristotle, *The Politics*, trans. T. A. Sinclair (Baltimore, Md.: Penguin, 1962), 192.
   16. Aaron Wildavsky, *The Rise of Radical Egalitarianism* (Washington, D.C.: American University Press, 1991), 235.
   17. Although the egalitarian impulse behind feminism, gay liberation and animal rights seems fairly straightforward, it is less clear that environmentalism has any particular connection with egalitarianism. Wildavsky argues that

> Attempts to protect the environment are prevalent but perhaps less obvious evidence of a rise in egalitarian culture than attempts to diminish power differences between people, or between people and animals. We have argued that these pursuits are mutually reinforcing. Egalitarians believe that the environment is threatened by man-made things, just as man is. Humanity's institutions, in the egalitarian view, are no less the source of inequalities among humans than they are the source of destruction for the environment. To defend the environment is therefore to erode inequalities. (74)

   18. Martha Nussbaum is right to see *The Princess Casamassima* as a source of insight about politics, but she strains credulity when she asserts that the novel endorses "socialism in the economy" and then strains it even more by identifying the "political stance" of the novel with "the Britain of the pre-Thatcher years":

> In short, there is, it seems to me, a political program, or at least a political stance, in this novel, and one that was going a long way toward executing, with its combination of socialist economic policies in health and nutrition with the protection of liberal freedoms, with its policies of free public access to museums and galleries, with its public parks and musical performances, with its schemes, however vexed with difficulty, of public education. (*Love's Knowledge: Essays on Philosophy and Literature* [New York: Oxford University Press, 1990], 205, 206.)

   19. Wildavsky, *The Rise*, xxxv.
   20. Wildavsky, *The Rise*, 96-97.

Chapter 3

Love, Law, and Rhetoric: The Teachings of Francesca in Dante's *Inferno*

Peter Kalkavage

> *"Watch how you enter and in whom you put your faith!"*
>
> —Inferno, *5.19*

The Circle of Passion

"Thus did I descend from the first circle down into the second, which girdles less space, and so much greater woe that it goads to wailing."[1] Here begins the most famous and beloved canto in Dante's *Comedy*. It is the canto that sings of Paolo and Francesca, the pair of lovers eternally swept around by a storm. The pilgrim Dante asks Francesca to tell her story. She graciously complies, while her lover Paolo accompanies her words with a constant strain of weeping. When her story is over, Dante ends the canto with the following words: "for pity I swooned as if I had died; and I fell down the way a dead body falls."

Our centuries-long love affair with Canto 5 is no surprise. We are deeply moved by this heartrending story of love, told so sadly—so beautifully—by its heroine. We find in her very sin something to admire, something we might even wish to experience. "Ah," we say to ourselves, "to be as rapt with love as Francesca, to abandon oneself so completely to the birdsong of *Amore* that one would even choose eternal damnation for love's sake!" Dante's sympathetic portrayal of Francesca thus invites our questions. How, we wonder, can something so beautiful end up in Hell? Why, exactly, is she in Hell? Why is Dante so overcome by what he hears that he falls down as if he were dead? By addressing these questions, I hope to shed light on how Dante in this canto functions as our teacher and guide.

Now, Dante's poem is a love poem. It tells of how the poet came to be reunited with Beatrice, with whom he fell in love when she was nine and he was almost ten.[2] But the *Comedy* is also didactic. It is full of teachings and lectures. Beatrice is the greatest of Dante's many teachers, as she gradually unveils to him, with all the composure of full knowledge, the nature of the heavens and the mysteries of bliss. This overt didacticism, like the many allegories, is to be taken seriously and is a central part of the poem. Dante, though, also teaches through the autobiographies of his characters. Here the teaching is neither overtly didactic nor simply allegoric. A story does not directly teach but only shows and tells. How, then, does Dante's portrayal of Francesca teach? What does Dante want us to learn through the experience of listening to her story? I shall anticipate myself here by saying that Francesca, like Beatrice, is above all a teacher. In the canto, she reveals to Dante not only the particulars of her past but also the universal principles which, to her, grounded and justified her adulterous love affair with Paolo. Teaching is for this reason the very topic as well as the mode of *Inferno 5.* Through the teachings of Francesca Dante shows us, among other things, that it is impossible to isolate the apparently private sin of illicit love and to separate it from the will to destroy the common good.

In Dante's carefully constructed plan of Hell, the circle of lust is the beginning of Hell proper. The first circle, that of the virtuous pagans, has neither pain nor wailing. Instead, there is the sole affliction of desire without hope (4.41); and the only sounds that greet Dante's ears are the sighs that come from "grief without torment" (25-30).[3]

All this changes abruptly as Dante goes down into the infernal home of Paolo and Francesca. The circle is more constricted than the previous one and is filled with "woeful notes" (5.25). And whereas the virtuous pagans live in "a blaze that conquered a hemisphere of gloom" (4.68-69), here, Dante ominously tells us, "I came to a place where every light was mute" (5.28).[4] The fact of increasing physical constriction has vast significance for the *Comedy.* As Beatrice announces in the *Paradiso,* the greatest gift God gave man was freedom of will (5.19-22). This explains why Hell is a funnel. Sin is the constriction of being, the narrowing and ultimate annihilation of our freedom. And so, as we go deeper into Hell, deeper into sin, we enter circles that are not only lower down but also less free. Freedom is lost by degrees. At the very end we come upon Satan, whose machine-like flapping of wings freezes lower Hell and imprisons him in eternal frustration. The circle of "hot lovers" is far indeed from this icy domain of cold-hearted treachery. The lovers fly around like birds, and the tempest keeps them in a state of constant motion. But the storm, the wind of love's passion, is also a prison. It forces the lovers to go where *it* will. Moreover, the storm isn't even an *it* but a random confluence of battling forces. The bird imagery suggests the heaven of freedom that carnal lovers seek; the storm is the randomness and compulsion to which they subjected themselves in seeking that heaven. Such is the torment of the sinners who, as Dante learns, "subject reason to desire" (38-39).

Dante carefully sets the stage for his heroine. This care is all part of the way in which his poem charms and terrifies as it teaches. To repeat: the opening of Canto 5 is not just the introduction to the carnal lovers; it is also the beginning of Hell proper. At its entrance stands Minos, the first of Hell's many monsters. Minos admonishes Dante with the words: "Watch how you enter, and in whom you put your faith" (19). As we shall see, this warning applies to the reader as much as to the pilgrim Dante.

The storm of sexual passion is depicted with unforgettable vividness: "The hellish hurricane, which never rests, sweeps the spirits with its rapine; whirling and beating, it torments them" (31-33). In the *Inferno* Dante objectifies and concretizes sin, thus making it accessible to imagination and experience. Sin thus becomes more real—and more terrifying. Here the storm is true to our experience of romantic love. It objectifies our feeling of being overwhelmed, swept off our feet, carried away. Along with the visual externalization of passion here in Canto 5, there come sounds: shrieks and lamentations. The storm also contains the raging cries of those who curse the divine power (*la virtù divina*, 36). All this Dante experiences just *before* Virgil tells him about the storm's inhabitants. The implied reaction is something like: "Oh no! You mean *that's* who's here?"

The imagery then switches, incongruously, to birds. The sinners swept by the storm of their passion are said to be like starlings and cranes. With this imagery Dante has begun to make Hell seductive. Yes, there is a storm; but now we are made to imagine lovely winged creatures cruelly beaten by that storm. Our hearts go out to the poor birds who struggle vainly against the quarrel (*la briga*) of the winds and who sing their "lays" as they go (*cantando lor lai*). We pity these bird-people, whose wings of eros are opposed and defeated by the winds of eros.[5] Our sentimentality makes us forget that they are suffering, not the external punishment of a vindictive God, but the constricting passion to which they freely yielded their whole being.

Dante wants to know who is in the storm, and so do we. Virgil gives him a catalogue of carnal sinners: Semiramis, Dido, Cleopatra, Helen, Achilles, Paris, Tristan—"more than a thousand shades . . . whom love parted from our life" (67-69).[6] There is a note of "alas!" in the concluding relative clause. The reference to *nostra vita*, "our life," reminds us of the same phrase in the very first line of the poem. We feel a bond with these fellow human beings whom love parted from that very life that we now enjoy, the life that is supposed to be sweet in goodness, fellowship and love. How unnatural and sad that love should bring on death rather than add immeasurably to life's sweetness! The sinners Virgil names are all worthy of remembrance. Recalling the many famous love stories that fill the human imagination, Dante refers to the sinners romantically as "the ladies and knights of olden times" (71). Semiramis is "the first of these of whom you wish to know" (52-53). In a sense she sums up the sin of this level of Hell: she made lust into law, that is, not only subjected her reason to desire but also tried to make this subjection publicly defensible and justified. Dido does something very similar in the *Aeneid*. Once she and Aeneas have begun their illicit romance, Dido calls the affair marriage, thus using a name, as Virgil tells us, as a pretext for her fault (*culpam*, 4.172). As we shall see, Francesca too makes lust into law.

The exemplars of tragic love are those who allow their private erotic necessity to subvert the public order. Semiramis perverted the law by erasing the distinction between private gratification and public sanction; Dido's tragic love for Aeneas diverted Aeneas from his divine political mission and brought the Carthaginian curse on the Roman Empire; Cleopatra, who bewitched both Julius Caesar and Marc Antony, was yet another sexual enemy of Rome; the affair of Helen and Paris brought ten years of war upon Troy, Rome's seed-bed; and Tristan, in the version of the story Dante is probably recalling, was killed when King Mark of Cornwall found Tristan with Queen Isolde. Even Achilles, who seems at first not to belong in the list, may be accused of sacrificing his loyalty to the Greeks to his love for the Trojan Polyxena.[7]

The Ennoblement of Having

Near the center of the canto's one-hundred-and-forty-two lines, we reach a turning point. Dante curiously invokes Virgil as "poet" and expresses his desire, or rather wish, to speak with "those two who go together, and seem to be so light upon the wind" (73-75).[8] The Roman poet, apparently moved by the spectacle of fallen love, responds gently and encouragingly. He bids Dante entreat them "by that love that leads them, and they will come" (76-78). Virgil's tone here is very different from the one he adopted in reference to the disgusting army of Neutrals or Nonlovers in Canto 3. *Guarda e passa*, he told Dante, "look and pass" (3.51). Dante must wait for the wind to do its mindless work and bring the lovers round. Once they are near, he "set his voice in motion" (*mossi la voce*): "Oh, wearied souls, come and speak to us, if One forbids it not" (80-81). God is never mentioned by name in Hell (except in blasphemy), and here Dante respects that fact. He does what the lovers here failed to do: he acknowledges that the proper completion of a desire is subject to the divine will.

The starlings and cranes are at this point transformed into doves, the birds of peace and love:

> Just as doves, who are called by their desire,
> with wings raised and fixed, come to the sweet nest,
>   born through the air by their will;
> So these lovers left the troop where Dido is,
>   coming to us through the malignant air,
> so strong was that affectionate cry of mine. (82-87)

Can we believe that we are in Hell? The lovely naturalness of the imagined scene, the delicate image of the birds' homecoming, Dante's affectionate cry—all this nearly rises above the miasma through which the lovebirds must fly. Dante's affectionate cry is like the call of Love itself that first summoned the lovers to their tragic union. Then as now, the call of Love proves irresistible, as Virgil reminds Dante (76-78). That Dido is mentioned here as the patroness of the troop brings the whole scene of modern Italian lovers into direct continuity with Virgil's poem. By singling her out, Dante arouses our wonder: What is Virgil's role in this meeting between Dante and Francesca?

At last we get to hear Francesca, whose two-part speech is one of the most breathtaking moments in the entire poem. Dante allows her to pose as our teacher in love matters. He presents her, as I have said, not only as the teller of a tale but also as a professor of love's universal principles and code—the erotic code of knights and ladies. Dante does not shield us from her seductiveness. On the contrary, by composing such beautiful music for her love talk, he causes us to feel the sweet pull of Hell, feel it even as we are called upon to judge Francesca and search for why she might after all merit eternal damnation. To understand Francesca we must allow ourselves to fall under her spell, if only for a moment. Only then will we know what we are judging. Thus does Dante teach—by plunging us into the thick of seduction and the labyrinth of our conflicted feelings.

"Oh creature gracious and benign," begins the courteous Francesca. The use of the word *animal*, which goes with all the bird imagery, echoes Dante's earlier address—"Oh wearied souls (*anime*)." In this word *animal* Francesca begins to reveal her idolatry of nature. Love, as impulse, is instinctive and natural. It is as natural as the birds that fly and seek their nest, as natural as the flowers and trees. Carnal lovers seek a purely natural union with one another, a union unguarded and ungoverned by laws and public authority. In a strange way, they seek a return to innocence through sexual fulfillment. It is ironic that Francesca's name should be what it is: she is a female (and perverse) St. Francis who endows Nature with a divine goodness but denies the Fall of Man as well as the authority of human institutions. Francesca's presumed innocence is thus a purely romantic pose. It is a lie: human beings are not birds or flowers, and freedom does not consist in giving way to instinct and natural impulse. Her lover's name, Paul, points to the apostle for whom love was the transcendence of nature and the ground of fellowship: "So faith, hope, love abide, these three; but the greatest of these is love" (1 *Cor*. 13.13). Francesca rejects the teachings of St. Francis and St. Paul on the subject of nature. She rejects the possibility of a love that calls us to rise above nature, mortal body and the lust for possession.

What we know of the real-life Francesca is summed up in Singleton's commentary on the *Inferno*. Paolo was Francesca's brother-in-law. Her husband found the lovers together and immediately murdered them both. As we hear from Francesca's own lips in Canto 5, the murderous husband (who, we must remember, killed his brother as well as his wife) will be imprisoned in the deepest circle of Hell: "Caina," the place that holds the followers of Cain, "waits for him who quenched our life" (107). Dante here reminds us that yielding to adulterous lust, as sins go, is a much lesser evil than the murder of one's own. It is not enough to know evil as evil: we must also come to know the degree and quality of specific evils.

As Francesca begins to speak to Dante, she defines herself and Paolo as those "who stained the world with blood" (90). She begins, in other words, with a reference to the horrible outcome of their illicit love. She reminds us that the world itself had been bloodied and defiled. Does she comprehend what she is saying? Does she have any pity for the world that was polluted by a double murder brought on by love? In any case, Francesca is genuinely moved by Dante's manifest pity for her and Paolo. Using the first person plural and avoiding the name of God, she says: "If the King of the universe were our friend, we would pray to Him for your peace, since you have pity for our perverse ill" (91-93). Clearly, Francesca is not one of those in the storm who curse the divine power. She defers to God, as a lady in a story would defer to the very king she had wronged. And yet, there is something pathetically childish, if disarmingly courteous, in her reference to God as someone who does not happen to be her friend. "Sorry, nice animal," she seems to say to Dante, "Paolo and I are on the outs with You Know Who. We are naturally inclined to help you—but we can't." She shows no understanding whatsoever of why she and her lover are in Hell. It's as if the extent of her understanding were summed up in formulas like "Rules are rules" and "You can't fight City Hall." We are reminded of how Virgil defined the damned at the beginning of Canto 3: as "the woeful people who have lost the good of the intellect" (17-18). As we move on in Francesca's speech, we descend more deeply into her self-deceived pose, her loss of intellect. We must remember at each stage, however, that even as we judge Francesca and come to know her self-deception, she remains pitiable and attractive. Dante's exquisite rendering immortalizes Francesca as alluring in her very sinfulness. He thus makes this canto permanently unsettling—and thereby instructive.

Francesca reminds Dante that the only reason speech is possible now is that the storm has momentarily died down (94-96). It seems unlikely that Paolo and Francesca can speak with one another within the storm: the storm of passion muffles discourse even as it prevents freedom of flight. When Dante first called to the lovers, he was said to move his voice (80). That is, as a still living being, he was free to speak. And while the storm has abated, Francesca too is free to speak. Her words "were born from them to us" (108). They were allowed, in Homer's phrase, to be *winged*. But wings are useless in a storm, including, we assume, the wings of words. Paolo and Francesca are moved eternally as a pair, but they seem not to have much to do with one another. There is no apparent interchange. Paolo seems eternally absorbed in weeping, and Francesca is eternally absorbed in her romance. They are eternally in love; but the storm of passion, which causes them to move together in Hell, also makes them curiously and permanently separated from each other. One wonders if part of their torment is to be eternally paired but never really united. Hell in this way grants their wish by giving them what they most wanted—an eternity of togetherness. But it also torments them with the full consequence and truth of that wish.

Francesca begins her story, not in Rimini (the city of her marriage, love affair and murder) but in her hometown of Ravenna. She sets the tone of nostalgia that permeates the canto like some heady perfume: "The earth where I was born sits on the shore where the Po descends to be at peace with its followers" (97-99). The explicit reference to peace is a sad reminder of precisely what these storm-tossed spirits do not have. Beautifully situated on the Po, Ravenna is the picture of natural serenity. It is a world not of conflicting winds but of harmonious waters. In recalling the very soil of her birthplace, Francesca reminds us again of the goodness of life, of lands that nurture their offspring and of our natural affection for the "sweet nest" where we were born. It is terrible that so courteous a lady, blessed with so beautiful and peaceful a birthplace, should come to such an unnatural end. In her nostalgia for a beautiful past, Francesca unwittingly reminds us of what she herself rejects: the Fall of Man and the Eden we lost through the lust for *more*.

After expressing nostalgia for her native earth, Francesca proceeds to the adopted country of her soul:

> "Love, which is quickly kindled in the gentle heart,
>   seized this one for the beautiful body [*persona*]
>   that was taken from me—and the way of it still afflicts me.
>
> Love, which absolves no loved one from loving,
>   seized me so strongly with delight in him,
>   that, as you see, it does not quit me even now.
>
> Love conducted us to one death.
>   Caina waits for him who quenched our life."
>   These words were born from them to us. (100-108)

Eloquent rhetoric and poetry apparently can exist in Hell. In the first of these tercets we hear how love in general is born, or rather, *ignited*. It is Francesca's first Law of Love: Love is kindled like a fire in the gentle heart. The courtliness of the language makes it sound as though love could never be associated with anything as low as lust. Love is delicate and refined, even if its call is ineluctable. In the first tercet Francesca combines a happy memory (the thought of Paolo's falling in love with her) with the sad recollection of her murder. The focal point for these contrary recollections is Francesca's physical beauty. Francesca's grief consists in her recognition of this irony: in her violent death, she lost the very thing that inspired Paolo to love her. We sense a certain narcissism in these lines, an all-too-acute awareness of one's own beauty. The most striking thing here is of course the repetition of *Amor* at the beginning of each tercet. The effect is that of an incantation. It is a spell that bewitches as it delights. Love is a god in these lines, and Francesca is the god's high priestess.

The central tercet begins with the romantic's second fundamental law: Love absolves no beloved from loving in return.[9] Love demands reciprocity. This is the law or code of Love, Love's *cortesia*. It is virtually a morality all to itself. Francesca had acted on a similar principle earlier when she told Dante that his pity for her and Paolo's "perverse ill" inspired her pity for him: she felt inclined to pray for him—if only she could (88-93). All this courtesy is a deceptive imitation of the gracious reciprocity we find throughout Dante's Paradise.

Francesca would have us believe that love is perfectly natural.[10] Let us notice the causal sequence at work here. First, there is the beloved's overpowering physical beauty. Corresponding to this beauty is the receptive, sensitive quality of the lover's heart. There is a certain analogy here with the Aristotelian-Scholastic relation of form and matter: form is that which by nature impresses itself on matter, while matter is that which is receptive to form. Beauty (in Latin, *forma*) and sensitivity are as naturally wedded as form is to matter. They are, as it were, made for each other and fated to unite. The very constitution of nature—the intimate relation between form and matter—thus seems to provide a sanction for the physical intimacy between lover and beloved. Francesca's enlightened discourse spells out the natural process by which the liaison between beauty and love takes place. Beauty begets love in the gentle heart, or rather, as Francesca puts it with a touch of delicious violence: Love *seizes* the lover with the desire to possess and enjoy the bodily beauty that attracts him.

Now comes the principle of erotic reciprocity: Love's law forbids the beloved not to love the lover in return. And that is why Francesca fell in love with Paolo: because he had fallen in love with her. Indeed, she fell in love so strongly that she continues to be in love even in Hell. In love, yes—but with whom? There is enough room for personification here to read in Francesca's *costui* (the "him" of line 104) a possible reference to Love himself (the boy-god Eros). In any case, Francesca does seem to be in love with Love. It is far from clear how present to her mind Paolo himself really is, so locked is she in the past moment of romance and her fulfillment of a romantic fantasy. A haze of self-enclosure hangs about her enlightened statement of Love's principles and causality. Perhaps that is what untempered, uneducated romantic desire does: it imprisons us in our feeling and makes us (contrary to what we might think) oblivious even of the beloved, who becomes grist for the mill of romance. Francesca's rhetoric uses natural causality to justify this dreaminess of passionate self-enclosure. In the rapture of Francesca, in the deification of feeling, Dante seems to be showing us the close bond that exists between Eros and Narcissus.

The canto might reasonably enough have ended with the hymn of Francesca. After all, she has identified herself for Dante and has told the story of her life from her birth in Ravenna to her murder in Rimini. She has professed her undying fidelity to her god Eros, and she has explained, in general, how love *works*. She has even told Dante where her murderous husband will end up in Hell. The sad story only intensifies Dante's pity and reduces him to silence. He bows his head and keeps it bowed until Virgil asks him what he is thinking (109-111). His response is perhaps much like ours: "Alas! How many sweet thoughts, what great desire, led them to the woeful pass" (112-114)!

But Dante wants to know more. He turns to the two lovers again and, addressing Francesca by name, tells her that her torments make him weep for grief and pity. And then he poses the question that is on his mind: "But tell me, in the time of your sweet sighings, on what occasion and how did love grant you to know your dubious desires" (118-120)?[11] Dante wants to know more precisely how Paolo and Francesca fell in love and realized that they were in love. He wants Francesca to reveal "the primal root" of her and Paolo's love (124). His deeply human, sympathetic question seems to take us light years away from any moralizing on the subject, any thought of good and evil. Why does Dante the poet take us into these perilous regions? Why does he emphasize the intimate beauty of the moment that engulfed the lovers and sent them to Hell? Let us see what light our teacher Francesca can shed on these questions.

This second part of her speech begins, as did the first, with the expression of a tragic nostalgia. "There is no greater woe," she tells Dante, "than to remember the happy time in misery; and this your teacher knows" (121-123). Who is the *dottore* or teacher to whom Francesca is referring here? Her formulation is very close to something Boethius says in his *Consolation of Philosophy*, a work Dante knew very well and loved.[12] But can we really imagine that such a book would be on Francesca's reading list? It is much more likely that "your teacher" refers to none other than Virgil, whose poem abounds in references to memory.[13] Furthermore, it is easy to imagine that Francesca read the story of unhappy Dido with great sympathy and perhaps admiration. By referring to Virgil as Dante's *dottore*, Francesca emphasizes a fact that is of central importance for her upcoming story: the fact that literature teaches by ennobling certain characters, situations and sentiments. If we take her as referring to Virgil, then it is unsettling to hear this modern Italian adulteress implicating the noblest Roman author in her nostalgia for unrestrained eros and, in effect, her justification of Dido. Francesca's sadly beautiful sentiment about memory pulls at our heartstrings. Nevertheless, as we shall see, the account she is about to give will take us deeper into the root of her sin. If Dante causes us to feel the pull of Hell, he also supplies the watchful reader with an antidote. The antidote to Francesca's wistful recollection of the happy time in present woe is this: there is nothing more horrible than recalling a time that we *thought* was happy but was in fact the beginning of our doom.

Francesca now reveals the "primal root" of her and Paolo's love:

> "One day for pastime we were reading
> of Lancelot, how Love constrained him.
> We were alone and had no suspicion.
>
> Many times did that reading urge our eyes
> to meet, and changed the color of our faces;
> but one point alone it was that conquered us.
>
> When we read that the longed-for smile
> was kissed by so great a lover,
> this one, who never shall be parted from me,
>
> all trembling, kissed my mouth.
> A Gallehault was the book and he who wrote it;
> That day we read no farther in it." (127-138)

In her first speech, Francesca revealed a general teaching about Love: Love demands reciprocity. And so, in obedience to the law of Love, when Paolo loved her for her physical beauty, she was duty-bound to love him back. Here in Hell she remains proudly loyal to this erotic code. In this second and more potent speech, Francesca paints an unforgettable picture of how circumstances conspired to bring her and Paolo together in sexual union.[14] Her last line is a classic meiosis or "lessening" and is in keeping with her refinement: "That day we read no farther in it." As Francesca makes the transition from Guinevere to herself, from ornamented fiction to stark reality, she moves us from *riso* or smile (133) to the blunt and graphic word *bocca* or mouth (136). It is as though the act of bodily gratification, the plain truth of carnal desire, dispels the noble illusions of romance.

Francesca depicts herself and Paolo (whom she does not name) as naive: they were all alone and yet had no suspicion (*sospetto*) of anything dangerous. How old are these people? Could they really not have known the trap they were setting for themselves? There they are—all alone, reading about the adulterous affair of Lancelot and Guinevere—just two beautiful people settling down for a nice read. The book is really the central character of Francesca's self-justifying story. It was the book that occasioned the initial closeness of the two; the book that, in their joint reading, drew their eyes together; and it was the book that told of the sublime moment of surrender, thus inspiring Paolo to play Lancelot to Francesca's Guinevere. Referring to the knight who brought Lancelot and Guinevere together and urged them to kiss, Francesca calls the book and its author a *Galeotto* or Gallehault (which also means Frenchman and came to mean *pander*).[15]

Francesca tells the story as though she and Paolo were simply the naive and hapless victims of circumstance. The book is her scapegoat. Here we reach the very center of Francesca's evil teaching. Francesca presents her and Paolo's deed, their yielding to their passion, as the work of unavoidable necessity. She denies freedom of the will and thus takes no responsibility whatsoever for what happened. In the story of Lancelot and Guinevere, she and Paolo read the ennoblement of their own erotic necessity. To her mind, she is thus the victim of a storm but not the maker of a storm. Her argument from necessity, which follows from her earlier elucidation of Love, is summed up in her understanding of Lancelot. Love *constrained* him, she says (*amor lo strinse*, 128). The denial of free will and responsibility is perfectly captured by the provocative line: "but one point alone it was that conquered us" (132). What does it mean to be conquered by a point? Francesca's account makes her and Paolo sound like a city that has at last fallen at the hands of an enemy. The point is a moment of time; it is a turning point in both the story of Lancelot and the lives of the Italian lovers. Paolo and Francesca are on a romantic voyage toward the abyss.[16] The voyage is mediated by a book that serves as their itinerary. They have many opportunities to see the danger that is right in front of them, *inside* them, but they press on, court the abyss. They willfully blind themselves to the glory of self-denial. They reject the possibility of a greater and more sublime romance that consists in the transcendence of nature (which, in Christianity, is a fallen or corrupt nature).[17] Carnal love, when left ungratified, stands the chance of metamorphosing into a higher love, a love that celebrates rather than destroys the clarity of intelligence and the harsh demands of responsibility. When Francesca says that she and Paolo stopped reading after their kiss, much is implied that the speaker fails to comprehend. The lovers indeed stopped reading; that is, they allowed the blindness of passion to over-come their capacity for reading *signs*, for seeing in their human experience the manifest clues of an impending fatality and the possibility of a higher, if more arduous, journey.[18]

There is a general romantic tendency among readers of Dante to prefer the *Inferno* and its Francesca to the *Paradiso* and its Beatrice. We appreciate the charm of the first lady but not that of the second. That is to say, we have a hard time understanding and accepting the education of desire and the possibility of transcendence. We find it hard to imagine a love that is not the desire to possess. But much as we want to dwell with Francesca, we cannot grasp the whole meaning of her story apart from the poem as a whole. As we finish reading the canto, we must say to ourselves: "But there is more."

So why is Francesca in Hell? Formally, she is an adulteress, who (like all the other carnal lovers) subjected reason to desire. But in her two-part speech we come to see the primal root of her damnation: she not only yields to illicit sexual passion but also, and more significantly, seeks to give such yielding a natural, indeed rational justification. The central part of that justification is the rejection of free will and the consequent stunting of spiritual growth, the constriction of one's being. This self-stunted growth is seen in all her charming but deceptive pretensions to naivete and natural innocence. The constriction of the second circle, the dark and violent storm that whips the spirits, the loss of sweet dis-course with one's beloved, the perpetual knowledge of the beloved's anguish, undying nostalgia for past sin and lost beauty, and an eternity of self-deception and sentimental rhetoric—all this is what Francesca has created. Her Hell is not just the place in which she finds herself: it *is* herself.

When Francesca ends her story, Dante reminds us that Paolo has been weep-ing the whole time, accompanying her tale like a piteous violin. We then hear in the famous last line of the canto the percussive alliteration of Dante's death-like fall: *e caddi come corpo morto cade* (142).

Why does Dante experience so strong a reaction to the tale of Francesca? No doubt Dante, like Paolo, is possessed of a gentle heart, a heart that is responsive, perhaps all too responsive, to female beauty. In the fall of Paolo and Francesca, Dante perhaps sees and relives his own betrayal of Beatrice, his own personal fall. He learns what happens when sweet sighs and great desire are taken to the limit and allowed to run their willful course. He is overcome to hear how Love, with all its heavenly promise, can lead to Hell. But there is more. Dante has just heard about how the written word, how literature, can itself seduce the soul and be an evil teacher, how it can induce spiritual death. Dante wrote secular love poems before he wrote the *Comedy*. Might not these, with all their virtuosity in the service of eros, possibly corrupt and mislead? Perhaps that is what Dante here recollects in making a book the central character in the story of a fall. Perhaps he is recalling his own secular poetic past, where "the straight way was lost" (1.3), his own potential for being an evil teacher. Indeed, the danger persists in the writing of *Inferno* 5, which might conceivably seduce the gentle reader into an uncritical sympathy with Francesca and her teachings. Dante gives us enough clues to be wary of Francesca's rhetoric: "Watch how you enter and in whom you put your faith." But the danger is still there. It is precisely this danger that Canto 5 keeps terribly alive in the reader's mind.

At this point we may hazard an answer to our earlier question: why does Dante the poet make Francesca so *attractive*? My guess is that he does this for the simple reason that he is interested in telling the truth about human experience. If Francesca had been made less alluring, if the bittersweet note of nostalgia had failed to be struck, the experience this canto is about would have been falsified. The extreme and terrifying vulnerability of the human heart would have been sacrificed to the easy moralizing of those who neither have felt nor can imagine love's sweetness and power.

Beyond Having

As we have seen, Francesca is possessed of a bodily beauty that possesses Paolo with a desire to possess her. Carnal love is all about possession and immediate gratification. The Italian lovers read a book that teaches them, in effect, how to blind themselves to the reading of signs that point to something beyond love as the desire to possess. What is this nonpossessive love, this *more* that Canto 5 points to but never reveals?

In *Paradiso* 11, St. Thomas sings the praises of St. Francis, Francesca's name-sake. St. Francis and Poverty are lovers (*amanti*, 11.74). Just as Francesca is "wedded" to Paolo, St. Francis is "wedded" to Lady Poverty, who is in turn "wedded" to Christ. The death of Christ opens the door to the higher love, a love that is impossible without a *death to self*. There are many ways to understand this death to self, but surely one thing it must involve is death to possessiveness. St. Francis came from a well-to-do family and was something of a *cavaliere* or knight. He literally divested himself of his chivalric worldliness, rose above his flamboyant nature, and became, in Dante's eyes, the Knight of Poverty or Need.[19] The crucified King bids us to marry our *need*, and Francis joyfully obeys.

Leaving Francis for the moment, we may turn to Dante's lady—Beatrice. Dante's love for Beatrice is the great exemplar in the poem of a nonpossessive love. Dante desires not to possess the Beloved but to share her world, to be where she is in the celestial city. It is of the greatest importance to note that when Beatrice at last returns to her celestial place, having descended into Hell for her lover's sake to summon Virgil, she is far above Dante (*Paradiso* 31.70-78). Yet he sees her now with enormous clarity and in the fullness of her being: "but to me it made no difference, since her image (*sua effige*) came down to me unmixed with anything in between" (77-78). Distance from the Beloved is an integral part of true intimacy with the Beloved. Why is this? Because the true function of love is not to blind but to illuminate, to cause the lover to see rather than to possess, and to be gratified by the natural rightness of things. The true object of love's desire is to see, that is, to comprehend, who and what the Beloved really is. Love aims above all at *insight*.

In the *Comedy* Dante recapitulates a Platonic teaching within the context of Christianity. The teaching is that eros, when thought through, is nothing less than the desire to know the whole of being. Beatrice opens Dante up to this love of intelligence and love of the whole. But he must first make himself worthy of so lofty an aspiration by climbing Mount Purgatory, walking through the flaming wall of lust, and enduring Beatrice's harsh rebuke and the "death" of self-accusation. At the moment when Beatrice, to make his purifying pain complete, lifts her veil, Dante experiences his second death-like fall in the poem. He reports, "Such self-accusation bit my heart that I fell, conquered" (*ch' io caddi vinto, Purgatorio* 31.88-89). It is in this second fall that Dante undoes the Siren song of Francesca, the deceptive birdcall of carnal love, and literally sees transcendent beauty. His "death" is the beginning of new life and—new poetry.

The love of Paolo and Francesca is a beautiful obsession. It is a love that fixates on the beloved and says "To Hell with the rest of the world!" Dante reminds us of this fact in the catalogue of carnal lovers, in which eros appeared as the enemy of human institutions and the common good they seek to promote. Hence the importance of Virgil in the canto: he knows, if anyone knows, how divine providence and world order can be opposed and poisoned by a love affair. He knew of Troy, which fell ultimately because of Helen and Paris; he knew of Rome, which was threatened first by Dido and then by Cleopatra. And yet, if we are to judge from his *Aeneid*, Virgil—an astute reader of the human heart and the poet who sang of the "tears of things"—was deeply moved by Dido's tragic love for Aeneas and her eventual suicide. Virgil's poem is thus the expression of an unresolved tension between the claims of Love and the claims of the City. Dante is unwilling to let this tension remain unresolved. He is unwilling to let Love and the City, the private and the public, be enemies, just as he is unwilling to let Love and Intellect be enemies. Beatrice is the figure who symbolizes the ultimate unity of these opposites. That Dante's love for her was not obsessive is beautifully conveyed by Beatrice herself in *Paradiso* 18, where she reminds her lover: "not only in my eyes is Paradise" (18.21).

Love, for Dante, when it is allowed to mature and be educated, opens our eyes to the divine goodness of world order and intellectual clarity. Its great result is not possession but transfiguration. By dying to the drive to satisfy our private lust, we become lovers of the very lawfulness and public order that the carnal sinners of Canto 5 scorned: rightness is made sweet to us. The *Comedy* is the grand elaboration of a truth at once simple and profound: love, when rightly understood, is our greatest teacher.

Notes

1. All translations are those of the author.
2. For the story of how Dante first met Beatrice and responded to her early death, see his *Vita Nuova*.

3. It makes sense that the virtuous pagans and the carnal lovers are infernal "next door neighbors": the first group represents the eternal frustration of intellectual desire, the second the eternal suffering of the mindless motion of carnal desire. Each group, in its own way, sought a heaven on earth.

4. Cf. *Inferno* 1.60, where Dante's dark wood of the soul is said to be a place "where the sun is silent."

5. The connection between eros and wingedness is given its most playful expression in Plato's *Phaedrus*, where Socrates suggests that the word *eros* derives from *pteros*, the word for wing (252C).

6. For details about Semiramis and the other famous carnal lovers, see Singleton's commentary on the *Inferno*, pp. 77-82, in Dante Alighieri, *The Divine Comedy*, translated, with a commentary, by Charles S. Singleton, Bollingen Series LXXX, (Princeton: Princeton University Press, 1970-76). Note that the entire list is composed of pagans. (The Christians Lancelot and Guinevere are not yet named.) The subjection of reason to desire, unlike suicide, is not a specifically Christian sin. Note, too, that Dido and Cleopatra are suicides but are ranked here among the carnal lovers. Dante respects the fact that pagan belief does not condemn suicide.

7. See Singleton's note on Achilles, Singleton, *Divine Comedy*, p. 80: "Dante's allusion to [Achilles'] death refers not to the Homeric story but rather to the accounts of the Trojan War current in the Middle Ages."

8. Singleton makes the valuable observation that Paolo and Francesca are "light upon the wind," that is, more tossed around by the storm than other lovers, because their passion was greater—they yielded themselves to Love more than others did (*Divine Comedy*, p. 82).

9. The most eloquent opponent of Francesca's second law is the shepherdess Marcela in *Don Quijote*. Marcela defends herself compellingly against the charge that she is unjust: "Heaven, you say, has made me beautiful—so very beautiful that you are moved, unable to help yourselves, to love me, and because of the love you show me I am obliged, you say, as also you desire, to love you. I know, by the natural understanding God granted me, that everything beautiful is lovable, but I do not understand how, because it is loved, that which is loved for its beauty is obliged to love whoever loves it" (Burton Raffel trans. [New York: A Norton Critical Edition, 1999], 77).

10. The most pointed formulation of the sheer naturalness of love is found in Guido Cavalcanti's famous poem, *Donna me prega*, "A Lady Bids Me." Cavalcanti was once Dante's "best friend," as we hear in the *Vita Nuova*. When Dante meets the heretics of *Inferno* 10, he has occasion to speak with Guido's father (10.52-72). Guido's poem rejects the transcendence of nature and replaces the theology of love with a physics of love. Guido, in short, is an anti-Dante who refuses to link love either to knowledge or to grace. Perhaps this is why, in Canto 10, the pilgrim Dante refers to Beatrice as "she whom your Guido held in disdain" (63).

11. On the various meanings of Dante's adjective *dubbiosi*, see Singleton, *Divine Comedy*, 92-93.

12. See Singleton, *Divine Comedy*, 93.

13. Francesca may be thinking of the beginning of Book 2 of the *Aeneid*, just before Aeneas begins his tale of woe for the listening Dido (2.3 ff.). A more heartbreaking invocation
of memory occurs in Book 4, where Dido, just before she commits suicide, sees Aeneas' clothes on her bed and recalls her all-too-brief happiness with him (4.643 ff.).

14. In his commentary, Singleton quotes the elaborate retelling of Francesca's story by Boccaccio (*Divine Comedy*, 84-89). Singleton remarks that Boccaccio's version is

"embroidered nicely to exculpate Francesca as much as possible" (p. 84). Like Cavalcanti Boccaccio rejected Dante's teaching about transcendent love, as is amply seen in the setting and the stories of his *Decameron*. Boccaccio was the first to append the adjective "divine" to the title *Comedy*, thereby opening up the possibility for another comedy, one that celebrates the delights of sexual love. For Boccaccio the desire for and belief in transcendence is a kind of disease or madness from which the *Decameron* seeks to deliver us. No wonder he brazenly gives the alternate name *Galeotto* or Gallehault to his masterwork, the name Francesca uses in referring to the book that brought her and Paolo together in sexual union. Can we doubt what he hoped reading his book would occasion? Like Cavalcanti Boccaccio defines his project as that of an anti-Dante who will reinstate the teachings of Francesca.

15. It is interesting that in the romance *Lancelot du Lac* it is Guinevere who first kisses Lancelot (Singleton, *Divine Comedy*, pp. 94-95). The reversal of the kiss in Francesca's story makes her even more the merely passive victim of the "advances" of all-conquering eros.

16. A deep connection exists between Francesca in Canto 5 and Ulysses in Canto 26. Romance is closely linked to adventure. Just as Ulysses exhorts his men to sail into the forbidden regions of the physical world (26. 112-142), Francesca, in her rhetoric, is the enchantress who beckons the gentle heart to the transgressions of love. Francesca and Ulysses are perverters of human bonds: she perverts the bond of marriage, he the bonds of comradery. Appropriately, each is punished with a partner in crime: she with Paolo, he with Diomedes (26.55-56). For a fuller account of Ulysses as a perverter of human bonds and the connection between Ulysses and Francesca, see my "Dante and Ulysses: A Reading of *Inferno* 26" in *The St. John's Review* Vol. XL, no. 3 (1990-91).

17. My reading here (and throughout my essay) is hugely indebted to Charles Williams and his book, *The Figure of Beatrice: A Study in Dante* (New York: Hippocrene Books, Inc., 1973). Williams writes: "The formal sin [of Paolo and Francesca] is the adultery of the two lovers; the poetic sin is their shrinking from the adult love demanded of them, and their refusal of the opportunity of glory" (p. 118).

18. The two books that most taught Dante about the proper reading of signs were the *Aeneid* and Augustine's *Confessions*. Reading is of central importance to the latter work. Augustine's goal is not primarily to confess his sins but to confess the presence of grace and providence throughout his life. Augustine's path to salvation is mediated by a complex series of divine signs. Indeed his eventual conversion in the garden is mediated by stories and books: the story he hears about the conversion of Victorinus (8.2); the book about the life of Anthony, who himself was admonished by a chance reading of Scripture (8.6); and the voice of the child who chants, "Take up and read; take up and read" (8.12). The *point* that masters Augustine proves to be a point of conversion. It is precisely the point that Paolo and Francesca reject.

19. A brief statement of the main events in the life of St. Francis can be found in Singleton's commentary on the *Paradiso*, *Divine Comedy*, 200-201. For a lively account of the importance of St. Francis for Dante's views on sacred history, see Erich Auerbach, "St. Francis of Assisi in Dante's *Commedia*" in *Scenes from the Drama of European Literature* (Gloucester, Mass.: Meridian Books, 1973), 79-98.

Chapter 4

Aliens Are Us? Walker Percy's Response to Carl Sagan on Wondering and Wandering

Peter Augustine Lawler

> *"I have undertaken a different kind of search . . . .*
> *Before, I wandered as a diversion. Now I wander seriously."*
> —Binx Bolling, in Walker Percy's The Moviegoer

From the beginning of the West, morally sensitive and politically astute writers have criticized the moral and political effects of the self-forgetfulness characteristic of natural scientists. Aristophanes, in *The Clouds*, laughs at the practical obtuseness of the natural scientist Socrates, who understands everything that exists but himself and his fellow human beings. For Aristophanes, Socrates was dangerously indifferent to morality because he abstracted theoretically from the distinctiveness of human nature, from human fears, passions, and longings. Plato, accepting that criticism, presents a different Socrates, one that remains philosophical but is attentive to the human difference, to the natural foundation of moral, political, and religious longing. The novelist Walker Percy, in his instructive mocking of the natural scientist Carl Sagan, seems to be the Aristophanes of our time. But his comedy, like Plato's, is in the service of philosophy rightly understood. Percy, a strange combination of novelist, philosopher, scientist, and Catholic, may show us better than anyone else how to correct our natural scientists' self-forgetfulness without abandoning science or philosophy. Percy, in my view, is a sort of Catholic Socratic, if by Socrates we mean the one portrayed by the philosopher/poet (the man who wrote dialogues or plays) Plato and not the one criticized so well by Aristophanes.[1]

Sagan and Percy both wrote prose and fiction that are wrongly called popularizing. They connected scientific knowledge to the fundamental questions of human life, and so no question was alien to either of them. Percy wrote his *Lost in the Cosmos: The Last Self-Help Book*, a hilarious and profound mixture of literary forms that includes a two-part space odyssey, partly to correct Sagan's elegant *Cosmos*, a huge best-seller as a book and, an equally successful television series.

Sagan's *Pale Blue Dot*, thoughts on the human condition, intelligent extraterrestrial life, the stars, planets, and comets, and a possible human future in space, was written after Percy's death, but it is the fullest and most inspirational version of Sagan's literary project. Sagan and Percy agree that human beings are naturally wanderers and wonderers, but they disagree on why human beings wander and wonder. So, they also disagree on both the likely benefits of space travel and on the nature of aliens. Although they were both prolific writers, I will, for the most part, limit my comparison to *Pale Blue Dot* with *Lost in the Cosmos*. My analysis of Sagan will come first, but from the very beginning my mind is on why Percy found Sagan so curious, and on why Percy, better than Sagan, understands why human beings wonder and wander.

Sagan on the Wanderer

Sagan knows that the attractiveness of vast expenditures for space travel faded with the end of the Cold War. Mere curiosity or wonder is never enough to animate the people or political leaders. So *Pale Blue Dot*'s first words are "We were wanderers from the beginning" (xi).[2] And we humans have almost always been wanderers, hunters, and foragers, until quite recently. We altered our way of life because we found better ways to satisfy our material needs, but "the sedentary life has left us edgy, unfulfilled" (xii). Despite our material success, we tend to believe that human greatness is past, that the best human efforts in literature, art, music, even science, are behind us. We even speculate "that political life on Earth is about to settle into some rock-stable liberal democratic world government, identified, after Hegel, as 'the end of history.'" We are edgy because there is nothing new to do, and no point in wandering. But our nature, our biological fulfillment, remains somehow as wanderers (384-85, 390). Sagan arouses a little nostalgia, that associated with anthropology: "Judging from some of the last surviving hunter-gatherers just before they were engulfed by the present global civilization, we may have been relatively happy" (390). And we make that judgment because we know we are relatively unhappy now. But there is no going back. We have forgotten how to be hunter-gatherers, and that way of life could not, of course, come anywhere near to supporting the number of people now on the planet. But most of all, Sagan contends, as hunter-gathers "we would be helpless before the impact catastrophe that inexorably will come" (383-84).

The original hunter-gathers roamed in the pursuit of survival. And we need to wander again for the same reason. We now know that "the chance is almost one in a thousand that much of the human population will be killed by an [asteroid] impact in the next century" (320). The impact will surely come eventually. The only way our species can perpetuate itself indefinitely is for some of us to abandon this planet. From another planet, we may be able to develop and use the technology required to deflect asteroids away from earth. Even if that technology fails and life is destroyed on earth, the species survives, because it will have dispersed among the planets. "The eventual choice" of all intelligent, planet-dependent species is "spaceflight or extinction" (327). And space travel must eventually be more than just planet-hopping. We should not be deceived by how "reliable" the sun has been so far (387).

We need to begin to wander through the planets and eventually solar systems and galaxies to give the species "a jolt of productive vitality" (284) and with the purpose of making it as safe as possible. Our time is extraordinary because of the unprecedented danger for self-destruction and the unprecedented opportunity for indefinitely postponing destruction, both the result of the present state of techno-logical development (373-74). Sagan quotes Bertrand Russell that space travel might "show to even the most adventurous of the young that a world without war need not be a world without adventurous and hazardous glory" (284). Purposeful, species-unifying adventure without war is just what we need today. Space travel will save us from both asteroids and each other.

We can wonder whether Sagan's analysis of wandering is too simply biological. But he does say that without the "escape hatch" of space travel, "we may have been locked and bolted into a prison of the self," and that we need to get our minds off ourselves and on to "something vastly larger" (405). And saying we cannot help but wander is of great help in explaining our dissatisfaction. Sagan disagrees with those who hold that we are homesick for our roots, for some stable and particular social order. He writes, in part, to make us at home with our homelessness. The strongest human longings, properly understood, do not hold us to any particular community, planet, or solar system.

Wondering About Cosmic Magnificence and Human Insignificance

Sagan says that human beings are passionate and inquisitive or wonderers by nature (36). They rightly wonder about the human place in the cosmos, about the vast, awesome, and magnificent universe considered as a whole, and about the possibility of intelligent extraterrestrial life elsewhere in the cosmos (54-56). Human beings "experience a stirring of wonder" when they first discover the simple truth that we are cosmic accidents and that the universe was not made for us (12). Sagan quotes Tolstoy: "The meaningless absurdity of life is the only incontestable knowledge available to man" (53). But our pretensions are as natural as our curios-ity and wonder; "our natural way of viewing the world" comes from the primates, who proudly privilege their own group. Natural is "a kind of ethnocentrism" (47).

We do, because of wonder, and do not, because of pride, want to view ourselves as modern science does, as accidents. Human beings want to believe in a providen-tial God or nature, that they are cared for and are the highest part of existence. But the progress of science has been the "Great Demotion" of man to a tiny, insignifi-cant being in no qualitative way different from the other animals. Proud or religious efforts to resist scientific truth "betray a failure of nerve before the Universe—its grandeur and magnificence but especially its indifference." The truth discovered by science is rational and impersonal; there are no grand and magnificent persons (50-51). Our wonder eventually overwhelmed our prideful and religious delusions: "As we began to indulge our curiosity, though, to explore, to learn how the universe really is, we expelled ourselves from Eden" (56). But who would choose to leave Eden? Pride, although natural, deludes us, and so it is conquered by wonder, which leads us to the truth.

Sagan refuses to say what some physicists today do: Our ability to understand how the universe really is, its order or design, is evidence that the human mind, at least, is somehow at home in the cosmos; human existence could not simply be accidental or insignificant. We may be specks of dust on a pale blue dot, but we can also crack the "cosmic code." Wondering about the cosmos or the whole of nature and our knowledge of that whole have no obvious survival value, and they are hard or impossible to explain in terms of some accidental process of evolution.[3] But Sagan skeptically refuses to say that our purpose is to know the cosmos, although he can say that we cannot help but wander and wonder. The scientists, Sagan contends, who adhere to some kind of Anthropic Principle, the view that life had an inherent tendency to evolve in the direction of consciousness, are infected by "residual pride" (38).

Sagan on the Sacred

Modern science, in Sagan's eyes, seems in some respects to show the truth of existentialism. Human life is absurd and insignificant, and human beings must be nervy or courageous enough to see that there is no providential God and that nature views their existence with indifference. Sagan says, "knowledge is preferable to ignorance," but not because it is enjoyable or comforting. "Better to embrace a hard truth," he asserts, "than a reassuring fable" (57). Courage and so pride, more even than wonder or wisdom, sometime seem to be the qualities that lead us to the truth.

But existentialism is not Sagan's final word. He admits "we crave some cosmic purpose," and apparently cannot be cured of it. Human beings were left without a "telos" when science eroded tradition and religious belief. But they still need "a sacred project," "a sanctified notion of humanity's potential" (403). And so Sagan says, "let us find ourselves a worthy goal" (57). And let us call that "long-term goal . . . a sacred project" (405). Worthy means according to nature, one that integrates our natural or biological inclinations to wander, wonder, and preserve the species. Sagan shows that his choice of human purpose, space travel, aims to satisfy together all three longings. In order to begin to wander effectively, "we [must] vastly increase our knowledge of the Solar System," or make discoveries that flow from our wonder (377). And of course, our wandering will open our minds as never before to the magnificence of the universe, for Sagan the most awesome source of wonder. Our wandering and wondering are rooted in the responsibility given the species by nature to survive. The "longing for safety," most fundamentally, is what leads us to wander, and if human beings were ever to become content with the species' duration, the wandering would end. But then our species would have evolved into something else (400). For now, meaning probably millions of years, we can make species safety our sacred cause. It is the one most solidly rooted in nature or relatively free from prideful delusion (399). We must notice Sagan's innovation. The liberal or bourgeois human thinkers, following Christian psychology, connected human wandering or restlessness to the individual's longing for safety, and the existentialists share that focus on the individual's fate.

There are at least two reasons for Sagan's correction of the individualism of liberalism and existentialism: Obsessing about one's own fate leads to a narrow fearfulness incompatible with courage and openness to wonder. And the individual, of course, cannot really do much to fend off his impending death. In the name of virtue and success, our attention must turn from the individual of the species. But are self-conscious beings—those who wander and wonder—really motivated all that much by the species' fate? Or can they be made to be so in the future? Concern for the species may be more solid or scientific than concern with God, but can devotion to the species really replace love of a God who cares for me in particular? Human beings really are individuals, each concerned with his or her own mortality. One of the ways Sagan employs to turn the focus away from human self-consciousness is to say that chimps are self-conscious too (31). And Sagan, the celebrant of wandering and wondering, does not really want us to revert to the consciousness of chimps, much less become unconscious. He searches for "myths of encouragement" to support our choice of "many worlds" over none. He notices that "Many religions, from Hinduism to Gnostic Christianity to Mormon doctrine teach that—as impious as it sounds—it is the goal of human beings to become Gods." Sagan proclaims for the record that he worries "about people who aspire to be 'god-like'" but for this encouraging purpose he lets that thought pass. He asks us to "consider the story in the Jewish Talmud left out of the book of Genesis," in which "God tells Eve and Adam that He intentionally left the Universe unfinished." The responsibility of our species "over countless generations" is to complete creation. Perhaps in the name of survival we can "rise to this supreme challenge" and eventually become Gods (382). If we really solve the problem of survival, we will become gods. Or will we? Each god is immortal, not the species of gods.

What must be regarded as Sagan's final word on religion is quite different. The truth is "science has far surpassed religion in delivering awe." Because we have focused our thoughts on ourselves and not on the universe, we have come up with a puny God who mirrors our insignificance. If religion would turn its attention to the universe in its grandeur, elegance, and subtlety, God himself would seem much greater, if quite indifferent to us in particular. Sagan's prediction is that "A religion, old or new, that stressed the magnificence of the Universe as revealed by modern science might be able to draw forth reserves of reverence and awe hardly tapped by the conventional faiths. Sooner or later, such a religion will emerge" (52). If we not only turn our attention from the individual, but from the species, we will finally find something worthy of our devotion.

Extraterrestrials and Intellectual Progress

Sagan wonders both about the stars and the possibility of extraterrestrial intelligence (ETI). The discovery of ETI need have nothing to do with space travel. The best method, in fact, is radio contact, and Sagan encouraged the American government to pour resources into both the space program and signaling ETI. He was distressed by the American government's lack of interest in pursuing such fundamental knowledge, observing that "every civilization in human history has devoted some of its resources to investigating deep questions about the Universe, and it is hard to think of a deeper one than whether we are alone."[4] Much of his writing is in support of that search.

Sagan is distressed that extraterrestrials are so often portrayed as aliens, as beings fundamentally different from and threatening to us. If they find us, the thinking goes, "they will come here and eat us." And so both space travel and sending out radio signals are foolish (353). Sagan reports that he convinced Steven Spielberg to make his two hugely successful films about benign ETs (355). He himself, with his wife, wrote a strikingly similar film script, based on the best-selling novel *Contact.* The film, more than the book, is an encouraging myth, a story with a vaguely but insistently religious dimension. It begins with a brilliant and lonely girl who becomes a scientist and spends her life searching through the world with a short-wave and later through the cosmos for contact. She finally discovers comforting, paternalistic, advanced beings, who have been watching over us and gradually and benevolently intervening in our affairs. Through this initial contact, otherwise unknowable secrets about the nature of the cosmos are revealed to a human being. This revelation mysteriously brings inspiration to people searching for meaning to replace discredited biblical religion.[5]

But in *Pale Blue Dot,* Sagan mocks all such pictures of fatherly providence as they have appeared throughout history. He too obviously manipulates the image of the biblical, paternal God to promote his more scientific view that ETI would likely be benign. Our fears about extraterrestrial intelligence, he says, are evidence of our "guilty conscience" about human history. They make no sense in terms of understanding a society more advanced than ours.[6] Given our obvious isolation in a particular part of the universe, Sagan can add: "The vast distances that separate the stars are providential. Beings and worlds are quarantined from one another. The quarantine is lifted only for those with sufficient self-knowledge and judgment to have traveled from star to star" (398). But that claim too is suspicious because of its connection with providence.

Yet even the skeptical, scientific Sagan cannot help but often really see something rather providential: His usual view is that technology and morality clearly evolve. Human conflict and violence are rooted in "the deep, ancient reptilian part of the brain." Human history is the movement away from violent, reptilian behavior and toward living scientifically and cooperatively, from pure body to pure mind.[7] With time, all intelligent life becomes less passionate and violent, or more benignly godlike. So even the biological desire to wander, he muses, might eventually fade away. The only glitch in this process is that moral evolution sometimes lags behind technological development, as is the case now on earth, raising the prospect of technological self-destruction. Extraterrestrials, he says, may aid us in moral evolution, saving us from ourselves. Their appearance at this crucial moment, especially when the government is dragging its heels on space travel, must be regarded as providential.

But in musings buried in a footnote, Sagan makes clear that he knows that the Spielberg-Sagan picture of benign ETs is not necessarily true. There are, in truth, several imaginable ways that an advanced extraterrestrial civilization might view our species. It might, in *Contact* fashion, seek us out, offering the good news that a high-tech society can "avoid self-annihilation." Or, having escaped self-inflicted catastrophe in its own development, such a civilization might fear discovery, might consider contact with other civilizations dangerous. But it might also be "aggran-dizing . . . looking for *Lebensraum*," or just aiming "to put down the potential competition" (372).

One way of speculating on which of these views is most likely true is to consider Sagan's view of our species' extraterrestrial future. We will abandon earth, which cannot support life forever. We will wander from planet to planet and solar system to solar system, consuming resources as we go. But the planets most useful to sustaining human life will be the ones already most likely to possess life, and Sagan admits that homesickness for earth will make those substantial and well-lit planets particularly attractive. We might find potential conflict well worth risking (391). Does Sagan want us to become planet-hopping, parasitical, life-destructive, resource consuming aliens like the ones portrayed in the film *Independence Day*? When it comes to the survival of the species he is "an unapologetic human chauvinist." Our exploration of our solar system will, unfortunately but necessarily, be a danger to any other life that may exist there (376). He even adds, "A less sympathetic observer might describe" such cosmic wondering "as sucking dry the resources of little world after little world." His rejoinder is simply to observe that "there are a million little worlds in the Oort Comet Cloud," which will just be the beginning of our journey. For all practical purposes there is an infinite amount of sucking to do (387). By thinking about ourselves, we can see that we have no particular reason to believe that extraterrestrials we contact will be good to us. A civilization must minimize internal conflict to wander the cosmos, but it might do so, like a band of pirates, to prey on others.

We are inclined to conclude that even Sagan himself is too hopeful about extra-terrestrial benevolence, because he hopes that intellectual development can save beings from their personal troubles. In his view, scientists are less screwed-up than ordinary people, and that view tends to the beginning of his hopeful imagining about beings more advanced and intelligent than our best scientists. But Sagan is less hopeful than he wants us to be. In encouraging the quest for contact, he is promoting a noble risk. His curiosity about ETI is greater than that for banal human troubles, and he actually expects that the fulfillment of his hope for the discovery of other intelligent beings will be the culmination of the beneficial lesson science has taught us. The discovery of ETI will show us that even our intelligence is nothing special in the cosmos. It will show beyond doubt, in Sagan's mind, the untruth of our anthropocentric biblical religion. Confident that we will eventually establish contact with any number of forms of intelligent life throughout the cosmos, Sagan nevertheless admits the small possibility that despite our best efforts we will never hear from anyone. But even that failure would be most instructive: "It would speak eloquently of how rare the living things of our planet are, and would underscore, as nothing else in human history has, the individual worth of every human being" (72-73). But the last thing Sagan wants to do is to focus us on individual worth. The implication is that if the search for ETIs succeeds, it will underscore the worthlessness of every human individual and how ridiculous individual self-obsession is. But the ETIs, in truth, will be worth no more than us, and our devotion will finally turn to the magnificence of the cosmos.

Sagan believes that human beings must both discover and become intelligent extraterrestrials to fully come to terms with the truth about their existence as insignificant cosmic accidents, with no purpose except species survival. Both of these projects turn us away from the ineradicable truth of individual contingency and finitude by submerging us in some more enduring natural whole. Perhaps Sagan's deepest teaching is that the incontestable truth affirmed by Tolstoy is too hard for him or us really to bear. Sagan, finally, does not make us at home with our homelessness but diverts us from what he believes to be the truth about how home-less we really are.

Percy's Self-Help Book

Percy's *Lost in the Cosmos: The Last Self-Help Book* rightly views Sagan's *Cosmos* as, most deeply, a failed attempt at a self-help book, and we can see that *Pale Blue Dot* is too. Sagan analyzes the plight of the wonderer and wanderer and offers a solution, and Percy does the same. But their understanding of both our predicament and what we might do about it are quite different.

The core of Percy's self-help is his explanation of "why it is that man is the only alien creature, so far as we know, in the entire Cosmos" (2).[8] The human being, Percy shows, is the being with the capacity for language by nature. Because of that capacity, he can come to understand pretty well everything in the cosmos except himself. The self, or the being that can know the cosmos, is always a leftover from any account of the cosmos. So as modern science explains more and more about the cosmos, the human being experiences himself as more and more an alien, and modern science tends to deprive that being of the language to articulate and come to terms with that growing experience of alienation. Percy disagrees with Sagan that that experience of human uniqueness is a prideful delusion. He also disagrees with the Marxist that it can be remedied by economic transformation, and with the behaviorist that it can be cured through behavioral or environmental change. He, finally, disagrees with Sagan that the remedy is wandering through space.

In Percy's first published novel, *The Moviegoer*, the protagonist Binx Bolling calls himself a wonderer and a wanderer. He begins as a self-forgetting scientist, a spectator or moviegoer, wondering about everything but himself. And his search barely diverted him from his despair. But soon he begins to wonder about himself, the searcher or wanderer. He discovers the true relationship between wondering and wandering.[9] The human being is a wanderer because he is a wonderer. The being who wonders cannot really account for or locate himself in the reality he can describe. He does not wander because he must hunt and gather, but because of his capacity for self-consciousness.

For Percy, the capacity for language and so consciousness is natural, but it introduced a fundamental discontinuity into nature that cannot be accounted for by the species' adaptation to its environment. "Neo-Darwinian theory has trouble accounting for the strange, sudden, and belated appearance of man, the conscious self which speaks, lies, deceives itself, and also tells the truth" (161). Percy imagines a conversation between two scientists in a stalled elevator in the Rockefeller Foundation building. The one who challenges the "post-Darwinian" asks "how do you account for the fact that with the appearance of man . . . almost immediately thereafter [follows] a train of disasters and triumphs which seem to have very little to do with adapting to an environment" from suicide through heroism to "child abuse and loving care for the genetically malformed" (197)? The dogma of modern scientists, Sagan's dogma, is the inability to acknowledge this discontinuity, and so the source of the unique joys, miseries, and perversities of human nature. Our species obviously exists for more than self-preservation; we are the only animals capable of consciously and perversely acting against self-preservation. We can commit suicide and murder, not to mention heroically risk our lives, for no natural reason. Language is a natural human capacity, and so consciousness, wondering, and wandering are natural too. But they cannot be explained in terms of the generally correct homogeneous theory of evolution. Human beings are by nature qualitatively different from the other animals. Percy introduces this "*thought experiment*" to show that Sagan's dogma prevents him, most of all, from understanding himself:

> Imagine that you are the scientist who has at last succeeded in puncturing the last of man's inflated claims to uniqueness in the Cosmos. Now man is proved beyond doubt to be an organism among other organisms, a species in continuity with other species, a creature existing in interaction with an immanent Cosmos like all other creatures, like all elements, molecules, gaseous clouds, novas, galaxies. Now, having placed a man as an object of study in the Cosmos in however an insignificant place, how do *you*, the scientist, the self which hit upon this theory, how do you propose to reenter this very Cosmos where you have so firmly placed the species to which you belong? Who are you who has explained the Cosmos and how do you fit into the Cosmos you have explained? (170)

Carl Sagan cannot locate Carl Sagan in the cosmos he describes; he has no place even in his own species. Percy understands and even sometimes shares the scientist's motivation to transcend absolutely the dreariness of ordinary life, and he knows the experience of the scientist or philosopher or artist that his activity is the most pleasurable for human beings, so much so that all other human activities "are spoiled by contrast" (143). But the trouble is that such transcendence cannot define a whole human life. Sagan cannot, in fact, become more than human by reducing, scientifically, all other human beings to beings just like the other animals. He remains a self or soul, born to trouble, and his science cannot tell him how to reenter the world of his own kind.

It is not surprising that Percy goes on to ask "Why is Carl Sagan so lonely" (173)? The first page of the two-part space odyssey that concludes *Lost in the Cosmos* includes a note where Percy acknowledges his debt to Sagan in writing them. He says that reading Sagan gives him great pleasure, and he agrees with his choice for the rigorous, self-correcting scientific method over superstition, including the various forms that now seem to "engage the Western mind now more than ever." But Percy adds that he finds reading Sagan more "diverting" than everything else, because everything he writes is infused with the "ignorance" of "unmalicious, even innocent, scientism." Scientism is the ideology which holds that all that exists can be explained the same, reductionistic way, and a diversion, according to Pascal, is something we use to get our minds off what we really know about the greatness and misery of the human condition (201-02).

Percy's complaint is that Sagan is not realistic at all; he does not give an account of what human beings, including the lonely, troubled Sagan, really experience and know. And Percy is amazed that Sagan can account for the whole history of science from the ancient Ionians to the present with no contribution at all from Christianity (201-02). But the Christians, such as Pascal, understand better than their Ionian or Greek predecessors why it is human beings wander, and the relationship between wandering and wondering. Christian realism, or the philosophy of St. Thomas Aquinas, is more scientific than Sagan's modern science, which is as much a diversion from as an expression of the truth. Human beings wander because they cannot, as wonderers, experience themselves as at home in this, natural world.[10]

The first part of the space odyssey concerns an earth starship's discovery of ETI, and the highlight is the conversation between the earthship and the extraterrestrials. The extraterrestrials describe themselves as possessing "The joy of consciousness and the discovery of the Cosmos through the mediation of symbols and the cooperation of others and the preservation of this joy against the incursions of boredom, fear, anger, despair, shame, and the love of war and death and the secret desire for the misfortune of others" (209). They enjoy being conscious and making scientific discovery without the characteristic perversities of being human. They are Percy's version of the benign ETIs of *Contact*.

These extraterrestrials are anxious to determine the nature of the consciousness of our species before allowing the earthship to land on their planet. They have discovered that "In some evolving civilizations, for reasons which we don't entirely understand, the evolution of consciousness is attended by a disaster of some sort. . . . It has something to do with the discovery of the self and the incapacity to deal with it" (210). The result is various forms of self-denial, "[p]laying roles, being phony, lying, cheating, stealing, and killing. To say nothing of exotic disordering of the reproductive apparatus of sexual creatures" (210). And these disorders produce beings who are cruel because they are sentimental (the teary compassion they claim to have for others they really have for their own disorders), and the ETIs are afraid of such civilizations. Beings with our kind of consciousness may be the only thing that can scare them. We are bound to be big trouble (211-12).

The extraterrestrial civilization has become free from this trouble because it became "aware of its predicament, sought help, and received it" (212). What this help is, is unclear, but we immediately think of God's grace. But it is clear that the predicament of the self cannot be cured by the self, and it does not evolve out of existence as intelligence increases. And it is equally clear that those on the human beings earthship, despite the fact that their civilization has self-destructed on earth, are unaware of either their troubled predicament or the need for help. So the extraterrestrials decide quickly and forcefully to order the earthship out of their planet's orbit, wanting to "Get them out of here" immediately (216). Their advice to what remains of our species is to "take your chances" with another screwed-up civilization on another planet (216-17).

Percy's thought on extraterrestrials is that they quite likely will be as "curious" and "murderous" as we are. A civilization that will have transcended the mixture of joy and misery of self-consciousness will have done so only with help beyond scientific understanding (216), and we have no reason to believe we will ever encounter such a civilization. Percy goes on to imagine the character Sagan ex-plaining to the ETIs that "We still have aggressive traits, but these can be explained by our residual reptilian brain" (217), allowing us to see how a genuinely advanced civilization would see that explanation as ridiculous self-denial. It is equally ri-diculous to think that the help we need will come from a superior extraterrestrial civilization. One freed from our troubles would have nothing to do with us, and one like us would surely be trouble for us. But Sagan's search might still be viewed as more than diversion. It is an acknowledgment, however misguided and incomplete, that even the scientist needs help he cannot provide for himself.

New Ionia versus Lost Cove

Percy's second space odyssey concerns a starship that was sent to follow up on what was thought to be a promising lead on extraterrestrial intelligence.[11] The mission failed to make contact, and the theme of this part of the odyssey is "what can happen if there is no one out there" (2). The focus of Percy's tale is the ship's captain, Marcus Aurelius Schuyler, a man with the same "dark" understanding of the human condition as the philosopher-emperor after whom he was named. He views human beings as more full of mischief and hatred than love. They are almost surely destined for self-destruction. But unlike the captain, they understand none of this, and their strongest motivations are unconscious. The captain's view is darker than the Christian's, but they are alike in being free from the diversion of scientific optimism or progressivism. "He was like a Christian," Percy writes, "who has lost faith in everything but the Fall of man." His view is that of the pre-Christian or stoic philosopher (228-29).

But Marcus is also "sardonic"; his dark view also has its pleasure. He enjoys being fully conscious of "playing the unflappable captain." He takes pleasure in living well with the strange contingency of human existence, and in not losing his bearings by "sticking with his decisions," even as they probably lead to failure. He also takes pleasure in the fact that, after leaving behind all his worldly possessions, including his woman, he feels no compulsion to look back. His sardonic role-playing is a form of pleasurable transcendence based on self-confident self-knowledge. It is evidence to himself that he can exempt himself from the conse-quences of the Fall (228-29).

The mission returns to an earth devastated by nuclear war. Landing in Utah, they find the astronomer Aristarchus Jones, who is as devoted to science as his Ionian namesake, three (two black and one Jewish) Benedictine monks, and about a dozen genetically malformed and misbegotten children. Aristarchus, named after the founder of science according to Sagan's *Cosmos,* and Abbot Liebowitz offer the captain two incompatible plans.

Aristarchus, like Sagan, thinks both about scientific truth and the perpetuation of the species, and he believes his plan to wander from earth is in the name of wondering. Life on earth is finished but might be reestablished on a firmly scientific foundation on a satellite of Jupiter. He is excited by the possibility of a "New Ionia," where people will live free from the "superstitions and repressions of religion," from the contentious mystifications of the Bible and Plato. They will live in peace, self-knowledge, and sexual freedom, and the arts and sciences will flourish uninhibited. In the name of science, or the species' perfection, the genetically malformed must be left behind. Nothing will be malformed in New Ionia (245-46).

The abbot says they must proceed to Lost Cove, Tennessee, where the effects of radiation may well be minimal and life sustainable. Siding with Plato and the Church against Ionian or apolitical science, he tells them to repopulate the cave. But this cave is "lost." It is for the lost, for beings who, as the Church says, will never feel completely home in this world.

The abbot's task is to perpetuate the Church, and the children born on the starship are potential priests. He gives an elegant, theological version of Percy's science, speaking not of the self but "ensoulment." He criticizes the Church, as a Catholic Jew, for not loving science and art more. He hopes to repopulate the University of Notre Dame with Jewish scientists. He realistically tells the captain and his party that they cannot escape the predicament of the soul or self merely by escaping planet earth; Sagan is wrong that planet-hopping can cure what troubles us as wanderers. The Church, not science, the earth, or some new physical location in the cosmos, points to the home they are seeking (247-51).

Percy does not have the captain make one choice or another. He does suggest that if he chooses Lost Cove it will be because of the influence of the woman he has unexpectedly come to love (who sees how religion protects marriage, the family, human community, and the mystery that is at the foundation of the love of one human being for another). The choice is left for the reader. But as an aid to choice, Percy imagines for us the consequences of each choice for the captain.

New Ionia's founding principles are freedom without God and self-knowledge through absolute honesty. Honesty is secured through "group self-criticism," which aims to abolish secrecy and lying. More generally, New Ionia is based on "The principles of Skinner's Walden II, modified by Jungian self-analysis, with suitable rewards for friendly social behavior and punishment, even exile, for aggressive, jealous, solitary, mystical, or other antisocial behavior." The principles are derived from Sagan's characteristically modern, scientific view that human behavior is not qualitatively different from that of the other animals. But New Ionia's aim is actually to suppress distinctively human qualities; a behaviorist utopia is a social order that works to *make* the Great Demotion true. In the name of self-knowledge, manifestations of human experiences of self are to be eradicated. In the name of honesty, antisocial or personal experiences are punished. But in truth, only the being ironic enough to lie and keep secrets can tell the truth to himself about himself or really be honest. And there are no real experiences of the goodness of human life in New Ionia. The substitute supplied to make life bearable is the "euphoria" caused by a drug. So much for self-knowledge.

The captain remains "somewhat ironical" about the group exercises, viewing them as a new sort of AA meeting. He finds no pleasure in his irony. It has become a reaction against human beings who have been or are just about free from the consequences of the Fall, thanks to behavior modification and drugs. His only pleasures are sex with any well-formed body or bodies (and so not with his old wife, who sulks, showing that she still has a self) and Shakespeare and Mozart, who remind him of his species' human or troubled past (256-57).

It might seem unfair to identify New Ionia with Sagan, or even Sagan with the behaviorist Skinner. Sagan holds that human beings will remain wonderers and wanderers as they leave this planet, but the problem is that thought contradicts his denial of human uniqueness. Skinner explains, more clearly than Sagan, the culmination of the way of thinking of modern science. Human beings are or will be completely determined by stimulus and response like the other animals.

The most important lesson Sagan should have learned from Percy is that it is impossible to see how the sciences and arts could flourish in New Ionia. There are no restless selves—those who wander because they wonder—longing for the truth and seeking absolute transcendence from the dreariness of ordinary life. There are just two miserable, superfluous selves—the captain and his wife. And if Sagan were there, he would join them in their misery. New Ionia has solved every human problem it seems, but that of the self or soul of the scientist or philosopher.

In Lost Cove, we find the captain "watch[ing] ironically yet not without affection" two black priests saying Mass in the cave. The community is flourishing with all sorts of human beings, including the most malformed and misbegotten, and the love and hatred of political life ("us against them") is returning, along with racism, feminism, war, and religious fanaticism. Wherever there is love of particular troubled selves for others, there is hatred too. The captain's thought is "Jesus Christ, here we go again," and he laughs.

Marcus sits "above the cave" (where you'd expect to find a philosopher) with a community of "good friends," a variety of dissidents and unbelievers known as the "heathen." When his wife asks him to come to Mass, Marcus responds "My cathedral is the blue sky. My communion is with my good friends." And she responds "Bull." The tension between the two somehow does justice to both reason and revelation, because each is, with some good reason, ironic about the limitations of the other.

The captain now enjoys his friends, the love and affection of others. He is happy with his wife, satisfied with being monogamous. He also likes liquor and pork and just being alive. He still does not believe; he remains somewhat detached or ironic, a wanderer and wonderer. But now ordinary life is more than bearable. He knows why he has affection for the priests and their Church. He knows, as he did not before, the limits of his independence. His freedom depends on the cave; his skepticism depends upon belief, and his pleasurable experiences of the goodness of life, even the theoretical ones, depend upon his love of others. He knows he is more alike than different from other human beings. He lives well with all sorts of misbegotten selves, because he knows that he is one too; he himself is far from being free of trouble or disorder. What the captain now knows is the true foundation of human wandering and wondering. He knows what Sagan did not: why it is that human beings can be scientists or philosophers, or restlessly in pursuit of the truth (258-62).

The Preposterousness of Wondering and Wandering

Percy also presents, as an aid to making the choice between New Ionia and Lost Cove, a thought experiment on "the relative preposterousness" of "Judaeo-Christianity" and the modern scientific consciousness of Aristarchus Jones. He begins by observing that "we are all Aristarchus Jones," that is, "rational, intelligent, well-educated, objective-minded denizens of the twentieth century, reasonably well versed in the sciences and arts" (252). Sagan merely expresses the pervasive scientism of our time. And Percy does not deny that Judeo-Christianity is preposterous from its view. So in the name of truth and courage, we characteristically refuse, like Sagan or even Marcus, to choose religious illusion over scientific fact.

But Percy adds a "new perspective" from which "the objective consciousness of our age is also preposterous." Consider that "The earth-self observing the Cosmos and trying to understand the Cosmos by scientific principles from which the self is excluded is, beyond doubt, the strangest phenomenon in all of the Cosmos." And that strangeness is evidence that "the self . . . is in fact, the only alien in the entire Cosmos" (253). What is most preposterous, finally, is that we are sometimes so far from self-understanding that we do not acknowledge the very existence of the self. Scientism attempts to dispense with human mystery and human uniqueness. But actually doing so would create a world not only without religion but without science. The Christian or Judeo-Christian explanation of our alien condition is surely not the only one, but it is one that understands and makes possible both wandering and wondering better than Sagan's scientism.

And who could deny that, after seeing the results of each choice, Sagan himself would choose Lost Cove over New Ionia, because he, like Marcus, could wonder and wander better there? Percy's self-help is not merely showing us that each choice is equally preposterous, and that we must choose. The choice for Judeo-Christianity, or at least the Judeo-Christian anthropology, is actually the choice for scientists and so science. The choice is not only for the truth or possible truth of biblical revelation but for what we really know about nature, including our own natures.

The preposterousness of Judeo-Christianity may be a reflection of preposterousness of our being lost in the cosmos, but only such lost souls or selves could come to know the cosmos, or be theorists or scientists. A world perfectly understood theoretically or scientifically would have no one to understand it, and both the self and the political community must remain disordered, like Marcus and his friends and Lost Cove, for human freedom to have a future. And so the Church actually protects the mystery that makes science possible. Knowing that alone should make us at home with our homelessness, or "[a]mbiguously at home" (139). We do somehow experience our true home as somewhere else, but that does not mean some other planet or star, and Sagan surely has misunderstood his deepest longing.

Notes

1. For a very clear and accessible account of the relationships among Plato, Socrates, and Aristophanes presented here, see Mary P. Nichols, *Socrates and the Political Community: An Ancient Debate* (Albany: State University of New York Press, 1987). The view of Percy given here is presented at much greater length in my *Postmodernism Rightly Understood: The Return to Realism in American Thought* (Lanham, MD: Rowman and Littlefield, 1999), chapters 3 and 4. Also see my "Walker Percy: Catholic Socratic?," *Modern Age* 40 (Spring, 1998), 226-31.

2. Numbers in parentheses in the Sagan sections of this chapter are page numbers found in Carl Sagan, *Pale Blue Dot: A Vision of the Human Future in Space* (New York: Random House, 1994).

3. For this line of criticism of Sagan, see the work of the physicist Paul Davies, including *Are We Alone?* (New York: Basic Books, 1995) and *The Fifth Miracle: The Search for the Origin and Meaning of Life* (New York: Simon and Schuster, 1999).

4. Carl Sagan, *The Demon-Haunted World* (New York: Random House, 1995), 396.

5. Carl Sagan, *Contact: A Novel* (New York: Simon and Schuster, 1985).

6. Carl Sagan, *Cosmos* (New York: Ballentine Books, 1985; first published 1980), 255-58.

7. Sagan, *Cosmos,* 269.

8. Numbers in parentheses in the Percy sections of this paper are page numbers found in Walker Percy, *Lost in the Cosmos: The Last Self-Help Book* (New York: Farrar, Straus, and Giroux, 1983).

9. Walker Percy, *The Moviegoer* (New York: Alfred A. Knopf, 1961).

10. On Percy's Thomistic realism, see my *Postmodernism Rightly Understood*, chapter 3.

11. Parts of this account of the second part of the space odyssey are borrowed from *Postmodernism Rightly Understood*, chapter 4.

Chapter 5

Shakespeare's *Henry V* and the Act of Ethical Reflection

Henry T. Edmondson III

> *"I and my bosom must debate awhile."*
> —Henry V

In his heroic history, *Henry V,* Shakespeare offers his audience a portrait of statesmanship.[1] The play is organized so that as it progresses, Henry's character unfolds, revealing successively the salient features of a virtuous leader. In the Prologue, the Chorus invites the reader to approach the play by parsing the various dimensions of his ethical character—"Into a thousand parts divide one man" (prologue:24-25).[2]

Henry's character is most visible in his introspection on the eve of the great battle at Agincourt. Ethical reflection, as Henry practices it, is the key to self-knowledge and the *sine qua non* of moral maturity. It is a skill; it is not performed on a whim, and if it is to guide one toward moral integrity, it should be practiced as a habit. It is the process of shining a flashlight into one's own soul. The taking of one's ethical inventory is especially important to the adult for whom moral consideration is both the means by which character is refined, and the sign that one takes seriously life's challenges and dilemmas. Aristotle explains that virtue may be acquired by three separate means: nature, acquired habits, and reason.[3] Nature has set her mark long before adulthood; even in adulthood, however, the sincere person can strengthen virtuous behavior and strive to attenuate vicious behavior. Guided by reason, the conscientious leader can continue life's moral education by the cultivation and preservation of moral reflection, a practice that frequently leads to the refinement of virtue.

Considered from a different perspective, ethical reflection is the process by which one is to acquire self-knowledge: in Socrates' immortal phrase, "The unexamined life is not worth living for a human being."[4] Yet, such self-knowledge is rare without a deliberate, purposeful attempt to acquire it. It is as much technique and habit as desire. Before looking closely at Henry's opportunity for self-examination in the Agincourt battle camp, a more general consideration of Shakespeare's famous play is important.

Shakespeare and the "Christian King"

"We are no tyrant, but a Christian king," contends Henry V to the French ambassador, using the royal first person plural to underscore the assertion (I:ii:241). Although there are competing interpretations of Shakespeare's play, the traditional interpretation has been that of the ideal Christian king. Hall states—if not overstates—the point:

> [His] life was immaculate and his living without a spot. . . . He was merciful to offenders, charitable to the needy . . . faithful to his friends, and fierce to his enemies, towards God most devout, towards the world very moderate, and to his realm a very father . . . He was a blazing comet . . . he was the mirror of Christendom and the glory of his country . . . the flower of kings past.[5]

More moderate is Shakespeare's own description, spoken by the Chorus in the epilogue to the play, where he concludes "This star of England . . . greatly lived" (V:iii:5-6).[6] The Chorus' assessment of Henry is important in divining Shakespeare's intentions, since their role is especially prominent in this play. Prior to the final scene in Calais where Henry sets the terms of peace with the French, the Chorus describes Henry's departure from London. They note that Henry refused an ostentatious display as both his humility and piety recommended against it: "He forbids it/Being free from vainess and self-glorious pride" (V:19-22). Introducing the important battle camp scene in Act IV, the Chorus explains that Henry's leadership is a buoy of encouragement and hope for his men in an otherwise desperate situation. In spite of the tattered condition of the army, "upon his royal face there is no note/How dread an army hath enrounded him," so that the most discouraged soldier under his command "plucks comfort from his looks" (IV:i:35-42).

More recent interpretations suggest that Shakespeare's intent was just the opposite. Shakespeare's purpose, they assert, was to undermine, however subtly, the reputation of a jingoistic, war-obsessed king. There are also those who recognize that Shakespeare meant to praise Henry V, but are uncomfortable with both the historic and poetic Henry V because of his militarism.[7] "No one bored by war will be interested in *Henry V.*"[8] Like it or not, "War was part of life in the sixteenth century and few, if any, dreamed of banishing war as an instrument for enforcing national policies."[9] Wilson and others attribute the intellectual genesis of this revisionism to Henry Hazlitt (1817) and Wilson notes that "*Henry V* is a play which men of action have been wont silently to admire, and literary men, at any rate during the last hundred and thirty years, volubly to contemn."[10]

Those who would criticize Henry V as bloodthirsty and driven by territorial greed can do so only by first refuting that Henry's campaign against France "was not naked aggression but the assertion of a legal right which it was his duty to enforce" even "at the expense of war."[11] Harold Bloom, in his contemporary best-seller on Shakespeare's works, quotes and perpetuates Hazlitt's cynicism.[12] Wilson summarizes the response of the traditionalists to the revisionists when he laments "Unhappy Shakespeare! He little dreamed that learned doctors would read their Holinshed or Holinshed's modern successors instead of his play, and so draw precisely those cynical conclusion, the evidence for which he had been at pains to erase from the record."[13] "Heroism is . . . the theme, and Henry the hero."[14]

Shakespeare then, invites us to view his portrait of the ideal leader as he sequentially reveals each dimension of his character, or his "many-sidedness" as one commentator describes it.[15] The Shakespearean Henry is a statesman: he is a leader governed by his integrity; a leader for whom "inward merit is the only basis of kingly right and rule."[16] The historical Henry V is the basis of Shakespeare's play.[17] "Shakespeare found the King highly extolled in Holinshed for his piety at home, and throughout his campaigns."[18] The king was twenty-six when he assumed the throne and the Parliament of the opening scene was the Parliament of the Spring of 1414. His marriage to Catherine of France, after that country's defeat pictured in Act V, took place in the Spring of 1420. Thus, the play spans four years. Henry based his claim for the throne of France on his descent from Isabella, Queen of Edward the Second, and daughter of Phillip the Fair, Henry being fourth in a line of direct descent from Isabella.

It is not necessary to believe that the historical Henry was the unexceptionally ideal Christian king. It is only necessary to understand that Shakespeare, in his desire to portray his concept of statesmanship, creates an *ideal* of the fifteenth-century English king. The ideal is based upon the real, but not limited by it.

The remainder of this chapter focuses upon Henry's capacity for moral reflection. This quality may be the most important for the statesman because, however virtuous he may be, the dilemmas with which he must grapple are likely to be complex and not given to mere spontaneous or instinctive resolution. That is to say, especially complex moral quandaries may require a combination of knowledge, wisdom, and fortitude that only personal integrity incubated in private moral consideration is able to direct. Such reflection, moreover, preserves in even the most accomplished leader a sense of humility. This humility is visible in a disposition to learn and openness to correction, without which any statesman is vulnerable to delusion and destructive pride.

Ethical Reflection

"I and my bosom must debate awhile," Henry tells his nobles on the eve of the crucial battle with the French (IV:i:31). In thus declaring his intention, the King reveals a habit of moral reflection demonstrated several times in the course of the play, especially evident on the eve of battle. In a sense, the moral climax of the play is not the famous battle but the previous evening of ethical introspection. But since Henry's ambition drives the action of the play, we must first ask if that ambition itself is ethical. Although great leaders are frequently driven by ambition, this powerful motivation is often associated with ruthlessness.

Although Shakespeare seems to approve of Henry's ambition, he clearly disapproves of a darker kind of ambition in both Richard the Third and Macbeth. The latter admits "I have no spur to prick the sides of my intent, but only Vaulting ambition, which o'erleaps itself/And falls on the others (*Macbeth* I:vii: 25-28). Abraham Lincoln sounds an unsettling warning when he prophesies that the generations of leaders who follow the American Founders may erect their own edifices even if that means razing the achievements of the predecessors. Yet these rulers can do nothing other than to follow their ambitious "ruling passion" intrinsic as it is to their nature.[19] Cervantes offers a similar warning when Scipio dourly observes, "Rarely or never is ambition fulfilled without causing harm to someone else."[20]

Though by ambition some soar to greatness, others are impelled to maleficent self-aggrandizement. Helpful in understanding the phenomenon of ambition is Tocqueville's distinction between "high" and "low" ambition, the essential difference being that with the leader of lofty ambition, ambition is achieved in the service of others, not at their expense.[21] For Shakespeare, then, Henry V is driven by Tocqueville's "lofty ambition" rather than the darker species of the same.[22]

Though zealous to rule France, Henry must first assure himself, by recourse to his prelates, that he has a just claim upon that country. He charges Canterbury to give him impartial counsel since he will act upon his judgment and that action could "awake our sleeping sword of war" (I:ii:22; also, I:ii:9-12).[23] To ensure his intent is clear to the churchman, Henry reiterates, "May I with right and conscience make this claim?" (I:ii:96). More to the legal point, Henry is interested in whether his right of inheritance trumps the claims of the Salic law. To be sure, it is on this point that some of the revisionist claims turn; namely, that ruthless ambition drove Henry to aggrandize his landholdings. In this view, his claim to rightful inheritance was but a pretense, yet Wilson responds,

> When the Henry of the play, therefore, affirms that he puts forth his 'rightful hand in a well-hallowed cause', he is speaking the simple truth. The war against France is a righteous war; and seemed as much so to Shakespeare's public as the war against the Nazis seems to us.[24]

Later in the play, the second and most important illustration of Henry's capacity for moral reflection occurs. The setting is the English camp near Agincourt on the eve of the decisive battle with the French. The somber anticipation engenders thoughtfulness in the English army. The entire episode is recorded in Act 4, Scene 1.

By contrast, in the previous scene, Act 3, Scene 8, members of the French army, who are more comfortably encamped nearby, are full of coarse swagger and irreverence. They entertain themselves by deriding the English, which activity itself soon degrades into debauched ribaldry. The French officers engage in a series of double entendres in which they compare horses with mistresses. Bourbon states that his horse is, in fact, his mistress; Orléans deliberately misunderstands him so that the conversation quickly speaks of "riding" one's horse/mistress and taming it/her as well: "Mine was not bridled" (III:viii:47). The conversation later runs to vile comparisons between the English and wild dogs.

Having established the profane and impudent demeanor of the French, the play visits the English camp. In light of the English tactical disadvantage, the mood is mildly anxious but the discussion is pregnant with insight.

> The poor condemnéd English
> Like sacrifices, by their watchful fires
> Sit patiently and inly ruminate
> The morning's danger; and their gesture sad. (IV:i:22-26)

As the King enters, he acknowledges the army's plight—"'tis true that we are in great danger"—but counsels an attitude that uses their distress as an opportunity for reflection—"The greater therefore should our courage be" (IV:i:1-2). In one of the most important and meaningful lines of the play, Henry declares, "There is some soul of goodness in things evil / Would men observingly distil it out" (IV:1:4-5). He reiterates the point a few lines later when he exhorts the others to "make a moral of the devil himself" by taking advantage of the night's pensive mood (IV:i:12).

In Henry's view, the eve of battle combined with the distressed state of the English army suggests that "we should dress us fairly for our end," that is, each soldier should prepare his conscience for the very real possibility of imminent death. Accordingly, he directs his noble, Sir Thomas Erpingham, to call the officers to a meeting in the King's pavilion. Meanwhile, Henry will enjoy a rare and unexpected opportunity to reflect upon his soldiers' state of mind, ruminate about the responsibilities of a leader, and debate the correlative responsibilities of a subordinate. The King, in the darkness, and wrapped in his cloak for warmth, finds that his own men do not recognize him. He first encounters Pistol who, with characteristically impulsive candor, speaks about the King more freely and casually than he should. He expresses his affection in his usual coarse manner: "The king's a bawcock and a heart of gold, a lad of life, an imp of fame, of parents good, of fist most valiant. I kiss his dirty shoe, and from heart-string I love the lovely bully." As an apparent afterthought he asks Henry, "What is thy name?" (IV:i:44-47).

Following the entrance of Gower and Llewellyn, and then the soldiers John Bates, Alexander Court and Michael Williams, the stranger (the King) tells them that he serves under Sir Thomas Eppingham. They ask, "[W]hat thinks he of our estate?" Hoping to lure the men into speaking their minds, the King glumly replies, "Even as men wrecked upon a sand, that look to be washed off the next tide" (IV:i:91-94). The two ask if Eppingham has spoken his mind to the King. He has not, Henry replies, but he should because "I think the king is but a man as I am."

> The violent smells to him as it doth to me. The element shows to him as it doth to me. All his senses have but human conditions. His ceremonies laid by, in his na-

kedness he appears but a man; and though his affections are higher mounted than ours, yet when they stoop they stoop with the like wing.[25]

For that reason, "no man should possess him with any appearance of fear" (IV:i: 96-105). Taking his own advice, Henry declares, "By my troth, I will speak my conscience of the king" (IV:i:111).

John Bates "takes the bait" and admits, "Then I would he (the King) were here alone." Henry then takes the King's part and defends his cause as "just" and his "quarrel honorable." The soldier Williams replies, "That's more than we know" (IV:I:119). Bates assumes the same agnosticism arguing that the King alone bears the moral responsibility for the military campaign; the only moral responsibility of the soldiers is to obey and the very act of their obedience absolves them of the wider guilt of an unjust conflict. At this point, the modern audience/reader must think of the Nuremburg trials, the Mi Lai incident, and every other conflict in which subordinates excused their heinous behavior by pointing to the authority of their superiors.

The soldier Williams follows Bates' faulty reasoning by arguing that "if the cause be not good" then it will be "the king himself" who will have a heavy reckoning to make "[w]hen all those legs and arms and heads chopped off in a battle shall join together at the latter day and cry all 'We died at such a place.' Now if these men do not die well it will be a black matter for the king that led them to it, who to disobey were against all proportion of subjection" (IV:i:123-133).

In response, Henry demonstrates by analogy that his soldiers cannot escape moral responsibility for participating in an unjust cause by pointing to the orders of their superiors. By their reasoning, "if a son that is by his father sent about merchandise do sinfully miscarry upon the sea," presumably carrying some sort of contraband, then the son would do nothing wrong, only the father. Henry asserts, "But this is not so" (IV:i:134-142).

He takes the logic one step further arguing that if a king's soldiers misbehave in battle, by rape, pillage, or premeditated murder, then, surely, that guilt would not be imputed solely to the king. Even if they escape the condemnation of ordinary civil or criminal justice, "they have no wings to fly from God," that is, they are still morally condemned. The point is that soldiers, although they may be subordinate to superior officers, are still moral agents, notwithstanding their protest that they were compelled to obey orders. Therefore, "no more is the king guilty of their damnation than he was before guilty of those impieties for the which they are not visited" (IV:i:144-152).

Henry eloquently concludes, "Every subject's duty is the king's, but every subject's soul is his own" (IV:i:159-160). For that reason every man must examine his own conscience: "Therefore should every soldier in the wars do as every sick man in his bed, wash every mote out of his conscience." This is the advantage of the dire circumstances in which the soldiers find themselves: it compels them to engage each in his own moral reflection and thus "death is to him advantage"—or "not dying"—because of the time spent in moral "preparation." For those who do not fall in battle, they will carry the benefits beyond the battle as they can employ their experience "to teach others how they should prepare." Williams seems convinced as he concedes, "'Tis certain, every man that dies ill, the ill upon his own head; the king is not to answer it" (IV:i:160-168)." In this exchange, Henry proves himself, not only a moral actor, but also a moral teacher to his men.

Shakespeare, though, will not leave Henry smug in his polemical triumph. Bates changes the subject by immediately challenging Henry's trustworthiness. "Although I do not desire that he should answer for me, I determine to fight lustily for him." Henry asserts "I myself heard the king say he would not be ransomed" (IV:i:171)." This is an important point because it means, if true, that the king will fight to the death as he expects of all his army, rather than, in the face of sure defeat, surrender himself to the French so that he might later be "bought" back by England. Williams sarcastically expresses his doubt that the King's promise might be little more than rhetoric meant to goad his army to the ultimate sacrifice: "Ay, he said so to make us fight cheerfully, but when our throats are cut he may be ransomed and we ne'er the wiser" (IV:I:2-3). Henry impulsively jumps to protect his own integrity, but can only offer the weak retort that if the King is duplicitous, "I will never trust his word after."

Williams mocks him:

That's a perilous shot out of an elder gun,[26] that a poor and private displeasure can do against a monarch. You may as well go about to turn the sun to ice with fanning in his face with a peacock's feather. You'll never trust his word after! Come, 'tis a foolish saying. (IV:1:175-9)

Williams' cynicism touches a raw nerve in Henry and it is well that it should. The subordinate expresses the frustration often felt against leaders that, at the end of the day, those in leadership do what they want, and often do so with impunity. Isabella makes the same complaint of leadership when she must confront Angelo's hypocrisy in *Measure for Measure*, as she says "Authority / Though it err like others / Hath yet a kind of medicine in itself / That skins the vice o' th' top" (II:ii:134-136). To be sure, Williams is not only doubting Henry's reliability, he is expressing the universal frustration of those who feel that leaders, in whatever political or religious form they appear, are often unaccountable. Henry is clearly disturbed by Williams' faithlessness in the King's integrity and loses his composure. He has no reasonable reply other than to turn his offense into an adolescent-like challenge as he whines, "Your reproof is something too round. I should be angry with you if the time were convenient." Williams responds in kind, "Let it be a quarrel between us, if you live," to which Henry angrily snaps, "I embrace it." The two then exchange gloves as a means of identifying each other after the battle at which time they plan to consummate the quarrel. Fortunately the exchange of gloves brings the contention to a temporary halt so that it degenerates no further, as Bates counsels the two, "Be friends, you English fools, be friends! We have French quarrels enough if you could tell how to reckon" (IV:i:180-198). In this last quarrel Henry is sufficiently sensitive to his duty to be troubled by the exchange. One might interpret the passage as revealing volatility and temper on Henry's part. A more apt interpretation is that

Henry is concerned about his reputation precisely because he seeks to be a responsive, trustworthy, and accessible leader.

As the soldiers exit the scene, the King is reduced to the despair and anguish that leaders experience if they appreciate the moral burden they carry. "We must bear all," he laments (IV:I:205). He complains, also, of the deprivations that public leadership brings: "What infinite heart's ease must kings neglect, That private men enjoy?" (IV:i:209-210). If a king enjoys a kind of god-like status it is an odd sort of divinity as such a god—if he be ethical—"suffer'st more / Of mortal griefs than do thy worshippers" (IV:I:214-215). He cannot "sleep so soundly as the wretched slave . . . with body filled and vacant mind / Gets him rest" (I:i:241-2). Such is and should be the plight of the Aristotelian king who rules, not in his own self-interest, but in the best interest of his subjects. That is to say, there is a measure of personal agony that should accompany moral leadership.

To Henry's credit, the next morning immediately before the battle, the French envoy Montjoy offers Henry a final escape by submitting himself for ransom, thus avoiding what appears to be sure defeat. By doing so Henry could avoid bloodshed—including his own—and eventually he could be restored to his present position with perhaps little worse than the *status quo ante bellum*. Henry refuses, predicting that, if his soldiers should fall in battle, their decomposing bodies will continue to make war upon France, the "smell whereof shall breed a plague in France" (IV:iii:102-3).[27]

Piety

Henry's unexpected midnight soul-searching reveals a leader at once ambitious, wise, sincere, vulnerable—and fallible. His fallibility especially requires that he possess one further moral quality: piety, which emerges at the conclusion of this nocturnal camp scene. He acknowledges the sin of his father Bullingbrook (later crowned Henry IV) who murdered Richard II and usurped his throne.

Not today, O Lord,
Oh, not today, think not upon the fault
My father made in compassing the crown.

Henry reminds the Deity in prayer that, as an act of penance, he has reinterred Richard's body and in doing so "have bestowed more contrite tears" than the bloodshed in the crime (IV: ii: 266-270). [28]

Some might call piety out of fashion. Even so, contemporary leaders of all philosophical persuasions seem incapable of resisting the temptation to invoke God's blessings after public addresses. Leaders frequently offer "thoughts and prayers" to the unfortunate. Victims of natural disasters and participants at Middle East summits, for example, are invariably the recipients of such benefaction. Contemporary practice as well as *Henry V* suggest that an attitude of piety borne of humility is always in fashion. No situation, moreover, seems as likely to induce piety as war.

On July 29, 1967, the supercarrier U.S.S. *Forrestal* suffered a disaster that permanently changed both construction and training for U.S. Navy aircraft carriers. While stationed off the coast of North Vietnam, an electric generator used to start jet engines sent a wayward electrical impulse to an A-4 jet on the flight deck of the carrier. The impulse caused a missile to fire across the deck hitting another aircraft that in turn ignited a jet fuel explosion followed by an uncontrollable raging fire. By the end of the day, the carrier had suffered nine major on-board detonations of the ship's own 500- and 1,000- pound armaments, and countless smaller missile explosions, including shrapnel-filled anti-radar ordinances.

The ensuing holocaust claimed 134 lives, including scores of sailors who were instantaneously cremated in below-deck sections of the ship while sleeping in their bunks. Many more were maimed or lost their lives to fire and explosions while heroically fighting to control the holocaust that threatened the entire *Forrestal* crew of five thousand and even nearby ships of the *Forrestal* battle group.

When the conflagration was finally contained, Commanding Officer Captain John K. Beeling, in perhaps the most challenging duty of his career, addressed the physically exhausted and emotionally shattered survivors, many of whom had spent hours collecting the charred remains or fragments of their fellow sailors. What does a leader say at such a time? What words can acknowledge the ship's immense tragedy and assuage the crew's deep grief, yet at the same time, initiate their difficult process of psychological and emotional healing while rejuvenating their sense of hope?

Beeling offered a prayer. He introduced it by conceding that "no words" could express the sentiment they shared, yet he would try, on their behalf, to express their thanks and acknowledge their "deep, deep, debt to Almighty God." The captain continued,

> Our Heavenly Father, we see this day as one minute and yet a lifetime for all of us. We thank You for the courage of those who gave their lives in saving their shipmates today. We humbly ask You to grant them peace and to their loved ones the consolation and strength to bear their loss.

Acknowledging the temptation to despair, the CO asked, "Help us to renew the faith we have in you." Resisting the natural tendency toward existentialist anguish in the face of a seemingly absurd disaster, Beeling instead turned the occasion toward greater faith:

> May we remember You as You have remembered us today. From our hearts we turn to You now knowing that You have been at our sides at every minute of this day. Heavenly Father, help us to rebuild and re-man our ship so that our brothers who died today may not have made a fruitless sacrifice.[29]

Piety may be broadly conceived as the acknowledgment that the leader is not the beginning and end of his own wisdom. The leader is not morally autonomous in the sense of being his own self-contained moral government; rather, if he is pious, he defers to some combination of Deity, tradition, history, and even colleagues who may possess moral wisdom greater than his own. The pious leader recognizes that he is answerable—somehow and to someone—for his decisions.

Demagoguery or Statesmanlike Rhetoric?

In regard to the spectacular English victory on the fields of Agincourt, Wilson argues that "the zenith of the play is not the victory . . . but the King's speeches before the battle is joined."[30] Winston Churchill called oratory "the language of leadership."[31] But it is also the weapon of demagoguery. Anyone who has heard Hitler's impassioned stentorian speeches has witnessed the power of speech misused by a fiend. Henry's memorable and stirring speech, on the other hand, is the combination of his skill and his integrity. Had it not been for his soul-searching the night before, he may not have enjoyed the confidence to deliver the same speech the following day.

Rhetoric is a tool for good or bad. The issue is explored in Plato's dialogue *Gorgias*, in which the interlocutor of the same name asserts that polemical political speech is a kind of craft involving the "power to persuade," just as carpentry is a kind of craft that carries the power to construct. This persuasive power leads to conviction, but the craft itself does not distinguish between what is just or unjust and may be simply a "knack" for "flattery." Speeches may be aimed at no higher goal than the "gratification" of the audience.[32] Speeches, according to Socrates, should be aimed not at what is most pleasant, but at what is best. Flattery is to be shunned, and rhetoric always must be aimed "in the direction" of justice. Such justice, among others things, consists of teaching others to be good in both private and public life, not merely to seem to be good. It includes acknowledging when evil is done and accepting the due consequence of such misbehavior. To live justly means to be genuinely "fine and good" and to "practice virtue."[33] There is, of course, no guarantee that rhetoric will not be misused just as there is no guarantee that the power of a firearm will not be misappropriated. One can only hope that the powerful tool of rhetoric will be wielded by men and women of integrity so as to encourage their audience to "just living."

But even those of integrity will speak most nobly and will be most effective if their important moments of oratory are preceded by ethical introspection. Such preparation will lend a moral confidence to the speaker that will be evident in the speech itself and in its effect. The juxtaposition of Henry's examination of conscience and his oratorical masterpiece implies that the success of the latter was directly proportional to the earnestness of the former. Henry, then, fulfills Socrates' admonition because of his moral integrity. In particular, he does so by his act of reflection not twelve hours before the famous St. Crispin's Day rally to his troops on the cusp of battle.[34]

To appreciate the speech one must understand the English army's desperate plight. Henry's army, already inferior in number to the French when he set sail from Southampton, has been reduced by one-third during the siege of Harfleur and during the subsequent march to Calais, primarily as a consequence of dysentery. The 150-mile march took sixteen days rather than the expected eight because the French had blocked the most convenient crossing of the River Somme. Arriving at Agincourt, "the men were wet, hungry and exhausted, and many were ill."[35]

As dawn breaks and the French are afforded a clear view of the English army they take great sport in mocking their bedraggled opponent. They observed, "Big Mars seems bankrupt in their beggared host" (IV:iii:43). The constable wryly notes, "They have said their prayers, and they stay for death" (IV:iii:56). Bourbon wonders if, before the decisive contest, it might be fairer if the French were to send the English dinner, fresh clothes, and provisions for their horses (IV:iii:57-9).

Exercising no more than common sense, the English soldier Westmoreland laments that there are ten thousand men of England otherwise idled by the holiday who would be useful in the fight. Henry retorts that if the army were larger, those present would be compelled to share the recognition of their noble cause. He says, "The fewer men, the greater share of honour" (IV:iii:22). Henry then elaborates upon this theme and in doing so demonstrates Aristotle's practical teaching on the use of rhetoric.

Aristotle teaches that the orator can, among other devices, make a deliberate emotional appeal to his audience, choosing carefully the "target" emotion. It might be fear, anger, indignation, or it could be honor.[36] Henry explains that he may not be greedy for material gain, but he lusts for something nobler.

> God's will, I pray thee wish not one man more.
> By Jove, I am not covetous for gold,
> Nor care I who doth feed upon my cost.
> It yearns me not if men my garments wear.
> Such outward things dwell not in my desires.
> *But if it be a sin to covet honour,*
> *I am the most offending soul alive.* (IV:iii:23-29; my emphasis)

Henry continues that he "would not lose so great an honour" by sharing it with any more than necessary; moreover, he wishes for even more (IV:iii:31). Henry mixes this appeal to honor by invoking the specter of the antithesis of honor, shame.

> [H]e that hath no stomach to this fight
> Let him depart. His passport shall be made,
> And crowns for convoy put into his purse. (IV:3:35-37)

The King so skillfully plays to the honor of the men that he creates in their mind the idea of an elite cadre of heroic men whose membership is a matter, not of necessity, but of privilege.

> This day is called the Feast of Crispian.
> He that outlives this day and comes safe home
> Will stand a-tiptoe when this day is named,
> And rouse him at the name of Crispian.

> He that shall see this day and live old age
> Will yearly on the vigil feast his neighbours,
> And say 'Tomorrow is Saint Crispian.'
> Then will he strip his sleeve and show his scars,
> And say 'These wounds I had on Crispin's day.' (IV:iii:40-48)

The names of the participants in the battle will become legendary as not a St. Crispin's day will go by "[b]ut we in it shall be remembered" (IV:iii:56-9). Their names will become household words, and the objects of moral lessons taught to sons by their fathers. The imminent battle will be a kind of blood initiation into an intimate sacred brotherhood that will render equal all those involved.

> We few, we happy few, we band of brothers—
> For he today that sheds his blood with me
> Shall be my brother; be hene'er so vile
> This day shall gentle his condition— (IV:iii:60-3)

Any Englishman not so privileged to be a part of this fight will forever be envious of his missed opportunity.

Henry's speech so inspires the Duke of York that he pleads with Henry to obtain the honor of leading the vanguard of attacking soldiers, a role almost sure to end in death. Henry consents, saying, "Take it, brave York. / Now soldiers, march away, / And how Thou pleasest, God, dispose the day" (IV:iii:131-2). The English, after a hard fight, enjoy a stunning victory over the French despite their many handicaps.

Conclusion

Henry's evening in the battle camp suggests several practical measures for the leader who wishes to cultivate the habit of ethical reflection. The first is illustrated by his understanding that "There is some soul of goodness in things evil, Would men observingly distil it out" (IV:i:4-5). The reflective leader must be opportunistic since some times are more fertile for reflection than others. The most promising opportunities are the important if not grave moments of one's life. The prospect of radical change, death, loss, or humiliation focuses the attention while stirring the passions. Although such occasions may provoke anxiety, best is the response that funnels that emotional energy into sober reflection.

The King's night of self-examination also teaches that ethical reflection need not be a solitary event. Solitary reflection for the morally mature is fruitful, but fruitful also is the time spent in counsel with a trusted colleague. Before one can accurately assimilate a personal moral inventory, one may often need the benefit of seeing an image of one's soul reflected back as in a mirror, from a friend. Indeed, as Aristotle teaches, friendship is an indispensable piece of one's philosophical equipment. True friendship among those pursuing a life of integrity is a kind of kinship in which each friend "encourages the other to reach the pinnacle of one's ethical maturity that will be seen in a life of noble action."[37] As the proverb has it, "Iron sharpens iron and one man sharpens another."[38] Such friendships for the leader, though, are difficult to obtain and enjoy because the associates of a man or woman of power are most likely to be keen "to serve and please." They rarely possess the "wit, insight, and flexible temperament" necessary to tactfully challenge and correct a leader.[39]

The eve of battle also suggests that if a leader genuinely wishes to gain a needful perspective on his role as leader, he needs the frank opinion of his subordinates. This is perhaps the hardest of all to achieve; only by Henry's cleverness and subterfuge was he so illuminated. More typical is the tendency for leaders to surround themselves with "flatterers" whom Erasmus, in his *Education of a Christian Prince*, identifies as perhaps the greatest danger facing any ruler.[40] Elsewhere, Erasmus notes that "the ears of Princes are strangers to truth, and for this reason they avoid those Wise men, because they fear lest some one more frank than the rest should dare to speak to them things rather true than pleasant; for the matter is, that they don't much care for truth."[41] Erasmus knew of what he counseled for he had the living example of his close friend, the King's Chancellor Sir Thomas More, for whom truth and conscience were more precious than life itself.

Morally rich literature offers the same opportunities for a kind of examination of conscience. The insights into human psychology and motivation in Dante's *Inferno* and *Purgatory*, the abundant philosophical principles and political warnings so manifest in the narrative and drama of Joseph Conrad's works, and the many moral lessons of Shakespeare, all offer ethical challenges to the reader humble enough to submit himself to the tutelage of the author.

To do so may require a conscious choice in the use of one's leisure time. Plutarch, whose *Lives* offer keen insight into public leadership, rues those who "misuse that love of inquiry and observation which nature has implanted in our souls, by expending it on objects unworthy of the attention either of their eyes or their ears, while they disregard such as are excellent in themselves, and would do them good."[42] Henry and his men could have spent the eve of battle as did the French, in bawdy, coarse, and superficial talk. Instead the English king offers an example of self-inquiry to all those who hold responsibility and must bear the weight of making difficult but wise choices and leading by the example of their integrity.

Notes

1. There are, of course, many editions of *Henry V*. The one used here is the Cambridge School Shakespeare edition. Marilyn Bell, Elizabeth Dane, and John Dane, (Cambridge: Cambridge University Press, 1997). The layout is pleasant, the footnotes are (barely) adequate, and each scene is both introduced and concluded with a short editor's discussion. The Oxford Shakespeare's *Henry V* not only offers a pleasing format but very thorough footnotes and an intelligent introduction. Gary Taylor, ed. (Oxford: Clarendon Press, 1982). The two film adaptations are the 1944 Laurence Olivier (now also on DVD) and the recent popular 1989 Kenneth Branaugh production. *Newsweek* calls the latter "a critical and commercial success" and the "flash point" for the new cinematic Shakespeare craze. ("Close-Up on Will," February 15, 1999, p. 15.)

2. Hudson notes that King Henry V is "the most complex and many-sided of all Shakespeare's heroes" other than Hamlet. Shakespeare, *King Henry the Fifth*. With introduction, and notes explanatory and critical, Rev. Henry N. Hudson, LL.D. (Boston: Ginn & Company: 1889), 16.

3. Aristotle, *Politics*, Carnes Lord, trans. (Chicago: The University of Chicago Press, 1984.) 1332a 41.

4. Plato, *The Apology*, Harold North Fowler, trans. (London: William Heinemann, 1933), 38a4-5. Also see *Philebus*, Harold N. Fowler, Ph.D., trans. (London: William Heineman, 1935), 48c12. Representing this important theme of self-knowledge among the Spanish mystics, see St. Teresa of Avila, *Las Moradas* (Sevilla: Apostolado Mariano, n. d.), I:8, p. 13.

5. Edward Hall, 1548, quoted in Shakespeare. *King Henry V*, Marilyn Bell, Elizabeth Dane and John Dane (Cambridge: Cambridge University Press, 1997), 220.

6. No doubt some of the more cynical revisionism of Henry V of the nineteenth and twentieth centuries were a reaction to the cloying excesses that stopped just short of Henry's canonization; e.g., Rolfe gushes, "And having vindicated the justice of God, and purged his country of treason, Henry sets his fact to France with the light of splendid achievement in his eyes." William J. Rolfe, Litt.D., ed., *Shakespeare's History of King Henry V* (New York: American Book Company, 1905), 18.

7. For an intelligent and balanced summary of this debate, see *King Henry V* John Dover Wilson, ed. (Cambridge: Cambridge University Press, 1947) xv-xlvii.

8. Shakespeare, *Henry V*, The Oxford Shakespeare (Oxford: Clarendon Press, 1982), 1.

9. Shakespeare, *Henry V*, Louis B. Wright and Virginia A. LaMar, eds. (New York: Washington Square Press/Pocket Books Publication, 1960), xiv.

10. Shakespeare, *King Henry V*. John Dover Wilson, ed., (Cambridge: Cambridge University Press, 1947), vi.

11. Wright and Lamar, *Henry V*, xiii.

12. Harold Bloom, *Shakespeare and the Invention of the Human* (New York: Riverhead Books, 1998), 321-4.

13. Wilson, *King Henry V*, xxii

14. Hudson, *King Henry the Fifth*, 16.

15. Rolfe, *Shakespeare's History*, 12.

16. Hudson, *King Henry the Fifth*, 17.

17. Shakespeare's main historical source was Raphael Holinshed's *Chronicles of England*, Scotland and Ireland (1587). In some places Shakespeare quotes Holinshed word for word. Holinshed, *The Famous Victories of Henry the Fifth*. See Bell, Dane, and Dane, *King Henry V*.

18. Hudson, *King Henry the Fifth*, 31.

19. Abraham Lincoln, "The Perpetuation of Our Political Institutions." Address to the Young Men's Lyceum of Springfield, Illinois. January 27, 1838. Available: http://www.founding.com/gohome.htm.

20. Miguel de Cervantes, *The Dialogue of the Dogs*, in *Exemplary Stories*, Lesley Lipson, trans. (Oxford: Oxford University Press, 1998), 262.

21. Alexis de Tocqueville, *Democracy in America*, J.P. Mayer, ed. George Lawrence, trans. (New York: Harper Perennial, 1969), 627.

22. Aristotle explains the problem of ambition in a different but compatible way. Ambition may be defined as the love of honor, but the love of honor easily slips into the love of flattery; accordingly noble ambition degenerates into the baser sort of ambition. Aristotle, *Ethica Nicomachea* (Oxford: Oxford University Press, 1986), 1159a12ff.

23. Sullivan offers an interpretation of Henry V casting him as the consummate Machiavellian: "Henry is Machiavelli's guileful prince of appearance." In this instance, for example, she accuses Henry of craftily placing the responsibility for war on his religious advisors. To the extent Sullivan demonstrates cunning on Henry's part, however, I find it to be a shrewdness not incompatible with integrity. Vickie Sullivan, "Princes to Act: Henry V as the Machiavellian Prince of Appearance," in *Shakespeare's Political Pageant: Essays in Literature and Politics* (Lanham, Md.: Rowman & Littlefield, Inc., 1996), 126, 125-152.

24. Wilson, *King Henry V*, 1947, xxiv.

25. An allusion to falconry.

26. Irony: that is, a (toy) popgun made of elder wood.

27. The most notable apparent inconsistency in this argument for Henry's integrity as commander-in-chief comes when he orders all the French prisoners slaughtered. According to the play, he does this in retaliation for the wanton murder of the English boys left behind to guard the English equipment and luggage (IV:vii:1-8). Both acts constituted violations of a sense of justice in war. Hudson (1947) offers this explanation:

> This incident is related in full by Holinshed. It appears afterwards, however, that the King, on finding that the danger was not so great as he at first thought, stopped the slaughter, and was able to save a great number. It is observable that the King gives as his reason for the order, that he expected another battle, and had not men enough to guard one army and fight another. Gower here assigns a different reason. Holinshed gives both reasons, and the Poet chose to put one in the King's mouth, the other in Gower's. (footnote, 141)

A difficulty in this interpretation of Henry V, traditional though it is, has to do with the "complex" problem of Henry's execution of the French prisoners after finding that the young boys guarding the English luggage behind the battle lines have been slaughtered by the French. Henry's retaliation has been interpreted as cold-blooded murder at Henry's hand. It is also suggested that his self-control escaped him upon finding the French. Indeed, the historian Hall's description of the scene is disturbing as he said, "pity it was to see and loathsome it was to behold how some Frenchmen were suddenly sticked with daggers, some were brained with poleaxes, some were slain with mallets, other had their throats cut and some their bellies paunched." Taylor explains, though, that Henry's decision would have been accepted by any Elizabethan audience who understood that Henry feared a second-wave counter-attack by the French at any moment. His badly outnumbered men could only look upon the captured French as a potential component of the imminent attack, a division already within Henry's own forces.

28. Kittredge explains that "For the intensely religious nature of King Henry, Shakespeare had ample justification in Holinshed." Kittredge, ed. Shakespeare. *The Life of King Henry the Fifth* (Boston: Ginn and Company, 1945), x. The only extant portrait of Henry, painted by an anonymous artist of the late fifteenth century, hangs in the National Portrait Gallery, London, England. The image supports Henry's pietistic character albeit to the point of suggesting asceticism.

29. *Situation Critical: The U.S.S Forrestal*, prod. by Brian J. Kelly, dir. By Peter Mullett, 50 min., Henninger Media Development, 1997, videocassette. I am indebted to many of the men and women aboard the U.S.S *Carl Vinson*, from whom I have learned a great deal about the life and operation of a nuclear aircraft carrier.

30. Wilson, *King Henry V*, 1947: xxxi

31. James C. Hume, *The Sir Winston Method: The Secrets of Speaking the Language of Leadership* (New York: William Morrow & Company, 1991).

32. Plato, *Gorgias*, Terence Irwin, trans. (Oxford: Clarendon Press, 1979), 455a 1-2, 462d 13, 463b 3, 46521e 10.

33. Plato, *Gorgias*, 521e 10, 527a 1,ff.

34. St. Crispin's day, October 25, a public holiday celebrating the martyrdom of the brothers Crispin and Crispianus, thrown into boiling lead for being Christians. (Bell, et al, *King Henry V*)

35. Bell, Dane, and Dane, *King Henry V* (Cambridge: Cambridge University Press, 1997), 138.

36. Aristotle *Rhetorica*, W. Rhys Roberts, trans. In *The Basic Works of Arisotle*. Richard McKeon, ed. (New York: Random House, 1941) 1355a 4-5, 1361a27ff. In regard to Henry's appeal to a kind of elite camaraderie see 1380-33ff.

37. Aristotle, *Ethica Nicomachea*, (Oxford: Oxford University Press, 1986) 1155, 13-15. My translation.

38. Proverbs 27:17. Revised Standard Version.

39. Aristotle, *Ethica* 1158a 30-33. My translation.

40. Desiderius Erasmus, *The Education of a Christian Prince*, Lester K. Born, trans. (New York: Columbia University Press, 1936). This is Erasmus' canvass of the ideas on statecraft of classical and medieval thinkers followed by his own discourse. Many classical thinkers warn against flatterers; e.g., Isocrates, 48-9; Xenophon, 51; Plutarch, 71; Dio Chrsostom,73; Marcus Aurelius 80, 84; Erasmus, 193-204. It may be helpful, in order to appreciate the relevance of this discussion for modern leadership, to note the tendency of many contemporary leaders "to hear what they want to hear," as the expression goes, instead of encouraging and recognizing constructive criticism.

41. Erasmus, *The Praise of Folly* (Oxford: At the Clarendon Press, 1931), 72.

42. Plutarch, *Plutarch's Lives*, The translation called Dryden's. Corrected from the Greek and revised. By A. H. Clough (New York: A.L. Burt Company, Publishers, Vol. I. n.d.), 290.

Chapter 6

Rabelais and Pascal: Wise Kings and Anguished Men

Pádraig Ó Gormaile

> *"The greatness of man is that he knows himself to be miserable."*—Les Pensées, *No. 397*

The French *tradition moraliste* refers to writers whose work has its origins and its purpose in provoking reflection on human nature, human behavior and human society. It refers in particular to writers like Montaigne (sixteenth century), Pascal, La Rochefoucauld, La Bruyère (seventeenth century) and Vauvenargues (eighteenth century), the most celebrated of the French *moralistes* and authors of reflections on the mores of an era and a people. The texts of the *moralistes*, a typically French term, are frequently brief and characteristically take the shape of thoughts, maxims or sketches. Peter France correctly states that "what the reader derives from these short texts is less a moral truth than a stimulus to self-examination, observation, reflection and discussion."[1] Much of the French moralist tradition concentrates therefore on addressing certain fundamental aspects of the human condition with a view to describing universal human conduct and with the purpose of encouraging the reader to engage in the process of self-knowledge. Such observations may include details of everyday human existence but may also refer to more serious topics like just wars and good government.

The French *moralistes* express the fundamental yet universal skepticism of those human beings, who, in T. S. Eliot's terms, live by thought and who either balk at the ultimate question or go on to discover faith. Eliot explains, "For every man who thinks and lives by thought must have his own skepticism, that which stops at the question, that which ends in denial, or that which leads to faith and which is somehow integrated into the faith which transcends it."[2] While the remarks of moralist writers touch on the fundamental truth of the human condition as it effects ordinary human beings, they also refer to these selfsame universal characteristics in the case of rulers and kings even though the latter were frequently held throughout history to be above the level of existence of mere mortals.

This chapter shows how two French thinkers-cum-writers, namely Rabelais and Pascal, one from each of the sixteenth and seventeenth centuries, reveal basic perceptions of human nature. Their insight informs our understanding of human behavior today, particularly with regard to the use of political power. More to the point, Pascal and Rabelais teach us that kings, no less than commoners, are morally inadequate creatures. Both political classes attempt to divert themselves from their moral misery by frivolous distractions. In the case of kings, however, such activity may have ramifications far beyond the personal life of the political ruler. The antidote to this state of affairs, as Pascal especially teaches, is the cultivation of self-knowledge. As self-knowledge is acquired, the ruler will recognize his moral inadequacy and seek to remedy it through spiritual growth.

Gargantua, by François Rabelais

Rabelais was born in the Loire valley, probably in 1494, and died in 1553. His father was a lawyer, and as a young man he frequented liberal monastic schools in the west of France where Greek was once again being studied as a direct consequence of the humanist renaissance. As a monk and a Greek scholar he became suspect to the Church authorities because of the effect of knowledge of Greek on biblical interpretation, and he subsequently temporarily abandoned the priesthood. Having turned instead to the study of medicine, he went on to teach the subject at university while authoring medical texts. He fathered two children, traveled in Italy on several occasions, and having practiced medicine, later returned to holy orders. At the center of the humanist movement, and having acquired a vast amount of learning, he published *Pantagruel*, in 1532. This story of the giant Pantagruel, the son of Gargantua, whose tale is told in his second published book entitled *Gargantua*[3] and published approximately three years later, parodies the received wisdom of the day, the classical tradition as well as the author's contemporaries. Rabelais' fiction recounts the tale of a family of giants with particular insistence on the birth, education, and military accomplishments of Gargantua and Pantagruel. In the mid-1540s the Sorbonne (i.e., the University of Paris), under the powers of censorship conferred upon that institution, was busy combating the success of humanism. Anxious to defend its conservative clerical ethos, it condemned the writings of Rabelais, and numerous other works by other theologians, philosophy and imaginative literature. Rabelais' work offended the clerics of the University by criticizing, among other things, the out-dated, irrelevant, and bookish education then dispensed in scholastic institutions. He further outraged the defenders of public taste by his bawdy if not scatological sense of humor which, far from intending to offend, in fact projects a deep respect for everything human and is expressed in a style which conveys a unique form of linguistic inventiveness.

The story of Rabelais' life is inextricably linked with the spread of humanism and the attempts of the evangelical movement to effect necessary reforms within the Church. His work is satirical in nature and pokes fun at religious practices that appear to him to have outgrown their usefulness, while also satirizing (harmlessly) institutions such as the papacy and condemning unjust wars. His linguistic style is unique in the history of French literature because of its inventiveness and its energy.

Rabelais reveals his standing as a humanist writer in the education of the giant Gargantua; and in the portrait of the despot Picrochole, whose instability leads to the declaration of the unjust Picrocholean war. Pircrochole is the perfect example of the bad or immoral ruler. The Picrocholean war is unnecessarily provoked as a result of a disagreement among country-folk, and King Picrochole avails of the opportunity to attack the territory of his neighbor, King Grandgousier (Gargantua's father). When attempts to avoid a war have failed and self-defense demands a reaction, Grandgousier recalls his son Gargantua to defend his people. Because of Picrochole's unbridled ambition, his bellicose manner and the extremely poor advice offered by his counselors, war becomes inevitable. The intervention of Gargantua and his troops is decisive and they defeat Picrochole's forces without difficulty, thereby confirming in passing Gargantua's worthiness to succeed his father as king in due course. When the hostilities are over Gargantua delivers a victor's speech, revealing his nobility of spirit and great generosity before sending the vanquished home laden with presents. The reader notes the burlesque satire of the epic hero-tale by means of which Rabelais holds the reader's attention. Reference to contemporary events and local detail add to the attractiveness of the text in which the major characters, many of them literally larger than life, have a strong symbolic meaning. Discussion here will be confined to *Gargantua*, chapters 25-50, i.e., the Picrocholean war, and will deal in particular with the theme of kingship and war: Grandgousier is the portrait of the wise and generous king; while Picrochole represents the weak and tragicomic despot.

In *Gargantua*[4] the king Grandgousier makes arrangements to replace the young prince's medieval and backward education by new humanist, pupil-centred methods of pedagogy. He then describes, in chapter 25, "How a great Quarrel arose between the Cake-bakers of Lerné and the people of Grandgousier's country, which led to great Wars" (G&P, 94). In a nutshell, while Grandgousier's shepherds were protecting the precious Autumn vines from attack by birds, the bakers of Lerné passed by on their way to town with a large consignment of cakes. We then read: "Now the said shepherds courteously requested the bakers to sell them some of their cakes for cash at the market price" (G&P, 94). Rabelais follows with a colorful comment on how delicious is the taste of "grapes and fresh cake" and on the beneficial effect of grapes on the constipated bowel; we must not forget that he was also one of the leading medical experts of his day. However, we are more interested in the violent and unprovoked reaction of the bakers, which also provides the storyteller with the opportunity to reveal his remarkable gift for colorful, embellished and descriptive language

The cake-bakers, however, were not at all inclined to accede to this request and, what is worse, they heaped insults on the shepherds, calling them babblers, snaggle-teeth, crazy carrot-heads, scabs, shit-a-beds, boors, sly cheats, lazy louts, fancy fellows, drunkards, braggarts, good-for-nothings, dunderheads, nutshellers, beggars, sneak-thieves, mincing milksops, apers of their betters, idlers, half-wits, gapers, hovel-dwellers, poor fish, cacklers, conceited monkeys, teeth-clatterers, dung-drovers, shitten shepherds, and other such abusive epithets. (G&P 94)

The shepherds initially react to these insults as puzzled, "honest neighbors" (G&P, 94) before one of their number is unwittingly drawn into a trap and attacked, after which a general mêlée breaks out. Finally, the shepherds demonstrate that they are not only just but generous as "they caught up with the bakers and took from them about four or five dozen cakes, for which they paid them the usual price, however, giving them a hundred walnuts and three baskets of white grapes into the bargain" (G&P, 95). The shepherds' gesture proves their good faith.

The peace offering of the shepherds is of no effect, however, and the bakers complain to King Picrochole about the beating delivered by their neighbors. Picrochole "promptly flew into a rage and, without any further question of why or how, called out his vassals great and small, commanding every one, under pain of the halter, to assemble armed in the great square in front of the castle at the hour of midday" (G&P, 96). The satirical names of his commanders prepare us for the "rash and disorderly fashion (in which) they took to the fields" (G&P, 96): Lord Hairychest, Blow-trumpet, Duke Rakepenny and Captain Swillwind. More significant still in the headlong, unplanned foray led by Picrochole is the unparalleled, wanton destruction carried out by his men against Grandgousier's people. The bravery of Friar John of the Hashes, monk of Seuilly, in saving the Abbey (and its precious vineyard) fails to stop Picrochole's advance and he goes on to take the town of La Roche-Clermault. Grandgousier reacts in disbelief at this news: "'Picrochole, my old and perpetual friend, united to me by blood and by alliance, has he come to attack me? Who is inciting him? Who is urging him on? Who is leading him? . . . It must be the evil spirit that has prompted him to outrage me now. Lord God, Thou knowest my courage, for from thee nothing can lie concealed'" (G&P, 102).

Grandgousier's natural reaction is, first, to question the truth of what he has heard, then, to ask for God's help. Finally, he consults his counselors and son for advice and assistance. The contrast with his adversary's rash and bellicose manner is striking: "Thereupon he ordered his council to be convoked, and set the matter before them just as it was. Their decision was that some prudent man should be sent to Picrochole, to find out why he had so suddenly broken the peace and invaded lands to which he had absolutely no claim" (G&P, 102).

Grandgousier meanwhile writes to his son, Gargantua. The letter, chapter 29, gives an insight into the basic Christian principles that inform Grandgousier's understanding of his kingship and that of course contrast dramatically with the unprincipled actions of Picrochole. Grandgousier writes in a manner reminiscent of the prayer of Saint Francis of Assisi: "My intention is not to provoke, but to appease; not to attack, but to defend; not to conquer, but to guard my loyal subjects and hereditary lands, which Picrochole has invaded in an unfriendly manner, without reason or excuse" (G&P, 103). The aggrieved king concludes, given the irrational behavior of his aggressor, that the latter is deranged and that it is his duty not only to defend his own people; but, to bring about the restoration of sanity in his neighbor's camp: "He (i.e., God) has entrusted me with the duty of recalling him to his obedience and bringing him to his senses by painful experience" (G&P, 103). Without insisting that Gargantua return to assist his father, the letter reminds the prince of his duty to "save and protect" his people. Even at this advanced stage, and in direct contrast with Picrochole's destructiveness, it is the king's intention that: "Our measures will be carried out with the least possible bloodshed. If it is possible, we shall by subtler expedients, by tricks and stratagems of war, save all souls and send them to their homes rejoicing" (G&P, 103). The position of self-defense, clearly justified in Grandgousier's case, will not to be used as a pretext to invade, confiscate or unnecessarily destroy Picrochole's property.

Grandgousier's emissary, Ulrich Gallet, communicates to Picrochole the displeasure of Grandgousier. He refers to their previous friendship, reminds him that procedures exist for grievances to be aired, and admonishes him to pay a fine for the damage already incurred by his men. Picrochole's response is inadequate, vulgar and childish: "Come and fetch them. . . . Come and fetch them. They've a good ballocky pestle, and a mortar here, and they'll knead some cakes for you" (G&P, 107). Ever anxious to establish the objective facts of what actually happened in the vineyard, Grandgousier carries out an investigation into the incident of the cakes to verify the facts. He awards the shepherds' leader for his bravery and honesty and offers retribution to Picrochole for any harm inflicted on his bakers. Picrochole reacts instinctively: "These clods are in a fine funk. By God, Grandgousier's shitting himself, the miserable boozer! He's not a fighting man" (G&P, 108). He therefore confiscates the peace offering of food sent by Grandgousier, intending to use it as rations for his ill-equipped army and heads into council with his advisers.

Chapter 33, "How certain of Picrochole's Advisers, by their headstrong Counsel, put him in extreme Peril," is a parody of the conqueror. Picrochole, weak when faced with the delirious ambitions of his advisers, appears as little more than an abstraction. His advisers, unrealistic and suffering from delusions of grandeur, are greedy, grasping and unrealistic. With their plans they rewrite ancient history, invade vast territories in their imagination, and create an absurd fantasy in which they control the world. Their plans and projects are absurd, and even the wise words of one of their own, "an old nobleman named Ecephron, a hardened warrior" (G&P, 112), fail to dissuade them from foolhardiness. This episode satirizes Picrochole's megalomania and with it of course the idle dreamings of would-be despots everywhere.

Chapter 46, "On Grandgousier's humane treatment of his Prisoner Touchspigot," illustrates the noble concept that the former holds of his office and with which he views his duty vis-à-vis his prisoners. His declarations are infused with wisdom. Regarding the megalomania of Picrochole he comments: "He who grasps at too much grips almost nothing" (G&P, 138). His thinking takes account of the progress that the Renaissance detected in human history:

Saracens and Barbarians of old called deeds of prowess we now call robbery and wickedness" (G&P, 138). In urging his prisoner to: "Remonstrate with your king when you see him to be in error, and never give him counsel with an eye to your private profit" (G&P, 138), Grandgousier condemns his adversary's aggression through psychological insight and wisdom. His release of Touchspigot—he sends him back to his master laden with presents—sets the scene for the last chapter upon which we shall comment here, namely chapter 50, "Gargantua's Address to the Vanquished."

In chapter 50 Gargantua confirms that he is indeed his father's son by referring to acts of clemency carried out by Grandgousier in earlier times. His ancestors, he claims, "have preferred to erect monuments in the hearts of the vanquished by a display of clemency, than to raise trophies in the form of architecture in the lands they have conquered" (G&P, 145). The gratitude of men is more highly valued than inscriptions on historic buildings "which are subject to the injuries of climate and all men's spite" (G&P, 145). In a display of generosity Gargantua provides irrefutable evidence of both the success of his education (according to Renaissance principles) and his ability to succeed his father in a noble and wise manner. He therefore absolves and frees the vanquished, gives them the financial means to restart their lives and appoints his own tutor, Ponocrates, as Regent of Picrochole's kingdom and as tutor of the vanished king's infant son. Too wise to give hostages to fortune Gargantua claims to emulate both Moses and Julius Caesar by retaining the troublemakers among Picrochole's people, including his "advisers, officers, and servants, who have incited, encouraged, or counseled him to cross his frontiers for the purpose of troubling us" (G&P, 148). Of course he also honorably buries the dead before duly rewarding his own victorious soldiers with gifts of money and property. Thus ends the unjust Picrocholean war, in which the good (and paternalistic) king Grandgousier, with the help of his worthy son Gargantua, defeat the unjustified ambitions of the unworthy king Picrochole.

The wise and generous king Grandgousier defeats the weak and ridiculous king Picrochole.[5] Rabelais deals with the dual theme of kingship and war by inventing a satirical fable that allows him to express his ideas on war and peace, the duties of a good king, and human nature. The tale unfolds by thesis and antithesis, opposing the good king to the bad. A moral contract links the just ruler to his people whereby the latter support their sovereign in return for his protection. Grandgousier, noble and handsome, is a humanist and a Christian ruler, inspired by the Gospels. He is averse to war, which, for Rabelais, Christianity has rendered anachronistic and he prefers a peaceful and pragmatic solution to conflict. When all other options fail, he accepts a war of self-defense in which the use of modern methods allows for minimum human and material destruction for all involved. In victory, the good king is generous toward both the vanquished and his own victorious troops, but is careful to prevent those responsible for the conflict from repeating their depraved misbehavior. Picrochole, the bad king, is the very example of the megalomaniac ruler, despotic and overambitious, whose vanity and greed lead inevitably to folly. Poorly advised by avaricious and self-interested counselors, he acts without just motive, provokes a war for which he is not equipped and comes to a miserable end.

Les Pensées, by Blaise Pascal

Moral misery is a fundamental theme in the *Pensées* by Pascal, a compendium of over nine hundred incomplete notes and essays that constitute a logical and impressive apologia for Christianity. Deeply aware of the weakness of human nature and the vanity of worldly activity, Pascal reveals a surprisingly modern understanding of human psychology. He expresses his insight into the psychology of leaders in a lucid scientific style and asserts timeless and essential religious truths.

Pascal was born in 1623 in Clermont-Ferrand and orphaned at the age of three. His father, a member of the *noblesse de robe* (i.e., the wealthy upper middle class), and later a tax commissioner for Normandy, raised and educated Pascal and his two sisters at home. Well educated in the classics, Pascal was also a brilliant mathematician from a very early age and published his first scientific paper in geometry at the age of sixteen. He invented a calculator ("la pascaline"), participated in important experiments on the vacuum and atmospheric pressure and thought up a system of inexpensive public transport for Paris. He died in 1662.

His family was profoundly influenced by contact with members of the Jansenist movement, a radical form of religious thought named after Cornelius Jansen, Bishop of Ypres. The Dutch theologian believed that man was powerless without divine grace, and that only a predestined elite would be saved. Pascal, who enjoyed very poor physical health (he died of stomach cancer at the age of thirty-nine), at first opposed his younger sister's decision to join the Jansenist convent at Port-Royal. He led an active and expensive life at the court and by the time of his religious conversion had gained extensive knowledge and understanding of human beings and in particular those of the fashionable world. High society eventually left him dissatisfied, but he was close to his saintly sister even while his health was declining. Following a particularly powerful religious experience on the night of 23 November 1654, when he sensed the presence of God, he became an ardent defender of the Jansenists, particularly against Jesuit attacks. His *Lettres écrites à un provincial* or *Letters to a Provincial*, are among the finest polemical works written in any language and had an undeniably powerful effect on the development of the modern French prose style.

In the final two years of his life he began to plan what we call the *Pensées*. T.S. Eliot has pointed out that it would "have been a carefully constructed defense of Christianity, a true Apology and a kind of Grammar of Assent, setting forth the reasons which will convince the intellect . . .[H]is book would have been also his own spiritual autobiography."[6] Pascal did not live to complete his planned defense of Christianity, of which the *Pensées* are but the preparatory notes, discovered in his room after his death.

Pascal sees human nature as displaying fundamental contradictions, contradictions that can only be explained by Christianity. Pascal describes many of the public relationships of his own day as essentially flawed and repeatedly asserts that human nature is plagued with an unavoidable sense of dissatisfaction. This vista of apparent gloom may be corrected and transformed through the quest for knowledge of God, a quest that culminates in the discovery of Jesus Christ. As John Cruickshank has written: "The *Pensées,* therefore, use an analysis of the problem of human nature in order to interest the reader in the Christian solution."[7]

His social background and his years in Paris gave Pascal first-hand insight into high society; and, in the *Pensées* he regularly uses figures of high social and political standing to illustrate his point, a technique that required considerable moral courage. For Pascal, "Man is obviously made to think" (no. 146).[8] It is man's intelligence and capacity for self-knowledge that distinguishes humans from the natural world because, "[t]hought constitutes the greatness of man" (no. 346). For Pascal, man is adaptable yet vulnerable, "A thinking reed" (no. 348), but "A vapour, a drop of water suffices to kill him." (no. 347) Man possesses, however, a nobility not available to the natural world in that "he knows he dies" and although he understands "the advantage which the universe has over him," the universe itself "knows nothing of this" (no. 347). Pascal imagines man as suspended "between those two abysses of the Infinite and Nothing" (no. 72); "The whole visible world is only an imperceptible atom in the ample bosom of nature." "It is an infinite sphere, the center of which is everywhere, the circumference nowhere" (no. 72).

In Pascal's view nature is corrupt—hence man's misery. Happiness is found only with God, a relationship made possible by the coming of the Redeemer, announced and recounted by Scripture. The reader, without having to agree with Pascal's conclusions concerning the truth of Christianity, may still accept the power of his logic. Through his depiction of corrupt human nature, he concludes that man's unhappiness comes from within, from "the natural poverty of our feeble and mortal condition" (no. 139). On considering the various activities which men choose, military men and courtiers in particular, Pascal concludes: "I have discovered that all the unhappiness of men arises from one single fact, that they cannot stay quietly in their own chamber" (no. 139). Although, "if we muster all the good things it is possible to possess, royalty is the finest position in the world" (no. 139), kings are no different from other mortal beings in that they too are prone to unhappiness. Men and women pursue positions of political power precisely because they bring with them the attractions of activity, ambition and intrigue that divert the attention from the basic human condition

> Yet, when we imagine a king attended with every pleasure he can feel, if he be without diversion, and be left to consider and reflect on what he is, this feeble happiness will not sustain him; he will necessarily fall into forebodings of dangers, of revolutions which may happen, and, finally, of death and inevitable disease; so that if he be without what is called diversion, he is unhappy, and more unhappy than the least of his subjects who plays and diverts himself. (no. 139)

Pascal offers more illustrations to argue his thesis: The gambler does not play solely for the winnings nor for the fun of playing: he deceives himself that he will be happy to win whatever he is playing for, that is he acts from a mixture of desire, anger and fear. Similarly the hunter pursues animals not from necessity but because it distracts him from his other concerns; he hunts for the chase, not for the quarry, because, "Without amusement there is no joy; with amusement there is no sadness" (no. 139).

A king (or political leader) surrounds himself with people to amuse him, because without amusement he will sense his own wretchedness. Attendants, courtiers—today's spin doctors and personal advisers—ensure that a king is never left alone to contemplate his own moral misery. And here Pascal proposes an image, which would be outlandish were it not true, of a king learning how to dance in order to escape contemplating the self

> Would it not be a deprivation of his delight for him to occupy his soul with the thought of how to adjust his steps to the cadence of an air, or of how to throw a ball skilfully, instead of leaving it to enjoy quietly the contemplation of the majestic glory which encompasses him? Let us make the trial; let us leave a king all alone to reflect on himself quite at leisure, without any gratification of the senses, without any care in his mind, without society; and we will see that a king without diversion is a man full of wretchedness. (no. 142)

Man permits himself to be willingly deceived by the imagination: lawyers and magistrates depend on their robes for some of their effect as defenders and dispensers of justice; physicians don special coats; guards of honor precede kings (no. 82). Custom, or habit as Pascal sometimes refers to it, fails to see in this mechanical inspiration of respect and awe for kings the illusion that it really is: "because we cannot separate in thought their persons from the surroundings with which we see them usually joined" (no. 308). In an echo of Rabelais' depiction of Grandgousier, Pascal states, "The pleasure of the great is the power to make people happy. The property of riches is to be given liberally" (no. 310). The *Pensées* echo the soldierly prowess (if unmonastic behavior) of Rabelais' Friar John of the Hashes by noting those instances when "force attacks humbug, when a private soldier takes the square cap off a first president, and throws it out of the window" (no. 310).

The ethical principles illustrated by Pascal in the *Pensées* mean that political power, as in Rabelais, is justified by the service of a greater good than the well being of the ruler or the pleasure he or she might obtain from using power. Kings, although seen to be apart from common mortals, are subject to the same experience of their own wretchedness as other human beings.

> The greatness of man is that he knows himself to be miserable. A tree does not know itself to be miserable. It is then being miserable to know oneself to be miserable; but it is also being great to know that one is miserable. (no. 397)

The moral onus upon kings and political rulers is therefore all the greater in that, to fulfil their mission, they must ignore the trappings of royalty and power that for many people are synonymous with influence. To be truly royal means surpassing the order of political power and accepting human weakness without being influenced by it.

Pascal's depiction of the human condition is initially depressing as well as remarkably modern. In one place, he compares man's situation to that of a cell of death-row inmates where each in desperation observes the departure of his companions while helplessly awaiting his own dreadful encounter with death. Yet, for Pascal, a Redeemer was born to save humanity. For him then, the religious history of the Jewish people is not simply the history of a particular Middle Eastern race; it becomes the history of the salvation of humanity. God's sovereignty, later expressed in Christ's kingship, is not of a merely political or human order; it transcends the human condition. Consequently, faith alters the perspective of the believer.

While on occasion Pascal concedes and even revels in the paradoxical nature of Christianity, and especially the paradoxical style of the biblical prophecies and parables, he proposes a remarkably clear and logical analysis of the interaction between the human and the supernatural. The three orders—*the body, the intellect and wisdom*—divide human endeavor into distinct categories. Kings and political leaders belong to the physical world of conquest and possession: "The greatness of clever men is invisible to kings, to the rich, to chiefs, and to all the worldly great" (no. 792). We can readily associate Rabelais' King Picrochole and his greedy advisers with the natural temptation of worldly rulers to emulate Alexander the Great and control as much of the physical planet as contemporary conditions allow. Grandgousier on the other hand does not draw his greatness from material possessions; rather he shares his wealth with his enemy; he takes no booty but rather restores their property to the vanquished.

Acknowledging the importance of intellectual cultivation—the second order—Gargantua makes arrangements for the princely education of his defeated adversary's offspring and future successor, thereby emulating the excellent Renaissance education that his own father had arranged for him. An important link between Rabelais and Pascal is to be found in the theme of education. Grandgousier replaced the ineffective medieval schooling, to which his son was initially subjected, by new, modern methods, which placed the growth of the individual (not the imposition of an outdated program) at the center of the educational process. Through the advantage of a humanist education, the future king understands the world in its natural, human and supernatural dimensions. Thinkers and scientists belong therefore to the second order, that of the mind, and are detached from desire for personal gain: "Great geniuses have their power, their glory, their greatness, their victory, their lustre, and have no need of worldly greatness, with which they are not in keeping" (no. 792).

The third order, that of supernatural wisdom, includes charity, and goes even further than the first two, as "[t]he infinite distance between body and mind is a symbol of the infinitely more infinite space between mind and charity; for charity is supernatural" (no. 792). Those therefore, who belong to the third and ultimate order—wisdom, love, sanctity—share in the supernatural: "The saints have their power, their glory, their victory, their lustre, and need no worldly or intellectual greatness, with which they have no affinity; for these neither add anything to them, nor take anything from them" (no. 792). According to the kingly ideal that Grandgousier transmits to his son, the ideal king/ruler/political leader is inspired, not by worldly gain or by intellectual achievement, but by the light of Christian faith. The ultimate kingship, for both Rabelais and Pascal, is the kingship of Christ, that is literally of another order, that of charity and wisdom, an order which neither the body nor the mind alone can produce. Rabelais, whose profound religious faith was accompanied by a fervent reforming zeal, preaches a return to the pure, simple and evangelical foundations of the Church where, as in the Abbey of Thélème, members are invited to: "Do what you will" (G&P, 159). Far from being an invitation to licentiousness, men and women are invited to discover the will of God the Father for them his children. Rabelais' use of satire, including the anti-clerical depiction of some churchmen and their practices (for example the papal pursuit of temporal power), is aimed at highlighting the abuses of the day; his ideal ruler is clearly the Christian model. The more intellectual Pascal, who sees faith as coming finally from divine grace, also believes in the importance of the quest whereby those who search earnestly, despite doubt and uncertainty, already share in anticipation that understanding which they seek. Sincerity and self-knowledge confer on those with leadership ability the judgment needed to become judicious rulers.

While Rabelais is not afraid to use satire as a means of unmasking the abuses of political tyrants, he proposes as the model king the example of the enlightened Grandgousier and his son Gargantua whose style is more paternalistic than constitutional and who does not boast of royal divine appointment.[9] Pascal is therefore courageous in suggesting the fundamentally arbitrary nature of many high social offices and positions of privilege. While his illustration of both the misery and spiritual grandeur of man is not a prerequisite for any particular form of religious faith, it does prepare the reader for Pascal's logical conclusion regarding the truth of Christianity. His king is not the ambitious, self-centered—even destructive—political leader whose misdeeds fill the books of world history. Kings/political leaders are subject to the same human weakness as those whom they rule. Knowledge of human frailty—self-knowledge— is Pascal's insight into maintaining the balance between the people and those who have power. Kingship here is not of a material order nor of an intellectual order; rather it is of the heart and points intuitively to aspirations beyond the material and the intellectual: "The heart has its reasons, which reason does not know" (no. 277).

Conclusion

The direction in which the French classical tradition ultimately pointed—the emancipation of Tradition by Reason[10]—sought to replace the medieval understanding of man with a more modern concept. The ideal created an obvious tension between Tradition and Antiquity on the one hand, and the driving force of critical Reason on the other. The reality and the aspiration are evident in the spirit both of Rabelais' *Gargantua* and Pascal's *Pensées*. Writers like Rabelais and Pascal, whose families belonged to the influential and affluent middle classes, crystallized in their very different writings a desire to break new ground. The fresh approach of the Humanist Renaissance, the renewal of the study of Greek for example, revolutionized the study of Scripture and later the concept of authority within the Christian community. Rabelais expressed a form of faith that is perennial because it is "a personal and mystical, not an orthodox or traditional faith."[11] Rabelais teaches that the way of fundamental human freedom, that is, inner freedom, is an enthusiasm for life itself as opposed to an obsession with any particular form of human activity, political or otherwise. Pascal, because of the insights afforded by the physical sciences and by the intensity of his metaphysical anguish, realized the true nature of man: "A Nothing in comparison with the Infinite, an All in comparison with the Nothing, a mean between nothing and everything" (no. 72). By applying his spiritual insights into human psychology to the topic of social and political hierarchy, Pascal underlined the common humanity of all, rulers and ruled alike. By placing wisdom at the top of the three orders he furthermore reminds today's reader that, despite the events of history, kings remain human.

This has frightening implications today since, in the words of one of the principal characters in Walker Percy's novel *The Second Coming* (an admirer of Pascal in fact), today's unbeliever seeks escape from contemplating his nothingness by eating, drinking and watching TV, until "to relieve the boredom and the farce (of which he is dimly aware) [he] goes off to war to shoot other people."[12] Today's rulers/political leaders are no less subject to folly than the archetypical Picrochole nor do they necessarily withstand the contemplation of their own human dissatisfaction. Pascal's king ludicrously learned how to dance and to play tennis; our leaders are likely to play infinitely more dangerous games to relieve their "moral misery." The remedy for moral misery as Pascal teaches is spiritual growth, a process that must begin with self-knowledge including an acceptance of one's moral poverty. Admittedly, though, if the courage and humility necessary for self-knowledge are hard to find among commoners, they are even harder to find among kings.

Notes

1. "Moraliste," *The New Oxford Companion to Literature in French*, ed. Peter France (Oxford: Clarendon Press, 1995), 545.

2. T.S. Eliot, "Introduction," *Pensées* (London: J.M. Dent & E.P. Dutton: 1931, reprinted 1940), xv.

3. *Pantagruel* contains little in the way of political commentary; the king rules unquestionably over the civil and religious domains. *Gargantua*, on the other hand, presents the portrait of the ideal king, Grandgousier, who, in a paternalistic manner, condemns wars of conquest, defends his land, negotiates and fights only in self-defense. When provoked he responds by causing the least possible material and human damage, refuses to confiscate his opponent's property, imposes no postwar embargoes and restores the loser's possessions to their rightful owners.

4. Rabelais, *Gargantua and Pantagruel* trans. J.M. Cohen (New York: Penguin Books, 1955). (Abbreviated here as G&P.)

5. Madeleine Lazard, *Pantagruel/Gargantua* (Hachette: Nouveaux Classiques illustrés, 1977), see p. 151, "La royauté et la guerre," for the following concluding remarks.

6. T.S. Eliot, "Introduction," *Pensées*, xi.

7. John Cruickshank, "Pascal," *The New Oxford Companion to Literature in French*, Peter France, ed. (Oxford: Clarendon Press, 1995), 601-602.

8. References to individual *pensées* are taken from the Dent (Everyman's Library) edition referred to above.

9. Lazard, *Pantagruel/Gargantua*, 33.

10. Albert Guérard, *The Life and Death of an Ideal* (London: W.H. Allen, 1957), 20.

11. John Cowper Powys, "Rabelais," *Enjoyment of literature*, 144.

12. Walker Percy, *The Second Coming* (New York: Ivy Books, 1990), 173.

Chapter 7

Chinua Achebe and the Nature of Social Change

Alan Levine

> *The question is how does a writer re-create [the] past?*
> *Quite clearly there is a strong temptation to idealize it—*
> *to extol its good points and pretend that the bad never existed.*
> *We cannot pretend that our past was one long, technicolour idyll.*
> *We have to admit that like other people's pasts*
> *ours had its good as well as its bad sides.*
> *—Chinua Achebe*

Chinua Achebe (1930-) is perhaps the most famous African writer in history. Born in the Nigerian village of Ogidi, which was one of the first centers of Anglican missionary work in Eastern Nigeria, Achebe attended a Western-style university in Nigeria, and left his first career in radio broadcasting at the outbreak of the Biafran civil war in 1966. Steeped in both Western and Nigerian traditions, he became a full-time academic and has held several teaching posts in Nigeria and the United States. He has won numerous international prizes for literature, been lauded as one of the "Makers of the Twentieth Century," and been credited with defining "a modern African literature that is truly African."[1]

While Achebe considers all writing to be political insofar as it threatens existing power structures, his particular political project follows from his assessment of his own historical situation. "The writer's duty," he says, is "to explore in depth the human condition. In Africa he cannot perform this task unless he has a proper sense of history."[2] As an African writer from a colonized country, Achebe is concerned with overcoming colonialism and its iniquitous legacies. In order to redefine and combat these legacies, he explores their numerous components—political, cultural, racial, religious, linguistic, economic, social, and psychological—through literature.

Achebe is concerned with how, if it all, it is possible to survive and thrive in a fractious cultural world. The main characters in the two novels discussed below choose opposite ways of dealing with cultural conflict. One seeks to keep his culture powerful and separate, the other pursues a path of assimilation and seeks a kind of universal harmony—the two possibilities that so nicely echo the separatist and inclusionary positions of debates over multiculturalism in America today.[3] Achebe's novels do not, however, address multiculturalism as it is discussed in late twentieth-century America. He does not explicitly write about affirmative action, questions of preferences, or debates over the academic canon. Rather, Achebe focuses on the heart of the issue: the basic struggle for self-respect and social dignity in Africa. He wants to help Africans celebrate their own ways: "I think it is part of my business as a writer to teach that boy [who would be ridiculed for writing on African topics] that there is nothing disgraceful about the African weather, that the palm tree is a fit subject for poetry."[4] Achebe's quest for African dignity is what he calls the "serious intention" of all his work.[5]

When asserting African dignity "not only for the enlightenment of our detractors but even more for our own education,"[6] Achebe is careful and cautious not to exaggerate his cause. Raised and educated in both Western and Igbo traditions, Achebe has incorporated both into his life. He de-anglicized his given name in favor of an African one and is clearly committed to the future of Africa.[7] Yet, he also writes in English and lives and works mostly in the West.[8] Just as he is a melange of cultures, so he does not uncritically embrace any culture, not even the traditional Igbo culture for which he seeks respect. He shows its cruel side and illustrates the fundamental tension that occurs when autonomous individuals live in a society with strong cultural beliefs. His main characters suffer from people outside their group, from people within it, and from their own individual character flaws. Thus, while making the reader feel the benefits of equal recognition and the dignity of cultures, Achebe's novels also serve as cautionary tales about the problems and pitfalls to be avoided when trying to remedy historical injustices, and his work shows the limits of what might realistically be achieved.

Achebe's first two novels, *Things Fall Apart* (1958) and *No Longer at Ease* (1959), together tell the tale of three generations of an African family named Okonkwo.[9] The Okonkwos are not an ordinary family, and they are not living through ordinary times. Each Okonkwo is a leader of his generation, with the generations corresponding to: 1) those who first encounter white men, 2) those who first cooperate with the whites, and 3) those who first try to excel in white society. The novels span a period of collapse and renewal, renewal and collapse. Times are not good, as the books' titles, *Things Fall Apart* and *No Longer at Ease*, indicate. But the decay and anxiety forecast in the titles is something of a misnomer. Things were never entirely "together" in either of these books, nor is it suggested that they can be in the future. Rather, Achebe portrays the disintegration of one legitimate but imperfect culture at the hands of another legitimate but imperfect culture. There are no easy answers or simple solutions. There is no escape into a "community" of any sort—neither into a modern, Western world nor into the ancient traditions of Africa. There is no "going back," no "return." Nor is "progress" inevitable. Politics cannot produce meaning and happiness; rather individuals must create and constantly struggle for them.

Traditional Igbo Life

Things Fall Apart, Achebe's first and most celebrated work, is the tale of an Ajax-like warrior tragically destined for suicide.[10] The story is set in late nineteenth-century Umuofia,[11] part of the Igbo nation, in modern day Nigeria, made up of about 10,000 people in nine villages within a day's walk of each other. The novel is essentially divided into two parts: the nature of traditional communal life before the coming of white men and the community's collapse after the whites' arrival.

Traditional Igbo society as represented by Achebe is a community that meets most human needs. It is materially and spiritually self-sufficient. It has all the physical necessities of life and unites everyone into a clan, giving them a sense of purpose and attachment. Its religion connects everyone to the heavens, to the earth, and to the land. It places everyone in the social order. In short, it is described as achieving everything that Plato thinks can only be achieved with a noble lie.[12] This has led some commentators to confuse Umuofia with a liberal utopia. For example, one commentator writes:

> What is remarkable about his Igbos is the degree to which they have achieved the foundations of what most people seek today—democratic institutions, tolerance of other cultures, a balance of male and female principles, capacity to change for the better or to meet new circumstances, a means of redistributing wealth, a viable system of morality, support for industriousness, an effective system of justice, striking and memorable poetry and art. Achebe appears to have tested Igbo culture against the goals of modern liberal democracy and to have set out to show how the Igbo meet those standards.[13]

However, this is not the case. Traditional Igbo culture has beautiful and stable aspects, but (for better or worse) it is not a liberal democracy. Rather, it is a warrior culture, happily hierarchical, harsh toward some of its own inhabitants, and cruel toward outsiders. The Igbo fight with other villages, kill each other, and ritualize brutality in a way that is most definitely illiberal. For example, they headhunt. Okonkwo has five human heads of which he is very proud, and he drinks from his first one on ceremonial occasions (14). The Igbo also have slaves (46). Slavery is accepted without controversy; we never see it challenged or its legitimacy questioned, and this is so because it is ritually sanctified. The Igbo fight only when they consider justice to be on their side (16), but their conception of justice is compatible with ritual cruelty and slavery. The Igbo practice ritual human sacrifice. The sacrifice of a young boy, captured in war and raised and loved by Okonkwo, is demanded and sanctified by "the Oracle of the Hills and the Caves" (56) and is one of the reasons why Okonkwo's son later rejects the traditional religion. Nonetheless, Achebe describes Umuofia without condemnation or flinching. His unsentimental acknowledgment of these facts precludes a celebration of the culture as liberal—but this does not mean that Umuofia is evil. To the contrary, Umuofia is full of beauty—in human relations, relations to the gods, in poetry, song, and sport. The moral system that blends the psychic sublimity and physical cruelty is, Achebe suggests, not inferior to liberalism but different from it.

Achebe's account of Igbo culture before the arrival of the white man corresponds to what Max Weber describes as an "enchanted world." In contrast to a scientifically ordered world, Weber describes an enchanted world as one where "mysterious powers existed" and where people must therefore have recourse to "magical means in order to master or implore the spirits."[14] Achebe describes the Igbo as "powerful in war and magic" (15), their magic being related to their religion. The Umuofians believe that the Earth and various animals are gods, tell tales in which animals speak and comprehend human language (13), and believe in ancestral spirits and personal gods called *chi* (29, 121). Weber is of two minds about the value of living in an enchanted world. On the one hand, Weber admires the spirituality that accompanies enchanted worlds. The intellectualizations and rationalizations that allow science to explain the world also demystify it. For this reason, the West suffers from what Weber terms the retreat of the "ultimate and most sublime values" from public life—something he regrets if his calls for "genuine prophecy," "genuine community," and "genuine passion" are indicative.[15] Achebe depicts Umuofia as having a strong sense of "ultimate and sublime values." The Umuofians have great spiritual strength, and their religion has "genuine passion."

But there is a price to pay for living in an enchanted world, which Achebe also depicts. Living in harmony with nature means they have not conquered, nor desire to conquer, it. As with all people who live in enchanted worlds, the Igbo suffer from many of the problems that the modern Western world overcame when it despirited and demystified its view of the cosmos, a process that began in the sixteenth century with the rise of the scientific description of everything as mere matter and motion. This disenchantment of the world may have profoundly contributed to the Western world's current sense of spiritual drift and malaise, but the conquest of nature enabled Europeans to conquer famine and disease. By contrast, the Igbo have not overcome famine and disease and thus suffer. For example, Achebe describes one woman who lost nine of her ten children in infancy (73-4) and a man who lost twenty-two children, all at young ages (124). The West's conquest of nature also leads to power, and, needless to say, Umuofia's enchantment cannot protect it from the European conquest of its land.

Enchanted worlds are also frightening. The West might fear some of the consequences of its technological successes, such as the possibility of nuclear war, ecological accidents, or the effect of the assembly line on the human spirit, but Umuofia suffers a more primordial fear. A part of Umuofia's surroundings, for example, is described as the "Evil Forest" (21, 33, 75, 85, 138-9). The Evil Forest is where people who died of "really evil diseases" are buried, and it is thus thought to be "alive with sinister forces and powers of darkness" (138). Darkness in general holds terror over the people: "Darkness held a vague terror for these people" because they are afraid of evil spirits (13).

A final aspect of traditional Igbo life that must be noted concerns gender roles: its men dominate the village at the expense of its women. The women have no share of political life, few roles in the religion,[16] and are essentially stuck in domestic roles—doing light farming, taking care of the children, and cooking for the men. Women do have a niche in which their authority is respected, but the general wisdom of Umuofia is that "a man is the head of the family and his wives do his bidding," and this inequality is institutionally enshrined by the practice of polygamy (123). Igbo society does not officially uphold misogyny or wife beating, but we see Okonkwo beat two of his wives, literally shooting at one of them (31, 39).[17] He "ruled his household with a heavy hand" and his wives and children live in "perpetual fear of his fiery temper" (16). Okonkwo argues that a man must be able to control his women (52), equates masculinity with violence (52), considers someone weak because he discusses important issues with his women (66), and uses "womanish" as a pejorative (52-3, 57, 62-3, 168, 184). He also believes that one should never treat a man the way he treats women or it would "kill a man's spirit" (28).

Achebe implicitly criticizes Okonkwo's excessive masculinity. Okonkwo acts this way, he writes, because "his whole life was dominated by fear, the fear of failure and weakness" (16). His insecurity drives his harshness. And his insecurity is reactive:[18] his father was weak, so he resists everything that his father represented. His ambition is driven by fear of weakness and ridicule. Indeed, at one point in the story, the religio-political authorities of the village decide that a boy Okonkwo raises—and loves more than a son—must be ritually killed. The village authorities tell Okonkwo he should remain a passive observer since the boy calls him father (56). But Okonkwo does not listen: "Dazed with fear, Okonkwo drew his machete and cut him down. He was afraid of being thought weak" (59). An oracle had said that it was necessary for the boy to die, so it would have been impious of Okonkwo to defend the boy despite their great mutual love. Nonetheless, Okonkwo's "manly" desire to do the deed himself is actually driven by insecurity. A more philosophical neighbor suggests a more moderate solution: "if the Oracle said that my son should be killed I would neither dispute it nor be the one to do it" (64-5). This same neighbor also wonders about the origins of cruel laws, such as the community custom of killing newborn twins (70-1,117-18). Through this level-headed neighbor, Achebe argues against the fanatical application of law and raises questions about the legitimacy of tradition. Igbo society is not ideal. Like everywhere else, it has cruel customs and beliefs. It has limits. To idealize Igbo culture is not to take it seriously. Achebe's position is more sensitive: Igbo culture, despite its limits, contains humanity and wisdom.[19]

The Coming of the White Men and the Tragedy of *Things Fall Apart*

The wisdom of Africa is especially apparent in contradistinction to the crassness of the arriving whites. Igbo wisdom and tolerance of other cultures is embodied in its recognition and acceptance of its own historical contingency—"what is good among one people is an abomination with others" (130). The whites coming to

Africa share no such tolerant outlook. While tolerance based on an acceptance of cultural diversity is part of certain philosophical traditions in the West (Hellenistic thinkers, Montaigne, Montesquieu, Locke),[20] it is clearly not part of the mind-set of the whites arriving in Umuofia in *Things Fall Apart*. The whites in the novel make little attempt to understand African customs and categorically condemn them as "bad" (162). Moreover, when white men first appear, they wipe out an entire village (127-30).

Within a few years of their arrival, the whites are entrenched and the traditional African world begins to fall apart. The whites in *Things Fall Apart* bring about what Nietzsche calls a transvaluation or revaluation of values. In *On the Genealogy of Morals*, Nietzsche distinguishes between two kinds of moralities: master and slave.[21] These names do not refer to the existence of actual master and slave classes but to the psychological drives underlying the moral codes. Master morality is warlike and inegalitarian and recognizes rank. Everyone in a society dominated by master morality wishes that he could impose his will on the world, as do the strong-willed heroes. Rather than condemn the strong for following their will, everyone wants to emulate them. This is very close to the warrior ethos that dominates traditional Umuofia as exemplified by Okonkwo. The pre-Christian Igbo world as described in *Things Fall Apart* illustrates the joy and free-spiritedness that Nietzsche associates with pre-Christian pagan morality. The strong follow their will, they are rewarded for their strength with honors and additional wives, and everyone wants to emulate them.

By contrast, slave morality, according to Nietzsche, is a morality of equality driven by resentment. Nietzsche argues that weak and resentful people who are not strong enough to get their way in this world seek to hold back the strong by affirming universal moral principles in the name of which the strong man should hold himself back. Failures of self-restraint, they argue, deserve moral condemnation and punishment. The Judeo-Christian tradition is the epitome of slave morality according to Nietzsche, and *Things Fall Apart* seems to bear out Nietzsche's viewpoint. The grandeur, heroic manliness, and magnanimity of the Igbo's traditional world is replaced by ignoble concerns and a humbling equality, insofar as everyone is to be restrained and meek. Like Nietzsche, Achebe says that the new religion appeals in particular to the "low-born" and the "outcast" (159), to the "ne'er do wells" and to Umuofia's "effeminate men clucking like hens" (142). No convert "was a man whose word was heeded in the assembly of the people. None of them was a man of title. They were mostly the kind of people that were called *efulefu*, worthless, empty men" (133). Not only was their council not listened to, but they are described as "the excrement of the clan" (133).[22] Like Nietzsche, Achebe suggests that Christianity "leveled everybody down."[23]

In a final accordance with Nietzsche's theories, in *Things Fall Apart*, resentment and revenge motivate those who are drawn to Christianity. Consider Okonkwo's eldest son, Nwoye, who converts to Christianity. His father, who considers him "degenerate and effeminate" (143), has never loved him. Indeed, Okonkwo wonders "how he could have begotten a woman for a son" and whether he had been cuckolded (143). When Nwoye converts, he gets a new name: Isaac, reminiscent of the first-born son from Genesis, whose father was willing to slaughter him. Christianity has several attractions for Nwoye/Isaac, including an escape from his father's condemning and murderous beatings. But Achebe emphasizes—and here is the similarity to Nietzsche's account—that his conversion is at least in part an attempt at spiritual revenge driven by resentment of his "brother's" sanctioned murder. Nwoye had loved Ikemefuna like a brother; but, on orders from the clan, he was torn from him and killed by Okonkwo—who had raised him as a son! Nwoye never forgives his father for this brutality and wishes to punish him by rejecting everything for which he stands. It is an act of spiritual revenge. Others who convert, such as a woman who keeps having twins and the *osu*, or outcasts, similarly do so not out of any lofty concern for things spiritual, but simply to gain power, to escape from their position on the bottom rungs of the clan's hierarchy (140-1). Their enthusiasm for the new religion is inversely proportional to their previously low status, with the most liberated becoming the most fanatical. The downtrodden, unfortunate, and persecuted shake off their shackles and find comfort and advancement in the new religion. As Nietzsche says, the religion of love gets its power from hate.

In sum, while Achebe never mentions Nietzsche anywhere in the novel, his psychological account of Christianity's appeal and triumph reads like a case study of Nietzsche's revaluation of values and the triumph of slave morality. What is nice about using Nietzsche's terminology to describe Achebe's plot is that it helps reverse the insidious values that the white Christians impose on the Africans. Nietzsche's language enables the Africans to be seen, psychologically at least, as strong and masterful and the whites as lowly and slavish. But whereas Nietzsche avows a strong preference for master morality, we have seen that Achebe's account of traditional Umuofian values is not as simple. Unlike Nietzsche, he is not willing uncritically to embrace some of master morality's darker aspects. This leads to a more complex and more tragic moral situation.

The tragedy of *Things Fall Apart*, the climactic clash between the Christians and the Umuofians, is precipitated by Christian intolerance. Under a fanatical priest, zealous converts become militant and openly hostile toward their former religion. One new Christian kills a sacred python, a crime so shocking that the Igbo had no legally prescribed penalty for *willingly* killing the sacred serpent, so inconceivable was it that anyone would ever do so (147).[24] Another unmasks an *egwugwu*, one of the ritually masked gods of the clan. This unmasking is actually considered to have "killed an ancestral spirit" and is described as "one of the greatest crimes a man could commit" (171). Christian violence and intolerance results in the destruction of the clan, which splinters under the pressure of the changes inaugurated by the new religion. The separation of kinsmen from kinsmen along religious lines breaks the backbone of traditional Igbo society.

Opposing widespread opinion, Okonkwo vociferously advocates eliminating the Christian intrusion. But, in fact, Umuofia decides to be tolerant. He tells the Christian priest, "You can stay with us if you like our ways. You can worship your own god. It is good that a man should worship the gods and the spirits of his fathers" (175). This is the most tolerant, multicultural moment in the novel. Igbo wisdom validates the ancestral, accepting that different customs can co-exist side by side.

But the Christians continue to proselytize and undermine Umuofia's traditional ways. When some exasperated Umuofians finally burn the Church building, Okonkwo is pleased; Achebe describes him as having a feeling "akin to happiness" and as "almost happy again" (176). "It was like the good old days again, when a warrior was a warrior" (176). Indeed, Okonkwo fights further: when the whites' government punishes Umuofia for its "offenses," an indignant Okonkwo chops off a messenger's head. He wants the village to fight for its traditions, but senses that it will not. Convinced that they are accepting new debased ways, Okonkwo hangs himself. The historically minded reader understands that even had the village fought, it would not have made a difference.

The ending of *Things Fall Apart* is bitter, offering but a faint glimmer of hope for the future based on Achebe's emphasis on the political importance of writing. The novel despairs that there was nothing that the villagers could have done to prevent the collapse of traditional Igbo society. Resistance was suicide, but in a sense, assimilation was also suicide—cultural suicide. The village's only choice was whether its destruction would be physical or cultural. But the power of writing offers a small hope for the future. As Okonkwo's body is cut down from the tree, the white District Commissioner imagines writing Okonkwo's story in a book:

> The story of a man who had killed a messenger and hanged himself would make interesting reading. One could almost write a whole chapter on him. Perhaps not a whole chapter but a reasonable paragraph, at any rate. There was so much else to include, and one must be firm in cutting out details. He had already chosen the title of the book, after much thought: *The Pacification of the Primitive Tribes of the Lower Niger* (191).

From the colonialist's point of view, Umuofia is merely a primitive tribe in need of "pacification." Okonkwo's life and death is not a terrible tragedy but merely an interesting paragraph. And so it would be to the readers of that—and all—colonialist writing, if that was all they knew. But as *Things Fall Apart* has demonstrated, the death of Okonkwo is no mere paragraph. Achebe indicates that if the Igbo do not tell Okonkwo's story—their story—the terrible beauty that was Umuofia will be lost forever. Since the teller of the story determines the tale that is told, Africans have the possibility—and the responsibility—to write and tell their stories themselves as correctives to centuries of books by District Commissioners. *Things Fall Apart* is exactly such an effort. By illustrating the civilization of Umuofia and the tragedy of colonial intolerance, Achebe at once gives his people dignity—and strikes a blow for toleration, African style.

The "Truer" Tragedy of *No Longer at Ease*

Whereas *Things Fall Apart* is the tale of the Ajax-like Okonkwo, *No Longer at Ease* chronicles the slow downfall of a senior clerk. Although it is less conventionally dramatic, Achebe suggests it is a more real, everyday tragedy. "Real tragedy," Achebe has his main character say, "is never resolved. It goes on hopelessly forever. Conventional tragedy is too easy. The hero dies and we feel a purging of the emotions" (45-6). Achebe beautifully and powerfully executes such a "conventional [Aristotelian] tragedy" in his first novel. This second, less celebrated, work, however, is less conventionally dramatic but more tragic according to this unconventional definition.[25] "A real tragedy takes place in a corner, in an untidy spot, to quote W. H. Auden. The rest of the world is unaware of it. Like that man in *A Handful of Dust* who reads Dickens to Mr. Todd. There is no release for him. When the story ends, he is still reading. There is no purging of the emotions for us because we are not there" (46).[26]

Achebe's first novel tells the tragedy of the collapse of traditional Igbo society, his second novel tells of the next generations' tragic failures at achieving authentic dignity within white society. Just as Okonkwo epitomized Umuofia's traditional warrior ways, so Obi epitomizes the new Umuofia that is trying to assimilate into white ways. *No Longer at Ease* tells the tale of Nwoye's son, Obi, the third generation of Okonkwos, who is the first in the village to get a university education and a well-paying job in the civil service. The clan stakes its future on getting the youth to "learn book," i.e., acquiring knowledge of the white man's ways, and after getting a university education in England, Obi wholeheartedly buys into Western ideals. But as with the first Okonkwo, his travails parallel the clan's: his unfamiliarity with the new ways (and his family's and clan's inability to embrace them fully) doom him to unhappiness and ultimately to ruin. The clan tries to internalize white values only to become "strangers in this land" (7). Far from being the manly, self-reliant people of their past, the clan says it is "prepared to fight to the last" to help Obi (6), but they "fight" not a war but in the law courts! Furthermore, they have adopted Christian language, describing themselves as having been "delivered by the blood of the Lamb of God" and liberated from their former "darkness" (12). (This liberation from "darkness," of course, is only metaphysical.)[27] Like the heroes of both novels, the first Okonkwo who fights the new order and his grandson who accepts it, Umuofia suffers. *No Longer at Ease* shows how the traditional Igbo world has been turned upside down since its defeat by the white conquerors.

Given the nature of the Igbo's situation within a colonial society, one might expect Obi's failures to result from white racism. This is partially true, but Obi's biggest problems result more from other problems than from racism. Obi lacks clear vision and decisive will, and his father Isaac cannot live up to his own professed rejection of traditional Igbo *moeurs*. This is not to say that Achebe favors African assimilation of white ways. Nor is Achebe arguing that Africans cannot escape who they are, that they have no choice but passively to surrender to and consciously embrace their past traditions and culture. The situation is more tragic than black versus white, traditional beliefs versus Western. Living in a multicultural world, Obi—and his society—fails to blend competing traditions into a happy synthesis.

Obi's difficulties are in two areas: financial and personal. Together they make him a lonely human being and bring about his ruin. Not one single character in *No Longer at Ease* understands the pressures and the silent torment that Obi undergoes. After obtaining his lucrative appointment in the civil service and then falling in love, his life seems set. Indeed, all of the characters in the novel think he is set. Yet, nothing works out as planned. Obi has serious financial difficulties that he cannot share with anyone and which no one understands. Having thoroughly bought into Western ideals, Obi almost alone of all the characters in the novel wants to do the "right" thing, but Nigeria seems to be organized in such a way that he cannot meet all of his financial responsibilities if he does not take bribes. Between paying back his educational loan, giving money to support his retired father and sickly mother, and buying the luxuries, namely a car, that someone in his position must have, he does not have much left over. Financial emergencies keep coming as he does not plan for the annual income tax, car insurance, electricity bill, and the like, which, being the first of his acquaintance to enter such a world, he did not know were coming. People only told him about his perks. No one explained the (hidden) costs. Nonetheless, he resists every temptation until a series of events completely crush his spirits. Therein lies his more "real," everyday tragedy. On the one hand, Obi's tragedy results from nothing more than the difficulties in everyday life, and is thus more mundane and more obscure than his grandfather's tragedy. No one knows what he is going through, but for this reason, Achebe seems to suggest, it is not less but more tragic. Being the first to have to deal with the difficulties of his elevated position, Obi has no one to share them with. He suffers alone, in silence, "off in a corner" as it were, while everyone else misinterprets his situation and motives.

No Longer at Ease begins with its end: Obi is being tried for corruption. No one, lawyers, judge, nor observers understand what went wrong. Yet, from the very beginning the trial is juxtaposed with the corruption rampant in colonial Nigeria. In later novels, Achebe unrelentingly dissects corruption by both Nigeria's civilian government (*A Man of the People* [1966]) and its military governments (*Anthills of the Savannah* [1987]). Here, corruption is ever present but not the novel's focus. Rather, it forms the background against which Obi must be judged.

Corruption exists in the novel in many forms on many levels. Even the novel's opening scene is fraught with fraud, as a lawyer lies to a judge and government clerks are described as having bribed doctors to get notes so they can skip work to watch the trial. Indeed, corruption is everywhere. When Obi comes back from England, the very first official he meets solicits a bribe (35). On the one hand, Achebe seems to explain this as a rational response to an "alien institution": "In Nigeria the government was 'they.' It had nothing to do with you or me. It was an alien institution and people's business was to get as much from it as they could without getting into trouble" (37). However, Achebe also illustrates how deeply corruption is woven into Nigeria's social fabric. For example, Obi profusely condemns the traditional African custom of buying a wife (47-8), and he witnesses a traditional market scam (54). These have nothing to do with alien white impositions—and it is rumored that plenty of white officials take bribes, too (38). Corruption seems to be almost universal, if particularly oppressive in Nigeria. The question is why it exists.

Nigeria's deeply entrenched corruption is explained in many ways throughout the course of the novel. From the point of view of the novel's main white character, Mr. Green, corruption is inherent in the African character. Green asserts that "The African is corrupt through and through" (3). He blames this corruption on climate and disease—not white discrimination. "I'm all for equality and all that," he says,

"I for one would hate to live in South Africa. But equality won't alter facts" (4). He seems oblivious to the fact, however, that as he utters this he is a colonialist sitting in an exclusive club. Indeed, his lack of self-awareness is reflected again later in the novel when he condemns the government's policy of extensive vacations as representing African laziness—until Obi points out that it was a policy originally set up by the whites for the whites (174-5). If Mr. Green is intended to be representative, the whites seem oblivious to their contribution to Africa's corruption.

Unlike Mr. Green, Obi (and Achebe) does not consider Nigeria's corruption to be due to an innate character flaw. Rather, he attributes it to a class of administrators that he calls the "old Africans," whose corruption is a product of ignorance and experience. His theory of the "old African" is as follows: "He has worked steadily to the top through bribery—an ordeal through bribery. To him the bribe is natural. He gave it and he expects it" (23). Being the first generation of African leaders in the white power system and having no education, they thought they had to be corrupt to get ahead. In any case, they saw nothing wrong with taking bribes.[28] Most Africans that Obi meets assume that he will be corrupt like the old Africans. Obi is contemptuous of such attitudes and originally has little doubt that with time such corruption will disappear. Not that he thinks the younger generation of administrators like himself are morally superior: "To most of them bribery is no problem. They come straight to the top without bribing anyone. It's not that they're necessarily better than others, it's simply that they can afford to be virtuous" (23). Throughout the novel even as pressures mount on Obi, he seems to be the embodiment of this new kind of African administrator. However, because Obi does not take care of appearances, everyone assumes he is corrupt, and when he does not play the necessary political games, others assume he is stupid or haughty, so his good intentions create problems for him. Whatever the cause—be it white imperialism, old African cronyism, or something else—Achebe seems to be saying that the difficulties of eradicating corruption stem from it being so endemic that those who do not partake are regarded as untrustworthy and obstructionist.

The story of Obe's life and career as a civil servant exemplifies Achebe's analysis of the limits of political idealism. Obi epitomizes the optimistic, Western-influenced African who believes that progress is inevitable as enlightenment spreads. His belief that the political or social world can be changed is, Achebe suggests, naive. Obi returns from his European university filled with hopes for the changes he will make in Africa. His idealism is symbolized by his absolute refusal to take a bribe of any kind; to do so would be to capitulate to old-fashioned corruption, but his refusal to do so leads him down a path toward economic and total ruin. The system was set up so that he had to succumb; resistance is nice but futile.

Achebe shows the naivete of Obi's views in the social and private sphere, too. His idealism is symbolized in his private relations by his falling in love with an *osu*, a girl whose family had been cursed in accordance with ancient Igbo traditions and who therefore was absolutely taboo in terms of marriage. In accordance with his "enlightened," Western attitude, Obi requests his father's blessing on his marriage, but his father, Isaac, opposes it, notwithstanding the fact that, as a Christian, he should be indifferent to an ancient, pagan superstition. Achebe even tells us that Obi made all the right arguments to his father, using "the very words that his father might have used in talking to his heathen kinsmen," but to no avail (151).[29] Despite adopting Christianity and believing "utterly and completely in the things of the white man" (143-44), Isaac is not indifferent to the *osu* curse, and he and his wife refuse their blessing upon Obi's choice. When Isaac tells Obi that this matter is "deeper than you think" (151), he is acknowledging the extent to which Igbo beliefs, which he has claimed to have uprooted, still remain a force within him.[30] Achebe's message is clear: individual transformation does not happen overnight— not even in one lifetime.While Isaac may "believe" in Christianity, his Igbo heritage runs deep, too. And the same may be said for many of their fellow clansman, who have accepted the new religion but nonetheless whisper about the "scandal" of Obi's desire. Culture is in the bone, and it cannot be redone easily, either on a personal or on a societal level.

The underlying question concerns which way to turn: should one affirm one's traditions or leave them behind in the name of some universal cosmopolitanism? Rather than giving a final answer to this question, Achebe poses it in a forceful manner. On the one hand, there are many beautiful aspects to traditional Igbo culture. But on the other, Obi's happiness is frustrated by an ancient Igbo curse, the legitimacy of which seems hard to accept. The curse has been passed from generation to generation, and now has rendered outcast the smart, beautiful woman with whom Obi has fallen in love. This woman has done nothing wrong. Should she— and Obi—suffer for an ancient tradition, the origin of which no one alive can explain? Achebe's point is to illustrate the tremendous difficulties that must be overcome for individuals trying to change themselves or their world. The difficulty of resisting, let alone changing, one's culture is reinforced by Obi's subsequent actions. Fearing to be an outcast more than he fears losing his love, he does not marry, falling instead into a state of depression. He had thought that he could transcend his culture, but he cannot at an acceptable price. A stronger-willed individual might follow his will regardless of his family's wishes. Perhaps Obi needs more of his grandfather's strength. But if Obi is not driven enough, Okonkwo was too driven. Just as the first Okonkwo exemplifies the limitations of a spirited effort to live a traditional life in the modern world, so Obi exemplifies the difficulties and limitations of an effort to live a Western-style life in Nigeria. We might imagine that somewhere in his corpus Achebe would depict someone who illustrates a healthy and happy blend of conviction and wisdom or of traditionalism and idealism, but he never does. Achebe offers no clear vision of how to reconcile the tensions inherent in a fractious multicultural world. If happiness is to be achieved at all, he seems to imply, people must wrestle individually with the competing claims of modernity and traditionalism, and find some balance that works for them.

Conclusion

Despite the meaning of Obi's name—"the mind at last is at rest" (7)—not one of the three generations of Okonkwos has a mind at rest.[31] The three Okonkwos are very different people who suffer very different fates, but each of their lives is tragic in its own way. The first Okonkwo commits suicide, the last is arrested for bribery. The middle Okonkwo rejects his father and is cursed by him, but then he frustrates his own son's happiness. To outsiders, it appears as if history has repeated itself, that in two successive generations sons have rejected their fathers (182). But the struggles are deeply personal. The first Okonkwo is captive to his fears and anger, the second captive to resentment and Christian ideology, which prevents his having human contact with his son, the third a captive to naive idealism and Enlightenment optimism in his belief that superstition and communal bonds can be overcome and everything can change. The easy temptation when reading novels such as these is to blame all the problems on white colonialism, and while that is a serious part of Africa's problem, Achebe indicates that the problems are deeper. Life in Umuofia before the white men come is in some ways beautiful and loving but in other ways cruel. According to Achebe, then, the answer does not seem to be to "go back." And just as backward-looking romanticism is eliminated, so too is the forward-looking romantic belief in quick progress and change. While we do see numerous changes throughout the novels, when push comes to shove, ancient ways keep asserting themselves. The novels show how slowly the world changes, even despite upheavals like colonialization and the introduction of a revaluation of values. Despite his rejection of Igbo traditions, Isaac cannot leave them behind. Despite his love, his best intentions, and his great idealism about the possibility for betterment and change, Obi gives in and collapses under the weight of social reality.

The lesson of the novels seems to be to take the world at its own pace. One ought to have a sense of self and ideals, but human beings cannot simply transcend the world but must live in it with its rhythms. Toward the end of *No Longer at Ease*, Achebe reflects on the nature of idealism: "The impatient idealist says: 'Give me a place to stand and I shall move the earth.' But such a place does not exist. We all have to stand on the earth itself and go with her at her pace" (190). Achebe discusses human illusions, which might temporarily lead to a kind of inner peace, but he seems to conclude that they cannot do so in the long run. The first two generations of Okonkwo's hid behind external ideologies, of the warrior and Christianity, respectively. Neither one really knows himself. Obi gains peace when he admits to himself what he is. But because the truth is so different from his previous idealism, the truth crushes him. The question is whether it is possible to know and to accept reality without being crushed.

Achebe seems to be suggesting that social change is limited by the deep connection between the personal and the political, and the preeminence of the personal. These novels could be about people caught up in events beyond their control, but they are only partly about that. Each generation's tragedy is due not to politics in any immediate sense, but to the characters of individuals. The first Okonkwo's tragedy would not have happened without Britain's cruel colonial policies, but he had problems that predated the arrival of the whites, and he was likely to continue to have them, even if the whites had more fully validated Umuofia's culture. Indeed, his clan had already exiled him for seven years for killing someone. Likewise, despite being accepted into the new white culture, Isaac and Obi still end up unhappy. Isaac tries to assimilate but fails. Ultimately he cannot leave his original

culture behind. Obi fully assimilates and accepts the Enlightenment ideal of progress, but he is nonetheless ruined by the traditional beliefs of his Igbo community
in which he does not believe. Like his father, he cannot escape his past. But whereas
Isaac chooses to keep the link (to honor the *osu* curse), Obi does not. He merely
chooses not to be ostracized. His main problem is not white racism but Igbo tradition and his inability to buck it. His idealism coupled with a lack of heart to execute
his plans is what leads to his downfall. Each character's individual weakness—
Okonkwo's anger, Isaac's ideological but incomplete transvaluation of values
motivated by revenge, and Obi's spineless idealism—is what seals his fate, not
politics. While the characters adopt numerous strategies for dealing with a
multicultural and conflicted world, their tragedies are brought on by events on three
levels: a failure to be accepted by the dominant element in one's overall society,
intragroup conflict spurred by the dominant element in one's own cultural group,
and the unique character of each individual.

Given the failures of all the characters' strategies, we are left with the ancient
transcultural question of "what is to be done?" At one point, Obi reflects on how
large-scale social change might be brought about:

> 'Where does one begin? With the masses? Educate the masses?' He shook his head.
> 'Not a chance there. It would take centuries. A handful of men at the top. Or even
> one man with vision—an enlightened dictator. People are scared of the word nowa-
> days. But what kind of democracy can exist side by side with so much corruption
> and ignorance? Perhaps a halfwayhouse—a sort of compromise.' (50)

Obi never finishes thinking this through, but he suggests that change from below
and above are both fraught with difficulties. The difficulties in figuring out how
change might happen are reinforced by the lack of individual character change in
the novels and by the deplorable role models provided by Nigeria's horrible experiences with "a handful of men at the top." Obi merely comforts himself that England
had been corrupt until not so very long ago, reminding the reader that change does
occur.

There is one character in the second novel who seems the best adjusted to the
flux and flow of the world: Christopher. He is a black man with the ultimate white
iconographic name. Unlike Obi, he embodies the less "enlightened" aspects of
Nigerian culture. He sees nothing wrong with accepting bribes (137-9), is "callous"
when he gets a girl pregnant (164-5), and adamantly avows that he would never
marry an *osu* (163). Christopher is also the character most "at ease" with his double
heritage (a critically important quality given the meaning of Obi's name and the title
of Achebe's second novel). Unlike the first generation of "civilized" blacks, he is
comfortable eating with his hands (because it tastes better), and he can masterfully
move back and forth between proper and pidgin English, depending on who he is
talking to and what message he wants to communicate. He is described as "rather
outstanding in thus coming to terms with a double heritage" (126). The point about
him, however, is that he is at ease in the world. Christopher achieves his personal
tranquility by having no "illusions" about love or "highfalutin" morality as Obi
does. He rejects "chaps like [Obi] who have wonderful ideas about love" (163). He

understands the significance of the *osu* curse, and even if he doesn't believe it, he acknowledges social reality and its role in life. Just as with the wise neighbor in *Things Fall Apart* (see page ninety-one), he does not demand that the world be other than it is, he merely tries to know what it is and make his way through it the best he can. Perhaps this seems quietist, but what else can be done? He knows that we all have to stand on the earth itself and go with her at her pace (190). Christopher and the wise neighbor's acceptance of social and political realities lead to inner peace, but Achebe notes the price: they accept cultural injustices. Thus, they too are not ideal.

Perhaps the only other avenue for change is education, as exemplified through Achebe's own writing. Despite Christopher and the neighbor's quietist happiness, Achebe is not quietist. He "fights" all the books of all the District Commissioners of *Things Fall Apart* and all of the readily volunteered opinions of all the Mr. Greens of the world.[32] Achebe's analytical essays state what I think he achieves with his novels: "Here then is an adequate revolution for me to espouse—to help my society regain belief in itself and put away the complexes of the years of denigration and self-abasement. And it is essentially a question of education, in the best sense of the word. Here, I think, my aims and the deepest aspirations of my society meet. For no thinking African can escape the pain of the wound in our soul."[33] Achebe's work seems to argue—and his deeds as a writer exemplify—that historical injustices cannot fully be righted by politics. Politics has a role—Achebe certainly is not indifferent to the end of colonialism and Nigerian independence—but this regime change (and a certain basic decency) seems to go a long way toward exhausting what can be expected from politics. The battlefield now, he says, is in the heart and mind—the "soul"—of each individual. The battle is fought by means of education, by writing and rewriting the inaccurate writings of the past. Achebe does not want a transparent ideological maneuver reminiscent of socialist realism, but the reclaiming of the present via accurate portrayals of a dignified but necessarily imperfect past.

The imperfections must be portrayed because Achebe's vision of all cultural and political spheres seems to be that they are flawed and tragic. This sobriety makes his self-appointed mission (of reclaiming the past as the beginning of the future) that much more effective, because he cannot be accused of simplifying or whitewashing history. He is not primarily interested in the daily slights covered by newspapers but in the more fundamental issues. "[A]s far as I am concerned the fundamental theme must first be disposed of. This theme—put quite simply—is that African people did not hear of culture for the first time from Europeans; that their societies were not mindless but frequently had a philosophy of great depth and value and beauty, that they had poetry and, above all, they had dignity. It is this dignity that many African people all but lost during the colonial period and it is this that they must now regain."[34] Achebe is successful, because he captures traditional African dignity while fighting the angry Okonkwos and the corrupt Africans, too. Achebe is aware of the political nature of his novels. "Perhaps what I write is applied art as distinct from pure. But who cares? Art is important but so is education of the kind I have in mind. And I don't see why the two have to be mutually exclusive."[35] He uses the white man's weapon, the book, on behalf of Africa, upholding the traditional wisdom that Umuofia displayed in its early years that everyone should be free to pursue his own path, to follow his own gods.[36]

Notes

1. *The London Times*, September 22, 1991, m55.

2. Chinua Achebe, "The Role of the Writer in a New Nation," in *African Writers on African Writing*, G.D. Killam, ed. (London: Cox & Wyman, 1978), 8.

3. I have in mind those who argue that cultural differences either cannot or should not be overcome (American black Muslims, the Amish, Québécois separatists) versus those who argue that special recognition of particular groups is needed only as a temporary measure to remedy historical injustices. This latter position argues that group recognition is merely a temporary means to, hopefully, an eventual universal inclusion based on equality and social dignity for all. See *Multiculturalism*, Charles Taylor & Amy Gutmann, eds. (Princeton: Princeton University Press, 1994), which includes an illuminating introduction by Gutmann, Taylor's celebrated "The Politics of Recognition," and thoughtful essays by Kwame Anthony Appiah, Jurgen Habermas, Steven Rockefeller, Michael Walzer, and Susan Wolf.

4. Chinua Achebe, "The Novelist as Teacher," in his *Morning Yet On Creation Day* (New York: Anchor, 1975), 71.

5. *Chinua Achebe* [videocassette]. Achebe interviewed by Bill Moyers, part of series *A World of Ideas*. 28 min. (NY: PBS, 1989).

6. Achebe, "The Role of the Writer in a New Nation," 9.

7. For Achebe's autobiographical account of his younger years, including his name change, see his "Named for Victoria, Queen of England," in *Morning Yet On Creation Day*, 115-24.

8. Achebe is very conscious of the problems and ironies of his writing in English. In "The Role of the Writer in a New Nation," 12, he argues that a writer should "try to push back" the limits of conventional English "to accommodate his ideas." And while he argues for "extending the frontiers of English so as to accommodate African thought-patterns," he also argues that writers "must do it through their mastery of English and not out of innocence." He wants to make English sing in African rhythms.

9. References are to the following editions: *Things Fall Apart* (New York: Fawcett Crest, 1984) and *No Longer at Ease* (New York: Anchor, 1994). The titles of these two works are derived from William Butler Yeat's poem "The Second Coming" and T. S. Eliot's "The Journey of the Magi," respectively. Achebe purposely uses white, Christian iconography in telling Nigeria's downfall to the Christian West. But he subverts standard Western iconography, because in his work, the second coming does not promise divine rewards. Nonetheless, the fact that he uses it at all shows the way in which he blends and mixes cultures to make his point. He uses Christian symbols to support African—not religious—liberation. See also A. G. Stock, "Yeats and Achebe," *The Journal of Commonwealth Literature* 5 (1968).

10. Ajax, one of the heroes of the ancient Greek world, is "consistently regarded as the most powerful Greek warrior after Achilles." As Okonkwo is the bulwark of Umuofia, so Homer calls Ajax the "'bulwark of the Achaeans,'" and stresses frequently his physical and military prowess." As with Okonkwo, perceived dishonor leads him to violent outlash and suicide. His life is described in Homer's *Iliad* and in Sophocles' play *Ajax*. Quotations from Whitney J. Oates & Eugene O'Neill, Jr., eds., *The Complete Greek Drama*, 2 vols. (New York: Random House, 1938), vol. I, 313.

Achebe explained the similarity between Okonkwo's and ancient Greek tragedy thusly: "the man who's larger than life, who exemplifies virtues that are admired by the community

. . . is still human. He can have flaws, you see; all that seems to me to be very elegantly underlined in Aristotle's work. I think they are there in human nature itself, and would be found in other traditions even if they were not spelled out in the same exact way." In Charles H. Rowell, "An Interview with Chinua Achebe," in *Callaloo* 13:1 (winter 1990), 97. On tragedy in Achebe's work, see Abiole Irele, "The Tragic Conflict in the Novels of Chinua Achebe" in *Critical Perspectives on Chinua Achebe*, C. L. Innes and Bernth Lindfors, eds. (Washington, DC: Three Continents Press, 1978), 10-21; and, Roger L. Landrum, "Chinua Achebe and the Aristotelian Concept of Tragedy" in *Black Academy Review* 1 (1970), 22-30. Michael Moses, *The Novel and the Globalization of Culture* (Oxford: Oxford University Press, 1995), 110, compares Okonkwo to Achilles.

11. See Robert M. Wren, *Achebe's World: The Historical and Cultural Context of the Novels* (Washington, DC: Three Continents Press, 1980), 26 & 77.

12. Plato, *The Republic*, 414b-415c.

13. Diane Akers Rhoads, "Culture in Chinua Achebe's *Things Fall Apart*," *African Studies Review* 36:2 (September 1993), 61.

14. Weber attributes enchantment to premodern, traditional, and "savage" societies. See Max Weber, "Science as a Vocation" in H. H. Gerth and C. Wright Mills, eds., *From Max Weber: Essays in Sociology* (Oxford: Oxford University Press, 1946), 139. No one that I am aware of has made this comparison between Achebe and Weber.

15. Weber, "Science as a Vocation," 155, and Weber, "Politics as a Vocation," in *From Max Weber*, 127-28.

16. Umofia has one female priestess, Chielo.

17. See Rhoads. Also, Arthur Ravenscraft, *Chinua Achebe* (Harlow, Essex: Longman, Green, 1969), 11, notes Okonkwo's personal shortcomings but does not consider it to be a cultural shortcoming. Robert Wren, *Achebe's World*, 47, argues that "Okonkwo's household, because of his harshness, is a poor example," but he still does not fully appreciate the limits of the different gender roles.

18. Compare to Uzbek in Montesquieu's *Persian Letters.*

19. Achebe writes, "I would be quite satisfied if my novels (especially the ones I set in the past) did no more than teach my readers that their past—with all its imperfections—was not one long night of savagery from which the first Europeans acting on God's behalf delivered them" ("The Novelist as Teacher," 72). Achebe is confident that Africa's "past with all its imperfections, never lacked dignity" ("The Role of the Writer in a New Nation," 9). The point is to show the Igbo as part of the exact same human condition as everyone else. See also Eustace Palmer, *The Growth of the African Novel* (London: Heinemann, 1979).

20. For a history of toleration in the West, see Alan Levine, ed., *Early Modern Skepticism and the Origins of Toleration* (Lanham, Md.: Lexington Books, 1999), ch.1. Whatever strengths may exist in the West's philosophical tradition of toleration, this must be distinguished from the colonial policy of "toleration" that was sometimes cynically employed. Under this policy, every culture was to develop on its own. This was often an excuse to neglect the indigenous people and to justify disproportionate spending on whites and blacks.

21. Friedrich Nietzsche, *On the Genealogy of Morals*, Walter Kaufmann, trans. (New York: Random House, 1969). On the distinction between master and slave morality, see the first essay and the third essay, aphorisms #13-15. See also, Alan Levine, "Chinua Achebe's *Things Fall Apart* as a Case Study in Nietzsche's Transvaluation of Values" in *Perspectives on Political Science* 28: 2 (Summer 1999). As far as I know, only Moses, *The Novel and the Globalization of Culture*, 123, has also noted the similarity between Achebe and Nietzsche.

22. Another similarity between Nietzsche's and Achebe's accounts of Christianity concerns its passive attitude toward the world. Those attracted to Christianity in Achebe's

Umuofia are seen as useless because they are foolish and lacking in prudence: "The imagery of an *efulefu* in the language of the clan was a man who sold his machete and wore the sheath to battle" (133). This echoes Paul's famous admonition to use "truth as a belt tight around your waist, with righteousness as your breast plate . . . carry faith as a shield . . . accept salvation as a helmet, and the word of God as the sword" (Ephesians 6: 14-17). Worldly foresight is not necessary because God will provide. Accordingly, the first priest in Umuofia counsels his congregation: "We cannot offer physical resistance to them. Our strength lies in the Lord" (172). Then instead of fighting, "They knelt down together and prayed to God for delivery" (172). The passive attitude toward the world is condemned by traditional Igbo culture and master morality but praised by Christianity.

23. Achebe, *No Longer at Ease*, 5.

24. Contrast the valuation of snakes in Umuofia's religion and in Christianity. Umuofia considers the python sacred, but because of the serpent's role in the garden of Eden, the snake might be Christianity's most hated animal.

25. Ravenscraft, *Chinua Achebe*, 20-21, discusses *No Longer at Ease* as an unconventional tragedy, but he impatiently rejects it as a failure.

26. Lest anyone be reluctant to equate the views of this character with Achebe's own views, in his writing elsewhere, Achebe offers a similar analysis. See Achebe's "Preface" to *The African Trilogy: Things Fall Apart, No Longer at Ease, Arrow of God* (London: Picador, 1988), x.

27. Indeed, even Umuofia's secular meetings to discuss practical issues are described in religious tones. They are called a "congregation" and repeatedly say "amen" (7).

28. Of the various theories put forward in this novel to explain Nigeria's corruption, Achebe seems to agree most with Obi's indictment of Nigeria's leaders. "The trouble with Nigeria," he writes, "is simply and squarely a failure of leadership." Against Mr. Green's contentions, Achebe argues that "There is nothing basically wrong with the Nigerian character. There is nothing wrong with the Nigerian land or climate or water or air or anything else." Achebe, *The Trouble with Nigeria* (London: Heinemann, 1983), 1.

29. Obi argues that "Our fathers in their darkness and ignorance called an innocent man *osu*, a thing given to idols, and thereafter he became an outcast, and his children's children forever. But have we not seen the light of the Gospel?" (151). Obi is not a "believer" and does not accept the premise of his own arguments, but he is making his points to try to persuade his father, who has dedicated his life to Christian principles. But it is precisely here that we see the limits in his father's ability to change.

30. The tragedy of Isaac's lack of self-knowledge is that he has lost genuine human contact with his son—and perhaps with the whole world. Despite Obi's disappointment in his father's refusal, he is described as having a "strange happiness," because he feels this is the first "direct human contact" he ever had with his father (153). By wrapping himself in a system in which he does not believe at the deepest levels of his heart, Isaac has tragically condemned his relation to his only son to be mediated by ideology. This crisis cracks Isaac's ideological armor; he had been relating not based on "direct human contact" or heart but mediated by white/Christian/foreign ideology.

31. More precisely, Okonkwo achieves happiness just before his suicide and Obi temporarily achieves inner peace, but only at the price of his ideals and longings. Also, Obi has a paradoxical reaction to his mother's death: a brief period of guilt quickly replaced by inner peace. "It [guilt] very soon vanished altogether, leaving a queer feeling of calm . . . 'Poor mother!' he said, trying by manipulation to produce the right emotion. But it was no use. The dominant feeling was of peace" (187). In short, he feels a "kind of peace. The peace that passeth all understanding" (187). The peace that Obi feels is as if "he, too, had died" (190).

32. Achebe calls attention to his fight with all the Mr. Greens of this world by having Obi say that he should write a novel on this theme (121-22). *No Longer at Ease* is Achebe's beginning of this project.

33. Achebe, "The Novelist as Teacher," 71.

34. Achebe, "The Role of the Writer in a New Nation," 8.

35. Achebe, "The Novelist as Teacher," 72.

36. Fuller versions of parts of this chapter are found in "Chinua Achebe's *Things Fall Apart* as a Case Study in Nietzsche's Transvaluation of Values," in *Perspectives on Political Science* (Fall 1999) 28:4, 136-42. Thanks to Joanne Molina for research assistance and to Marianne Noble for commenting on earlier versions of this essay.

Chapter 8

A Place in the World: Delinquency and the Search for Liberty in Cervantes' *Rinconete and Cortadillo*

*Juan José Sendín Vinagre**

> *"The place I came from is not my own . . .*
> *All I have in it is a father who doesn't treat me as his son*
> *and a stepmother who treats me in the way stepchildren are usually treated.*
> *I am going where chance directs."*
> —Rinconete and Cortadillo

At first glance, the short novella *Rinconete and Cortadillo* seems no more than a lighthearted picture of habits and customs among sixteenth-century Spanish juvenile delinquents. It seems to lack the intellectual profundity and imagination characteristic of literature of Spain's Golden Age, especially Cervantes' major accomplishment, *Don Quixote*. Yet, closer examination reveals a story at once brilliant and subtle in which the author not only offers keen insight into life but communicates his own ethical convictions as well.

At times, one may ask whether the study of literature has any useful purpose; and, although the necessity of studying narrative and poetry may be conceded, its study is not always pleasant. In this regard, literary scholars are wont to repeat the admonition of the Latin poet Horace "All agree that the best literature is that which combines what is morally useful with what is pleasant, delighting the reader while instructing him."[1]

To be sure, literature often has been the most agile mode of divulging scientific knowledge, philosophical convictions, aesthetic values, religious beliefs, and the moral principles of a society when such knowledge first appears. In order to understand best the ability of literature to be simultaneously both pleasing and useful, we note the echo of these verses of Horace in Spanish writing at the end of the sixteenth century and the beginning of the seventeenth. For example in 1617, Francisco Cascales published his *Tablas Poeticas*[2] in which he repeats

---

* Translated by Henry T. Edmondson III

the conviction of the Latin poet and notes disapprovingly that much literature of the previous century did not give equal weight to both the agreeable and the morally useful.[3] A few years earlier, in 1583 the young Lope de Vega proclaimed this same idea in *Arcadia* in which a romantic tale is built upon a structure of moral instruction.[4] Fray Luis de León, in decrying the success of merely romantic or adventure literature, calls for all talented authors to intertwine their work with stories that exalt virtue and good manners, even as it is done in sacred Scripture.[5]

The "Exemplar" and the Novellas

In the story at hand, *Rinconete and Cortadillo*, the protagonists behave outside of the moral norms of society. The author, in one subtle way or another, reinforces conventional morality by his deprecation of the counterculture in which the two young delinquents find themselves. At the same time, society at large does not escape the author's criticism. Interestingly, in this type of story, which has its context in the margins of society—the "picaresque" novel of the first half of the sixteenth century—most authors other than Cervantes do not seem to have the least intention of broaching the subject of social injustice.

The literary form that has best served to teach moral lessons has been that of the "exemplar"—a narration in which the author introduces principles woven into the plot, personalities artfully arranged within the story, whether amusing or dramatic, who encounter failure by following conduct contrary to the predominant values of their society.[6] In 1554, the "picaresque novel" was introduced with the publication of *La Vida de Lazarillo de Tormes y de sus Fortunas y Adversidades* by an anonymous author. The book deals with the life and changes of fortune of a young boy, revealing as much about his society as his life. This work and those that follow in its genre fit nicely with the description by Franciso Cascales who speaks of works that present personages "worthy of commiseration, of whom even the very wise learn something as their story stirs in us fear and sadness."[7]

In contrast with later novelists who would explain social marginalization and personal misery as a function of social injustice or inequality, the picaresque novel generally teaches that the unfortunate life of those outside of established society is a consequence of not adhering to prevailing moral standards. These cases do not invite the reader to question or criticize the norms of society, rather the reader is encouraged to adhere more closely to them. We cannot speak, however, of an undeviating complicity between the authors of the period and their society as social criticism is not entirely unknown in this literature. Works like the aforementioned *Vida de Lazarillo de Tormes* (1554), *Guzmán Alfarache* by Mateo Alemán (first part, 1599, second part, 1604) or *El Buscón* by Francisco de Quevedo (1626) clearly show the disastrous consequences of a life lived apart from established virtue; nevertheless, the contemporary reader will readily perceive a subtle indictment of a maladjustment between proclaimed social ends and the behavior of those individuals charged with achieving them. This criticism is evident, but implicit.

In order to develop his *Exemplary Stories* (1613), Cervantes chooses the "example" or the "exemplar" as his literary type and combines it with the form of the novella, a genre imported from Italy where it had enjoyed dazzling success since Boccaccio's *Decameron*. With this work in mind Cervantes announces the introduction of the same genre in Castillian Spanish:

> I am the first to write short stories in Castillian. For the many examples that are already in print in Spanish are all translated from foreign languages, while these are my very own, neither imitated nor stolen.[8]

This concept of the novella, inherited from the Italian *novella*, is different from previous works such as *Lazarillo* in that Cervantes' novellas feature short stories characterized by his customary preference for action and adventure over reflection and theoretical discourse. Cervantes' novellas instruct and warn through their entertainment, not apart from it. As he affirms in the prologue, "I have called them 'exemplary', and on close examination you will see that there is not one from which you cannot extract some profitable example."[9]

The portrait that Cervates paints of himself in the "Prologue" is that of a sixty-six-year-old man, different than practically all the other writers of the time with whom he shares success and popularity in the royal court such as Lope de Vega, Francisco de Quevedo, and Luis de Góngora. It is well known that Cervantes had lived a colorful life outside of the courtly circle. He was exiled as a young man, served as a soldier in Italy, Flanders, and Lepanto, was captured by Algerian pirates and held captive for five years. He later returned to work as an obscure bureaucrat in Spain, and always suffered familial and economic problems because of his chronic failure as a dramatist and poet.

> The man you see before you, with aquiline features, chestnut-colored hair, smooth, unwrinkled brow, bright eyes, and curved though well-proportioned nose, silver beard that not twenty years ago was golden, large moustache, small mouth, teeth neither large nor small—since he boasts only six of them, and those he has are in poor condition and even worse positions, for not one of them cuts against another—of medium build, neither tall nor short, a healthy colour in his cheeks, fair rather than dark complexion, slightly stooping, and not very light on his feet. This, then, is a description of the author of *La Galatea* and *Don Quixote of la Mancha* and the man who wrote *Journey to Parnassus.. . .* He is commonly known as Miguel de Cervantes Saavedra.[10]

One can appreciate in this portrait the melancholy, the pride, and the humor of an intelligent man at the end of his life (he would live only three more years) as he makes an accounting of who he was and who he had been. The same sharp irony and brilliance of this self-portrait is often present in his works. For this reason, the reader must be attentive to the constant games Cervantes plays with words and concepts, a technique that adds a second and at times a third dimension to all that he writes. He contradicts that which he affirms, he affirms with irony so that he means the contrary of what he says, he guides the reader down unexpected paths that carry him to paradoxical conclusions and make him a partner in an interminable game of such subtlety that even the most attentive reader may perceive his meaning but experience difficulty in reducing Cervantes' message to logical terms. In the work under consideration in this chapter, *Rinconete and Cortadillo*, we find at times insinuations that permit the author to put into play implicit criticisms and allusions from which the reader must draw his own conclusions. Although the tone is of carefree nonchalance, beneath the superficial appearance of his prose is a profound message about human nature.

Cervantes' *Exemplary Stories* is a collection of twelve exemplary tales, written by means of the classical formula of instructing and entertaining. They propose a variety of situations, always uniquely resolved. Each of the stories has a moral intent; at the same time, even when the author censures attitudes and habits, the censure is clothed in a refined sense of humor. Cervantes explains, "It has been my intention to set up a billiard table in the public square of our nation, where anyone may come and amuse himself without injuring anyone else."[11] Joaquín Casalduero offers an explanation of ten of the twelve works.

> The twelve novellas are a continual marvel that carry us from the first of the collection *The Little Gypsy Girl*, whose beauty is untarnished by the harsh life that surrounds her, to the last novella in which two dogs pass the night in a rare and magical opportunity for serious conversation (*The Dogs Colloquy*). Between these novellas we pass through *The Generous Suitor*, a story of heroic deeds and virtue; *Rinconete and Cortadillo*, an astonishing but tongue-in-cheek picture of Spanish low life; and, *The English Spanish Girl*, a story of two souls who find themselves united only as they consecutively move apart in order to be truly reunited. *The Glass Graduate* describes the strange changes and perturbations of a student; the abuse and prodigious recuperation of a young girl is the theme of *The Power of Blood*; and, *The Jealous Old Man from Extremadura* is the psychological portrait of extraordinary jealousy. . . . *The Deceitful Marriage* is a story of incredible but everyday events and *The Two Damsels* describes the dangerous pilgrimage of two young women who seek their lost lovers.[12]

When Cervantes published his *Exemplary Stories* at the publishing house of Juan de la Cuesta, in Madrid, Castillian literature was in one of its most brilliant moments. Authors such as Lope de Vega, Luis de Góngora or Francisco de Quevedo had converted the Court into one of the most priviledged places in all of Europe for the cultivation of the letters. Their works, together with the works of a second tier of authors whose works matured in their shadow, were published by Juan de la Cuesta or copied elsewhere. These works passed through a virtual poets' universe whose beneficiaries were to be found in salons, literary academies, and palace gardens—as well as in taverns, markets, hostals, and brothels where the genius and inspiration of these poets, dramatists, and novelists was celebrated. Even the literary inheritance of the previous century was recollected and enjoyed again. All celebrated the brilliance and foolishness of the "Man of La Mancha." In this context we are reminded of the anecdote of Philip III who, upon seeing a page laughing to himself uncontrollably, said to those who accompanied him, "Either this lad is crazy or he is reading *Don Quixote*." The immediate success and popularity of the works of the golden age of Spanish literature was comparable to—if not superior to—the success of novellas of chivalry and romance of the previous century.

An Empire and a City

The Spanish political situation in Cervantes' day had passed from that of the extensive Spanish empire with indisputable international predominance, to that of an empire rapidly deteriorating, precariously deployed on diverse foreign fronts. Phillip II had not been able to prevent growing religious and political tensions in Germany and the Netherlands. He tried to maintain control of these areas through his favorite, the Duke of Lerma, yet they progressively drifted out of the sphere of Spain's influence. Military failures, especially the spectacular defeat of Phillip II's Grand Armada against the English in 1588, had severely undermined the political prestige of Spain in Europe as well as the authority of the Spanish Crown in its far flung possessions.

Spanish society had never been the community of unanimity that those in power had pretended; but now, Spain suffered the political and ideological recession of the grand empire first undertaken by the Catholic Queen and King, Isabella and Ferdinand. Financial and economic difficulties, although nothing new, contributed even more to the demoralization by which the Spanish citizenry in general and the writers in particular perceived their own national situation. In general, there was in Spain a diffused but palpable sense of disillusionment.

The literary reflection of this state of affairs is, nevertheless, one of unparalleled brilliance. Despite a repressive mentality that impeded the manifestation of fresh philosophical and spiritual ideas contrary to the prevailing orthodoxy, the pages of artists like Cervantes describe the way of life of a community in conflict with—or ruptured from—its own convictions.

This troubled political atmosphere gave birth to an increase of delinquency and other expressions of the marginal life that give place—in a sense especially interesting to this study—to a growing public curiosity with the "bad life" (*la mala vida*) that became popular among readers. Since the earlier appearance of *Lazarillo*, two parallel literary interests coexisted: the attraction for books of chivalry and an appetite to know more of the picaresque antihero and his way of life at the edge of the law. This latter genre called the reader's attention to the counterculture swarming about him in the shadowy corners and back alleys of the city, populated by persons that in another life could have been the reader himself. In 1605, Cervantes offers us a map of the Spanish underworld when, at the beginning of his adventures, the misguided Don Quixote asks the coarse innkeeper to perform the service of "knighting" him. The innkeeper offers a sympathetic, but hilarious parody of Quixote's noble aspirations:

The innkeeper, who . . . was pretty crafty and had already a suspicion that his guest was wrong in the head . . . decided to fall in with his humour. He added that he too, in the day of his youth had devoted himself to that honourable profession and travelled in divers parts of the world in search of adventures, not omitting to visit the Fish Market of Malaga, the Isles of Riaran, the Compass of Seville, the Little Market Place at Segovia, the Olive Grove at Valencia, the Circle of Granada, the Strand of San Lucar, the Colt-fountain of Cordova, the Taverns of Toledo and sundry other places, where he had exercised the agility of his heels and the lightness of his fingers, doing many wrongs, wooing many widows, ruining sundry maidens and cheating a few minors—in fact, making himself well-known in almost all the police-courts and law-courts in Spain.[13]

In the *Exemplary Stories*, the theme of adventure is often united with that of the picaresque protagonist. For Cervantes, this combination is one of the most frequent narrative themes that he uses in order to avoid more mundane, even monotonous life and a secure family. This is true not only in *Rinconete* but also in *The Little Gypsy Girl* and *The Illustrious Kitchen Maid* where the adventure of the protagonists unfolds in just such a context. As Casalduero has indicated, there is a radical difference between the picaresque persona in Cervantino novellas and those of more typical picaresque novels such as *Lazarillo* or *El Buscon*; the Cervantino heroes generally remain immune from the reformative influences of the world in which their adventures take place; the typical moral posturing of this genre is absent with Cervantes. His moral warnings are more subtle, his actors more complex; and, in the midst of the spectacle of their lives, it is the sum total of their comportment through which the author offers his counsel rather than through explicit discourse. Though they take place at the margins of society, Cervantes' stories are distinct from the conventional picaresque stories that unswervingly warn against the alienation from societal norms. Especially in *Rinconete and Cortadillo*, the author offers an implied but brilliant and optimistic defense of individual independence, of the quest for freedom along the road of adventure. Yet, in the end, the reader encounters an unexpected idea of liberty and social norms peculiar, unique, and just as emphatic of those the two young delinquents have escaped. The tone of this kind of search is expressed clearly in *The Illustrious Kitchen Maid*:

> Carriazo was little more than thirteen years of age when he was inspired to try the picaresque way of life. Without being forced into such action by an ill treatment on the part of his parents, but by a mere whim and fancy of his own, he cut loose, as the slang of his generation would have it, from his parents' home and ventured out into the world. He was so content with the freedom of the road that even in the midst of the discomfort and hardship that came with it he did not miss the luxury of his father's house; travelling on foot did not tire him, the cold did not offend him, and the heat did not annoy him. As far as he was concerned each season of the year was like a mild and gentle spring; he slept as soundly upon unthreshed corn as he did upon a mattress; he bedded down in the hay lofts of inns with as much pleasure as if he were lying between fine linen sheets. All in all, he became such a successful *pícaro* that he could have taught the famous Alfarache himself a thing or two in the art of being a rogue.[14]

Cervantes is no mere disinterested portraitist of this form of adventure—he is an enthusiast. In contrast with other picaresque novellas where authors see in the life of the *pícaros* the root of all evil and failure, Cervantes praises without restraint the free life of adventure; for example, in his description of the "tunny fisheries of Zahara, the *ne plus ultra*[15] of picaresque activity":

That is where you will find unmitigated squalor, plump fatness, urgent hunger, abundant satisfaction, undisguised vice, endless gambling, incessant brawling, sporadic deaths, vulgarities at every turn, the kind of dancing you find at weddings and the type of *seguidillas*[16] you find in print, ballads with refrains and poems without. . . . That is where liberty reigns and work is conspicuous by its absence.[17]

One of the centers of this life is Seville, the city where the gold of America was collected and a portion of it was stored. This converted Seville into a place where, more than any other, the abundance of riches became the symbolic clock by which the Sevillanos ordered their lives. It "was the port to the Indies, the place of departure and arrival for the American flotillas. For this reason, it became the fountain of gold and silver."[18] In these decades, Seville is the Mecca of picaresque Spain in the same way that literature and cinema has engendered organized illicit activity in such cities as London, Paris, Tangiers, Marseilles, Chicago, or New York. Seville sported "organized picaresque activity not unlike that of the modern day Mafia. Fraternities of thieves and criminals [were] corporately organized. . . . They parceled out urban territories and the activity therein was regulated scrupulously with established means of cost accounting and booty distribution."[19]

The Adventure of Rincón and Cortado

In *Rinconete and Cortadillo*, Cervantes sketches for us an entertaining picture of southern Spain (Andalusia) at the beginning of the seventeenth century including the officials, the habits, the places, but above all, the clandestine flavor of the environment. As the reading of the novella unfolds, there is scarcely a censure—until the end of the story—of this dissolute way of life. Rather, Cervantes' energy seems to be directed toward outlining the parallels and subterranean connections and ironic parallels between the life outside of the law and the rest of society.

The story is of "two boys of about fourteen or fifteen"[20] who abandon their families to seek a new way of life. Cortado leaves his home because the "'restricted life of the village and my stepmother's unloving attitude made me fed up (88)'" while Rincón (like Carriazo in *The Illustrious Kitchen Maid*) has not embarked upon his adventure because of tension at home but rather simply because the opportunity presented itself, or perhaps for a simple impulse to escape:

"[My] father is a person of quality, being an officer of the Holy Crusade, by which I mean that he is a seller of papal bulls, or a pardoner as the common people call them. I went with him on his rounds once or twice, and I learnt his trade so well that the man who is reckoned to be the best seller of bulls in the world couldn't beat me at it. But one day, being more fond of the cash from the bulls than the bulls themselves, I made off with a bag of money and ended up with it in Madrid." (87)

The two boys having met at siesta time on the front porch of a roadside inn, set out together. Cervantes offers a description of the two that, except for the outdated clothing and weaponry, seems quite modern:

> They had no cloaks; their breeches were of drill and their stockings-of bare flesh. It's true that their footwear made up for it, because one of them wore rope sandals, but worn so much that they were in fact worn out, and the other had shoes which were full of holes and with the soles off, so that they were more like stocks than shoes. One of them wore a green hunting-cap; the other a hat without a band, low-crowned and broad-brimmed. In a bag on his back fastened round him one carried a greasy, chamois-colured shirt; the other was empty-handed and with no baggage [...] The two were sunburnt, with long, dirty fingernails and hands none too clean; one had a cutlass, and the other a knife with a yellow horn handle, of the sort they call a cow-herd's knife. (85)

They then describe to each other their respective talents—Cortado is a pickpocket and Rincón is a card sharp—and decide immediately to unite for their mutual advantage. Their first victim is a muleteer who, upon emerging from the inn, is quickly fleeced by Rincón in a quick card game on the porch. They join a group of travelers to Madrid and the next day Cortado slices open the traveling bag of a Frenchman in the group and pilfers "two good shirts, a sundial and a little memo book" (91). Upon arriving in Seville, Cortado steals a small purse from the church sexton; at the same time the delinquents are introduced into the craft of basket carrying by a lad from the Asturias.

> The Asturian had told him about this trick; and also that when they were carrying small fish, such as dace or sardines or plaice, they could take a few out by way of samples, at least against the day's expenses; but that this had to be done with care, so that one should not lose one's good reputations, which was what counted most in that trade. (92)

The two next sell the booty collected earlier from the Frenchman and Cervantes offers us a snapshot of the city as they explore it:

> they sold the shirts in the second-hand shop near the Arena gate, and made twenty *reales* out of them. After this they went to look at the city, and were amazed at the size and splendour of its cathedral and the vast number of people by the river, because it was at the time when they were loading up the fleet. There were six galleys[21] there, the sight of which made them sigh and dread the day when a mistake on their part would lead them to spend the rest of their lives in them. (90)

Eventually, the young Asturian reveals to Rincón and Cortado the existence of a fraternity of delinquents headed by a certain Mr. Monipodio of which he is a member. He first asks if they are already members, "'Tell me, gallant sirs, do you belong to the bad set or not'"(94)? They indicate they are not, nor do they really understand the question.

> "Don't you understand," said the youth. "Well I'll make you understand, and I'll feed it to you with a silver spoon. I mean gentlemen, are you thieves? But I don't

know why I'm asking you this, for I already know you are. Tell me, how is it you haven't been to Mr. Monipodio's customs house?" (94)

Rincón asks, "'Do you pay duty on thefts in this part of the country, gallant sir?'" The boy explains the rules that govern illicit activity among juveniles in Seville: "'If you don't pay at least you register with Mr. Monipodio, who is the father, master and protector of thieves; and so I advise you to come with me and pay your respects to him'"(94). The Asturian then leads them to a patio where the fraternity is gathering; its members include two youths of about twenty disguised as students, "two basket-boys and a blind man," and two old men carrying "a rosary of jingling beads." Soon "there were about fourteen persons assembled in the patio in different dress and belonging to different professions" (97). When all had assembled, their chief, Monipodio appeared who "looked about forty-five or forty-six years old." He was "tall, dark, beetle-browed, and with a very thick black beard and deep-set eyes." There was a "veritable wood" upon his chest, "so thick was the hair . . . In fact, he looked the most clumsy and hideous ruffian you've ever seen" (98).

Monipodio submits them to an exam in which he calibrates their abilities but, most importantly, their capacity for apprenticeship and their future potential. He is pleased with his conclusions but must ascertain whether they can withstand a public whipping without revealing their connections: "'I should like you also to be able, if necessary, to stand half a dozen *ansias* without opening your mouth or saying a word'" (100). Cortado assures Monipodio that they have firsthand experience with *ansias* and that "'we're ready for anything'" knowing that "'what the tongue says the neck pays for'" (101). "'Stop, that's enough,' said Monipodio at this point.'" "'This statement alone convinces me, and obliges me to let you become full members at once and dispense with the year of probation'" (101). The boys rejoice as this judgment automatically means generous exemptions.

[It] involved not having to pay half the proceeds of the first theft they made, not to do menial jobs all that year, such as taking bail to the prison for a senior member or going to the brothel on behalf of those who had contributed. They could drink wine without water in it, have a party whenever, however and wherever they wished, without asking leave of their chief; have a share straight away in the winnings of the senior members of the brotherhood; and other things which they considered to be a great privilege, and for which they thanked the company in the most civil manner. (101)

Having superseded this rite of passage, Rincón and Cortado are baptized with the more dignified names of "Rinconete" and Cortadillo" and become members in full of this society within a society.

Juan José Sendín Vinagre

A Place in the World

Along the road of discovery, the dream of independence that seemed so exciting to the two boys on the porch of the inn where they met—fleeing the narrowness of their life, the rigor of monotony and pursuing their adventure—dissipates and gives way to another type of hierarchy much more demanding. It is the patio of Monipodio where the norms are inflexible and where each member must comply voluntarily with the sovereign rule of Monipodio, a mixture of paternalism and inflexible tyranny. As the Asturian had explained, he is "'the father, master and protector of thieves,'" but if one should "'dare to steal without his authority, it'll cost you dear'" (94). Monipodio himself warns, "'Let no one make light of breaking our rule in the slightest degree, or it'll cost him his life'" (102)! The order that exists in the patio of Monipodio is parallel to any other order, with precise assignments and recognized offices. For example, certain boys were assigned the office of "hornet," their job being "to go round by day to see which houses they could break into by night, and to follow those who got money out of the Contración, or Mint" (108). The patio is, in effect, a small court where the monarchical Monipodio dictates what each member of the fraternity should do and determines those who have been obedient to his instructions. The efficiency and harmony of this "court" is based upon the complimentary rigor of the established rules and the arbitrary orders of Monipodio, as well as the equity by which benefits are shared. Each one recognizes his duty and is obligated to its fulfillment; for that, he receives a predetermined stipend.

> "What you have to do," answered Monipodio, "is to go to your posts, all of you, and not to leave them until Sunday, when we'll all meet here and have a share out of anything that's come our way, without doing injury to anyone." (117)

The work of each member of the community and their assignments are recorded in a notebook. The computation and accounting of these tasks, an activity itself learned from "legal society," is carried out with the same scrupulosity of any professional registry. During an assembly on the patio, Monipodio, standing in the middle of the group, "took out a notebook which he had in the hood of his cloak." Rinconete was instructed to read its contents (because Monipodio could not read). He began

> *List of knifings for this week*
> The first, to the merchant at the crossroads; price fifty crowns. Received thirty on account. Executor, Chiquiznaque. (115)

On another page he read he continued under the heading "*List of beatings*" (115). Monipodio's judicial proceedings in admitting Rinconete and Cortadillo to the fraternity and the exemptions they receive are similarly documented:

> Whereupon Monipodio took from the hood of his cloak a paper, on which was a list of the members of the brotherhood, and he told Rinconete to put his and Cortadillo's names on it; but as there was no inkpot he gave him the paper to take away

and get it written at the first apothecary's putting "Rinconete and Cortadillo, members; probations, none; Rinconete, card sharper; Cortadillo, pickpocket;" and the day, month, and year, not mentioning parents or birthplace. (118)

This hierarchy so severe, that the boys have accepted so freely—in contrast with the familial hierarchy from which they fled—provides them a certain paradoxical independence. It is an independence in which they "make it" by their own efforts in the world, assuming "adultlike" positions of responsibility on which depend their security, prosperity and the physical liberty they enjoy. This rite of passage from custodial adolescence to the autonomous life of adults is underscored with their new baptism: they are no longer Rincón and Cortado but "Rinconete, The Cardsharp," and "Cortadillo, The Pickpocket." The only thing lacking in these proceedings is the formal recognition of the law.

In contrast with those stories to which cinema and television have made us accustomed, in which, in one way or another, delinquents fall into the hands of the law, *Rinconete y Cortadillo* ends with a vague understated censure at the end of this upbeat and sympathetic tale of juvenile delinquents. In this story, injustice is described only as poor administration. For example, when "a young gentleman came to the door" and demanded of Monipodio why his crime for which he had contracted "had been so badly carried out," Monipodio then demands an accounting of the juvenile Chiquiznaque. The delinquent protests that the intended victim was too small to leave the agreed upon "fourteen knife wounds"; instead, he knifed his "lackey" administering "the best quality wounds" (113-14).

The ethical values upon which the protagonists sustain the fraternity are practically identical with those of "legal society" including the primordial religious values that reinforce the validity of established norms and even sanction them. All involved expect to be saved by means of the faithful attendance to their devotions, independently of their reprehensible acts. Rinconete is "especially amused" at one of the delinquent girls when she said that "heaven would offset against her sins the labour she had put into gaining the twenty-four *reales.*" Rinconete "was also amazed by the assurance they had and their confidence that they would go to heaven because they didn't fail to perform their devotions, when they were up to their eyes in stealing and murder and offences against God" (119).

Earlier we alluded to the moral recapitulation found at the end of this story that is somewhat more explicit than the subtlety that characterizes the rest of the tale. Cervantes offers an admonition to the reader and protagonists alike as all find themselves at an unexpected point in an adventure that had seemed to be preceding happily but now seems more grim, even hopeless. At this point, although Cervantes has painted the picture of an illicit society, it is not a particularly unfavorable portrait; he must now, however, leave us on "the right side of the law" if he wants to maintain a position of moral authority over his readers. This then seems to motivate the final discussion; although, Cervantes is still unwilling to abandon a sense of irony and use of nuance as he puts the finishing touches on the story of Monipodio's patio. Rinconete becomes our guide as he finds himself astounded at the "obedience and respect" the fraternity all "felt for

Monipodio," when their leader was "such a barbarous, uncouth and soulless wretch" (119). Also,

> he was shocked by the slackness of the law in that famous city of Seville, where such pernicious and perverted people could live almost openly; and he made up his mind to advise his companion that they should not spend much time in that evil and abandoned way of life, so uncertain, lawless and dissolute. But all the same, carried away by his youth and lack of experience, he spent some months longer with the community. (119)[22]

Rinconete seems to accept that this form of life has no future even though, at least for Cervantes, such an adventure is motivated in part by an elemental love of life. One suspects that although the author must register his disapproval of Monipodio's patio, the ex-soldier, ex-captive, and ex-wanderer can only do so with some reluctance.

The reader suspects as well that Rinconete and Cortadillo's search is not so much for freedom as it is for community and accountability. Although the two are driven by a sense of adventure and an apparent lust for liberty, their quest is satisfied after a time and with its passing they ultimately find themselves dissatisfied with a life that is excessively free.

Rinconete's final musings at the conclusion of the story suggest that the search all along has been a search for community and order—a "place in the world." In his earlier introduction, Cortadillo had not complained of a life that was restricted; instead, he expresses his unhappiness with an existence without meaningful identity and definition: his place is not his "own" and he is in subjection to "a father who doesn't treat me as his son and a stepmother who treats me in the way stepchildren are usually treated." The careful reader will also infer that the two seek a morally coherent life, one where religion and sincere ethics are not mutually exclusive, or at least a pattern of living where external religious practice is not a cover for a morality based only upon convenience.

Cervantes' novella demonstrates that a life without authority is an illusion. Those who seek completely to escape authority will inevitably embrace another form of the same, and the newer expression may be more authoritative and less accountable than the first. Criminals who abandon normal society inevitably find themselves members of "bands" or groups of some kind that without exception are led—if not ruled—by authoritarian figures. True freedom seems to be the opportunity to choose that rule to which one submits, not to escape it.

Finally, Cervantes' unique portrait of the picaresque life offers yet one other surprising suggestion: the author, no doubt informed by his own life experience, seems to suggest that an indispensable element of a rich life is *adventure* and that a life from which the adventurous is absent will be an existence that leaves the individual restless and unfulfilled. It is not so much illicit adventure for which human beings long; it is simply adventure. If this experience is not available by legitimate means, it may be sought illegitimately until the restless soul finds "a place in the world."

Notes

1. Horacio, *Epístola a los Pisones* , en *Aristóteles, Horacio. Artes poéticas*, Aníbal González, trans. (Madrid: Taurus, 1987), 141. The original Latin reads "Omne tulit punctum qui miscuit utile dulci, / lectorem delectando pariterque monendo," vv. 343-344, ibid. 157.

2. Francisco Cascales, *Tablas Poeticas* (Murcia: Luis Berós, 1617).

3. "De manera que el poema no basta ser agradable, sino provechoso y moral, como quien es imitación de la vida, espejo de las costumbres, imagen de la verdad. ¿Quién duda, sino que leyendo los hombres las obras de poesía, o hallándose en las representaciones tan allegadas a la verdad, se acostumbran a tener misericordia y miedo." Francisco Cascales, *Tablas poéticas*, Benito Brancaforte, ed. (Madrid, *Clásicos castellanos*, 1975), 37-38.

4. Lope de Vega, *la Arcadia, prosas, y versos de Lope Vega Carpio* (Madrid, Luis Sánchez, 1598). "El oficio del poeta . . . es verdaderamente, escriuir para enseñar, y para deleitar, y este es el fin, a q[ue] su principio de dirige." Lope de Vega, *la Arcadia, Obras completas de Lope de Vega*, I, Joaquín de Entrambasaguas, ed. (Madrid: CSIC, 1965), 1-753, 85.

5. "Como quiera que siempre aya sido provechoso y loable escrivir sanas doctrinas que despierten las almas o las encaminen a la virtud, en este tiempo es assí necesario, que a mi juyzio todos los buenos ingenios en quien puso Dios partes y facultad para semejante negocio tienen obligación a occuparse en él, componiendo en nuestra lengua, para el uso común de todos, algunas cosas que . . . les quiten de las manos, succediendo en su lugar dellos, los libros dañosos y de vanidad." Fray Luis de León, *De los nombres de Cristo*, Cristóbal Cuevas, ed. (Madrid: Cátedra, 1984), 144.

6. In the Spanish literature prior to the epoch we are studying, we could speak quite extensively of this class of novel; it is sufficient, though, to mention *Milagros de nuestra Señora*, by Gonzalo de Berceo (s. XIII); *El conde Lucanor*, by Don Juan Manuel; *Libro de buen amor* , by Juan Ruiz (s. XIV); or, finally, *El Corbacho*, by the Arcipreste de Talavera (s. XV) in which each of the chapters proposes the excellencies of a particular virtue and propounds upon the consequencies of neglecting its practice.

7. Francisco Cascales, *Tablas Poeticas*, 38.

8. Cervantes, *Stories*, Lipson, 5.

9. Cervantes, "Prologue," *Stories*, Lipson, 4.

10. Cervantes, "Prologue," *Stories*, Lipson, 3.

11. Cervantes, "Prologue," *Stories*, Lipson, 4.

12. Joaquín Casalduero, extract from *Sentido y Forma de las "Novelas ejemplares,"* in Carlos Blanco Aguinaga y Joaquín Casalduero, "Las novelas ejemplares," *Historia y Crítica de la Literatura Española* , II, 636-39, 638.

13. Miguel de Cervantes Saavedra. *The Adventures of Don Quixote*, J.M. Cohenm, trans. (London, England: Penguin Books, 1950), Part I, Chapter III, 41-2.

14. Cervantes, *Exemplary Stories*, Lipson, 185.

15. Translator's note: *ne plus ultra*, "no further," is a well-known phrase in Spain. It is the slogan once painted upon Spanish ships indicating that Spain, geographically, stood at the edge of the known world. After Columbus' discovery of the New World, Queen Isabella ordered that the word *ne*—that negates the phrase—should be removed.

16. Translators note: A poem containing four or seven verses used in popular songs; a traditional Spanish dance. *Concise Spanish-English Dictionary* (France: Larousse, 1993)

17. Cervantes, *Exemplary Stories*, Lipson, 186.

18. Bartolomé Bennassar, *La España del Siglo de Oro* (Barcelona: Crítica, 1983), 325.

Juan José Sendín Vinagre

19. Bennassar, *La España*, 223.

20. There seems to be a contradiction in the text as Cervantes describes the boys as being "about fourteen or fifteen"; yet, immediately above he says "neither of them was more than seventeen." Cervantes, *Exemplary Stories*. C.A. Jones, trans. (London: Penguin Books, 1972), 85. All parenthetical references refer to this edition.

21. Translator's note: At the turn of the sixteenth century in Spain, convicted criminals were often sentenced to years of slave labor on these ships, a sentence so harsh that many did not live to complete their sentence.

22. Translator's note: Cervantes' original could as easily be translated to say that Rinconete was troubled with the way of life in which he found himself because it was "so uncertain, so *free* (*libre*) and dissolute" (my emphasis). The Lipson edition translates *libre* as "libertine."

Chapter 9

The Great-Souled Woman: Jane Austen as Public Moralist

Gregory R. Johnson

> *"And what are you reading Miss-?" "Oh, it is only a novel," replies the*
> *young lady "[O]nly some work in which the greatest powers of the mind are*
> *displayed, in which the most thorough knowledge of human nature,*
> *the happiest delineation of its varieties, the liveliest effusion of wit and*
> *humour are conveyed to the world in the best chosen language."*
> —*Jane Austen,* Northanger Abbey

There is a surprising amount of literature on Jane Austen as a moralist, including works by such distinguished philosophers and scholars as Alasdair MacIntyre, Allan Bloom, Gilbert Ryle, Eva T. H. Brann, Iris Murdoch, Judith Shklar, and Henry Veatch.[1] Austen's moral sensibilities have been characterized as Aristotelian, Hobbesian, Lockean, Humean, Smithian, Rousseauian, Kantian, and even as proto-Marxist. But Austen seems an unlikely candidate for a *public* moralist. All six of her novels are set entirely in the private realm and focus exclusively on the quests of their female protagonists for husbands. All six end with weddings—sometimes two or three. Her stories usually take place in the country, not the city, and when Austen's protagonists venture into the city, they are found in drawing rooms and ballrooms, not in the chambers of state. Soldiers are present in *Pride and Prejudice*, but nothing is said about who or why they are fighting. Austen, in short, seems as apolitical a novelist as one can name.

Nonetheless, Austen is an important teacher of public ethics, because for Austen, as for Aristotle, the highest virtue is magnanimity or "greatness of soul" and the most amiable and excusable vice is irony or dissimulation. Excellence in public life requires the cultivation of both greatness of soul and irony.

Greatness of soul is a necessary good and irony is a necessary evil for two reasons. First, they promote the well being of society by helping to negotiate the tensions between the practical necessity of creating and maintaining social hierarchies and the moral necessity of recognizing the dignity of all men, no matter what their place in the hierarchy. Second, they promote the well-being of the individual by helping to cultivate and maintain inner freedom and detachment in the midst of public offices.

What is Greatness of Soul?

For Aristotle, greatness of soul is a virtue.[2] Aristotle regards a virtue as a perfection of the soul that is conducive to worldly happiness. For Aristotle, well being (or happiness) comes from the actualization of our potentialities for excellence; well-being is the perfection of human nature. According to Aristotle, greatness of soul is a virtue having to do with self-knowledge and self-esteem. A great-souled individual is a person of superlative worth, and he knows it. Greatness of soul is a mean between two vices. On the one hand is small-mindedness or pusillanimity, the vice of underestimating one's worth, of chasing after and being too easily satisfied with things beneath oneself. On the other hand is pretentiousness, the vice of overestimating one's worth.

Greatness of soul is not, however, simply a sense of complacent self-satisfaction. The great-souled individual may take pride in his achievements, but he does not rest upon them, for he is also aware of his capacity for improvement, and he strives always to live up to his capacities. Indeed, his awareness of his own worth contributes to its further augmentation. In his pride, he sets and meets only the highest standards for himself.

What is the standard of worth by which the great-souled individual measures himself? The standard is virtue—moral worth. This is his highest good. Thus the central concern of a great-souled individual is his own moral perfection, the care of his soul. Thus the great-souled individual is concerned to become and remain as virtuous as possible.

Great-souled individuals are also concerned with secondary and external goods. The greatest of these is the recognition of their virtue by others, i.e., honor. But their interest in honor is not unqualified. First, they are not interested in the opinions of all men, but only the opinions of the highly virtuous, i.e., their peers. Second, they are not immensely gratified by the praise of their peers, for they feel that such praise is not a gift, but is merely their due. They are gracious in accepting it, though, for no one can offer them anything better. Third, great-souled individuals are not concerned to please other human beings, except for their friends, for an excessive desire to please others is a sign of servility and a lack of self-respect. Fourth, great-souled individuals are entirely uninterested in receiving recognition for small actions and minor traits, for they consider an occupation with small things to be beneath them. Fifth, they are not impressed with being honored for whatever other external goods they may possess, such as power, wealth, good fortune, or high birth, for the only thing they think worthy of honor is goodness. Nor, finally, are they interested in the praise of those whom they regard as inferiors in virtue or judgment, for the opinions of such people cannot be trusted to be accurate.

Because of this detachment from the opinions of others, the great-souled individual does not like to speak of himself. Nor does he like to praise or blame others. He is not easily pleased, and so is not given to praising others. And because he expects little of his fellow men, he is seldom disappointed, and thinks it unimportant to complain about them. Thus he is not a gossip, and he speaks no evil, not even about his enemies, unless provoked.

The great-souled individual cultivates a high-minded detachment from small things that is often mistaken for disdain. He prefers to ignore the trivial details of day-to-day life, but if he is forced to deal with them, he deals with them in a desultory and detached manner. He is neither overwhelmed by bad fortune nor overjoyed at good fortune, particularly when they affect small things. He does not dally with trifles or stoop to petty advantages; thus he opts out of most affairs. He regards haste as a sign of attachment to small things, and since he regards few things as great, he is slow and deliberate in action. But he moves decisively when great things are at stake. He does not risk his life over small things, although he is willing to lose it over great things, for he does not regard life as unconditionally good and thinks that it is not worth living under certain circumstances. He takes more pleasure in doing favors than in receiving them, for the former heightens his independence whereas the latter decreases it. He overlooks small slights and does not bear grudges or remind people of unpleasant things in the past, for this too is a sign of attachment. Although the great-souled individual cultivates detachment from merely useful things, he prizes fine and beautiful things that have no utilitarian value, such as art and music. Aristotle even remarks at how great-souled individuals are thought to be soft-spoken, and to have low voices, for raised, high-pitched voices are signs of regarding small things as great.

Many commentators have found Aristotle's portrait of magnanimity to be rather unattractive, primarily because greatness of soul is a kind of pride, and Christianity brands pride a sin. So it makes sense to ask: How, precisely, is greatness of soul a virtue? How does it contribute to well-being? First, since greatness of soul presupposes the other virtues, its presence is a sign that one is already well equipped to attain well-being; hence, Aristotle styles greatness of soul as a crown or ornament of the other virtues. But greatness of soul also involves a moral idealism that contributes to maintaining and developing one's virtues. This moral idealism requires the cultivation of the inner life and detachment from external things. Thus greatness of soul contributes to one's integrity and independence; thus the well-being of a great-souled individual depends more upon inner resources than external ones, a policy that makes one's well-being easier to gain and harder to lose. By liberating us from an excessive attachment to external and petty goods, greatness of soul also promotes tranquility of mind, an important component of happiness.

Greatness of Soul in Austen's Novels

Those who are familiar with Austen's novels will immediately recognize that in Austen's moral world, greatness of soul plays a central role; for Austen, magnanimity is the greatest virtue and pusillanimity the greatest vice. For brevity's sake, let us consider only her three most widely read novels: *Sense and Sensibility*, *Pride and Prejudice*, and *Emma*. Each of these novels contains two characters who display genuine greatness of soul. In *Sense and Sensibility* the character of Elinor Dashwood is a vivid portrait of greatness of soul, and Colonel Brandon is a less fully realized example. In *Pride and Prejudice*, the central characters of Elizabeth Bennett and Fitzwilliam Darcy are both great-souled individuals, Elizabeth being the more perfect example of the two. In *Emma*, both Emma and the appropriately named Mr. Knightley show greatness of soul, Mr. Knightley being the more perfect of the two. All of these characters are characterized by their high sense of self-worth. Like Aristotle, Austen has a most un-Christian view of pride. For Austen as for Aristotle, pride, when merited, is a virtue. Like Aristotle, when one fails to hit upon the virtue of pride, one can fall into two associated vices: pretentiousness and pusillanimity, vices richly displayed by John and Fanny Dashwood, Robert Ferrars, and Lucy Steele in *Sense and Sensibility*; by Mr. Collins, the Bingley sisters, and Lady Catharine de Burgh in *Pride and Prejudice*; and by Mr. and Mrs. Elton in *Emma*.

All of Austen's heroes and heroines are of high moral worth. Yet none of them are morally complacent. Indeed, they are given to self-examination and self-criticism, which makes possible their continued moral improvement. All of them are characterized by well-developed inner lives and by independence of mind. This orientation toward inner goods goes along with a detachment from outer goods. There is one realm of external goods from which they are not, however, detached, and this is precisely because this realm is so closely connected with the goods of the spirit: the realm of love, friendship, and conversation.

Austen's most well realized portrait of a great-souled individual is Elinor Dashwood. Elinor is characterized by remarkable moral earnestness and strength. She acts rightly, and she takes pride and solace in this fact. When she promises to keep confidence with Lucy Steele, only to discover that Lucy has been secretly engaged to Edward Ferrars, the man whom Elinor loved and who she was certain loved her in return, Elinor keeps her promise and keeps the secret. She does not connive to split up Edward and Lucy; she does not tell her mother and sisters; she simply endures. Now, many of Austen's readers have regarded Elinor as a masochist and a martinet, which are hardly exemplary qualities, and are far more sympathetic with her ardent sister Marianne. But Elinor's course of action is the only one consistent with virtue *and* happiness. She would think it beneath her, and it would lower her, to connive to break up Edward and Lucy or to break her promise. Besides, she knew her mother and sisters well enough to realize that their reactions would be so emotional that she would end up consoling *them*. So she endures, and she takes solace in the fact that she is doing the right thing. This moral self-approbation gives her tranquility of mind.

Some readers find Elinor inhumanly detached even in the midst of heart-break, but a comparison with Marianne shows that Elinor's detachment promotes her long-term well-being, whereas Marianne's more passionate nature nearly kills her. Both sisters have managed to fall in love with men who at the time did not, or could not, consider marrying them. When Elinor found out, she suffered, but her suffering only went so deep, for with her characteristic caution, she had not fully given her heart to Edward, for he had not explicitly indicated that he would reciprocate. With her inner strength and sources of satisfaction came a measure of detachment even from the man she loved. Finally, her sorrow was consoled by her knowledge of her own rectitude.

When Willoughby jilted Marianne, however, she was utterly devastated, grew careless of her person, fell sick, and nearly died. With her characteristic lack of caution, she gave her heart totally without requiring any concrete sign of reci-procity. Lacking Elinor's inward nature and sources of happiness, she invested all of her hopes for happiness in a relationship with a man, forming an attach-ment that was so deep that it nearly tore her heart out when it was removed. And afterwards, her suffering was not mitigated by a sense of her own rectitude, but exacerbated by self-reproach for her own folly.

There are other points of comparison between Elinor and Aristotle's great-souled individual: Elinor does not merely esteem herself, she is clearly con-cerned to make herself *worthy* of the esteem of others. But she values only the esteem of those with good judgment, and is utterly indifferent to the flattery of Lucy Steele. Although Elinor is far more attentive to conventional proprieties than Marianne, Elinor has greater critical distance from conventions and enjoys greater liberty of mind than her sister, who is sabotaged by Romantic common-places and silly prejudices about petty things such as flannel waistcoats. Elinor is also relatively detached from material goods. When she and her sister Marianne compare their conceptions of comfortable living, Marianne's minimum income is double what Elinor regards as comfortable. Elinor is reticent to speak of herself. She expects less from her fellow men than her sister and is therefore less liable to disappointment. She is not inclined to gossip or to speak ill of others. Because of her detachment, Elinor enjoys a greater equanimity and tranquility of mind than her sister. Elinor is also less inclined to haste in judgment and action. But the most strikingly Aristotelian characteristic of Elinor and Austen's other mag-nanimous characters is their use of irony.

What is Irony?

Aristotle does mention, quite unobtrusively, that the great-souled individual does have one vice. Or, perhaps it would be better to say that one of the virtues of the great-souled is a vice in lesser men. This vice is "irony." What Aristotle means by irony, however, is something different from literary irony. Literary irony is a figure of speech in which something contrary to what is said is understood. When words are used ironically, they mean something other than their settled, literal meanings. In Plato and Aristotle both, however, irony refers to a kind of "white lie."

Aristotle describes the great-souled individual as outspoken concerning his loves and hates, for he cares more for truth than for reputation and he is contemptuous of secrecy, falsity, and fear. Thus, "he will be truthful, except when he is ironic, and if ironic, it will be only toward the many."[3] The "many" here are specifically the many people who are his inferiors. Aristotle claims that great-souled individuals will fully display their sense of dignity only when dealing with people of high position and good fortune. When dealing with inferiors, they affect an unassuming manner. For, as Aristotle puts it, "it is difficult and impressive to be superior to the former but easy to be so to the latter; and whereas being impressive to the former is not the mark of a lowly man, being so to the humble is crude—like using force against the weak."[4] To avoid this crudity, the great-souled individual must lie; he must condescend; he must pretend to be less than he really is. This is irony in the Platonic and Aristotelian sense.

If Aristotle regards irony as a vice, then why does he find it forgivable? Aristotle regards virtues as perfections of the soul that are desirable in and of themselves, regardless of their worldly consequences. But he also regards them as traits that are conducive to worldly happiness, when and if fortune cooperates. Let us try, then, to understand the vice of irony in accordance with the same standards.

How does irony contribute to the perfection of the individual soul? Irony contributes to self-perfection, insofar as man is a political animal, and any human being who is better than his peers incites their jealousy and malice, which can prevent further self-perfection. The ironical man avoids this by dissembling his virtues in the presence of potentially jealous and malicious inferiors. Irony is also a sign of self-perfection: a sign of sensitivity, prudence, and self-control.

How does irony contribute to worldly success? All societies have to strike a balance between two competing forces: the existence of social hierarchies and the universal human desire for respect. Some hierarchies are assuredly arbitrary and unjust. Others, however, are both necessary and just. But both sorts impose moral burdens on those who live in them, for all hierarchies are inegalitarian. This brings them into conflict with the desire for respect, which chafes against all forms of subordination. Magnanimous irony and forbearance promote worldly success by lubricating the frictions between social classes. They conceal social inequities, allowing one both to preserve social hierarchies and respect the dignity of those on the lower rungs.

Irony in Austen's Novels

The classical conception of irony is important for understanding both the content and the form of Austen's novels. First, important elements of the plots of *Pride and Prejudice* and *Emma* turn on beautifully dramatized failures of irony. Second, virtually all critics agree that Austen is a deeply ironic writer. Allan

Bloom beautifully describes Austen's irony in his last book *Love and Friendship*, the title of which is itself a tribute to Austen:

> Real irony has a lot to do with the virtue missing in modern thought, moderation. It is the tone of superiority politely exposing inferiority without wounding it, leaving things in their place while nevertheless understanding them. It is a certain art of deception, the mode of radical thought that accepts conventional life while itself remaining free. Irony flourishes in the disproportion between the way things are and the way they should be while accepting the necessity of this disproportion. It is the classical style, because the ancients did not expect that reality could become rational. Stupidity they thought to be inexpungible. Moderation, rather than being the expression of a timid or easygoing soul, was for them the expression of one who has overcome hope and therefore indignation.[5]

In *Pride and Prejudice*, Elizabeth Bennett rejects Mr. Darcy's first proposal of marriage because of his lack of magnanimous irony.

> After a silence of several minutes, [Darcy] came towards [Elizabeth] in an agitated manner, and thus began:
> "In vain have I struggled. It will not do. My feelings will not be repressed. You must allow me to tell you how ardently I admire and love you."
> Elizabeth's astonishment was beyond expression. She stared, coloured, doubted, and was silent. This he considered sufficient encouragement; and the avowal of all that he felt, and had long felt for her, immediately followed. He spoke well; but there were feelings besides those of the heart to be detailed, and he was not more eloquent on the subject of tenderness than of pride. His sense of her inferiority—of its being a degradation—of the family obstacles which judgment had always opposed to inclination, were dwelt on with a warmth which seemed due to the consequence he was wounding, but was very unlikely to recommend his suit.
> In spite of her deeply-rooted dislike, she could not be insensible to the compliment of such a man's affection, and though her intentions did not vary for an instant, she was at first sorry for the pain he was to receive; till, roused to resentment by his subsequent language, she lost all compassion in anger. She tried, however, to compose herself to answer him with patience, when he should have done. He concluded with representing to her the strength of that attachment which, in spite of all his endeavours, he had found impossible to conquer, and with expressing his hope that it would now be rewarded by her acceptance of his hand. As he said this, she could easily see that he had no doubt of a favourable answer. He *spoke* of apprehension and anxiety, but his countenance expressed real security. Such a circumstance could only exasperate farther, and, when he ceased, the colour rose into her cheeks.[6]

She refused his utterly graceless and humiliating proposal. Darcy reveals rather than conceals his struggle not to propose to Elizabeth. He heightens rather than downplays the differences between their social classes. His words conceal—but his actions reveal—that he takes her acceptance for granted. And this astonishingly tactless display of condescension produces the result one would predict: resentment, then anger, then refusal. If virtues are perfections of character that are conducive to happiness, then Darcy's frankness is no virtue and magnanimous irony is no real vice.

A failure of magnanimous irony or forbearance is also a pivotal event in *Emma*. The scene is the pastoral fiasco of the Box Hill outing. Frank Churchill suggests a game. Each of the parties present must offer Emma, "either one thing very clever, be it prose or verse, original or repeated; or two things moderately clever; or three things very dull indeed; and she engages to laugh heartily at them all." Upon this, the amiable and good-hearted chatterbox Miss Bates exclaims, "'Oh! very well . . . then I need not be uneasy. Three things very dull indeed. That will just do for me, you know. I shall be sure to say three dull things as soon as ever I open my mouth, shan't I?' (looking around with the most good-humoured dependence on everybody's assent.) 'Do not you all think I shall?'" To this, Emma could not resist replying, "Ah! Ma'am, but there may be a difficulty. Pardon me, but you will be limited as to number—only three at once."[7] This comment, predictably, was deeply humiliating to Miss Bates, although it could be argued that she invited it with her buffoonish self-mockery.

After the gathering had broken up, Mr. Knightley took Emma aside and rebuked her for her failure of magnanimity:

> While waiting for the carriage, [Emma] found Mr. Knightley by her side. He looked around, as if to see that no one were near, and then said:
> "Emma, I must once more speak to you as I have been used to do; . . . I cannot see you acting wrong, without a remonstrance. How could you be so insolent in your wit to a woman of her character, age, and situation? Emma, I had not thought it possible."
> Emma recollected, blushed, was sorry, but tried to laugh it off.
> "Nay, how could I help saying what I did? Nobody could have helped it. It was not so very bad. I dare say she did not understand me."
> "I assure you she did. She felt your full meaning. She has talked of it since. I wish you could have heard how she talked of it—with what candour and generosity. I wish you could have heard her honouring your forbearance, in being able to pay her such attentions, as she was for ever receiving from yourself and your father, when her society must be so irksome."

At this point in their conversation, Emma acknowledges the truth of Mr. Knightley's tactful rebuke although she first tries to make excuse by reference to the weakness of Miss Bate's personality. Mr. Knightley concedes the accuracy of Emma's characterization, but argues Emma's own point to urge her again to magnanimity.

> "Oh! cried Emma, "I know there is not a better creature in the world; but you must allow, that what is good and what is ridiculous are most unfortunately blended in her."
> "They are blended," said he, "I acknowledge; and, were she prosperous, I could allow much for the occasional prevalence of the ridiculous over the good. Were she a woman of fortune, I would leave every harmless absurdity to take its chance; I would not quarrel with you for any liberties of manner. Were she your equal in situation—but Emma, consider how far this is from being the case. She is

poor; she has sunk from the comforts she was born to; and if she live to old age must probably sink more. Her situation should secure your compassion. It was badly done, indeed! You, whom she had known from an infant, whom she had seen grow up from a period when her notice was an honour—to have you now, in thoughtless spirits, and the pride of the moment, laugh at her, humble her—and before her niece too—and before others, many of whom (certainly some) would be entirely guided by your treatment of her. This is not pleasant to you Emma—and it is very far from being pleasant to me; but I must, I will—I will tell you truths while I can; satisfied with proving myself your friend by very faithful counsel and trusting that you will some time or other do me greater justice than you can do now."[8]

Emma and Miss Bates are unequal in many respects. Emma is rich, Miss Bates poor. Emma is young and nubile, Miss Bates a middle-aged spinster. Emma's prospects are bright, Miss Bates' dim. Emma is intelligent, Miss Bates a scatterbrain. These inequalities are exacerbated by the fact that their positions were recently reversed. When Emma was a child, the attentions of Miss Bates were an honor. Now that Emma is grown, it is her attentions to Miss Bates that are an honor. Only the first form of inequality is conventional, and it is by no means obviously arbitrary and unjust. The other inequities are entirely natural. But to emphasize either form of inequality can only offend Miss Bates's dignity. Hence the seriousness of Mr. Knightley's rebuke. Emma's failure of magnanimity is a sign of a lack of sensitivity, prudence, and self-control, the presence of which perfect the soul. It also has practical repercussions, for it renders her less socially attractive in her small community, which can only detract from her happiness. Only by practicing irony and forbearance can Emma retain both her liberty of mind and the advantages of society. Again, frankness turns out to be no real virtue and magnanimous irony and forbearance no real vice.

The Greatness of Jane Austen's Soul

Finally, we note the greatness of soul of Austen herself. Austen's novels alone should be ample evidence of her greatness of soul, for only such an individual could execute such vivid and sympathetic portraits of greatness of soul with such fine classical irony. But for those who protest that these are just fictions and that Austen's heroes and heroines need not reflect Austen's own character, there are telling examples of magnanimous irony in Austen's correspondence.

Consider, for example, the case of one Reverend J. S. Clarke, who suggested that Austen, "write a novel about an English clergyman, including a disquisition on the benefits of taking away tithes (of which he himself was ardently persuaded), and a description of the clergyman's having to bury his own mother because the High Priest of his parish failed to pay her remains the proper respect (which had been his very experience)."[9]

Reverend Clarke's recommendations are silly because they propose that Austen treat very small and uninteresting things with greater seriousness than is due. That he offers these recommendations is a sign of an (albeit benign) ego-centrism and pusillanimity. That Austen regarded the Reverend Clarke and his advice as such is apparent from her hilarious, posthumously published, "Plan of a Novel, According to Hints from Various Quarters," in which the heroine's father is described as follows:

> The Father to be induced, at his Daughter's earnest request, to relate to her the past events of his Life. This Narrative will reach through the greatest part of the 1st vol.—as besides all the circumstances of his attachment to her Mother & their Marriage, it will comprehend his going to sea as Chaplain [at which point Austen wrote in her margin, "Mr. Clarke"] to a distinguished Naval Character about the Court, his going afterwards to Court himself, which introduced him to a great variety of Characters & involved him in many interesting situations, concluding with his opinion of the Benefits to result from Tythes being done away, & his having buried his own Mother.[10]

To the risible Reverend Clarke himself, however, Austen showed a very different face, declining his suggestions with tactful gentleness and respect:

> The comic part of the character I might be equal to, but not the good, the enthusiastic, the literary. Such a man's conversation must at times be on subjects of science and philosophy, of which I know nothing; or at least occasionally abundant in quotations and allusions which a woman, who like me, knows only her mother tongue, and has read very little in that, would be totally without power of giving. A classical education or at any rate, a very extensive acquaintance with English literature, ancient and modern, appears to me to be quite indispensable for the person who would do justice to your clergyman. And I think I may boast myself to be, with all possible vanity, the most unlearned female who ever dared to be an authoress.[11]

Austen in fact read both French and Italian and was widely read in English literature. She did not have a classical education *per se*, but members of her family did, and her works quietly reflect a deep acquaintance with and a genuine understanding of the classics, particularly the moral philosophy of Aristotle.

So Austen is lying. But her willingness to condescend to the small vice of irony is a clear sign of greatness of soul. For her lie is noble not base in that it aims to protect both the liberty of her own judgment and the feelings of Reverend Clarke. In a far from perfect world, classical irony is often the only way of doing justice both to one's own dignity and the dignity of others.

Notes

1. See Alasdair MacIntyre, *After Virtue: A Study in Moral Theory* (Notre Dame: University of Notre Dame Press, 1981); Allan Bloom, *Love and Friendship* (New York: Simon and Schuster, 1993); Gilbert Ryle, "Jane Austen and the Moralists," in *Critical Essays on Jane Austen*, ed. B. C. Southam (London: Routledge and Kegan Paul, 1968); Eva T. H. Brann, "The Perfections of Jane Austen," in *The Past-Present: Selected Writings of Evan Brann* (Annapolis, Md.: St. John's College Press, 1997); Iris Murdoch, *Ex-*

istentialists and Mystics: Writings on Philosophy and Literature (New York: Allen Lane, 1998); Judith Shklar, *Ordinary Vices* (Cambridge: Harvard University Press, 1984); Henry B. Veatch, *Swimming Against the Current in Contemporary Philosophy: Occasional Papers and Essays* (Washington, D.C.: The Catholic University of America Press, 1990).

2. Aristotle's primary discussion of greatness of soul is *Nicomachean Ethics*, Book 4, chaps. 7-9.

3. Aristotle, *Nicomachean Ethics*, 1124b 30; cf. 1127b 22-35, tr. Hippocrates G. Apostle (Grinnell, Iowa: The Peripatetic Press, 1984).

4. Aristotle, *Nicomachean Ethics*, 1124b 20-25, tr. Apostle.

5. Bloom, *Love and Friendship*, 193.

6. *Pride and Prejudice*, ch. 34, in *The Complete Novels of Jane Austen*, vol. 1: *Sense and Sensibility, Pride and Prejudice, Mansfield Park* (New York: Modern Library, 1992), 408.

7. *Emma*, ch. 43, in *The Complete Novels of Jane Austen*, vol. 2: *Emma, Northanger Abbey, Persuasion* (New York: Modern Library, 1992), 269-70.

8. *Emma*, 273.

9. Quoted in Brann, *The Perfections of Jane Austen*, 34.

10. Jane Austen, "Plan of a Novel, According to Hints from Various Quarters," in *Sanditon and Other Stories*, ed. Peter Washington (New York: Everyman's Library, 1996), 473-4.

11. Quoted in Brann, *The Perfections of Jane Austen*, 34.

Chapter 10

True and False Liberalism: Stolypin and His Enemies in Aleksandr Solzhenitsyn's *August 1914*

Daniel J. Mahoney

> *The loud mouth, the big fist, the bomb,*
> *the prison bars are of no help to you,*
> *as they are to those at the two extremes.*
> *Following the middle line demands the utmost self-control,*
> *the most inflexible courage, the most patient calculation,*
> *the most precise knowledge.*
> —November 1916: The Red Wheel II

The Russian Revolution of 1917 had an undeniably dramatic impact on the destiny of the twentieth century. The first, ostensibly democratic revolution of February 1917 overthrew the *ancien regime* and closed off the possibility of a peaceful Russian evolution toward European-style constitutional monarchy. In the midst of war, it pushed Russian politics irrevocably to the Left, and created a power vacuum that was filled by the most militant and "totalitarian" of the revolutionary sects. With the October Revolution of 1917, the Bolsheviks, under the leadership of Lenin, withstood the opposition of almost every stratum of society, and began their monumental effort at establishing "utopia in power." In the process they undid all of the principal reforms introduced in the final period of the Tsarist regime (1860-1917). They eliminated the hard-won acquisition of the rule of law, destroyed the independence of civil society, abolished the constitutional order established in the aftermath of an earlier revolution, and ferociously attacked the legitimacy of the Churches, the aristocracy, the bourgeoisie and the independent peasantry. They even managed to do what the Tsars had never come close to doing: destroy the proud socialist and revolutionary parties of the non-communist Left. By taking advantage of the war, by introducing communism, and later with the full-scale collectivization of agriculture, the Leninist regime restored serfdom, but in a new ideological guise and accompanied by rivers of blood. Besides demolishing Russia's opportunity for a humane and liberal modernization consistent with her national traditions, the October Revolution opened this century's great ideological schism. It gave rise to the heated triangular conflict between liberal democracy and Left and Right totalitarianisms, the first phase of which ended with the defeat of Nazi Germany in 1945, the second only with the unexpected implosion of European communism between 1989 and 1991.

In the Marxist-Leninist vulgate, the collapse of the Russian old regime and the victory of communism were *inevitable*, preordained by the laws of historical dialectic. But the communists could never anticipate that their long revolutionary project would culminate seventy years later in a desperate effort to restore constitutional politics and a "normal" civil society, a "restoration" made all the more difficult by the pernicious legacy of Red October.[1] Today, only a few die-hard leftists believe that the Bolshevik Revolution was in any way preordained by the laws of history. In contrast, the majority of analysts in Russia and the West alike still welcome the February Revolution as an unqualified victory for democracy over absolutism. They forget that there could be no October Revolution without the February one and that it was the February Revolution that put an end to the prospects for stable constitutional development in Russia.

In his great cycle of historical novels, *The Red Wheel*, beginning with *August 1914*, Aleksandr Solzhenitsyn sets out to examine and "de-construct" claims made on behalf of the inevitability of the communist revolution. *The Red Wheel* is first and foremost an attempt to restore Russian national memory, but it is also an effort to explore, through the medium of literature, fundamental historical and philosophical questions that have implications beyond the Russian tragedy. Some Western observers have been perplexed by the historical character of *The Red Wheel* and have denied that it is a novel in any recognizable sense of the term.[2] This perplexity is the result of what Alexis Klimoff has called "the Western tendency to draw a sharp distinction between fiction and non-fiction" in contrast to the Russian tradition's emphasis on the simultaneously "cognitve, ethical and aesthetic goals" of great literature. In the Russian tradition, "literary achievement was not seen in the ability of a powerful imagination to create a vivid world *ex nihilo*, but rather in the writer's skill in selecting, shaping, and ordering the data of reality, in this sense re-creating it in aesthetically compelling ways."[3] Solzhenitsyn explicitly identifies with this ethical/realist understanding of the literary enterprise. In response to a particularly ferocious attack on *Lenin in Zurich* (whose chapters are culled from several volumes of *The Red Wheel*), Solzhenitsyn emphatically affirmed "that I am not simply a belletristic writer, but . . . in all my books I place myself in the service of historical truth."[4]

At present, only two of the five volumes of *The Red Wheel* have appeared in English, the augmented *August 1914* published in 1989 as well as *November 1916*, published early in 1999.[5] What is apparent on the basis of these two massive volumes alone, is that, in Solzhenitsyn's view, the decadence and decrepitude of the old regime in no way suggests that Russia was predestined to experience communist totalitarianism. Not that Solzhenitsyn has any illusions, whatsoever, about the solidity of the old order. *The Red Wheel* is a powerful indictment of the senile petrification of the old regime in its final period, marked by incompetent military leadership, a propensity to fatalism on the part of its leaders,[6] a mediocre Tsar, a meddling and superstitious Tsarina, and an uncomprehending bureaucracy that failed to see that Russia's only hope lay in far-reaching reforms. But Russia's problems in that period are in no way attributable to the blindness of the regime alone. Russian society, too, failed to appreciate sufficiently that its real interest lay not in indulgence toward violent revolutionaries but in a prudent reconciliation with those healthy forces in the regime committed to a free, prosperous and civilized Russia. Alas, the liberals "were as immoderate as only Russian liberals could be" (507)[7] and generally sided with revolution over reform. The genuinely progressive elements in Russia, represented in *August 1914* by Solzhenitsyn's fictional hero, Georgi Vorotynstev, supported the reform of the regime in a manner compatible with inherited traditions and constitutional government, but they were increasingly isolated and outmaneuvered by the extremists on the Left and Right. Yet Solzhenitsyn suggests that Russia knew one exceptional statesman, her greatest in perhaps two centuries, who set out "to steer Russia along this new and strange middle channel" (506) that was the road of her salvation. That statesman was Pyotr Stolypin, Prime Minister of Russia between 1906 and 1911. Stolypin combined repression of revolutionary terrorism with far-reaching reforms and tried to govern in conjunction with society's representatives in the elective Duma. After five years of tumultuous rule, he fell victim to an assassin's bullet in September of 1911. For Solzhenitsyn, the death of Stolypin meant the effective end of the prospects for constitutional government and social progress in Russia. Solzhenitsyn dramatically concludes that what the assassin's bullet had slain was nothing less than the dynasty itself. The assassin Dmitri Bogrov's bullets "were the opening shots of the fusillade at Yekaterinburg" (573) that brutally destroyed the historic monarchy once and for all in July of 1918.

The Stolypin Cycle

The fifteen chapters in what the author calls the "Stolypin cycle" (vi) in the augmented *August 1914* (Chapter 8, 60-73), are a veritable tractate on statesmanship. Solzhenitsyn tells the story of Stolypin's courageous efforts to save Russia and the dynasty within the context of the ongoing conflict between the Russian state and the Russian society. Respectable representatives of society, such as the progressive-minded Aunts Adalia and Agnessa in *August 1914,* mindlessly celebrated the moral heroism of the populist and socialist terrorists. The extreme Russian Right and the tsarist courtiers were equally resistant to political good sense and the requirements of social progress. They "did not want to know about reform and progress, about new ideas, above all about concessions, [and] believed in nothing but prayerful prostration before the Tsar, in petrified immobility, century after century" (617). Solzhenitsyn is as equally scornful of Russian reactionaries as Russian liberals, and contrary to legend, expresses no nostalgia whatsoever for tsarist immobility or absolutism.

The Red Wheel is written as a series of "knots," what Solzhenitsyn calls "narrative(s) in discrete periods of time." The original edition of *August 1914,* published in Russian in Paris in 1971 and in English in 1972, limited itself to the immediate events leading up to the very earliest stage (e.g., the Battle of Tannenburg) of the First World War.[8] But Solzhenitsyn soon concluded that it was impossible to address the question of the supposed inevitability of October 1917 without examining in detail the most sustained effort to reform the old regime. He concluded that it was necessary to closely examine Stolypin's five-year tenure as Prime Minister. He thus introduced a series of flashbacks to previous knots, including a dense historical chapter (#65) on Stolypin's life and statecraft, as well as riveting accounts of the assassin's plot, the attack on Stolypin at the Kiev Opera, Stolypin's death and the reaction of both the regime and society to it. The fifteen chapters of the Stolypin cycle, while undoubtedly interruptions in the orderly flow of the novel, are justified by the fact that Russia's prospects in the war, and more broadly, her hopes for peaceful, piecemeal and humane political development, were dealt a crushing blow by the assassination of Stolypin.

Chapter 65 of the augmented *August 1914* is entitled "Pyotr Arkadievich Stolypin." It is a long, somewhat dense, but fascinating biographical and historical account of Stolypin's life and statesmanship. The first several pages of the chapter are an integral part of the "novel" itself, eloquently discussing the central idea that gave "high purpose" (495) to Stolypin's statecraft, namely, the liberation of the peasant from the tyranny and penury of the repartitional commune. The final pages of the chapter provide a riveting account of Stolypin's premonition of his impending death and of the final, dramatic moments at the Kiev Opera on September 14, 1911, when Stolypin was shot in the presence of the Tsar. The eighty or so pages in between are in small print and are intended for "the most indefatigably curious readers" (496). These pages provide a detailed account of Stolypin's career from 1905 until 1911. Solzhenitsyn apologizes for "such a crude distortion of the novel form." It is justified, he writes, only because "Russia's whole history, her very memory" had been "distorted in the past, and her historians silenced" (496). But this apology should not mislead the reader. The historical character of the "small printed" section of Chapter 65 does not take away from the clarity or eloquence of Solzhenitsyn's account. His is a carefully limned portrait of a "great-souled man" worthy of Plutarch's *Lives*. In addition to its salutary character, the chapter is an essential element in Solzhenitsyn's dissection of the Marxist-Leninist dogma that the Revolution was somehow historically inevitable. Solzhenitsyn challenges the leftist dogma that communism, whatever its defects, was an advance over the "absolutism" that preceded it.

Solzhenitsyn admires Stolypin both for his manly character and his well-grounded but visionary ideas. He describes Stolypin as "firm" and "self-possessed," "a figure of epic presence" (526). He embodied authority in a natural and unforced way, and his unapologetic defense of his principles as well as of the regime's unequivocal right to defend itself against its armed opponents, impressed even his most inveterate opponents. Stolypin's impressive qualities startled an intelligentsia that habitually "revell(ed) in their intellectual superiority to an obtuse and decrepit government which had never, as far as anyone could remember, produced an orator, thinker or statesman" (502).

Stolypin was a constitutionalist and a convinced monarchist. But he was not scrupulous in his attachment to constitutional forms as were some otherwise like-minded leaders such as the zemstvo leader D. M. Shipov.[9] Stolypin did not believe that Russia could afford such moralism in the face of a genuine revolutionary challenge to the existence of the regime. In contrast to the mediocrity of Tsar Nikolai II he was "the pillar (stolp) of the Russian state" and "his qualities were, in truth, kingly" (548). Solzhenitsyn subtly suggests the superiority of natural aristocracy to conventional or hereditary monarchy. Stolypin tried to be faithful to the mediocre but decent monarch and he was appalled by advanced society's ridiculous caricature of him as "short-sighted, stupid, malicious, vengeful, callous" (544). In truth, Tsar Nikolai II "diverged no further from the mean of mediocrity than the average monarch" and his mediocrity was made up for, in some part, by his abundant "goodness of heart" (545). But the "hangers-on" at the royal court did not reciprocate Stolypin's magnanimity. They did not hesitate to attribute the most self-serving motives to Stolypin since they knew nothing of statesmanship or service to the common good. Stolypin had tried to build a far-reaching coalition in the Duma on the model of George III's alliance of "the King's Friends."[10] In Stolypin's view, this coalition would include a range of liberals and conservatives loyal to constitutional monarchy and committed to sensible reforms. The petty reactionaries in the court could see in such far-sighted prudence only personal self-aggrandizement.

Stolypin's Central Idea

The centerpiece of Stolypin's vision was his deep conviction that the Russian peasant could not be free and that Russia could not be a great and prosperous nation if the peasant did not own his own land.[11] If Stolypin (and his latter-day partisan Solzhenitsyn) share a "Slavophile" conviction that the land is sacred, if they share a "feeling for the land, for the upturned soil," they most certainly do not uphold the traditionalist view of the peasant commune, with its "compulsory egalitarianism," as the embodiment of that feeling and sense of responsibility. Stolypin was convinced, "sure as holy writ," that the Russian peasant "would never prosper while he was shackled by the commune." The peasant or repartitional commune, which survived the emancipation of the serfs by Tsar Aleksandr II in 1861, required the peasants to re-divide their lands in a way that made improvements "senseless." The compulsory repartition of the land "made it impossible for the peasant and his land to grow together, perpetuated holdings each consisting of widely separated, long, narrow strips of arable and meadow." Stolypin certainly admired the skill and communal solidarity of Russian peasants. But the Russian strip-farming system was "excruciatingly wasteful" (in contrast to the enclosed farms of peasant proprietors in Belorussia and Ukraine) and it stifled peasant initiative and independence. Stolypin was rightly convinced that neither the maintenance of the communal system nor the redistribution of the gentry's land to a "land-hungry" peasantry could begin to address the problems of the Russian countryside. All the redistribution in the world could not outpace the dramatic increases in the peasant population of

European Russia in recent decades (for quotations in this paragraph, see pp. 495-496).

Solzhenitsyn states that "Stolypin's idea was one of shining simplicity—yet too complicated to be grasped or accepted." It was opposed by traditionalists, by Slavophile romantics, by selfish gentry who feared a self-reliant peasantry, and by revolutionaries and leftists who associated the commune with "socialism." Yet Stolypin was determined to break the back of the repartitional commune and to give the peasant "permanent property" in the land. Only then could the peasant have "freedom and prosperity." Stolypin (and Solzhenitsyn) know all the romantic, "Slavophile" arguments for the commune. In this romantic rendering, the commune demands self-denial and "the harmonization of the will of the individual with that of the commune." Stolypin was certainly convinced that there is something higher than freedom and prosperity, namely spiritual greatness, and that it ultimately lies in the "eternal subordination" of the individual to the common good. But Stolypin (undoubtedly speaking for the author), knows that such spiritualism ultimately "makes action impossible." Human beings need to live with property and prosperity "as we live with all the temptations of life" (see p. 496 for this and preceding quotations). The failure to distinguish between a general recognition of the primacy of spiritual goods and the advocacy of a utopian "spiritualist" politics, is at the source of the systematic misunderstanding in the West of Solzhenitsyn's major public pronouncements, such as the Harvard Address of 1978. Solzhenitsyn's Stolypin appreciates that the real-life commune has little in common with the subordination of the individual to spiritual concerns. Much as Aristotle insisted that the abolition of private prosperity in the name of civic unity would paradoxically undermine virtue and sow discord among citizens,[12] so Stolypin believed that in practice the supposedly "communal" commune "created a good deal of discord amongst the peasants" (496).

In his view, there was "a deep-seated fault in the structure of peasant life" (500) that was feeding revolutionary unrest and turning the peasantry, the traditional base of Tsarism, against the regime. But neither the peasants nor society at large, with its relentless clamoring for land redistribution from the gentry and thoughtless romanticism about the commune, understood the nature of the Russian disease. Stolypin's mission was to convince all who would listen that the repartitional commune "was an unsurmountable barrier" to the establishment of an order of "independent and prosperous farmers" (500). One of Stolypin's provincial reports as Governor, laying out his modernizing vision, was read by the Tsar himself (Solzhenitsyn suggests wryly that this was something of a miracle since the Tsar was "not noted for his assiduity as a reader or thinker" [500]). The result was that Stolypin was brought to St. Petersburg to become Minister of the Interior in 1906 and, shortly thereafter, Prime Minister under Russia's first authentically constitutional government.

Stolypin believed that the paternalism of both the Left and Right obscured the real causes of peasant discontent: the peasant's "lack of land that was truly his, land that he felt to be his, was what undermined *his* respect for everyone else's property" (519). The true barrier against revolutionary socialism was a peasantry whose *natural* desire for property was satisfied. Stolypin rejected the argument of leading "liberals" that ordinary Russian peasants were incapable of handling the responsibility of proprietorship free from the guidance of the commune. These liberals feared that too many peasants would squander their resources on drinking and leave their families destitute. Stolypin told the Duma (i.e., the Russian parliament) that such thinking was needlessly paternalistic and ignored the inherent strength of the majority of the Russian population. Stolypin famously argued that Russia must wager on "the sensible and the strong, not the drunken and weak" (541). He did not place his hopes on "land-grabbing Kulaks" as revolutionary and communist propaganda would later insist, but rather on hard-working and energetic farmers who were willing to take risks for their families and country.

Stolypin's wager on the independent and self-reliant peasant bore immediate fruit in his resettlement policy that allowed peasants to settle on unoccupied lands east of the Ural mountains (549-551). Not only did resettlement relieve rural poverty and overcrowding in European Russia, but it allowed independent peasants to operate in complete independence from the residual tyranny of the peasant commune.

Stolypin wished "to follow a specifically *Russian* line" (534) of social development. He supported an ambitious program of social and political reforms and was committed to general principles of civil rights and constitutional government. But like Solzhenitsyn himself, Stolypin opposed slavish imitation of western European models of liberal democracy. He hoped that Russia could combine a commitment to self-government, especially that local self-government that educates citizens in the give and take of political life, with a recognition of the central role that Christianity has historically played in giving shape to Russian national consciousness. (Although Stolypin actively opposed what he saw as senseless and cruel disabilities against Russia's Jewish population [see pp. 521 and 566].) On this front, he met opposition from an obdurate Tsar who seemed to think that the maintenance of petty anti-semitic laws was an obligation of Christian monarchy (see p. 521).

Above all, Stolypin believed Russia needed time in order to successfully navigate her own path to modernity, one that would not foolishly squander her national inheritance. The radical liberals believed that uneducated, inexperienced people could become responsible, enfranchised citizens at one stroke and hence they supported—and manipulated—universal suffrage. In contrast, Stolypin believed that the peasants needed to be given a real stake in the social order, and then encouraged to responsibly defend and articulate their interests through institutions of local self-government (see pp. 518 and 532). Stolypin was a Russian nationalist but one who rejected the ideological chimera of pan-Slavism and the temptation of an imperialist foreign policy (546-547 and 567). In his view, Russia must limit herself in order to become strong, and one mark of Russian national greatness was the capacity for prudent self-restraint. His "policy became the rallying point for all those educated people—as yet alas, so few—in whom some unchilled remnant, or some hesitant beginning of Russian natural sentiment and Orthodox belief could be detected" (549). Stolypin supported a synthesis of tradition and modernity, of conservatism and liberalism, that offered Russia an opportunity to escape the futile "civil war" between regime and society that had hampered Russia's development since the Decembrist revolt of 1825. In Solzhenitsyn's view, "a second Peter ruled Russia . . . . as radical a reformer, but with ideas that distinguished him from Peter the Great" (548-549). The first Peter had destroyed the independence of the Church, continued the persecution of the Old Believers, pursued a policy of relentless imperial expansion, and modernized Russia through despotic means and with contempt for many of her best traditions. Stolypin, like Solzhenitsyn, is deeply ambivalent about many aspects of the Petrine inheritance. But the ambivalence of these Russian patriots is that of conservative liberals concerned with the strength and freedom of the Russian nation and not that of reactionaries nostalgic for a premodern or feudal Russia.

Fighting Revolution as a Statesman

It was during his brief tenure as Minister of the Interior that Stolypin would begin his determined campaign against revolutionary terrorism, a campaign that would continue during his first years as Prime Minister. Solzhenitsyn makes clear that Stolypin's "thoughts were those of a statesman" (501). Ultimately, one had to fight the revolution "as a statesman not as a head of the police" (520), as Solzhenitsyn eloquently suggests. But there could be no constitutional order in Russia if revolutionaries were free to murder governmental officials and civilians alike, to rob banks, to destroy the economic infrastructure of the country and to encourage peasants to destroy estates and to set the countryside on fire. On August 12, 1906, a little more than a month after replacing the uninspired Ivan Goremykin as Prime Minister, Stolypin himself was the target of an assassination attempt.[13] Terrorists, disguised as gendarmes, threw briefcases with explosives into his home on Aptekarsky Island in St. Petersburg, while he was receiving visitors. As a result, twenty-seven people, including ordinary petitioners, were killed and another thirty-two were injured. Stolypin's three-year-old son and one of his daughters were badly wounded. These attacks made Stolypin all the more determined to stamp out revolutionary terrorism as the *sine qua non* for the success of his reformist program. In the course of the misnamed "Stolypin terror," "field courts" were introduced for "especially serious . . . cases of looting, murder and attacks on the police, on the civil authorities and on peaceful citizens, so as to bring trial and sentence closer to the time and place of the crime" (514). As the historian Richard Pipes notes, governors and military officials in eighty-two of Russia's eighty-seven provinces were given the authority to turn civilians "whose guilt was so obvious as to require no investigation" over to military courts for the administration of summary justice.[14] The field courts had "to convene within twenty-four hours of the crime and read a verdict in forty-eight hours. There was no appeal from their sentences, which were to be carried out within twenty-four hours."[15] According to Pipes, about 4,682 people were sentenced to death for violent political crimes between August 19, 1906, when the policy was decreed under Article 87 of the constitution, and the end of 1909.[16]

Stolypin's "first task, a strange one to him, was to lead the police into battle—such a battle as Russia's revolutionaries had never encountered or expected" (501). Without order, there could be no rule of law nor prospects for social development. Stolypin believed that firmness at the beginning would save many lives and prevent a full-scale revolutionary upheaval in Russia. "He would use conciliatory methods where persuasion was possible" (512). But in a situation where so-called liberals such as the Kadets or Constitutional Democrats were positively "pant(ing) for revolution" (525), excusing terrorist attacks and fighting salutary reforms, the regime had a duty to maintain public order. At the same time, it needed to remain scrupulously committed to the path of constitutional government, laid out in the Tsar's Manifesto of October 30, 1905, and the constitution or "Fundamental Laws" of May 6, 1906. The constitution may have been hurriedly adopted, unwisely imitating English and French models of universal manhood suffrage and parliamentary procedure (504). But "there could be no back-tracking . . . A constitution had been granted. The country had to learn to live by it" (529). Many, even most, of the same liberal and leftist parliamentarians and publicists who condemned "Stolypin's terror" and fulminated against "Stolypin's neckties" (the noose) remained silent about and even applauded revolutionary terror. It was in these difficult circumstances, so unpropitious to constitutional political development, that Stolypin had to pursue his precarious "middle channel," surrounded by "swarms of enemies . . . on both wings" (506-507).

Solzhenitsyn reflects at some length on the following paradox: Stolypin often had to pursue his centrist, constitutional path through extra-constitutional or at least questionably constitutional means (557-558). Solzhenitsyn criticizes Stolypin for excessive use of Article 87, which granted the government the power to promulgate laws when the Duma was not in session, even if the use of such an extraordinary step was sometimes necessary. He attributes this propensity to Stolypin's impatience with the longstanding resistance of nearly all segments of Russian society to necessary reforms. He also sympathetically notes that all of Stolypin's reform efforts, from the dismissal of the ineffectual and Left-dominated First and Second Dumas to the introduction of far-reaching agrarian reforms, initially got off the ground as a result of the invocation of Article 87 (558).

In discussing Stolypin's use of Article 87, Solzhenitsyn raises the problem of political founding and the related question of the statesman's handling of extreme situations. The wise founder of a political order, even a constitutional one, must have a certain freedom, at least at the beginning, "to legislate without parliament" (558). This is especially true in the Russian case where the center confronted an unholy alliance of reactionary anti-constitutionalists and revolutionaries of various stripes. Solzhenitsyn observes that even long-established parliamentary systems have been confronted "with great trials" in the twentieth century sometimes calling for the resort to extra-constitutional means to preserve liberty. "Russia was overtaken by these trials earlier than any other country and at a time when it was less well prepared" (558). Solzhenitsyn is warning against a doctrinaire liberalism that ignores the essential preconditions of a free society and demands moral purity from those statesmen trying to preserve a civilized order from fundamental assault.

Stolypin's and Russia's dilemma raises a question of political philosophy that is incapable of any simple or universal resolution, namely the question of "the correct relation between parliamentary procedure and the individual will of the responsible statesman" (558). Solzhenitsyn's Stolypin eschews both a Machiavellian disregard for constitutional government and a liberal legalism or formalism that, under Russian circumstances of the time, would only aid the cause of those who preferred revolution to reform. Throughout *The Red Wheel*, Solzhenitsyn suggests that many so-called Russian liberals tactically appealed to a scrupulous understanding of the law in order to undermine the prospects for ordered liberty in Russia. The aversion of many liberals to the requirements of legitimate authority, and their concomitant indulgence toward revolutionaries of the left, are not distinctively Russian phenomena. This problem first arose in classic form in Russia in the final half of the nineteenth century but would become a commonplace dilemma of liberalism throughout the world in the twentieth.

Stolypin's Visionary Program

After his confrontation with the State Council and Duma over the western zemstvo bill in the spring of 1911,[17] Stolypin set out to confront the enemy from within, the intransigent bureaucracy that had been suspicious of his every move. "The healing of the legs, the lower limbs, the peasantry, was proceeding splendidly; the time had now come to heal the bureaucracy" (565). In May of 1911, he dictated a visionary program of reform to his secretary, a program confiscated by the government after his death. His program was arranged systematically and laid out changes for each of the branches of the state administration. A new ministry would give support to the zemstvos (local self-governing councils) in carrying out administrative, welfare and educational tasks. A new Ministry of Labor would "draft laws to improve (the position) of Russian workers, and to make the rootless proletarian a partner in the constructive work of the state and the zemstvos" (565). Stolypin outlined plans for greater financial support for the education of clergy and expressed support for the restoration of the Patriarchate—and hence the establishment of a genuinely independent Orthodox Church (565-566). Special emphasis was placed on education, including the goal of universal free primary education by the year 1922 and a huge expansion in the number of state-supported intermediate educational institutions and high schools. At the summit of the educational system, Stolypin wished to establish a national academy to train civil servants. "A dazzling array of specialists and experts would take their place in the Russian governmental machine" (566). The Tsar would then be able to draw on competent professionals in government and would not be dependent on the advice of courtiers for the choice of ministers. Stolypin insisted that the precondition of his reform program was peace abroad and a rejection of grandiose projects of Russian territorial expansion (567). Russian national greatness depended upon a reform of the state apparatus and active efforts to improve the lives of ordinary people. Maintenance of a European peace and the cultivation of good relations with the United States were also important pillars of his program (567).

Stolypin's reform agenda aimed at nothing less than the comprehensive recon-struction of Russia by 1927-32. Of course, Solzhenitsyn's readers know that a very different plan was imposed on "Soviet" society during those years, a plan that relied upon class struggle, collectivization, forced industrialization—and the use of terror. Solzhenitsyn leaves no doubt which was the genuinely humane and "progressive" plan for Russia's reconstruction. Solzhenitsyn sadly notes that Stolypin's project "vanished, was never published, discussed, exhibited, or indeed recovered—all that survived was the testimony of the man who helped Stolypin to draft it" (568). Tragically, the communists' first Five-Year plan "coincided with what would have been the last five-year period of Stolypin's project" (568).

Dying Alone

The final pages of Chapter 65 (no longer in "small print") follow immediately upon the description of Stolypin's remarkable reform program. The reader sees a Stolypin apprehensive about Russia's future, and "full of foreboding of his own death" (568).

Officials in the Tsarist inner circle and bureaucracy already acted as if Stolypin were a former Prime Minister. Stolypin was required to attend a major ceremony in Kiev with the Tsar commemorating the fiftieth anniversary of Aleksandr II's emancipation of the serfs; but, he was left out of the official Court program on the occasion and was not even given a bodyguard. The self-serving Interior Minister General Kurlov had picked up the appropriate signs from the Court and was con-vinced "that Stolypin was no longer worthy of respect nor even of attention" (569-570). Even though the duplicitous Bogrov had sent a letter to the police on Septem-ber 8 warning them of an impending attempt on Stolypin's life, Stolypin was informed belatedly on September 14 and without any details about the threat to his life. No additional security precautions were taken and Stolypin himself did not take the threat seriously since no bomb (the chosen weapon of Russian terrorists) had been discovered. To make matters worse, the Okhrana informer and terrorist Bogrov was admitted to the Kiev Opera on the evening of September 14, 1911, *with the knowledge of Russian police officials*. During the second intermission of the program, Bogrov shot Stolypin within eyeshot of the Tsar.

For several days, Stolypin precariously hung on to life and for a short while even seemed to be improving. He learned from his doctor that he had been shot by Bogrov, the terrorist and sometime secret police informer. He spent several days anxiously waiting for the Tsar to appear. But the Tsar remained mindlessly com-mitted to his itinerary despite the extraordinary assassination attempt against his Prime Minister. Stolypin desperately wanted to speak to the Emperor, to convey to him for one last time the absolute necessity to proceed with reforms for the sake of Russia and the dynasty (609). Solzhenitsyn's Stolypin is overwhelmed by a sense of the tragedy of having to depart "at forty-nine, and still at the height of his power" (610). He knew that he was "leaving behind a Russia still rent by the radical hostil-ity of civil society towards the imperial power" (610). After taking a turn for the worse, Stolypin died on September 18, fearful for his country and mindful of the

Tsar's "weakness," his terrible inability "to face unpleasant realities" (615). Stoly-pin accepted his death with "rare equanimity and self-possession" (616). Solzhenit-syn concludes Chapter 69, which culminates in Stolypin's death, with explicitly biblical language to describe the great statesman: "He Brought Light To The World And The World Rejected Him." Stolypin offered Russia *political* salvation, a middle channel between absolutism and revolution, a path that aimed to respect the mutual requirements of liberty, social progress and national greatness. He respected Russia's Christian traditions and he brought a sense of religious obligation to his tasks as statesman. As a statesman and a Christian, he respected the autonomy of politics without forgetting its moral underpinnings.

Stolypin was despised by "progressive" society, which feared that he might suc-ceed in defeating the revolution with statesmanship. He was equally hated by the reactionaries and courtiers who could not forgive his support for constitutionalism, his refusal to jettison the October Manifesto or the difficult task of working with the Duma. The Tsar, in a supreme act of indifference and ingratitude, managed to miss Stolypin's funeral. "Everybody could see that the Autocrat of All the Russias had shown no pity for the wounded man" (617). Only a few foreign newspapers cap-tured the nature of Stolypin's greatness and the true extent of Russia's loss. *The Times of London* rightly observed that he "had adopted the political life of Russia to representative institutions more quickly and in a more orderly fashion than it had ever been done in any country" (618). A Viennese paper noted that Russia's terror-ist socialists "called themselves freedom fighters in an attempt to conceal their revolting barbarism but succeeded only in hindering the work of peaceful develop-ment" (619). Only fifty parliamentarians attended Stolypin's funeral (619-620). The same Left-Right consensus that came together in defense of the regressive peasant commune, united once again in one final expression of contempt for Stolypin's heroic efforts to save the honor of Russia. Solzhenitsyn ends Chapter 70 with a final, fitting tribute to Stolypin's courage. He writes that Stolypin's enemies "had never succeeded in frightening him. Only in killing him" (620).

Conclusion

The "Stolypin cycle" in *August 1914* is a defense of moderation and public-spirited statesmanship in a context in which both regime and society were driving "Russia toward the abyss".[18] Russia needed an intelligent and courageous politics of the center that had the foresight to mold together order and liberty, tradition and modernity, social innovation with enduring national and religious principles. The intellectuals, even the so-called liberals such as the Kadets, were in fact radicals who opposed constructive reforms if they would in any way strengthen the existing regime and social order.

These false liberals could see no enemies on the Left and failed to appreciate that liberalism must defend itself against the impatience of "progressives" as well as the inertia of reactionaries. The partisans of autocracy rejected the sensible conservative insight, best articulated by Aristotle and Burke, that balanced reform is the best means of conserving a political order.[19] Russia's "civil war" was the first of several in the twentieth century in which an ossified old regime confronted the forces of hyper- or radical modernity with a weak center marginalized on the edge of the battle.[20] In a memorable passage in *November 1916,* Solzhenitsyn pays tribute to the difficulty of pursuing "a middle line" of social development, particularly in an age of ideological politics. "The loud mouth, the big fist, the bomb, the prison bars are of no help to you, as they are to those at the two extremes. Following the middle line demands the utmost self-control, the most inflexible courage, the most patient calculation, the most precise knowledge."[21] This passage beautifully captures the character of Stolypin's achievement. His greatness is in no way negated by the fact that his prudent statesmanship was finally insufficient to prevent the "Red Wheel" from churning relentlessly forward.

Notes

1. On the "ideological" character of the Soviet regime as the key to the entire communist misadventure, see Martin Malia, *The Soviet Tragedy: A History of Socialism in Russia, 1917-1991* (New York: Free Press, 1994). On communism as a fundamental obstacle to genuine modernization, see Malia, *Russia under Western Eyes: From the Bronze Horseman to the Lenin Mausoleum* (Cambridge, Mass.: Harvard University Press, 1998), especially Parts 4 and 5.

2. See for example, D. M. Thomas, *Alexander Solzhenitsyn: A Century in His Life* (New York: St. Martin's Press, 1998), 479.

3. Alexis Klimoff, "The Sober Eye: Ivan Denisovich and the Peasant Perspective" in Alexis Klimoff, ed., *One Day in the Life of Ivan Denisovich: A Critical Companion* (Evanston, Ill.: Northwestern University Press, 1997), 6-7.

4. Aleksandr Solzhenitsyn, "An Exchange with Boris Souvarine on *Lenin in Zurich*" in John B. Dunlop, Richard S. Haugh, and Michael Nicholson, eds., *Solzhenitsyn in Exile: Critical Essays and Documentary Materials* (Stanford, Calif.: Hoover Institution Press, 1985), 338.

5. See Aleksandr Solzhenitsyn, *The Red Wheel I: August 1914*, translated by Harry Willetts (New York: Farrar, Strauss and Giroux, 1989), with paperback versions available from The Noonday Press and Penguin, and *November 1916: The Red Wheel II*, translated by H. T. Willetts (New York: Farrar, Straus and Giroux, 1999). Subsequent volumes, already available in Russian, include two volumes of *March 1917* as well as *April 1917*, which concludes with a long excursus covering events through the year 1922.

6. For excellent accounts of Solzhenitsyn's critique in the augmented *August 1914* of both Tolstoyan and Marxist historicism and pietistic fatalism, see Vladislav Krasnov, "Wrestling with Lev Tolstoi: War, Peace and Revolution in Aleksandr Solzhenitsyn's New *Avgust Chetyrnadtsatogo*," *Slavic Review* (Vol. 45, Number 4, Winter 1986), 707-719 and Alexis Klimoff, "Inevitability vs. Will: A Theme and its Variations in Solzhenitsyn's *August 1914*" in *Transactions of the Association of Russian-American Scholars in the U.S.A.* (Vol. 29, 1998), 305-312.

7. All internal citations are to Aleksandr Solzhenitsyn, *The Red Wheel 1: August 1914*, H. T. Willetts, trans. (New York: Penguin Paperback, 1990).

8. For the original version of the book, see Solzhenitsyn, *August 1914*, translated by Michael Glenny (New York: Farrar, Strauss and Giroux, 1972).

9. For a sympathetic account of Shipov's strengths and limits as a leader, and an implicit critique of his moralistic approach to politics see *November 1916*, 60-80, esp. 65-66.

10. On this point see Richard Pipes, *The Russian Revolution* (New York: Knopf, 1990),

169.

11. To be sure, Stolypin had "three favorite lines of policy" (555) that defined his "liberal conservatism" (510) as Solzhenitsyn calls it; although, a comprehensive discussion of all three of these elements is beyond the scope of this chapter. He was committed to "advancement of the peasant" through his liberation from the traditional commune, he supported the zemstvo or local self-government as the best means to promote civic consciousness among the people, and he encouraged patriotism or "Russian national awareness," though he resisted imperialism or pan-Slavism. These policies remain pillars of Solzhenitsyn's own practical political agenda as outlined in *Rebuilding Russia*, an agenda that might reasonably be called neo-Stolypinite in character and inspiration. See Solzhenitsyn, *Rebuilding Russia: Reflections and Tentative Proposals* (New York: Farrar, Strauss and Giroux, 1991).

12. *Politics*, Book 2, Chapter 5.

13. This was the second attempt on Stolypin's life. The first occurred in the Fall of 1905, when the Adjutant-General in Saratov was blown up by a bomb in Stolypin's home.

14. Pipes, *Russian Revolution*, 170.

15. Pipes, *Russian Revolution*, 170.

16. Pipes, *Russian Revolution*, 170.

17. Stolypin wished to change the old zemstvo law in order to give greater representation in the western provinces of the Russian empire to Russian peasants over the Polish gentry who were the chief beneficiaries of the differential franchise. He was chiefly motivated by a patriotic desire to maintain the Russian character of these provinces. In Solzhenitsyn's view, Stolypin underestimated the commitment of the regime to the principle of aristocracy (it not surprisingly preferred the conservative rule of Polish aristocrats to the potentially disruptive dominance of the Russian peasants open to manipulation by intellectuals). He also showed a "stubborn" disregard for the importance of constitutional forms by insisting that the Duma and State Council be suspended for three days so that the Western Zemstvo Act could be promulgated under Article 87 (p. 557). Solzhenitsyn is uncharacteristically harsh in his judgment: "The occasion did not warrant his [Stolypin's] resignation, nor the wrecking of the Council, nor the application of Article 87" (p. 557).

18. *November 1916*, 57.

19. See Book V of Aristotle's *Politics* and Edmund Burke, *Reflections on the Revolution in France* (Oxford: Oxford University Press / World Classics, 1993), especially pp. 21-23. Burke writes: "A state without the means of some change is without the means of its conservation. Without such means it might even risque the loss of that part of the constitution which it wished the most religiously to preserve."

20. The Spanish Civil War of 1936-39 is perhaps the classic example of a civil conflict where the party of the constitutionalist center was almost completely marginalized by the forces of the authoritarian (Carlist and Falangist) Right and the proto-totalitarian (Stalinist) Left.

21. *November 1916*, 59.

Chapter 11

The Alchemy of Power and Idealism: Dostoevsky's "Grand Inquisitor"

J. Patrick Dobel

> *"There are three powers, three powers alone,*
> *able to conquer and to hold captive forever the consciences*
> *of these impotent rebels for their happiness—*
> *these forces are miracle, mystery, and authority."*
> —The Brothers Karamazov

Idealism inspires public service. The moral energy and direction of idealism fuels the motivation and commitment of individuals seeking to make the world a better place. Ideals evoke visions of a world in which justice and happiness prevail over oppression and misery. Dedicated men and women often accept less money and endure the travail of public life fired by the reserves of moral vitality and outrage that ideals generate.

Ideals, though, can also haunt us. The moral distance between the ideal and the real creates cognitive dissonance and pain and this dissonance makes living with the goals inspired by ideals a gnawing source of distress and temptation for those who hold them. Because so many people enter public service inspired by ideals and the desire to achieve good, managers and leaders must view idealism as a great moral resource while recognizing it as a unique challenge for leadership.[1] Managing ideals, then, is a central task for public leaders.

At their best, ideals provide the vision and energy to sustain grueling public service. They motivate, guide and direct action while providing a framework from which to criticize society. Yet their strength, beauty, and urgency compel action and often plague individuals with a sense of moral incompleteness or failure; this experience often pervades the life of committed people and erodes their idealism and passion. Their disappointment induces cynicism, burnout, or withdrawal and ideals may even transmogrify into a sordid quest for power gilded by hollow words or become warrants to rule and dominate. Fyodor Dostoevsky's, "The Legend of the Grand Inquisitor," the most famous chapter of his last novel *The Brothers Karamazov*, provides a forceful study of the dilemmas

of acting upon ideals that illuminates the paradoxes they bring to the exercise of
power in public service.

The Story

Dostoevsky finished *The Brothers Karamazov* in 1880, a month before he
died.[2] He meant the novel to be his masterpiece, and many consider it one of the
great works of world fiction. The story chronicles the tale of a Russian family
and the murder of its overbearing and corrupt patriarch Fyodor Pavlovich
Karamazov by one of his four sons. Dmitri, the eldest, serves in the army as a
lieutenant and embodies his father's sensual love of life and earth. He flirts with
personal and physical corruption and loves the same woman his father desires.
Ivan, the second son, has studied abroad and is a brilliant intellectual committed
to the primacy of reason and will. The new socialist ideals inspire him, and he is
appalled by his father's vain, greedy life. Ivan struggles to make sense of the
suffering of the world and rejects both God and the state. Alyosha, the third son
and Dostoevsky's nominal protagonist, lives as a novice monk seeking God. The
famous elder and mystic Father Zosima mentors him. The bastard son Smerdyakov lives at the house as a lackey and sometime cook.

The novel throbs with great obsessions—the nature of good and evil, the
possibility of redemption, the laceration of the soul between spirit and flesh, the
battle of faith and reason. Each fully developed character represents a possibility
within these conflicts of the human soul. Dostoevsky's great literary and philosophical strength lay with his immanent critique in which he explores ideas with
powerful characters.[3] Within the drama of this family, the tensions of Russia,
life, politics, and religion emerge as each character reveals an existential stance
toward life.

Relatively early in the novel, Alyosha and Ivan accidentally meet at a bar.
Alyosha is entering the world for a time to deepen and test his faith. Ivan is preparing to leave the troubled family with its gritty melange of desire and power
that both repel and fascinate him. The meeting occurs in a section of the book
entitled "Pro and Contra" where Dostoevsky lays out, in the most powerful
terms he can muster, the battleground between faith and reason, belief and un-
belief, and spirit and flesh. At this fateful meeting, Ivan recounts to Alyosha the
reasons for his own rejection of the family, Russia, and the church.

Ivan's passion and rebellion arise from his hatred of the suffering woven into
the fabric of human life. In the critical chapter prior to "The Grand Inquisitor"
entitled "Rebellion," Ivan narrates excruciating stories of suffering children,
stories drawn upon Dostoevesky's own recollection of true events in which
family, friends, soldiers, fathers, and mothers all torture children. The children
die innocently in neglected pain, vainly waiting for God's help. Ivan reaches the
conclusion reached by many caring humans over history,

> "I must have justice, or I will destroy myself. And not justice in some remote in-
> finite time and space, but here on earth and that I could see myself. . . . I've only
> taken the children, because in their case what I mean is so unanswerably clear.
> Listen! If all must suffer to pay for the eternal harmony, what have children to do

with it, tell me please? It's beyond all comprehension why they should suffer, and why they should pay for the harmony. . . . Too high a price is asked for harmony; it's beyond our means to pay so much to on it. And so I hasten to give back my entrance ticket, and if I am an honest man I am bound to give it back as soon as possible. And that I am doing. It's not God that I don't accept, Aloysha, only I most respectfully return Him the ticket." (14-16)

In his rejection of God and the moral balance sustained by an afterlife, Ivan rejects all metaphysically justified limits to human action. For him, "everything is lawful." Using this idea as a point of departure, he articulates the moral and philosophical foundations of reason and will that justify revolution and the creation of "heaven on earth."

Dostoevsky sought to defend faith and redemption against the seduction of western enlightenment and the lure of moral nihilism and power; yet, he suffered the same problem Milton did in *Paradise Lost* where Satan's power and defiance dominated the story at the expense of a pallid vision of God and angels. His character Ivan Karamazov, full of wounded idealism, intellectual brilliance, and a passionate hatred of injustice and suffering, dominates the intellectual heart of the book. In the end, Ivan's assertion that in the world without God "everything is lawful" becomes the warrant for Smerdyakov to murder the father and let Dmitri be falsely accused. Ivan is appalled that Smerdyakov took him at his word and had never truly understood the implications of his own position. Propelled by love for his brother, whom he despises, he desperately attempts to save Dmitri but collapses with brain fever on the witness stand. At the end of the novel Ivan is hospitalized, Dmitri goes to jail for a murder he did not commit, Smerdyakov commits suicide, and Alyosha contemplates his future quest for God.

Before this unfolds, when Alyosha brings up Christ as the one who can atone for suffering, Ivan, in response, recounts a poem—"a ridiculous thing"—to Alyosha (17). Ivan calls his poem "The Legend of the Grand Inquisitor." During the height of the Spanish Inquisition in Seville where the air chokes with the smoke of burned heretics, Jesus returns to earth. Fifteen hundred years have passed since the crucifixion and resurrection, and humanity waits upon God with the "same faith and the same love." Humans may not see "signs from heaven" but they still wait with faith (19-20). Jesus visits "his children only for a moment and there where the flames were crackling round the heretics." "He came softly, unobserved, and yet strangely to say, everyone recognized him." He moves silently and "the sun of love burns in His heart, light and power shine from His eyes, and their radiance, shed on the people, stirs their hearts and responsive love." His touch causes the scales to fall from the eyes of the blind. A funeral procession stops before him as he rests on the steps of the Seville cathedral. The mother begs him to restore her daughter whose corpse lies hidden by flowers. The coffin is laid before him and in his only spoken words, Jesus whispers "Maiden, arise" (20-21).

At this moment, a cardinal, the Grand Inquisitor, walks by. "He is an old man, almost ninety, tall and erect, with a withered face and sunken eyes, in which there is still a gleam of light." Unlike many Roman Catholic ecclesiastics who, by means of their united political and spiritual power live like proud princes, the Inquisitor, wears "his coarse, old monk's cassock." The austere ideals of love and commitment remain in his heart uncorrupted by wealth and privilege. Yet at a raised finger, his guards seize Jesus and "such is his power, so completely are the people cowed into submission . . . [that] the crowd immediately makes way for the guards." The crowd kneels before him and "he blesses them in silence and passes on" (22).

In the silence of the deepest night "fragrant with laurel and lemon," the Inquisitor enters the dungeon to meet Christ. "Is it thou? Thou?" he asks. Receiving no answer, he adds, "don't answer; be silent. What canst Thou say indeed? I know too well what Thou wouldst say. And Thou hast no right to add anything to what Thou hadst said of old. Why, then, art Thou come to hinder us?" The Inquisitor informs Jesus that "tomorrow I shall condemn Thee and burn Thee at the stake as the worst of heretics. And the very people who have today kissed Thy feet, tomorrow at the faintest sign from me will rush to leap upon the embers of the fire" (23).

The rest of the poem is the Inquisitor's soliloquy before a silent Jesus. The Inquisitor justifies why he and his kind have "vanquished freedom and have done so to make men happy" (24). He did this to correct "thy work and founded it upon *miracle, mystery*, and *authority*," which three concepts have become the foundation and rationale of the Inquisitor's tyranny (30). In the end, the Inquisitor, and the elite of the state-church alliance work with the "wise and dread spirit, the spirit of self-destruction and nonexistence" whose temptations in the desert Christ rejected (25, 34).

"The Grand Inquisitor" can be read at many levels—an allegory of faith and betrayal, an attack upon the pretensions of reason, or an assault upon the moral nihilism of revolutionaries. Each level touches an aspect of the story, but this chapter focuses on how the story delves into the twists and turns of human idealism. In this perspective, Dostoevsky identifies the moral and psychological undertow that affects everyone holding position and power.

The Ordeal of Ideals

Ideals possess a unique role in moral life. They do not dictate deductively clear principles or action based upon reason, nor must they possess logical rigor.[4] Unlike specific moral and intellectual virtues, they do not prescribe those particular emotional and moral habits that guide our everyday decisions and behavior.[5] Ideals do, however, embody moral imperatives: they place strong claims upon the way we live our lives. Ideals enable us to weld together everyday activity with transcendent moral beauty; they provide a moral and social vision that shows how we might act and structure our life in order to achieve a morally perfect world. This vision offers an inspiration for public service beyond a simple sense of duty.

The moral role of ideals enfolds noble aspirations into a garment of motivation and action. This function of philosophical ideals resembles what modern management theory calls "a vision." Organizational or political visions provide a strong common direction that elicits loyalty and commitment from individuals, thereby providing meaning and coherence to mundane actions. Peter Senge explains how individuals can have different attitudes toward visions and ideals. Many might go along with an ideal or vision as an act of "compliance"—"going through the motions" with differing degrees of sincerity. Others will "enroll" and adhere to a vision by acting upon its norms and requirements; finally, some will "commit" to the ideal or vision and make it a fundamental part of their personal and moral orientation and a source of their initiative.[6] Ideals possess great importance not only for individuals, but they can also anchor the identity and community of an organization or polity. Psychologically and morally, ideals entwine themselves with the deepest aspects of our selfhood—of the way we perceive ourselves—supporting essential but idealized self-images. This self-definition provides us with substantial moral power and urgency, but the inevitable failure to live up to such ideals means a failure of integrity.

Viewed from the Platonic perspective, the archetype of ideals and idealism remains Plato's theory of the forms. He argued that ultimate reality could not be described simply by looking at the natural world. Its swirl of change and the ebb and flow of desires that rack humans cannot capture the deeper truth of the moral or physical world. He postulated eternally existing forms within which all individuals participate. Leaving aside his metaphysical claims about the eternal nature of the forms, Plato argued that for humans, the existence of ideal forms provokes an infinite sense of longing and incompleteness. The beauty and stability of the ideal forms tantalize us while bringing fulfillment and clarity to public life in a way that no material aspirations can do.[7] Plato thus identifies an important element of embracing ideals—they always find reality wanting.

The distance between the gleaming ideal of justice and the moral squalor of reality stirs a person to act because idealists know the world can be a better place. The rich, powerful, and unjust do not easily surrender their riches and power; the oppressed, marginalized or vulnerable often do not have the strength, resources or time to better their position. These never ending contradictions reduce some to despair but others, strengthened by the idealistic, may pursue the public service, working within public institutions.

Two personal challenges lie implicit in holding ideals. First, an ideal is unrelenting in its demands for perfection and obligation. Few can live the life called for by rigorous adherence to ideals. It demands consuming discipline and commitment to live a model life and transform the world. Persons must subordinate personal desires and interests to live up to the austere demands of the ideal life; this is a focus and intensity of life, however, that few can maintain.

Second, reality will never match the ideal. As with Plato's forms, all life, institutions, and accomplishments only approximate the grandeur and moral beauty of ideals.[8] Worse, humans, even at their best, cannot sustain the behavioral and moral requirements of an ideal world. Their obstinate mortality will thwart the perfect. Holding ideals means risking condemnation to a world of endless disappointment that leads us either to grudging compliance or a state of "burn out."

The Inquisitor accuses Christ of creating just such a dilemma for his disciples. By offering humans "the promise of freedom" and requiring of them universal love, Christ bestowed "fire from heaven" (25, 26). The people at large rush to embrace freedom, but the restless dissatisfaction and rebellion in their souls lead them to unleash chaos and misery in their world. The charge to "love one another" is a hopeless aspiration. Ivan and the Inquisitor stare with a bleak eye upon the human penchant for hatred, envy, and anger. Ivan asserts: "To my way of thinking, Christ-like love for men is a miracle impossible on earth. He was God. But we are not Gods" (7).

The Inquisitor accepts the command to love all humans and interprets it as the charge to end unhappiness. The range of suffering and misery in the world appalls him. Repelled by the horror of human history—the unending cycle of war, famine, conquest, towers of Babel built and fallen—he concludes "nothing has ever been more insupportable for a man and a human society than freedom" (25). The evidence suggests that humans cannot live up to absolute freedom or their obligation to love and care for each other.

In trying to live out the ideals of love and self-sacrifice, the Inquisitor discovers how little help Christ provides those who seek to make humans happy. Even more to the point, the Inquisitor rebukes Christ for having rejected the very things that would have made governance possible—the three temptations of the Evil One in the desert.

The Gospels record that Jesus, living alone in the desert, had just finished fasting for forty days and nights. He then entered the final moment of grace and reflection before he began his public ministry. At this point, the "Tempter" visits him. The Devil says, "'If you are the Son of God, tell these stones to turn into loaves.'" But Jesus replies "'Man does not live by bread alone but on every word that comes from the mouth of God.'" The Tempter then took him to the holy city, made him stand on the parapet of the Temple. He challenged Christ: "'If you are the Son of God, throw yourself down so that angels will minister to you.'" Jesus replies "'You must not put the Lord your God to the test.'" Finally, taking Jesus to "a very high mountain, the Devil showed him all the kingdoms of the worlds and their splendor. 'I will give you all these,' he said, 'if you fall at my feet and worship me.'" Then Jesus replied, "'Be off, Satan! For Scripture says: You must worship the Lord your God, and serve him alone.'"[9]

In his refusal, Christ underscores his insistence that human worship, love, and community must be built upon freedom. The Inquisitor, though, condemns Christ for failing to realize that the three gifts—temptations—of the Devil represent the essential tools needed for successful governance; namely, "miracle," "mystery," and "authority." Like a good Machiavellian, the Inquisitor chides Christ for his reluctance to "enslave man" by exploiting these concepts (29).

The realist in us warns the idealist in us that few humans can live ideally. Like Machiavelli, the Inquisitor concludes that Christianity's emphasis upon love and freedom is simply not a foundation for a just and good state.[10] "'Thou didst think too highly of men therein . . . man is weaker and baser by nature than Thou hast believed him . . . Thou didst ask far too much from him—Thou has loved him more than Thyself'" (29). The Inquisitor's idealism led him, at one time, to live "in the wilderness." He confesses,

> I too have lived on roots and locusts, I too prized the freedom with which Thou hast blessed men, and I too was striving to stand among Thy elect, among the strong and powerful, thirsting 'to make up the number.' But I awakened and would not serve madness. I turned back and joined the ranks of those *who have corrected thy work.* (33)

In a long tradition of disillusioned idealists confronting history and their experience, the Inquisitor concludes that universal love and freedom are not possible for most humans. God's gifts bring only unhappiness and misery.

The Inquisitor's insight is not for the timid—only those strong enough to know and bear his truth have the right to rule. Even Plato concluded that most humans could not live up to the ideals of justice and truth. To provide happiness and stability, he created a guardian class made up of those who gained the truth of the ideal forms after intense study and effort. To secure legitimacy for the state the guardians create a "noble fiction," and all members are socialized to accept the lie imbedded in the founding myth of the state. The Inquisitor knows that in a world without God or natural law, "everything is lawful" (37). The moral elite's love and care justify them to lie to provide the happiness of the whole.[11] Unlike Christ with his impossible demands, they "care for the weak, too" (26).

After hearing the Inquisitor's (and Ivan's) justification for power, Alyosha bursts out that it hypocritically masks the "lust for power, for filthy earthly gain, for domination." In response, Ivan laughs and denies that all tyrants must be hypocrites. He points out that it is entirely possible that committed lovers of humanity could fall into self-deception or become disillusioned with human freedom. The Legend ends with the Inquisitor staring at the prisoner's face longing for a reply. Christ approaches "the old man in silence and softly kissed him on his bloodless, aged lips. That was all his answer." The Inquisitor shuddered and opened the door, "Go, and come no more. . . . Come not at all never." Christ leaves and "the kiss glows in his heart, but the old man adheres to his ideas."

The Human Condition and the Gifts of the Devil

In Dostoevsky, the idealism of Ivan and the Inquisitor founder upon the reality of human nature. A relentless honesty drives them to face the unblemished facts of humanity. The stories of suffering children reveal that humans display an "intoxication of cruelty" and demonstrate a terrifying "love of torturing children" (12). Ivan believes, based on the evidence, that "In every man . . . a demon lies—the demons of rage . . . , the demon of lawlessness let off the chain, the demon of diseases that follow on vice" (12). Humans add to the list daily—the holocaust, World Wars I and II, the Khymer Rouge, slavery, apartheid, and ethnic cleansing. The Devil feels more real and alive in human life than God's care, and Ivan acknowledges that man "has created him in his own image and likeness" (9).

For the Inquisitor, the critical point about human nature is that human evil is not an artifact of social forces or class; although these aggravate problems, the capacity for evil lies deep in human nature. Consequently, human inclinations must be tamed, not liberated, to create a just order supporting human happiness.[12] For a disillusioned idealist, the ideal of love and freedom is impossibly high and unsustainable for most people. The Inquisitor believes Christ made a mistake, both by respecting humanity too much and by asking too much of ordinary human beings. Real love would ask less because humans are "weak and vile" (26, 29).

The Inquisitor shows that the capacity for evil is aggravated by the imperatives of survival. People fight and claw for bread and basic needs. Scarcity brings out the worst in humans, and one cannot expect nobility or integrity from hungry humans. Any solution to human nature must provide for bread and for social order and peace, otherwise humans will destroy each other; the motto of reformers becomes "feed men, and then ask of them virtue" (26). To address human nature, then, requires that a regime constrain the tendency to evil, provide social peace, and meet basic physical needs.

In the Inquisitor's view, these actions are reinforced by another aspect of human nature. To overcome the isolation of existence, people need a community to support and anchor their sense of meaning and identity. Community provides the internalized norms and social and symbolic support to control and shape one's conscience. This need for community and identity plays out as an "everlasting craving" to find "someone to worship." To have a stable identity, social place, and peace, humans need rules and belief that are "established beyond dispute, so that all men would agree at once to worship it." This "community of worship" need not be a traditional religion but must provide references and myths that all hold in common and that provide accepted answers. Community gives people a place, purpose, and connections. Communities, however, aggravate the tendency to war for peoples will "set up gods and challenge one another, 'Put away your gods and come and worship ours, or we will kill you and your gods'" (27)! The allure of identity politics never ceases since it solves so many human needs and weaknesses.

The Inquisitor's assessment of human nature and man's social condition provides the fulcrum for the Inquisitor's defense of his methods. His defense begins with his attack upon Jesus for rejecting the gifts offered by the Devil. To the Inquisitor, these are the tools of modern governance; they are the key to bringing happiness to the masses.

And so the Inquisitor reprimands Jesus for rejecting the gifts of the Devil. Given the human condition, rulers cannot succeed without exercising miracle, mystery, and authority. The Inquisitor charges that Jesus, by increasing human freedom, "burdened the spiritual kingdom of mankind with its sufferings forever", and laid the foundations of "the destruction of Thy kingdom." The Inquisitor challenges him, "There are three powers, three powers alone, able to conquer and to hold captive forever the conscience of these impotent rebels for their happiness—these forces are miracle, mystery and authority. Thou hast rejected all three . . . Thou didst proudly and well, like God; but the weak and unruly race of men, are they gods" (28)?

The Inquisitor sees another way. Mystery creates the conditions of rule and obedience. Mystery teaches people "that it's not the free judgment of their hearts, not love that matters, but a mystery which they must follow blindly, even against their conscience" (30). Mystery provides a backbone for most authority structures by stopping discussion and warranting obedience. It does this by placing the grounds of justification beyond rational questioning. All workable ideology, myth, and even science depend upon stopping places of discussion. Mystery leads people to follow those few who have insight into the grounds of the mystery. The quest for God or meaning ends with most people bowing before masters who have deeper insight into the mystery. The need for mystery to solve the contradictions of reason and meaning is evident in the proliferation of mystery cults, saviors, or paths to wisdom ransacked from other mysterious traditions. The success of mystery works best with dispossessed individuals whose social underpinnings have been destroyed. Such seekers, in their quest for mystery and meaning, may find the Inquisitor.

Mystery accentuates the distance between the governing authority and the capacity of most people to understand it; they are left only to accept it. The miracles are actions that ordinary citizens could not achieve on their own but that the elite can produce because of their access to the mysteries of power. Any system of knowledge and professional expertise creates this dynamic, and institutionalizing it amplifies the distance and power. Mystery and miracle compel people to defer to clerics and experts who have knowledge and insight due to their discipline and sacrifice; a situation many welcome since they have neither the time nor the interest in knowing how their jobs and resources arrive each day. People who control resources gain leverage and gratitude, as well as resentment from the people they serve as ritual, pomp, and symbol augment the mystery, secrecy, and miracle (29).

These rituals and symbols conceal the sword of Caesar that the Inquisitor and his kind accept. Any government must exercise authority backed in the end by brute coercion. The coercion and power behind law enable rulers to set boundaries and deal with rebels. "Then, and only then, the reign of peace and happiness will come for men" (31). This happiness for the mass of people will dull the edge of their rebellion and "all will be happy and no longer kill or destroy one another as under Thy freedom" (31). In a sense, the elite can rely upon the fact that the "fierce and rebellious will destroy themselves, others, rebellious but weak, will crawl fawning to our feet and whine . . . save us from ourselves" (32). Ivan lays out the logic of the new authoritarian leaders of the twentieth century. By the force of their will, they create happiness by offering peace, basic needs, identity, and meaningful community. Bread and community along with miracle and mystery will sustain this internalized authority bounded by the coercive power of the sword and state. In the Grand Inquisitor's view, the Devil's gifts are bounteous—and essential, "For who can rule men if not he who holds their conscience and their bread in his hands. We have taken the sword of Caesar, and in taking it, of course have rejected Thee and followed *him*" (31).

Living with the Devil's Gifts

"The Grand Inquisitor" reminds us of the poignant paradoxes involved in doing good—everyone holding position and power accepts, in some measure, the Devil's gifts. To govern successfully requires bread, mystery, miracle, and authority. Institutions need resources to pay workers and to provide service. Professionals use expertise not available to or understood by others. Officials and leaders exercise judgment that combines training, experience, skill, and relationships. Citizens rely upon expertise and judgment to perform the background activities of civilization, such as public health or environmental protection. None of these activities could succeed without the miracle and mystery surrounding the expertise of trusted and skilled managers and leaders. Intimate knowledge of arcane procedures and rules or access to complex networks of power and knowledge are beyond the ken of most people.

Sustained success in public endeavors also depends upon legitimate public authority. Law, promulgated by legitimate public authority and supported by the sword of executive enforcement, is designed to prevent oppression and create the conditions of peace. Without basic security, individuals cannot hope to find either happiness or freedom or community. While Dostoevsky's concerns may seem distant to us, the psychological and moral reality of public service is that organizational structure, hiring and firing, technique, and process conjoin authority, mystery and bread in the daily life of public managers and leaders.

For Dostoevsky, the idealism to serve humanity and bring people safety, happiness, and meaning inevitably leads to the Devil's gifts. Most public servants would prefer to ignore this disquieting aspect of leadership and its inherent temptations. Many individuals attracted to public service distrust power yet must learn to exercise it.[13] Indeed human frailty, need, anger, and a capacity to enjoy domination—all of these phenomena should trouble and alarm any sane person holding office and power. Yet, fine people achieve good things, imperfect things, but good things, all the time. They live lives of integrity and commitment without becoming cynics or zealots or surrendering to the temptation to dominate. Western liberalism was born in the struggle to answer just these provocations; the democratic insistence upon accountability, due process, participation, deliberation, and separation of powers, are all processes that must grapple with this paradox.

If the paradox is not resolved in these ways, Dostoevsky's "The Grand Inquisitor" prepares us for the manner in which elite authoritarian leaders will justify their rule. The Grand Inquisitor's ideology has dominated twentieth-century politics and it will not disappear. The story lays bare the timeless dynamics and temptations of authoritarianism. These justifications begin with the moral and psychological power of ideals by which we derive our most basic motivation. Those who hold them may ardently believe in the purity and consecrated nature of their own ideals and often of the superiority of those ideals.[14]

The ideals, though, collide with the limits of human nature revealed in centuries of moral squalor, endless suffering, failed attempts at self-rule, and endless un-met promises. The goal of maximizing human happiness often stops at the real-ity that humans exercising freedom spawn misery and squalor because people "will never be capable of using their freedom . . . these poor rebels can never turn into giants to complete the tower" (34-35).

The question, then, inevitably becomes: who should rule? The Inquisitor claims that a privileged group can (and should) assert the right to rule. This elite justifies their rule by claiming a kind of moral preeminence: first, they claim to possess a pure idealistic commitment to human happiness unencumbered by the pollution of self-interest and material pursuit. They love and care for humanity and recognize its needs, frailties, and limits. Second, their austere lives prove their moral purity and imperviousness to the allure of self-interest as they com-mit to reform or revolution and eschew the pleasure and seductions of wealth, family, friendships or the blandishments of position. Third and most important, they possess special knowledge that legitimates ruling over others less idealistic, pure, and knowledgeable than themselves: this is the knowledge of good and evil that Ivan possesses and the Inquisitor embodies.

Mystery, miracle, and authority combine to create immense distance between the rulers and the ruled in their access to knowledge and insight denied to the governed. It could be the power of technical and analytical expertise, a claim to divine revelation, the privilege of race or gender, or historical insight. The source of special knowledge, whatever it is, gives the rulers immunity from ac-countability to others. In some way, every teacher with students, every service provider with clients, every judge with defendants, and every superior with sub-ordinates recognize these problems and temptations.

The self-serving assertion of some leaders that they endure self-sacrificial lives creates an even greater distance between the ruled and their rulers.[15] This group will use immoral measures, such as lies and deception, to attain their ver-sion of good for the rest. As self-defined suffering servants, they accept the con-sequences for their souls and grief involved in protecting others while the gen-eral population are allowed to live the "good life" free from the burden and guilt of responsibility for the morally problematic actions needed to build a state.[16] The progress of humanity toward happiness means that some must, martyr-like, bear the burden of the truth and dirty hands.[17] This elite will not achieve self-interested happiness for they live the curse of the true "knowledge of good and evil" (33).

Myth, mystery, miracle, bread and sword fortify the regimes of authoritarian reformers committed to transforming society and bringing happiness. The re-gime claims to end injustice, misery, and oppression as well as establish correct moral behavior and belief in citizens; yet, the frailties of humanity that haunt the Inquisitor guarantee that each regime ends the same way: humanity will always disappoint an idealist. Their ideals are undermined by their diagnosis of human-ity, and the Inquisitor's own desperate disillusionment reflects this conclusion. Over time, failure and frustrated objectives hollow out the idealism and com-mitment of many. Every elite possesses a few true believers, but many will see through the noble lie. They will ultimately live the lie themselves and fail to sustain the contradiction in their lives. Their life, like the bloated Cardinals, will become one of privilege and wealth ornamented by ideology and mystery. The regime built upon ideals and run by idealists will end as a sham with hollow ideals. Cynicism and even despair fester at the heart of governmental and daily life. The ruins of the Renaissance papacy, Cromwell's England, Napoleon's France, communist Russia, or Mao's China all serve witness to the hubris of idealism so clearly sketched by the Grand Inquisitor.

Committed people will be tempted by the Inquisitor's logic of rule; using the Devil's tools possesses its own disorienting allure. Every public leader should think through the risk of holding ideals and meeting responsibility in an imperfect world. In the end, the story reminds people that love and compassion begin in silence and a kiss—an opening to possibilities, not a closure in certainties.

Notes

1. Charles Goodell, *The Case for Bureaucracy: A Public Administration Polemic*, 3rd ed. (Chatham, N.J.: Chatham House: 1994), 25-49; 103-132.

2. The best edition of *The Brothers Karamazov* is the Norton Critical Edition edited by Ralph E. Matlaw using the Constance Garnett translation revised by Ralph Matlaw, W. W. Norton & Co. New York, 1976.

3. Several independent editions of *The Grand Inquisitor* have been published as stand-alone books. I will use the *Grand Inquisitor*, Hackett Publishing, 1993 with an introduction by Charles B. Guignon. This edition uses the traditional translation by Constance Garnett and has the huge advantage of having the two prior chapters entitled "The Brothers Make Friends" and "Rebellion." These two lay out Ivan's own attack upon the world and religion. They provide the motivational basis for Ivan and his idealism and nihilism as well as the love of humanity and despair that drive the Inquisitor. This edition also has the later chapter entitled "The Russian Monk," which Dostoevsky wrote to provide his own prophetic response to Ivan's argument.

4. William Frankena, *Ethics*, 2nd ed. (Englewood Cliffs, N.J: Prentice Hall, 1973), chaps. 1, 2, 6.

5. David Norton, *Democracy and Moral Development: A Politics of Virtue*, (Berkeley: University of California Press, 1990); Stephen G. Salkever, *Finding the Mean: Theory and Practice in Aristotelian Political Philosophy* (Princeton, N.J.: Princeton University Press, 1990), especially chs. 3 and 4.

6. Peter M. Senge, *The Fifth Discipline: The Art and Practice of the Learning Organization* (New York: Doubleday, Currency, 1990), 205-233.

7. Plato, *The Republic,* trans. G. M. A. Grube (Indianapolis: Hackett Publishing, 1974), lines 476-480; 522-526.

8. Plato, *The Republic*, Books IV, V, VI.

9. Matthew 4: 1-15 *The Jerusalem Bible: Readers Edition* (Garden City, N. Y: Doubleday and Company), 1968.

10. Niccolo Machiavelli, *The Discourses*, Bernard Crick, ed. (Harmondsworth: Penguin, 1970), Book I, 11 & 12.

11. Plato, *The Republic*, lines 414-417; see also on deception, 376-379; 459-461.

12. Richard J. Regan, *The Moral Dimension of Politics* (Oxford: Oxford University Press, 1986), 3-29; 37-75; James Wiser, *Political Theory: A Thematic Inquiry* (Nelson Hall, 1986), 149-169.

13. Lester W. Milbrath and M. L. Goel, *Political Participation: How and Why Do People Get Involved in Politics*, 2nd ed. (Chicago: Rand McNally College, 1977).

14. Isaiah Berlin, *The Crooked Timber of Humanity: Chapters in the History of Ideas* (New York: Alfred Knopf, 1991), 1-20; 175-207.

15. Sebastian de Grazie, *Machiavelli in Hell* (Princeton: Princeton University Press, 1996) provides a brilliant analysis of the logic of self-sacrifice for the good of the state.

16. Michael Walzer, "Political Action: The Problem of Dirty Hands," *Philosophy and Public Affairs*, (Winter, 1973): 160-180.

17. Michael Walzer, "Political Action" (Winter, 1973): 160-180, presents a remarkable analysis of the nature of dirty hands and the complex psychological and moral stances one can take to come to terms with it. J. Patrick Dobel, *Compromise and Political Action: Political Morality in Liberal and Democratic Life* (Lanhan, Md.: Rowman & Littlefield, 1990), further discusses the complexity of dirty hands.

Chapter 12

Democratic Envy in Sinclair Lewis' *It Can't Happen Here*

Paul C. Peterson

> *[Shad Ledue] had thought, when he was a hired man,*
> *that there was a lot more fun in being rich and famous.*
> *He didn't feel one bit different than he had then! Funny!*
> —*It Can't Happen Here*

Sinclair Lewis, Novelist for Middle-Class America

Of major American novelists, Sinclair Lewis seems to be held in the lowest regard. In 1937, Robert Cantwell wrote that Lewis "has, in fact, been one of the most plunging and erratic writers in our literary history; unpredictability, waywardness, unevenness are his distinguishing characteristics."[1] A quarter-of-a-century later, Lewis' most prominent biographer, Mark Schorer, would conclude his 813-page biography noting that Lewis was "one of the worst writers in modern American literature."[2] It is certainly a mark of Lewis' decline as a significant force in understanding American culture that Schorer's biography, the only comprehensive biography of Lewis to have been published, is now out of print. And, of Lewis' twenty-two novels, only eight remain in print.

Whatever defects Lewis had as a writer, his most enduring contribution, a contribution that has not proven to be as enduring as one once might have thought, was in creating vivid characters such as Carol Kennicott, George F. Babbitt, and Elmer Gantry. As Walter Lippmann said of Lewis, he "is a maker of stereotypes."[3] As with successful stereotypes, Lewis' most notable creations became part of the American language for a time. Babbitt and Gantry would instantly bring to mind images of the presumed absence of soul of the American businessman and of the presumed sham of evangelical tent revivalism. Perhaps the most significant measure of Lewis' decline is that even Babbitt and Gantry have largely dropped out of American language as symbols of any sort, not to mention the powerful symbols that they once were. Most American college graduates of the last two decades would have a difficult time explaining who George Babbitt and Elmer Gantry were and what they represented. This failure of recognition would probably be true of English majors as well as the general body of college graduates. It is telling that several years back when the world of Christian evangelicalism went through its wave of scandals involving Jim Bakker, Jimmy Swaggart, and Robert Tilton that the most obvious cultural reference for older Americans, Elmer Gantry, was barely mentioned at all in the various accounts of these scandals.

Lewis' vivid characterizations were attached to what was thought, at least in his major works, to be an insightful portrayal of American middle-class life in the first half of the twentieth century. Thus, while Schorer calls Lewis "one of the worst writers in modern American literature," he goes on to say that without Lewis' writing "one cannot imagine modern American literature. That is because, without his writing, we can hardly imagine ourselves."[4] Cantwell continued in describing Lewis as "the historian of America's catastrophic going-to-pieces" of the middle class "with no remedy to offer for the decline that he records, and he has dramatized the process of disintegration, as well as his own dilemma, in the outlines of his novels, in the progress of his characters, and sometimes, and most painfully, in the lapses of taste and precision that periodically weaken the structure of his prose."[5]

To the extent that Lewis has a reputation that makes him worth reading, that reputation is built on his five great novels of the 1920s—*Main Street*, *Babbitt*, *Arrowsmith*, *Elmer Gantry*, and *Dodsworth*. This prodigious effort would be rewarded in 1930 with Lewis becoming the first American recipient of the Nobel Prize for Literature, an award that was itself controversial in American circles. Lewis' career is commonly—and correctly—pictured as a long decline from 1930 until his death in 1951. Lewis would publish another nine novels in the last twenty-one years of his life, with one more being published posthumously. By all accounts, none of the post-Nobel Prize novels ranks with any of the big five. But while it is true that none of the post-Nobel Prize novels ranks with the big five, it does not follow that there was nothing of worth in what was produced by Lewis during his declining years.[6] By most accounts, *It Can't Happen Here*, Lewis' 1935 portrayal of a fascist takeover in America, is perhaps the strongest of the books of this period of Lewis' life. Yet, whatever its strengths, it, too, is a far cry from the big five, although not as far a cry as some might think. In many respects, *It Can't Happen Here* is a topical potboiler. With the collapse of republicanism throughout Europe in the years immediately preceeding, Lewis imaginatively presents a similar collapse in America.

It Can't Happen Here and "Shad" Ledue

Perhaps because *It Can't Happen Here* is a lesser Lewis work, it has received little critical attention. While Schorer could state in 1961 that "[r]eading *It Can't Happen Here* today, one is impressed by its qualities as a tour de force," he, nevertheless, devotes only three of his 813 pages to the plot and characters of the book.[7] There have been only a few serious treatments of *It Can't Happen Here*, and those have tended to focus on the book's big story and its major characters, most notably the small-town Vermont journalist, Doremus Jessup, and the Huey Long-inspired, Senator Berzelius "Buzz" Windrip, who is the political leader of the fascist movement that will take over America through the electoral process. The real strengths of *It Can't Happen Here*, however, are found elsewhere, and these strengths have never been commented on. Just as Cantwell described Lewis as the "historian of America's catastrophic going-to-pieces," Lewis portrays the real going-to-pieces of the middle class as it is manipulated by a fascist movement in *It Can't Happen Here*.

The gem in *It Can't Happen Here* is Lewis's supporting character, Oscar "Shad" Ledue. Ledue is a character who ranks with George Babbitt and Elmer Gantry as a powerful and memorable portrayal of a certain type of individual. Ledue is, among other things, representative of certain dangerous yearnings in at least some elements of the middle and lower classes. Since democracy gives fuller vent to the political understanding and aspirations of the middle and lower classes than any other political system, the dangerous yearnings of a Shad Ledue are particularly threatening in democratic political orders. Lewis, like other thoughtful people, had seen all of this unfold in contemporary European politics. As its title suggests, *It Can't Happen Here* was a warning to Americans. While the fascist takeover of America portrayed in *It Can't Happen Here* did not come close to happening, Lewis' portrayal of certain psychological tendencies in the middle and lower classes, tendencies represented in the Shad Ledue character, has a timeless quality to it that the larger and more immediate theme of the book does not. Curiously, the Ledue character is virtually missing in all of the critical and scholarly discussion of *It Can't Happen Here*. In the one reference to Ledue in Schorer's analysis of the book, Schorer manages to misspell Ledue's name.[8] There is only one reference in Perry Meisel's introduction to the Signet Classic edition of *It Can't Happen Here*. Stephen Tanner in his 1990 study of the novel, "Sinclair Lewis and Fascism," mentions the Ledue character not at all.[9] Axel Knoenagel, in what appears to be the most recent study, makes one fleeting reference to Ledue.[10]

Lewis first introduces us to Ledue in an indirect manner in Chapter Three. The novel's protagonist, Doremus Jessup, is inconvenienced by the incompetence of his handyman, Shad Ledue. Upon arriving home, Jessup

> cursed competently as, on the cement walk from the garage to the kitchen, he barked his shins on the lawn-mower, left there by his hired man, one Oscar Ledue, known always as "Shad," a large and red-faced, a sulky and surly Irish-Canuck peasant. Shad always did things like leaving lawnmowers about to snap at the shins of decent people. He was entirely incompetent and vicious. At least twice a day, Doremus resolved to fire him, but—Perhaps he was telling himself the truth when he insisted that it was amusing to try to civilize this prize bull.[11]

Ledue is as vicious as he is "incompetent." Most of Lewis' examples of Ledue's incompetence are preconceived acts designed to annoy or inconvenience people who Ledue thinks have no business being his social and economic betters. Although the thought is never expressed directly in the text, Ledue seems to think that he is a hired hand rather than an employer, only because of some freak social accident. Those who give Ledue orders are no better than he is; only economic necessity keeps him in this otherwise unnecessarily subordinate social position. Indeed, in Ledue's mind not only are those who are giving him orders no better than he, they are in fact ultimately inferior to him. The few pleasures that Ledue can gain out of life are to create these annoyances for those people who are his social superiors but, in his mind, natural inferiors. Lewis tells us that "Shad *always* did things like leaving lawnmowers about to snap at the shins of decent people." Ledue is described in this passage as "surly," which he most assuredly is throughout the novel. Throughout his being under the employ of Jessup, Ledue shows nearly open contempt for his employer.

The first time that we directly encounter Ledue is in the preparation for an old-fashioned picnic to be enjoyed by the extended Jessup family. We are told that "the only stain on the preparations for the picnic was the grouchiness of the hired man, Shad Ledue. When he was asked to turn the ice cream freezer he growled, 'Why the heck don't you folks get an electric freezer?' He grumbled, most audibly, at the weight of the picnic baskets, and when he was asked to clean up the basement during their absence, he retorted only with a glare of silent fury." Philip Jessup, the adult son of Doremus and Emma Jessup, tells his father, "'You ought to get rid of that fellow, Ledue.'" Doremus responds, "'Oh, I don't know.'" And in a passage that echoes the first Ledue-related passage, he adds: "'Probably just shiftlessness on my part. But I tell myself I'm doing a social experiment—trying to train him to be as gracious as the average Neanderthal man. Or perhaps I'm scared of him—he's the kind of vindictive peasant that sets fire to barns.'" Doremus adds, a bit incredulously, "'Did you know that he actually reads, Phil'" (44-5)?

Each of these first two passages that introduce us to Ledue suggests the possibility of Jessup educating, improving, and civilizing Ledue. This project is certainly consistent with the benevolent and decent liberalism that characterizes Jessup. Both passages also suggest that the educational project might be a cover for a deeper psychological truth, namely, that Jessup is afraid of Ledue. "Perhaps [Jessup] was telling himself the truth when he insisted that it was amusing to try to civilize this prize bull." And as Doremus later confides to his son: "'Or perhaps I'm scared of him—he's the kind of vindictive peasant that sets fire to barns.'" Certainly if Jessup was afraid of Ledue, he had every right to be. Reason for such fear is telegraphed to us in nearly every passage dealing with Ledue; subsequent events of the novel demonstrate that the fear is justified. If anything, Jessup underestimates the possibilities for treachery in his hired hand. In a later incident Jessup arrives at home to find an anonymous note on his front porch, stating: "'You will get yrs Dorey sweethart unles you get rite down on yr belly and crawl in front of the MM [the MM were the Minute Men, a quasi-military organization that served Buzz Windrip's movement as the SS served the Nazis] and the League [of Forgotten Men] and the Chief [Windrip] and I [signed] A friend'" (98). Although anonymous, one cannot help but wonder if Ledue is in fact the author of this note. Given his disdain for Jessup and his easy access to the Jessup household, he would certainly be a likely suspect. It would certainly be consistent with what we know of Ledue's character.

Ledue could be accurately described by a famous passage in which William Alexander Percy describes Mississippi Senator Theodore Bilbo in *Lanterns on the Levee*: "[He] was a pert little monster, glib and shameless, with that sort of cunning common to criminals which passes for intelligence."[12] Cunning and an unfocused yearning for something better, indeed the idea of an entitlement to something better, are what best characterize the Shad Ledue that Lewis has given us. Lewis does not tell us much about Ledue's economic circumstances. Working as a handyman in depression-era Vermont, Ledue obviously cannot be well off. But he is evidently able to get by. What drives Ledue more than economic betterment or the economic envy of those who are better off than he is the desire for recognition and respect. The class conflict of which Ledue is representational is a conflict based on social standing rather than economic position. For Ledue, economic well being is significant chiefly because it is a necessary ingredient to the social standing that he craves. As we shall see, when Ledue betters himself economically (and even, to a certain extent, socially), he will still be characterized by the same frustrations that torment him at the outset of the novel.

Shortly after Senator Buzz Windrip receives the 1936 Democratic party nomination for President, Jessup has a brief conversation with Ledue, asking him how he plans to vote. Ledue responds, "'Well now, I'll tell you, Mr. Jessup.'" That "Mr. Jessup" is one of the few at least apparently polite and deferential references Ledue makes to Doremus. But Lewis quickly adds: "Shad struck an attitude, leaning on his ax. Sometimes he could be quite pleasant and condescending, even to this little man who was so ignorant about coon-hunting and the games of craps and poker" (64). This would be an accurate characterization of how someone such as a Shad Ledue would view a Doremus Jessup. One of the few ways in which Ledue would be superior to Jessup was Ledue's size and physical strength. Thus, he would see Jessup as "a little man." For Ledue, Jessup's comparatively small physical size would translate into a smallness in moral matters as well, given Ledue's understanding of the moral world. And that reference to "Mr. Jessup" would be, as Lewis explicitly states, condescending.

Ledue tells Jessup in this conversation that he is supporting Windrip primarily because of a plank in Windrip's platform that pledges $4,000 annually to every citizen. Ledue sees in this $4,000 the economic opportunity to better himself. He plans to start a chicken farm, and he believes that "'I can make a bunch of money out of chickens!'" Reflecting the envy that so dominates the character of Ledue, he adds, "'I'll show some of these guys that think they're so rich!'" Jessup, however, reminds Ledue that this would not be his first effort at a chicken farm. Evidently he had tried to raise chickens once before and the project failed because as Jessup states, "'You, uh, I'm afraid sort of let their water freeze up on 'em in winter, and they all died, you remember.'" Ledue tosses this failure off as nothing significant: "'Oh, them? So what! Heck! There was too few of 'em. I'm not going to waste my time foolin' with just a couple dozen chickens! When I get my five-six thousand of 'em to make it worth my while, *then* I'll show you! You bet'" (64). Ledue, who has so little going for him anyway, found it not worth his time to deal with a small flock of chickens. But give him a sufficient opportunity to make it big and then the world would see great things.

Ledue and the Onset of Fascisim

Ledue will never enjoy success in the business world. His success, such as it would prove to be, comes in the political world as a minion in the fascist movement that will take Windrip to the White House. Ledue becomes a secretary in the second Fort Beulah chapter of The League of Forgotten Men, an association put together by Bishop Paul Peter Prang, Sinclair Lewis' fictional counterpart to noted 1930s radio pundit Father Charles Coughlin. (Fort Beulah is the fictional Vermont town where most of the action of *It Can't Happen Here* takes place.) The League is an initially independent organization that supports Windrip. After Windrip gains power, Ledue will receive a political appointment as a county commissioner.

As a county commissioner (which in the reorganized America of *It Can't Happen Here* has considerably more clout, if only to make life miserable for others, than we would usually associate with such an office), Ledue participates in two incidents that are revealing of the envy that dominates his character. In one case subversive books are to be rooted out and burned. Ledue knows that Jessup has a substantial library and so Ledue, with his henchmen, arrives at Jessup's house and looks "at the fireplace to which he had once brought so many armfuls of wood and snickered." Jessup asks Ledue to sit down in the other room, to which Ledue responds, "'I will like hell just sit down in the other room! We're burning the books tonight! Snap to it, Jessup!'" As Ledue's henchmen are looking for books, Ledue reflects upon his past experience working in the Jessup household: "'I know this house, Ensign. I used to work here—had the privilege of putting up those storm windows you can see there, and of getting bawled out right here in this room. You won't remember those times, Doc—when I used to mow your lawn, too, and you used to be so snotty!'" If we could see contemptuous behavior in Ledue toward his presumed social betters when he was politically powerless, we should expect the level of his contemptuous behavior to escalate when he does assume political power. And that is exactly what happens. Jessup has anticipated an invasion from book burners and has carefully removed from his library the most obvious targets of the book burners. Ledue, however, is certainly not likely to leave Jessup's house without having found a single book to burn. To avoid what would be such a humiliation to him, Ledue instructs that a deluxe edition of the works of Dickens, an edition that has been in the family for three generations, be burned. Ledue justifies the burning of the Dickens set because "'That guy Dickens—didn't he do a lot of complaining about conditions—about schools and the police and everything?'" One of Ledue's henchmen notes the weakness of Ledue's argument: "'Yes, but Shad—but, Captain Ledue, that was a hundred years ago.'" Ledue's earthy response to this intervention is that it "'makes no difference. Dead skunk stinks worse 'n a live one.'" When Jessup, in almost a reflexive move, grabs an arm of one of the Minute Men, "Shad lumbered up to him, enormous red fist at Doremus's nose, growling, 'Want to get the daylights beaten out of you now . . . instead of later'" (198-200)?

This escalated level of display of contempt, along with the continuing display of envy, toward Jessup is found again in a later confrontation with Jessup. Jessup is seeking to formally quit the editorship of his newspaper that has been informally taken over by the government. But for whatever reasons, the local officials do not want Jessup's name disconnected from the paper. After making his request of County Commissioner Ledue, he is told by Ledue: "'But I can tell you, right here and now, Jessup, without any monkey business about it, you're not going to leave your job. I guess I could find enough grounds for sending you to Trianon [the closest concentration camp] for about a million years, with ninety lashes, but—you've always been so stuck on yourself as such an all-fired honest editor, it kind of tickles me to watch you kissing the Chief's [Windrip] foot—and mine!'" Jessup responds, saying, "'I'll do no more of it! That's certain! And I admit that I deserve your scorn for ever having done it.'" That response leads to this comment from Ledue:

"Well, isn't that elegant! But you'll do just what I tell you to, and like it! Jessup, I suppose you think I had a swell time when I was your hired man! Watching you and your old woman and the girls go off on a picnic while I—oh, I was just your hired man, with dirt in my ears, your dirt! I could stay home and clean up the basement!" (219)

The second major incident involving Ledue as a county commissioner occurs when he is sent to review and, if necessary, censor a lecture by Lionel Adams, an African American anthropologist with a Ph.D. from the University of Chicago. It is not difficult to see Ledue having trouble with an African American Ph.D., and Lewis plays the scene for all that it is worth. In a nice touch, Lewis tells us that "Ledue sat hulked down in a chair at the back of the hall. Aside from addresses by M.M. officers, and moral inspiration by his teachers in grammar school, it was the first lecture he had ever heard in his life, and he didn't think much of it." Not surprisingly, Ledue

was irritated that this stuck-up nigger didn't spiel like the characters of Octavus Roy Cohen, one of Shad's favorite authors, but had the nerve to try to sling English just as good as Shad himself....Shad signaled his squad and arrested Adams in the midst of his lecture, addressing him, "You God-damn dirty, ignorant, stinking nigger! I'm going to shut your big mouth for you, for keeps!" (283-4)

Professor Adams is sent to a concentration camp. As it turns out, Ledue, in the next paragraph, winds up a prisoner at the same concentration camp, where he will meet a grisly death.

Prior to his death, Ledue had come to a realization that for all the advancement he had gained in the politics of President Windrip's America, there was still something missing. Just as had been the case when he was working for the Jessup family, Ledue still thinks that he has not been treated fairly. As Lewis tells us: "Shad Ledue, back in his hotel suite, reflected that he was getting a dirty deal. He had been responsible for sending more traitors to concentration camps than any other county commissioner in the province [the 48 states had been replaced by eight provinces], yet he had not been promoted." And although Ledue now held a position of some political prominence, he was still a social outsider. Having returned from a dinner given in honor of the Provincial Commissioner, "Shad felt discontented. All those damn snobs trying to show off!" Even fascists, it turns out, can be social snobs. There they were talking about shows and art and other subjects about which Ledue knew little or nothing and in which he had no interest. Even worse, "they had paid no attention to Shad when he had told his funny story about the stuck-up preacher in Fort Beulah." They had "not paid one bit of attention to him . . . though he had been careful to be refined in his table manners and to stick out his little finger when he drank from a glass."

As Ledue continued in this self-pitying mode, he is perhaps lonelier than he has ever been before. He is outside the social circle of his new colleagues, those who had been responsible for his climb to some degree of political power and, in Ledue's mind, the prestige that would go with that power. But also his former acquaintances, "the fellows he had once known, in pool room and barber shop, seemed frightened of him, now" (281-2). To the extent that Ledue could have a romantic interest in a woman, he carried something of a torch for "Sissy" Jessup, the daughter of Doremus Jessup. This was a "relationship" that Ledue would handle in a clumsy fashion. Of course, the idea that Sissy Jessup would have a romantic interest in Ledue is preposterous. But knowing of Ledue's feelings for her she is not above playing on those feelings to gain information that might benefit her father and other interested parties about the dealings of the local authorities. Although not able to see the entire picture of Sissy's manipulation of him, Ledue knows that in spite of his new found status and political power, he seems to be no further along with Sissy than at any other time. At one point, Ledue, in frustration, says to Sissy,

"Oh, shucks! You think I'm still just a hired man! Even though I am a County Commissioner now! And a Battalion-Leader! And prob'ly pretty soon I'll be a Commander!" He spoke the sacred names with awe. It was the twentieth time he had made the same plaint to her in the same words. "And you still think I ain't good for anything except lugging in kindling." (245)

Ledue "had thought, when he was a hired man, that there was a lot more fun in being rich and famous. He didn't feel one bit different than he had then! Funny" (282)!

Envy as the Abuse of Equality

There is a dark passage regarding human nature at almost the exact midway point of *It Can't Happen Here*. Jessup has written an editorial—the last of the kind that he will write as a newspaper editor—critical of the actions of the new Windrip government. His editorial sparks a crowd that will become a mob surrounding the building where his paper is written and printed. Jessup observes in this crowd "dozens of people there unknown to him; respectable farmers in town for shopping, unrespectables in town for a drink, laborers from the nearest work camp and all of them eddying around M.M. uniforms. Probably many of them cared nothing about insults to the Corpo state [as the Windrip government was widely referred to], but had only the unprejudiced, impersonal pleasure in violence natural to most people" (166). If there is indeed an "unprejudiced, impersonal pleasure in violence natural to most people," then serious questions would have to be raised about the viability of democracy. Certainly, Lewis shows us the conditions in which such violence can be given a relatively free rein. Clearly, Shad Ledue is meant to be a reflection of this "impersonal pleasure in violence." The chapter that presents this dark view of human nature concludes with a scene where Ledue is marching a man out to be shot by a firing squad: "Shad marched out with them, pulling his automatic pistol from its holster and looking at it happily" (178).

In Schorer's view, Lewis meant Ledue "to be the American equivalent of European riffraff rising with the fascist tide to sinister and brutal power" and that Ledue "never ceases to be a simple-minded, ill-mannered lout."[13] The first part of this observation—Ledue as "the American equivalent of European riffraff rising with the fascist tide"—is correct. Of course, riffraff are found in America as well as Europe. In the case of a political revolution such as the one that Lewis presents in *It Can't Happen*, we should expect such a social upheaval in America as well as elsewhere. The second part of the characterization is only half true. Ledue is always an ill-mannered lout, but I have tried to raise questions about whether he is as simple-minded as Schorer sees him and as Jessup seemed on occasion to see him. The incompetence that Jessup saw in Ledue was, as suggested earlier, a contrived effort to annoy or inconvenience those that Ledue saw as his illegitimate social superiors. Ledue has a vague ambition, but he wants somebody or some providential force to hand him the means and the blueprint for achieving success. There is a low-level cunning to his actions. And when opportunities present themselves, he is certainly willing to take advantage of them, although these opportunities have to be those that involve little effort and not much in the way of deferred gratification.

In certain crucial respects, Ledue is an embodiment of certain fears of Alexis de Tocqueville in *Democracy in America*. Tocqueville warns that equality, not freedom, forms "the distinctive characteristic of the age" in democratic times and democratic regimes. Tocqueville tells us that "equality daily gives each man in the crowd a host of small enjoyments. The charms of equality are felt the whole time and are within the reach of all."[14] While Tocqueville says "equality daily gives each man in the crowd a host of small enjoyments," there are many for whom the enjoyments are not a host or are not there at all. Such a man is Shad Ledue. Ledue sees the relative well-being of Doremus Jessup and his family and he sees the relative well-being of other families in Fort Beulah, so in his mind the question emerges as to why is there not a similar well-being in his own social and economic circumstances. Seeing what others have and failing to see the connection between social and economic achievement and some form of individual virtue, Ledue feels the dangerous passion of envy. In Ledue, the passion of envy is so strong that he will do nearly anything to gain what he believes to be his just entitlement. Tocqueville tells us that in democratic ages "the passion for equality seeps into every corner of the human heart, expands, and fills the whole." Envy is a pathological form of equality and for Ledue, it is not so much equality that fills his heart, but envy. Envy exists in all times and virtually all places. Characters such as Shad Ledue are not unique to democracies. But envy becomes particularly dangerous in democratic ages, that is, in times where "the passion for equality seeps into every corner of the human heart." When, for large classes of individuals, equality assumes this pathological form of envy—"democratic envy"—as it does with Ledue in *It Can't Happen Here*, the political consequences, as well as the individual consequences, can be disastrous.

Concerns about the pathologies of democracy and the weaknesses of individuals in those political systems have a long standing in political science. Aristotle tells us that "there are two conceptions which are generally held to be characteristic of democracy. One of them is the conception of the sovereignty of the majority; the other is that of the liberty of individuals. The democrat starts by assuming that justice consists in equality; he proceeds to identify equality with the sovereignty of the will of [the many]." But this reasonable identification, Aristotle warns us, often becomes perverted. Democrats often wind up "with the view that 'liberty and equality' consist in 'doing what one likes.' The result of such a view is that, in . . . extreme democracies, each man lives as he likes—or as Euripides says, 'For any end he chances to desire.'" This is to say that in this perverted or extreme view of democracy, the rule of law and the idea of self-control are severely diminished. They are diminished to such an extent that what Aristotle calls extreme democracy is indistinguishable from anarchy. Aristotle warns that "to live by the rule of the constitution ought not to be regarded as slavery [as it comes to be seen in extreme democracies], but rather as salvation."[15]

In *The Republic*, Plato gives us a powerful poetic image of tyranny arising from democracy. The tyrannical soul is at war with human excellence. In a passage that rings even truer of Shad Ledue than of Buzz Windrip, Socrates says in *The Republic* that the tyrant "look[s] sharply to see who is courageous, who is great-minded, who is prudent, who is rich. And so happy is he that there is a necessity for him, whether he wants to or not, to be an enemy of all of them and plot against them until he purges the city."[16] Pettiness of soul can often lead to tyrannical impulses. We do not always see this because most of the petty do not have the power to carry out those impulses. In *It Can't Happen Here*, Sinclair Lewis shows us what can happen when someone with a petty soul has the opportunity to play out his fantasies and ambitions in the political arena. The petty soul would be, as Plato indicates, hostile to the courageous, the great-minded, the prudent, and the rich. The virtues of courage, great-mindedness, and prudence would be dismissed as aristocratic airs and pomposity. To a certain extent, Doremus Jessup embodied at least pale versions of these virtues. And it was precisely to the extent that he embodied these virtues that Ledue loathed him. While Jessup was not wealthy by most objective standards, from the vantage point of Ledue he was wealthy. Ledue saw that wealth as unjustified, a function of a cruel fate. Fate was, of course, being cruel because it had bestowed wealth and social position on the diminutive Jessup and not Ledue. The connection of Jessup's relative economic well-being and his social position to his virtues is a connection that never enters Ledue's mind.

Playing on these same themes from Plato, Aristotle, and Tocqueville, C. S. Lewis, in *The Screwtape Letters*, shows us how the democratic era transformed envy into an acceptable, if not virtuous, characteristic. In his famous toast, Screwtape illustrates how "'you can use the word *democracy* to sanction in [the] thought [of modern man] the most degrading and (and also the least enjoyable) of all human feelings. You can get him to practise, not only without shame but a positive glow of self-approval, conduct, which, if undefended by the magic word, would be universally derided. The feeling I mean is of course that which prompts a man to say *I'm as good as you*.'" Screwtape relates that one of the strengths of getting a man to say "'I'm as good as you'" is that it induces "'him to enthrone at the centre of his life a good solid, resounding lie.'" Screwtape adds:

"No man who says *I'm as good as you* believes it. He would not say it if he did. The St. Bernard never says it to the toy dog, nor the scholar to the dunce, nor the employable to the bum, nor the pretty woman to the plain. The claim to equality, outside the strictly political field, is made only by those who feel themselves in some way inferior. What it expresses is precisely the itching, smarting, writhing awareness of an inferiority which the patient refuses to accept.

"And therefore resents. Yes, and therefore resents every kind of superiority in others; denigrates it, wishes its annihilation."[17]

Ledue represents a variation on C. S. Lewis' theme. It is hard to imagine Ledue saying to Doremus Jessup or anyone else, "I'm as good as you." Ledue more likely sees himself as better than Jessup and most other people with whom he comes in contact. If he sees himself as better than others then his relatively low social and economic position would make him itch, smart, and writhe even more. Although Ledue would not likely say "I'm as good as you," the underlying psychology of his envy and resentment is democratic in form, and is best understood in light of the passages from Tocqueville and C. S. Lewis that I have cited.[18] C. S. Lewis notes, through Screwtape, that the "I'm as good as you" phenomenon is not new. "Under the name of Envy it has been known to the humans for thousands of years." What the democratic era did was give it a new name and make it respectable. In the past, "those who were aware of feeling [envy] felt it with shame; those who were not gave it no quarter in others. The delightful novelty of the present situation is that you can sanction it—make it respectable and even laudable—by the incantation of the word *democracy*."[19]

Fascist and communist movements, while not democratic, build on the pathologies of democratic times and manipulate those pathologies to their own ends. Thus, it is that Tocqueville can see how the democratic era can lead to tyranny. Tocqueville recognizes that democratic peoples love freedom, but if there exists a tension between freedom and equality they will choose equality. According to Tocqueville, democratic peoples "want equality in freedom, and if they cannot have that, they still want equality in slavery. They will put up with poverty, servitude, and barbarism, but they will not endure aristocracy." To Shad Ledue, Doremus Jessup and family represented a form of aristocracy. Anybody who was better off than Ledue would represent aristocracy. For Ledue, any aristocracy that did not include him would be, by definition, a fraudulent aristocracy, an aristocracy of showoffs. Most galling to Ledue is that these "aristocrats" were not entitled to what they had, or, at least, they were not entitled to have more than Ledue or to have the things that Ledue wanted but did not have. It is, therefore, only just that such people be put in their place. Ledue would do whatever was necessary and whatever was in his power to put them in their place, whether this would take the form of designing petty annoyances to inconvenience them, or to speak contemptuously to and of them, or to send them to concentration camps. Ledue would not see himself as a democratic man and his interest in equality would end once he had the social and economic position to which he thought he was entitled. He is, nevertheless, a democratic man in the sense understood by Plato, Aristotle, Tocqueville and C. S. Lewis, in the sense that his soul reflects the deepest pathological passion of the democratic age. And Sinclair Lewis did a masterful job of portraying the ugliness and danger of that soul.

Notes

1. Robert Cantwell, "Sinclair Lewis," in Mark Schorer, ed., *Sinclair Lewis: A Collection of Critical Essays* (Englewood Cliff, N.J.: Prentice-Hall, Inc., 1962), 111. The Cantwell essay was originally published in 1937 in Malcolm Cowley, ed., *After the Genteel Tradition*.

2. Mark Schorer, *Sinclair Lewis: An American Life* (New York: McGraw-Hill, 1961), 813.

3. Walter Lippmann, "Sinclair Lewis," in Schorer, *Sinclair Lewis: A Collection of Critical Essays*, 93. The Lippmann essay was originally published in 1927 in a volume titled *Men of Destiny*.

4. Schorer, *Sinclair Lewis: An American Life*, 813.

5. Cantwell, "Sinclair Lewis," 118.

6. While the critical evaluation of Lewis is that he went into artistic decline following the Nobel Prize award, he would, nevertheless, enjoy even greater commercial success in the 1930s and 1940s than he had in the 1920s. *It Can't Happen Here* would be the best seller of Lewis' career to that point. The 1947 novel, *Kingsblood Royal*, would be the best seller of Lewis' career. *It Can't Happen Here* is one of the eight Lewis novels remaining in print. In retrospect, *It Can't Happen Here* and the first post-Nobel Prize novel, *Ann Vickers* (also still in print), are not all that far an artistic drop from Lewis' most acclaimed work.

7. Schorer, *Sinclair Lewis: An American Life*, 610.

8. Schorer, *Sinclair Lewis: An American Life*. In Schorer's rendering Ledue manages to come out Larue.

9. Stephen L. Tanner, "Sinclair Lewis and Fascism," *Studies in the Novel* (Spring, 1990, 22:1).

10. Axel Knoenagel, "The Historical Context of Sinclair Lewis' *It Can't Happen Here*," *Southern Humanities Review* (Summer, 1995, 29:3).

11. Sinclair Lewis, *It Can't Happen Here* (New York: Signet Classic, 1993), p. 32. In a later passage, Lewis sarcastically writes of Ledue: "It was after seven that morning when Doremus came home, and, remarkably enough, Shad Ledue, who was supposed to go to work at seven, was at work at seven. Normally he never left his bachelor shack in Lower Town till ten to eight, but this morning he was on the job, chopping kindling." Oh yes, reflected Doremus—that probably explained it. Kindling-chopping, if practiced early enough, would wake up everyone in the house" (63). All parenthetical references in the text refer to this edition.

12. William Alexander Percy, *Lanterns on the Levee: Recollections of a Planter's Son* (New York: Alfred A. Knopf, 1959 printing of the 1941 original edition), 148.

13. Schorer, *Sinclair Lewis: An American Life*, 610.

14. Alexis de Tocqueville, *Democracy in America*, trans. George Lawrence and ed. J. P. Mayer, two volumes in one (Garden City, N. Y.: Doubleday Anchor Book, 1969), 505. All other quotations from Tocqueville are from this same chapter, "Why Democratic Nations Show a More Ardent and Enduring Love for Equality Than for Liberty."

15. *The Politics of Aristotle*, ed. and trans. Ernest Barker (New York: Oxford University Press, 1958), Book V, Chapter IX, 1310a 14-16.

16. *The Republic of Plato*, trans. Allan Bloom (New York: Basic Books, Inc., 1968), Book VIII 567c.

17. C. S. Lewis, *The Screwtape Letters* (New York: Macmillan Publishing, Co., Inc., 1977), 162-63. Emphasis in the original.

18. See a related and useful consideration of some of these same themes in Paul Eidelberg, *A Discourse on Statesmanship: The Design and Transformation of the American Polity* (Urbana: University of Illinois Press, 1974). See particularly Chapter X, "Economic Laissez-faire and the Degradation of Statesmanship" and pp. 124-131. For all of the strengths of this book, it is flawed by the fact that Eidelberg has a defective understanding of the original design of the American political order. Put another way his discussion of the design of the American polity is not as strong as his discussion of its transformation.

19. Eidelberg, *A Discourse*, 63.

Chapter 13

Natural Right, Conventional Right, and Setting Things Aright: Joseph Conrad's "The Secret Sharer"

Michael Platt

> *It is only the young who are confronted by such clear issues.*
> *— "The Secret Sharer"*

Joseph Conrad's "The Secret Sharer" introduces us to a young man meeting his first complete responsibility in life and in circumstances of novelty and solitude, for this young captain is new to his ship and its sailors and can, being the captain, have no friend to share his thoughts with. He is then like a teacher meeting his first class, but without any fellow teachers nearby, or like an orphaned oldest child left with the duty to rear his brothers and sisters, or like an entrepreneur starting his own business.

Ill at ease, unsure of himself, the very first evening of his command, Conrad's young captain gives the veteran crew the night off. Taking the watch himself, he suddenly sees right beside the ship in the water a fugitive and against all duty, the young captain not only lets the fugitive swimmer aboard but, upon hearing the man's story, hides him in his own cabin. According to the man (named Leggatt), he, though only the chief mate, saved his ship in a storm by felling an habitually malingering, malevolent sailor, and yet his captain clapped him in irons for later capital trial on shore. To escape that inevitable sentence, he was willing to swim miles in dangerous waters, would again, and would accept lifelong exile.

To appreciate how Conrad's young captain reconciles his admiration for Leggatt's courageous good deed with its bloody injustice, how he remains true to nature and to convention, to the sea and to the land—to appreciate all that this compact, rich short story has to teach, you would best read it first to the end. Meanwhile, this chapter poses the most profound issue the story treats and then the most personal, which is also the most political in our century filled with fugitives.

Is it sometimes naturally right that natural right be violated by conventional right? That the exception submit to the rule? That the noble bow to the mediocre? And that the just suffer?

The beasts, who are natural, do not need to ask such questions; neither the distinction nor the things distinguished are intelligible to them; and the intelligent gods, who are naturally right, they do not care about such questions, unless they should become human.

We humans, we seldom just ones, long for justice. Our hearts long for justice for ourselves, our souls want it for others as well, and our minds would be deeply pleased to discover it in the fundamental order of the whole. Yet all this is hard. To be sure, often what is just is clear and the hard part is to do it. But sometimes what is just is hard even to see.[1] Should the small boy receive the small coat that fits him, rather than the large boy to whom it belongs by inheritance, by gift, or by purchase? After a conquest, migration, or settlement how many years have to pass to make a land into a homeland? More generally, what is the relation of justice and law? Is what is just by nature also what is right by convention? Most of the time? Some time? Seldom? Does the truth about justice ever accord with opinion about it, even the best? And if and when justice and opinion are not in accord, how should a just man act? How should a just man act in an unjust regime? A philosopher in a city?

Many are the answers. Most profound are those of Plato and Aristotle, of Thomas, and of Machiavelli and the train of his captains.[2]

Among the poets who have addressed such questions is Joseph Conrad. In his fine story "The Secret Sharer,"[3] the young Captain, having erred at first, eventually satisfies, rather well I think, the conflicting claims of natural right and conventional right. In doing so, he learns much about himself, about justice, and about statesmanship. However, because Conrad's story gives, as poetry does, such intelligent support to conflicting views, readers must think things through, perhaps even philosophize, before they can arrive at Conrad's teaching. Thus, this story makes a fine beginning for students of justice, of statesmanship, and for teachers.[4]

Truth

Why are we being told the story of "The Secret Sharer"? Presumably for our sake. We may benefit from it, especially if we are young. Will the teller benefit too? If he has never told it before, perhaps he will now discover its full meaning by telling it, as Pierre and Natasha do in *War and Peace*, for truth strengthens by appearing in a story. It is no wonder that statesmen often write memoirs, not just to serve their country, their cause or themselves, but, some at least, for self-knowledge, as Tocqueville wrote his *Recollections*, the purity of his motive, being protected by writing it for no living human being (not even Beaumont), or even soon to be living one, just for himself alone. He sought self-knowledge in solitude. Is that the best way? Perhaps by speaking to a listener, a friend, or potential friend, Conrad's narrator is seeking such self-knowledge.[5] And if we are the same age as the narrator, then perhaps we, as we approach the end of the long gauntlet of life, will have the pleasure of finding someone with the same understanding of the things that matter. It would be good if the speech of old men, even unto garrulity, benefited young men.[6] And young men who are too impatient to listen to advice will sometimes listen to a story.[7]

There is a special clarity in stories. In them the vistas do not trail off into infinity; within their borders there is everything we need to know; in "history" you might always learn something else that might cause you to revise your view. Those who participate in a great war know some things; as Coolidge said of the Great War "What the end of the four years of carnage meant those who remember it will never forget and those who do not can never be told." Yet the participants do not know some other things, for example what the enemy was planning each year, which had they know it at the time, they would have done differently and won; and those who come fifty years later, who can read all the memoirs, on both sides, get to know even more, things neither side knew about their own side; but all these after-livers do not know some things the participants knew all too well; and even the "historians" who have finished their books, do not know what is still in the files, or attics, or secret memoirs, or code books, that may still emerge, or may not. In "history" the vistas pass off to infinity on all sides. Thus, by fixing the facts, and excluding infinity, poetry can put forward moral questions more cleanly, more starkly and yet also more subtly and richly, and thus more philosophicly.

If stories are more philosophical than histories, they are so by being more personal as well, and thus more the cause of self-examination. (Self-knowledge and knowledge of the whole proceed together, as Socrates was the first to learn.) Thus, this story by Conrad, "The Secret Sharer," asks every reader a personal question. What would you do if a man arrived in the dark of night at your door? What if he were naked, exhausted, and probably pursued? Would you invite him in immediately? Invite him in first and only later hear his story? Or would you insist on his story first and be ready to turn him over to his pursuers? And if his story included killing a man, would you believe his explanation of it? And even if you did, would you then hide him from the authorities on his trail? Or would you instead let the authorities and institutions take over? In our century a truly terrible number of persons have had to face such questions, from a suppliant at the door, but no century can be without them. We humans get in trouble, need help, and sometimes must ask for it from strangers in situations so urgent that not much examination is possible.[8] How will it be decided? By a look in the eye, a chance connection, a slight mistake, an intuition of trust, a sweeping predilection, or a sweeping prejudice.[9]

Veracity

Just as with *Hamlet* we see everything through the eyes of the young prince, so in "The Secret Sharer" we know everything through the young captain. Yet there is more than perspective to secure our trust. The story of the young captain is told by the older man he became during his youthful first command. Stepping on board, that young man "suddenly . . . rejoiced in the great security of the sea as compared with the unrest of the land, in my choice of that untempted life presenting no disquieting problems, invested with an elementary moral beauty by the absolute straightforwardness of its appeal and by the singleness of its purpose." But the older man, now telling his story, knows "it is only the young who are ever confronted by such clear issues."[10] When a self-critical man tells a story of his youth we are not inclined to doubt it.

All Conrad's art makes us fall in with the young captain's immediate, intuitive identification with the unknown swimmer in the water, fall in naturally and easily; in truth, uncritically. Our youth, like his, makes us side with a virtuous man who killed a vicious man. His sense of the mediocrity of his crew inclines us to share his delight in Leggatt's presence. "Who would I look forward to talking to on such a long voyage ahead?" we may ask ourselves. To the red whiskeradoded chief mate ready to waste hours wondering how a scorpion got on board? Perish the thought! Everything is designed by Conrad to make us side with the Captain siding with Leggatt—our unsureness about ourselves, our keen desire to find a friend, and the clear high standards we youths exult in, that we judge everything by, and hope to live up to in the lives before us.

Thus, we never doubt his story and we never doubt Leggatt's story. Not really. Initially perhaps a bit—and if we later question his conduct, still we do not question the veracity of his story. On only one point may we have a doubt: whether it was the captain of the *Sephora* or Leggatt who gave the order to put up the reefed foresail that saved the ship. However, meeting captain Archbold of the *Sephora* will shortly convince us he never gave that order. He, the captain, seeking the fugitive, with all the resources of authority, and country, and even civilization backing him, shows himself weaker than the lone fugitive hunched in a corner of that tiny cabin, listening without agitation, to his dogged pursuer. We too, or the youth in us, side with Leggatt, just as the young captain does.

Conrad knows that no captain, no man in command, no prince can enjoy friendship with those he rules. Every prince is an island. But the young captain didn't know this and the mature narrator hides it from us, in order to lure us into the discovery of it, and much more.

Justice versus Law

Thus, despite all that inclines us to side with the young captain taking the side of Leggatt, we must ask, as Conrad intends us to: Was what Leggatt did just? Was it good? Was it the best thing to do? Might he have done better? Been more just? Found a way to save the ship and not kill the man? (And as we ask these questions about Leggatt's conduct, we are on our way to asking the general and permanent questions the story provokes: What is justice? What is good? What shall we do? And: how shall we live?)

First, we must ascertain the facts in the case. In a storm, chief mate Leggatt killed a man. When the man resisted his authority, Leggatt knocked him down with a blow, and when the man then came at him just as a terrible wave descended, Leggatt locked his hands on his neck. And when that great wave passed, the two were found together, Leggatt's hands still on his neck, squeezing, tight, the man's face black and his tongue hanging out hideously, and then Leggatt was put in the brig to stand trial later, back in England.

The incident was not isolated. Leggatt had joined a ship accustomed to lax discipline. Captain Archbold had his wife on board. Probably, from time to time, he was, as Leggatt claims, drunk. When not drunk, he was, anyway, habitually weak. The crew was used to this weakness. They must have resented any effort of Leggatt to introduce good discipline. No wonder they united against him later. In the storm itself, they were just as reluctant to do what needed to be done as they ever had been. The man Leggatt killed was more reluctant, and not only reluctant. He was not only shiftless; he was not only a malcontent. He was a rebel, the kind of man who "knows all about his rights and nothing about his duties."[11] This rebel already had a following among the crew. Worse, he was supported by the captain who has never reprimanded his malingering men nor punished any of his fomenting crew, who, in short, had not exercised proper authority. If at some earlier time, Leggatt had asked Captain Archbold to confront the rebel, he might have said, in the idiom of our time, "Oh, we have to have a spirit of community here. He's a sensitive fellow. And, you know, we have to watch out for a suit, too." And then sighed, "Oh, if only everybody would just be nice to each other!"[12] As it happens, in the storm, Leggatt rids the ship of a poison apple, delicious to an infected crew, and kept by a negligent captain. "Lak of Steadfastnesse," as Chaucer said.

Still, did Leggatt act justly? Of course, as chief mate he was not called to reform the ship. It was not his duty to do what the captain would not do; unless the captain had assured him he wished to restore discipline and that he would back his efforts to do so (as Vincentio would Angelo in *Measure for Measure*). Only then would it have been Leggatt's duty to restore discipline. The captain did not intend this: He had not chosen Leggatt as mate, and he surely would not welcome it. Yet, Leggatt may well have tried to restore some discipline anyway. That he was disgusted with the lack of discipline on board is evident. That he and this rebel had clashed before the killing is also evident. Perhaps then Leggatt erred in prudence. Perhaps he tried to move too fast, too far, too much out ahead of his captain, or entirely without his support. Perhaps, like Churchill, he tried to run the whole show from a subordinate position, which when forcing the Dardanelles turned into dying in the trenches before Gallipolli, Churchill confessed was a mistake. If it fails, you get all the blame, and yet you had not enough in your power to make success all depend on you.

Nevertheless, although Leggatt probably made such mistakes, one cannot say that in that storm he erred. Then survival demanded reformation. Then survival required heroism. Then survival called for the best man to rule.

In a storm, virtue shines. In a storm, a mariner shows his stuff, and in a great storm, the great mariner shows it greatly, as he could not in any thing less. And in a storm, he who can by his art calm the winds, or by his art run safely before the wind, also rules. His excellence makes him the ruler.[13] Moreover, in a storm, the best want to rule (contra Plato). And, most important, in such a storm, the best man rules justly. What is good for him is good for all others.

In a storm, in a storm that will capsize the ship and drown all those whose life depends on it, Leggatt issues the order, gets the sail up, and saves the ship. He saved twenty-four or so lives; and, the man not saved, the man strangled, was resisting the man who was saving the ship. The good, the common good, the good that includes each, is superior to the just, certainly to the just as understood as mere fairness, and perhaps to justice in any sense. Certainly to any law. *Salus publica, suprema lex.*[14]

But wait. The sail, which did save the ship, was already up when Leggatt locks his hands on the man's throat. The order had been given, the crucial thing had been done, safety was in sight. Nothing more needed to be done. So, couldn't Leggatt have merely knocked the man down again as he had already done once? Did he need to strangle him? A second blow would have served well enough for reproof. And why did Leggatt not call upon the crew to hold the rebel and put him in the brig? Probably in the midst of the storm, and just at that terrible moment, with that great wave descending, the latter was not possible. And then again, the man was making for Leggatt, making for him, to get him, perhaps to kill him. Was it not self-defense then? Strangle or be strangled? However, since neither Leggatt nor the young captain make this defense, we must set it aside.

Thus we must face the choice starkly and reply like this: if you say Leggatt should have merely struck a second blow, you do not understand storms and you do not understand the spirit of the singular man capable of overcoming one. It is no wonder that Leggatt went for the neck the second time. There was a great force, a great force for good, mighty in him at that moment. He and he alone was capable of making the men obey the order that they, quaking and undisciplined as they were, had not the stuff to leap to by themselves, nor even the stuff to obey an order to do so, except that Leggatt give it. At such moments a good man may do with an evil one standing in the way what he wishes. It seems that at such times virtue is beyond good and evil, certainly beyond good and evil as the land and the law are likely to understand them. That mutinous sailor was killed in a fit of duty. And nature expects every man to do his duty.

Statesmanship

Ah, but would not the truly virtuous man have acted sooner, with foresight, with patience, with cunning, and long before the storm arose? Leggatt knew the man was a bad apple. Could he not have lured him into some false step, one so egregious that it left him without the support of Captain Archbold and even without the support of his fellow crew members, a step so false that his fellow crew members were for once sore at him, perhaps because he was claiming something for himself alone that they wanted for themselves as well—and thus a false step so unsupported that not even the weak Captain would shield the man? To foresee evil way off in the distance, over the horizon, like an AWAC pilot, and then to do away with it even before it is visible to others—that is heroic prudence. That is the achievement of a great statesman. And clearly, Leggatt did not have such prudence.

Still, that is heroic virtue. Must one require it of all who act from natural right? Leggatt was not the captain. It is not easy to rule from the second position, especially when all aboard are used to ease, to being slack, and to having things overlooked. Maybe a DeGaulle, or a Churchill, or a Lincoln could have done so. Still, would it be just to punish Leggatt for not having the far-seeing prudence of the greatest statesmen? In Leggatt, I suppose we are talking about a lesser man—but make no mistake—he is a worthy man.

Moreover, those great men actually did not get into a position to rule until the storm was pelting everyone, flooding the plains, and at last obvious even to houseless fools. Though they tried, they were not able to head off the gathering storm. Churchill did not convince Hitler to choose peace;[15] he did not convince his party to stay vigilant, his nation to stay armed, to resist each small aggression, and, when they did not, to expect more, and more, and more. DeGaulle did not convince Petain about tanks, he did not convince the politicians of the Third Republic to establish a professional army capable of acting beyond a fixed defensive line, and later he did not convince Premier Reynaud to fight on outside metropolitan France. Lincoln did not convince his fellow countrymen to maintain the Missouri Compromise, to overturn Taney's declaration that Dred Scott was no man, and to reject Douglas and his popular sovereignty. Only by being elected did Lincoln begin to achieve these roll-backs, and then hasty South Carolina led others into secession. And then a war came, whose bloody length required the nation to rededicate itself to its founding principles. The tasks of these three were great but not the same. Churchill's task was hard: to save a nation from slavery and extinction (or capitulation, which would have led to extinction). DeGaulle's task was harder, to lead a nation from defeat and capitulation to victory and then to give it a new regime, capable of healing its 150-year-old open wound. Lincoln's task was hardest: to risk his nation's extinction in a war, which he partly provoked—at least invited—that the nation might return to its principles. All who succeeded did so greatly, but none did so without the storm of war. If they, great as they were, did not head off such evils earlier in peace, then perhaps Leggatt can be excused for not doing so too.

Thus, in judging Leggatt, our standard should not be the farest-seeing statesmanship. We may wish he had somehow introduced discipline before the storm, but we cannot insist that he have done so to receive our measured praise, or our exoneration. We must merely ask whether what he did in the storm was just. Was Leggatt just? Did he do right?

It is a hard question. Perhaps there are situations in which only heroic virtue "escapes whipping," where it is better to do nothing than to do something middling. And thus where it is better to refuse subordinate command, as T. E. Lawrence did after his great desert exploit, knowing that intermediate command will inevitably require you to pass on injustice from your superiors to your subordinates.

Still, we cannot ignore the truth. A whole crew, a whole college, and even a whole nation, can corrupt. We do not want to say, "Unless you are the supreme ruler you should stand aside, keep quiet, seek shelter," let alone, "Go along, get along." Churchill, DeGaulle, and Lincoln did not. Nor do we want to say "Only success is worthy." Say that, say that no risk, or great risk, should be taken and you go against the long history of man, both the successes that would not have been a success without risk, and the noble failures, too.[16]

Say "Only success is worthy" and you declare yourself indifferent to virtue, indifferent to its beauty. After all, only in grave situations, in situations where failure is probable, does virtue really shine. In that storm, Leggatt radiated that brightness. In truth, virtue is what stands out in life. It alone can satisfy the man who wants to respect himself, it alone is noble, Every human being worthy of the name glories in it, wants it to rule, longs for natural right. Moreover, virtue alone is capable of reviving a crew, an institution, or a nation. Every army in flight that ever turned and fought, says Aristotle, did so because first one soldier stood, and then another, and then another.[17] Ask Rosa Parks.

Yet on the other side, we do not want to put aside convention, consent, and law with juries, even though these juries be "land dwellers." Such juries may well never face, and thus never understand Nature, the stern teacher, who sends storms to test men and to perfect a few. Why? Is it because often we are among such as cannot prevail in a storm? Are like the crew of Leggatt's ship the *Sephora*? Maybe. Is that our reason for not wanting to do without convention and law? Partly. Yes, we are like that crew. (Such Leggatt acknowledges, too, when he says they were not to be much blamed for being terrified by that storm.) Every hero is also a human, and certainly the law, in its regularity, in its impartiality, in its complication, its thickness, and even in its obscurity, and also in its process, the very slowness of it, offers protection.

Yet, there is another justification, not based on our vice or on our weakness, but on our human condition (including its weakness). Although we are not like others, we recognize that human societies cannot but exist on a basis that dilutes natural right. The truths upon which any society can be founded will always, even the best, have a strong residue of opinion in their make-up—we are lucky if these "truths" are noble opinions, noble lies, rather than base ones. We are not sovereign, independent, free, not enough. We need others and therefore must needs, in some measure, accommodate ourselves to them. We must submit to the law.

There is a higher supporting justification as well: we think it noble to treat human beings better than they deserve. A noble man does not insist others be as good as himself. The hero who requires others to be heroic is less heroic thereby. As it turns out, Leggatt is made of such stuff. Thus, he acknowledges that that storm was simply terrible. He felt all the apprehension that in others was unheroic. Though he did not succumb to it, he felt it, and feeling it, he does not blame to crew. He was a hero. The storm was terrible. Both are true. Thus also, upon hearing Captain Archbold say that he gave the order to set the reef foresail, Leggatt does not insist the man lies, only that he may now really believe he gave the order.

Whether Leggatt is made of the greater stuff, the stuff of charity, that not only does not require others to be heroes, but dedicates itself to their good we may doubt. One way to express that dedication would have been to have faced trial. But Leggatt is a young man and, who knows, he may find, in exile, a situation that calls such virtue out of him. And the young captain is also young and may do better next time.[18]

Torn between the Twain

What is the disposition of our young captain, who is telling the story, toward all this? Clearly, at first, even before Leggatt appeared, he felt he might not meet the test of sovereign command. Though having some sea experience, he has never commanded a ship. Never before has he been responsible for everything in his sight. This command has come to him suddenly. He has not had time to think much, imagine much, or foresee much. He does not know the ship, he does not know the men, and, in truth, he does not know himself. Although none of his crew knows himself—can a man really know himself if he has never had the responsibility of command?—they do "know" each other. They have been together. They are used to each other. They "know" the ship. He is younger than all but one of them. He and he alone is a stranger.

Right off the young captain commits an error. Aware of his inferiority to the crew, above all of his uncertainty, he excuses all hands from the night watch. It is a mistake, and he realizes it right away, with chagrin. Going easy on the crew, violating the custom of their labor, will just make them think him strange or, worse, weak.

As a consequence of this mistake, the ladder is there for the nearly exhausted Leggatt to cling to. Thus, without the imprudence of our captain, Leggatt wouldn't be there. There he is, and without the slightest hesitation, our captain takes him in. ("Because it was he, because it was I," as old Montaigne said of his instant, exalted friendship with Étienne de La Boétie.[19]) There is no question, no doubt, just immediate intuition, immediate trust, never shaken conviction, and steadfast loyalty. And yet there is agony. From the moment the captain invites Leggatt up the ladder, he is a divided man.[20]

The agony begins immediately, it never lets up, not until it teaches our captain. First, it teaches him to be on guard, alert—"hyper-alert." It teaches him to be foresighted, too—"hyper-foresighted." He has to think how to prevent discovery. He must hide Leggatt, he must head off potential discoveries, and he must hide the agitation that this creates in himself. He must be more than usually alert and more than usually self-controlled. And he must do so without compromising his authority even further.

Ah, but what is Authority? That too is something he learns about. Authority is something men see in another, and that the "authority" knows is something in them, not him, which he must encourage, even cause, in them, but which he did not create, just as Shakespeare's Henry V did not create the "ceremony" that cannot comfort him for the solitude it imposes on all monarchs. What could be more absolute than the authority of a ship's captain, and yet how limited! He can order anything, and yet he dares not lock his cabin door. He, his soul, is bound to Leggatt, his secret sharer, and he, his office, is bound by the opinions of his crew. The low does in some measure control the higher.

Later the young captain must plan more fully. He must anticipate and he must prepare, not just react. Thus, he must expect the captain of the *Sephora* to come searching, he must anticipate his questions, and he must prepare answers. By his over-polite manner, by his feigned deafness, and by his "showing off" his ship, our young captain is able to put off this obstinate yet spiritless man—but only barely. One direct question would have discovered everything. Being young, our captain is not used to lying for the good. (That a lie might be required to prevent natural right from destroying conventional right and that a lie might be required to prevent conventional right from destroying natural right, he has no basis as yet for even supposing.)

Does our young captain learn more than to lie? Yes, but not for a while. He nearly breaks under the strain. Always he is thinking of two things at once, anticipating discovery with anxiety, watching his authority with his crew melt away. He is powerless to stem it, thinking of Leggatt, his double, his better self, the personal incarnation of the virtues he looks up to and hopes he has. It is nearly unbearable. Being true to Leggatt and to his command, true to natural right and to conventional right, is almost more than he can bear. He wonders if he is going mad and admires Leggatt's self-mastery. Left to himself the young captain would continue this intolerable situation, which is bound to lead to eventual discovery, and to the loss of Leggatt's life and his own career, the only one he knows himself suited for. And it is not he who hits upon a solution.

Justice and Law

How might justice and law, natural and conventional right be united? Only when the philosophers are elected by the people, or when they come to command absolute power over nature and thus men, will natural and conventional right be united. As to the first, it is very unlikely; only in dire straits will a people elect even a statesman such as Churchill and as soon as they are breathing easy again, they will caste him aside. As to the second, it would mean the mastery of nature, such as Shakespeare's Prospero enjoys over the seas and winds, and his rival Bacon schemed for. Both lie outside the horizon of Conrad's story. No one is going to elect Leggatt captain and the minute it is known that the young captain is harboring him there will be a mutiny. And neither of these friends has the power to calm or raise the winds like Prospero, to power the ship like Homer's Phaiakians, or to command the sea and Leviathan in it. However, if no unity of justice and law is on the horizon, still perhaps some good relation of justice and law, short of unity, may be attained.

It is Leggatt who understands the discontinuity of nature and law. Perhaps he always did, or perhaps he only came to it in the long inactive time on the *Sephora* after his arrest. Just after the killing, he seems to consider only how right he was, but gradually he seems to recognize some right on the other side. Although he has some contempt for landlubbers and juries, he also has some care for them, including his parson father. Thus, Leggatt understands, in some measure, or comes to understand, that both nature and law have a claim on a man. And that if a man cannot unite them or harmonize them, then he must suffer their discontinuity.

Thus, Leggatt does not ask Captain Archbold to let him escape when they reach port, only to escape where he will have to risk his life swimming. In other words, he accepts such hardships and accidents as just punishment for his just deed. Yes, his deed in the storm was just, but it is also just that he suffer for it. He killed a man. True, he saved the ship; true, the man was bad and the cause of badness in others. But no society, or at least no democratic society, can permit individuals to make such judgments and not be judged by their peers. Thus, Leggatt never says, as we may say for him, that he acted justly in the storm, or that a land jury that found him guilty would be unjust. He says only that they are incompetent to really judge. It is enough that a society accords a ship's captain nearly dictatorial powers. To a mate, even a chief mate, however just he act, it cannot do more. Leggatt knows this and he accepts it. Thus he is willing, without complaint, without rancor or inward moral resistance, to accept as a price for his just deed, exile and all its enduring ills, and also the chance that he drown and never make it to exile.

Does Conrad think that such violent deeds as Leggatt's are what found societies, but that no society can acknowledge such a beginning of morality in immorality? That a lie will always create conflict between the foundation of a society and the self-respect it needs to continue after its founding? That such a lie must never be unmasked? And does Conrad write accordingly, exposing the truth to a few and yet covering it from all others? If Conrad thinks so, he gives no hint. Although his story is about saving a society, not founding one, it would have been easy to make a single comparison of the virtue in Leggatt to that in some founder, such as Moses, Cyrus, Romulus, Theseus, and the like. Conrad also differs from Plato and from the Gospels. For his just crime Leggatt is not to suffer death, as Socrates argues he should in the *Crito*, nor is he to suffer death as Christ, by his suffering the Cross, shows He should. Leggatt is, instead, to suffer exile. Exile if he, a proud swimmer, can make it. Trial by suffering is a good way to settle the conflicting claims of natural right and conventional right, justice by sea and justice by land, as they meet in him through his deed, which was both just and a murder.[21]

It is naturally right that natural right suffer for conventional right. As Nietzsche said, the exception must not wish to become the rule.[22] All the noble share this secret. Leggatt discovers it and gradually teaches it to the young captain. This secret is what they share most.

Prudence and Luck

It is Leggatt who first finds a way to be true to both natural and conventional right. Leggatt knows that our young captain is willing to keep him hidden virtually forever, certainly as long as it takes to reach some port where his undetected disappearance might gain him freedom. When first sheltered, Leggatt may hope for such a deliverance, for Singapore is only a week of normal sailing away. Leggatt is, of course, grateful to his benefactor, the captain, but more is required. Since the killing, the young captain is the only human being who has helped and sheltered Leggatt, and the only one who has "understood" him. All that time before, Leggatt had been alone; alone and surrounded by opposition on every side, he had to insist on the truth, and while holding tight to it, not lose the qualifications and conditions intrinsic to that truth. Now, however, there is something new. Leggatt has a friend. And just as that proudest and loneliest of heroes, Achilleus, the superhuman, is connected to humanity, and to its laws, by his friend, Patroklus, so is Leggatt connected by his friend. It is all very well, when truly alone, to insist 'I am subject to no human judge and jury. Only God can try me, as he did Cain.' But what if your friend will suffer thereby? Leggatt comes to care for his friend; he sees him suffering more anxiety than he does; and he does not want him to suffer much more of this torture. So Leggatt insists he cannot stay on board until he can be smuggled ashore in safety; he insists that he must soon cast off into the sea, with only the chance to swim to some distant shore.

It is then that the two friends find a way to satisfy the two obligations pulling the young captain apart (and through him Leggatt, too). Acknowledging the rightness of Leggatt's choice, the young captain devises a plan to steer his ship close to the Cambodge shore, where Leggatt may swim for it. It is easy to see how this fulfills his obligation to Leggatt, a man he admires, and who thanks him above all for his understanding. Is the course chosen just? Is it just to the ship and its crew? Leggatt's deed was a part of saving a whole ship. Our captain's deed will risk a whole ship. He would not ordinarily steer so close, he says. And, of course, steering the ship in those uncharted waters will make him seem even odder to the crew. However, unlike his earlier eccentricities, this one is stern. It compels the crew to obey. And our captain does take a good pleasure in forcing them to, in reproving them, and in showing a steadiness that he is far from feeling.

Yes, he would not have to pursue this course had he not compromised his authority earlier, even from the beginning, when he took the first watch and later by all his odd shifts to conceal Leggatt. Perhaps we might say, with Thomas Aquinas, if ever you find yourself in a bind, when it seems you cannot but do evil that good come, it is because at some earlier point up the trail you chose wrong. (Does Thomas appreciate that even Christ acted so that he Himself wished He did not have to die? That is, not all His foresight was enough to avoid what he Himself considered a choice with enough evil in it to ask His Father that it not happen—that He not be delivered up to evil, to quote from the prayer He left us.)

Perhaps we might also think of some foresight that the true statesman would have devised and thus not have found himself in such a situation. Maybe so. Assuredly, the torture the statesman will meet with in a purgatory fittingly devised just for him is to recognize how he might have avoided such a situation. As Auden might have said, "Then they will show you how really sage you would have been, how by hitting upon this other way, you would have secured an even greater good, and also without committing a lesser evil, and then you would really have been a statesman."[23] That would be torture indeed, fitted perfectly to the man, to the best in him, to his virtue and his discernment. It would be a perfect torture, because it would measure him by his own highest standard, the one he cares the most for.

Nevertheless, must we not say that given the situation as it is now, there could be no better way to restore the young captain's authority than for him to command the crew to do something they fear, that they do not understand, and that, nonetheless, they will submit to? If the soul of discipline aboard ship is the "exact performance of small things," isn't the soul of duty in a subordinate the performance—without protest—of a big thing you don't understand?

In the end, the course the two friends plan is blessed with success. Conrad arranges this result beautifully, for the hat that our captain gives Leggatt, out of singular sympathy, thinking of the sun beating down upon his friend, proves to be the marker that he needs to steer the ship by. Looking at that hat floating in the water, our captain could have again felt how hard the sun would be on

Leggatt. He doesn't. He thinks of the good of the ship. First given as an expression of his still excessive identification with his friend's plight, the hat becomes the means of the ship's safety, the crew's, and the young captain's ascendancy to command. Only when that hat becomes a marker in the water does the captain get things right and learn the lesson of Leggatt.

Thus, something given out of sympathy becomes the aid to duty. Something given out of a passion enables a virtue. Something given in obligation to Leggatt in recognition of the truth of his action in the storm—becomes the decisive thing in saving the ship. Thus, the captain at once meets the obligation to his ship and to Leggatt. It does not always happen that way. Our mistakes, our excesses, our passions, don't always lead to good, and our divided duties are seldom divided satisfactorily, let alone united in a harmonious success. Failure was nigh to success; the ship might have run aground, it might even have sunk, and then the young captain never would have had another command. In this case, even pity, merely a passion, and one felt in a degree approaching or becoming weakness, tends toward the good, the good of the better man, Leggatt. He first acknowledges that he, though just, deserves punishment, and the good of the younger captain, his student, whose authority over his crew is restored by his holding to such a dangerous—and to his crew so incomprehensible—a course. And things luck out (and are so arranged by Conrad).

Leggatt is a good teacher and the young captain an apt pupil. Both are attentive to the way things are, more exactly to the way things, such as natural right, and conventional right, are. It could have been a tragedy. But that is always true of the situations where the virtues of the statesman prevail. And sometimes the two, tragedy and statesmanship, are so close, they nearly coincide, as for example the result of World War II, which Churchill entitled *Triumph and Tragedy*. This is not so in this Conrad story, because Conrad wished to teach something about natural right and conventional right, virtue and suffering, justice and law. He wished to teach that sometimes it is naturally right that natural right be violated by conventional right, that the exception sometime submit to the rule, that the noble sometime bow to the mediocre, and that the just sometime suffer.

Of course, it is the exceptional man who must decide when that "sometime" is. Since the distinction is invisible to most, to the unexceptional, they cannot decide at all. Only the exceptional can choose such nobility, which is a choice, in one sense, against himself; in another sense, for himself utterly. The tragedy underlying that nobility could not be spoken of in any other way than in a story. In any other mode it would pit natural and conventional right directly and publicly against each other; it would damage both, it would contradict itself, and it would show a want of sagacity in the author. Conrad's wonderful "Secret Sharer" allows us to understand why of all modern writers, since Shakespeare, he is most fit to rule a country.[24]

Notes

1. On our twofold relation to the good, see my "The Good, the Great, and the Small," based on the first precept of law, according to Aquinas (*Su. Th.* I-II, Q 94, a. 2, c):"The good is to be done, and followed, and evils shunned" in *Faith and Reason* Vol. XXIII, nos. 3-4 (1997-98), pp. 323-354.

2. For a succinct survey, see Leo Strauss, *Natural Right and History* (Chicago: Univ. of Chicago Press, 1953), Chapters IV especially, which treats the relation of natural right and natural law, wisdom and law, purposes and laws, and the prudential question of when to follow the rule and when to allow the exception, the balance in Machiavelli tilted to the founding exception versus the balance the other way in Aristotle, and in Thomas.

3. I have used the old paperback edition of Albert J. Guerard (New York: Signet, 1950), but there are so many editions, the text is stable, and the tale is so short that page references would not help the reader; Bruce Harkness' *Conrad's Secret Sharer and the Critics* (Belmont, California: Wadsworth, 1962) includes the articles in *The Times* [of London] of 5 July and 4 August of 1882 reporting events on the *Cutty Sark* that are the source for the tale and pages from an alternate account published after Conrad's death; the man the Leggatt figure killed was black and there was no storm; the mate escaped and got a new position immediately; Captain Wallace had let him escape, the crew knew it, and Wallace committed suicide four days later; some years later the mate was sentenced to hard labor, after which he worked his way up to an Atlantic command, lived to a ripe old age, and could have read "The Secret Sharer."

4. If a first class meeting is long enough to read this story aloud, the natural course of the following discussion, driven by the students, will arrive at the questions statesmen face and political philosophers ponder.

5. When Jesse Conrad read the story, she chided Joseph, "You never told me that," and he chuckled, "It's pure fiction." See her *Joseph Conrad and His Circle* (1935), p. 77.

6. I once knew a young man beginning to teach. In the week before his first classes, ones he was wholly responsible for, he read this story and one other, by Lionel Trilling, about teaching. Yet reading them did not prevent him from erring a few years later, by giving a grade to a remarkable student solely on the basis of his promise of later work. Why did he do this? Early on, this young teacher had discovered that time spent in class with students is almost always more fruitful than time spent with colleagues. This, of course, makes your best students much more dear to you than colleagues. How could it not? You and your students are students of the same things, as colleagues seldom are in the modern college with its specialized, coreless curriculum. Nevertheless, he later came to see, and not because this student failed to turn in the promised work, that nothing justifies such a violation of conventional right, certainly not the good of that outstanding student, which would have been better served by receiving the "failure" his tardiness deserved.

7. Young nations too, such as America; "I have not given up all hope that human beings and nations may be able . . . to learn from the experience of other people," writes Solzhenitsyn in the Foreword to the abridgement for English-speaking readers he permitted of the *Gulag Archipelago: 1918-1956* by Edward Ericson (New York: Harper, 1985).

8. It is impossible to read this story (or any like it) without examining oneself. All stories provoke parallel thoughts. Must I give mine? Here is a bit: from the first morning I would have made sure the Steward brought two pots of coffee. My friends would suspect nothing, and that crew would just count it another eccentricity, as perhaps one's friends already do. As to other parallels, to each his own self-examination.

9. For such, see *The Rescuers* ed. Gay Block and Malka Drucker (New York: Holmes and Meier, 1992).

10. For some reason Conrad never tells us the name of his young captain. To be sure, his narrator treats us as already intimate, a friend, a nephew, or protege. But Conrad could have found a way around that, as he does by having his Marlow introduced before he tells the tale of Kurtz in the Congo. (Is this too Marlow, but unnamed?) Maybe Conrad wanted to make it difficult for us to refer to the story, to always be saying "the

young captain," just to remind us how hard it is to speak the truth so deeply embedded in this story, and according to that truth, so rightly embedded deep. For another nameless young man growing into a statesman, see Owen Wister's *Virginian.*

11. I believe this phrase comes from Conrad's *Nigger of the Narcissus.*

12. For keen reflections on the type, see Montaigne's "Cowardice, The Mother of Cruelty" in his *Essais,* (II, 26) and Tocqueville on soft despotism, in *Democracy in America,* Vol. II, Part 4, Chapter 6. Reading Tocqueville, you would think that agents of soft despotism would be pliant, gentle, or in a word, soft, but today there are despots of softness, enforcers of therapy, energetic deans of frailty, joke police, litigators of victimization, and stern administrators of sensitivity. The spirit is soft, the spread of it gradual, all as Tocqueville foresaw, but the agents are as hard as nails. Good shepherds beware. Some sheep now have teeth.

13. Thus, in the opening scene of *The Tempest,* the nobles, highest by convention and on land, must obey the Boatswain, highest by natural right, on the sea. For more, also on *Laws* 709a-712a, see my "Shakespeare's Apology for Poetry," in *Shakespeare and the Arts: A Collection of Essays from the Ohio Shakespeare Conference—1981,* eds. C. W. Cary and H. S. Limouze (Lanham, Md.: University Press of America, 1982), 231-244. The situation of the *Tempest,* in which one man, Prospero, controls the winds is an exhibition of what the pure natural right solution to the dilemma of "The Secret Sharer" would be; for natural right to rule entirely without dilution of conventional right or consent, it would have to have power over the tempest, power to invoke it, direct it, in other words, the power to command Ariel, that suffering come to each on board according to his crimes or inclinations to crime. Yet this too is limited, as Prospero appreciates, for the mutual affection of his daughter and Ferdinand must be free, and when Antonio will not repent, reform, forgive, Prospero must recognize that it is better to forgive than to destroy him. Moreover, Prospero's last use of the winds, before giving them up, is to get all persons from the mainland back to the mainland, where conventional right, such as hereditary inheritance, will be restored, and Italy will be united by the marriage of his daughter Mirada to Ferdinand (a gentle slap at Machiavelli that).

14. Or, as the American Constitution acknowledges, analogously: "The Privilege of the Writ of Habeas Corpus shall not be suspended, unless when in Cases of Rebellion or Invasion the public Safety may require it." (Article 1, Section 9)

15. A little after Hitler came to power, Churchill wrote a piece, to be found in his *Great Contemporaries* (London: Thornton Butterworth, 1937; rprt. University of Chicago Press) entitled "Hitler and his Choice" in which he praises Hitler for raising the spirits of his nation but tries to dissuade him from continuing along the path indicated by the methods he had so far employed. Cf. *The Gathering Storm,* pp. 304-305 for Hitler's missed chance to meet Churchill and pp. 224-225 for Churchill's later disinclination to meet Hitler.

16. In the early 1980s, fifty Mujahadeen from Afghanistan were brought to Dallas for medical attention. Learning of them, meeting them, realizing that they were seeing only the insides of hospitals and convenience stores, I proposed a trip to the Alamo, to Rep. Dick Armey, whose assistant said, "I know the congressman will be for it, but the first thing we have to think about is insurance." To which I replied, "Let's us Americans have a moment of silence to think about what you just said. If those men at the Alamo had thought of insurance, there would be no Texas. And if two Afghans, brothers, have one pair of shoes, one is always wearing them, looking for a Soviet officer to kill, not thinking about insurance." In the end, the trip did not happen. The man who wanted to drive the donated school bus lacked the proper driver's license. However, before the warriors returned home to fight, I secured for each a pair of small, light, powerful

binoculars, from L. L. Bean. To some potential subscribers, I said "It may save a man's life." To others the fuller truth, "With this a Mujahadeen can hunt a Soviet invader better." One subscriber, he knows who he is, has yet to pay up what he pledged to defend his liberty.

17. That the metaphor comes during Aristotle's discussion of insight (*Posterior Analytics*. II, 19; 100a11-13) is pertinent.

18. Conrad returned to such a situation in *Lord Jim*, which starts with a young idealist abandoning a ship that did not sink as expected and ever after, in the exile of disgrace, seeking a situation to do better, and when he finds it, not doing better, through his idealism; as a student of mine, Amy Bonnette, once said on an exam, "The nation that thinks Jim is a hero is in for trouble." Yet some young men have done better. As a young man, Jim Bridger was persuaded to leave a man for dead; when the man awoke and crawled 60 miles across the prairie, caught up with him, and vilified him, Bridger went on to become the most trustworthy mountain man the West ever saw.

19. Montaigne's celebrated account of friendship and his remarkable friend is in "Of Friendship," Chapter XXVIII in volume I of his *Essais*; for their conspiracy to change the West, see my "Montaigne, Of Friendship, and On Tyranny," in *Freedom Above Servitude: Montaigne, La Boétie, and "On Voluntary Servitude,* ed. David Schaefer, with essays by David Schaefer, Randall Runion, & Daniel Martin (Westport: Greenwood Press, 1998), 31-85.

20. There is a lot of language in the story suggesting that Leggatt is a "double" of the captain; he is, but the "psychological" critics, even the best, such as Albert Guerard (in the preface mentioned above and in his *Conrad the Novelist* [Cambridge: Harvard University Press, 1958]), misapprehend the point; the captain "identified" with Leggatt but he also remained himself; being both, he is divided, painfully so; how to be true to the truth in Leggatt and how to be true to his command is very hard for him.

21. See Isak Dineson's story "Sorrow Acre," for a remarkable example of justice under the Ancien Regime and a justification of it. Another story that by its merits is fit to start a course on Statesmanship is "Paso Por Qui" by Eugene Manlove Rhodes, in which the sheriff (being Pat Garret), the representative of conventional right, recognizes natural right and bows to it. Cf. Dorothy Johnson's "The Man Who Shot Liberty Valance" and Jack Schaefer's *Shane* for the distinction of natural and conventional right embodied in differing characters.

22. *Jenseits von gut und böse*, II, no. 26.

23. As Auden says, "You hope, yes, your books will excuse you, save you from hell: nevertheless, without looking sad, without in any way seeming to blame . . . God may reduce you on Judgment Day to tears of shame, reciting by heart the poems you would have written, had your life been good." From "The Cave of Making," in *About the House* (New York: Random House, 1965), 13; Hannah Arendt uses these telling lines as the epigram to her essay on Bertolt Brecht.

24. Solzhenitsyn might be a candidate. Maybe Jane Austen. I am grateful to my fellow panelists at the APSA convention in Washington in 1996, to Marlo Lewis especially, for asking how the story would go if natural and conventional right were united, and to Will Morrisey for a detailed reading informed by an appreciation of Leo Strauss' remark, to a forgotten nonwriter, "I write, you publish."

Chapter 14

The Beauty of Middle-Class Virtue:
Willa Cather's *O Pioneers!*

James Seaton

> *"Isn't it queer: there are only two or three human stories,*
> *and they go on repeating themselves as fiercely*
> *as if they had never happened before; like the larks in this country,*
> *that have been singing the same five notes over for thousands of years."*
> —Carl Linstrun in O Pioneers!

Willa Cather and "Bourgeois Morality"

In the last decades of the twentieth century, some commentators have argued that bourgeois morality, with its opposition to sex outside of marriage, its elevation of prudence over passion, and its celebration of hard work has no deep roots in human experience but is instead a recent and ephemeral event. Allegedly supported by no cultural text more authoritative than the televised situation comedies of the 1950s, like "Leave it to Beaver" or "Ozzie and Harriet," this "bourgeois morality" was outdated almost immediately by technological innovations such as birth control pills and automation. From this point of view, Willa Cather's fictions can be taken seriously only if one rejects their straightforward affirmations of middle-class moral standards and instead assumes they are written in a kind of code that obliquely champions a lesbian sensibility.[1]

Against this view, novels like Willa Cather's *O Pioneers!* affirm a morality that might be characterized as "bourgeois" or "middle class" is not tantamount to equating their artistic accomplishment or even their moral depth to that of 1950s sitcoms. After all, so-called bourgeois values, stressing the virtues of marriage, family and hard work, have been affirmed by voices whose authority has not depended on Neilsen ratings. The Hebrew authors of the Book of Proverbs taught that sex outside of marriage was not only a sin but a folly, and "whoso committeth adultery with a woman lacketh understanding" (6:32), in the words of King James Version. They emphatically endorsed the work ethic and the rewarding of work, observing with approval that "He becometh poor that dealeth with a slack hand; but the hand of the diligent maketh rich" (10:4). From a very different perspective but one equally distant from twentieth-century America, Aristotle pointed out that the virtues of the middle class were important sources of political stability, since, Aristotle observed, members of the middle class

> do not, like the poor, covet their neighbours' goods; nor do others covet theirs, as the poor covet the goods of the rich; and as they neither plot against others, nor are themselves plotted against, they pass through life safely. . . . Thus it is manifest that the best political community is formed by citizens of the middle class.[2]

Just as some today believe that our putative "postmodernism" renders the past irrelevant, so in the nineteenth century some Americans, including Ralph Waldo Emerson, believed that the new situation of Americans required the renunciation of the authority of both biblical religion and Greek philosophy in favor of "self-reliance," in the hope that, as Emerson put it, "A nation of men will for the first time exist, because each believes himself inspired by the Divine Soul which also inspires all men."[3] Emerson, however, was to be disappointed by the unwillingness of most Americans to see the necessity for a cultural revolution to complement their political revolution. Unlike Emerson, Alexis de Tocqueville was surprised and delighted that Americans combined innovation in politics and technology with adherence to traditional moral principles and religious beliefs. The dominance of middle-class rather than aristocratic attitudes led the new society to emphatically reaffirm Proverbs' celebration of work. Tocqueville noted that "Not only is no dishonor associated with work, but among such peoples it is regarded as positively honorable; the prejudice is for, not against, it."[4] The social equality that Tocqueville found so striking not only encouraged a renewed commitment to the work ethic but also to the sanctity of marriage. Tocqueville observed that

> Certainly of all countries in the world America is the one in which the marriage tie is most respected and where the highest and truest conception of conjugal happiness has been conceived. (268)

Tocqueville thought that such a commitment to traditional morality was especially necessary in a democracy, since he had no answer to his own question: "How could society escape destruction if, when political ties are relaxed, moral ties are not tightened" (271)?

O Pioneers! embodies Willa Cather's own mature awareness that she was most true to herself as an artist when she was most faithful to her origins as a child of the Middle West and the middle class. A comparison to Thomas Mann may illuminate the significance of Cather's acknowledgment. Unlike Willa Cather, Thomas Mann was a child of the city rather than the country, but like her he moved from an early emphasis on the opposition between art and middle-class morality to a recognition of their connections. Mann, who in *Buddenbrooks* and other works plumbed the hypocrisies and anxieties of middle class life, came to see that his fiction was not so much a rejection of middle-class culture as an expression and even an affirmation of what the radicals dismissed as "bourgeois" ideals. He recognized that his own literary achievement depended on the creative tension between "the purely aesthetic impulse" and "the ethical bent," "the perception for the duties of life," which Mann characterizes as "the bourgeois spirit applied to life."[5] Speaking against those who in the 1920s were spreading the news that "the middle class way of life" is "finished, condemned to death, doomed" (xxii), Mann replies that "that way of life is far too closely bound up with the idea of humanity and of all human culture for it ever to be alien, ever to be dispensable, in any humane world" (xxiii).

The moral and political affirmations of Cather's fiction carry all the more weight because they are generally implicit, since Cather refused to take up the role of social prophet and moral teacher. Even in the 1930s, when, as she noted, writers were being "told that their first concern should be to cry out against social injustice," she replied that "industrial life" would have "to work out its own problems" without the assistance of writers. Not that writers, or even philosophers and scientists, had any special wisdom to offer in any case. She herself doubted that if Tolstoi and Goethe and Viollet-le-Duc and Descartes and Sir Isaac Newton were brought together and induced to work with a will, their opinions, voiced in their various special languages and formulae, would materially help Mayor La Guardia to better living conditions in New York City.[6]

For Cather the token of greatness in art was a quality that seemingly has little to do with either personal morality or social justice, a quality that resists exact formulation. Every "fine story," she declared, leaves "an intangible residuum of pleasure" that the reader can recall but "can never absolutely define," a quality whose elusiveness and evocative power is like "the summer perfume of a garden."[7] In perhaps her most important literary statement, *The Novel Démeublé*, Cather attempted again to describe what differentiates art from entertainment or journalism:

> Whatever is felt upon the page without being specifically named there—that, one might say, is created. It is the inexplicable presence of the thing not named, of the overtone divined by the ear but not heard by it, the verbal mood, the emotional aura of the fact or the thing or the deed, that gives high quality to the novel or the drama, as well as to poetry itself.[8]

One reason Cather did not look to literature for new insights about politics and morality was because she did not believe that there were any new moral truths to be discovered and communicated. Freudians, Marxists and progressives of every stripe of course believed that they possessed important new truths that rendered bourgeois morality obsolete, but Willa Cather doubted that very much that was truly important had changed over the years. Carl Linstrum seems to speak for the author when he comments in *O Pioneers!* that there are only two or three human stories, and they go on repeating themselves as fiercely as if they had never happened before; like the larks in this country, that have been singing the same five notes over for thousands of years.[9] Professor Godfrey St. Peter echoes that judgment when he tells his students that modern science has done nothing to alleviate what he calls "the old riddles," which are in any case "insoluble."[10]

Although Willa Cather refuses to link literature with morality, she repeatedly associates art with religion. Godfrey St. Peter seems to speak for Willa Cather when he discounts the importance of science in favor of art and religion: "Art and religion (they are the same thing, in the end, of course) have given man the only happiness he has ever had," while science has only succeeded in "making us very comfortable." The professor assimilates religion to art while allowing morality a merely instrumental value:

> The Christian theologians went over the books of the Law, like great artists, getting splendid effects by excision. They reset the stage with more space and mystery, throwing all the light upon a few sins of great dramatic value. (138)

Godfrey St. Peter finds the age of faith superior to our own time not because he is a believer or because morality has declined but because life today lacks the dramatic quality the Christian theologian-artists infused in it:

> As long as every man and woman who crowded into the cathedrals on Easter Sunday was a principal in a gorgeous drama with God, glittering angels on one side and the shadows of evil coming and going on the other, life was a rich thing. The king and the beggar had the same chance at miracles and great temptations and revelations. And that's what makes men happy, believing in the mystery and importance of their own little individual lives. (137-8)

The connection between art and religion Godfrey St. Peter finds in medieval Europe is also evident in the ruins of the ancient Cliff City discovered by Rodney Blake and St. Peter's student Tom Outland. Father Duchene tells the two that the long-extinct tribe's evident "feeling for design" suggests that "they lived for something more than food and shelter." He imagines them making their mesa more and more worthy to be a home for man, purifying life by religious ceremonies and observances, caring respectfully for their dead, protecting the children, doubtless entertaining some feelings of affection and sentiment for this stronghold where they were at once so safe and so comfortable (233).

Father Duchene, unlike the professor, does connect religion to morality as well as to art. The tribe, he speculates, "developed considerably the arts of peace" but in doing so they "possible declined in the arts of war, in brute strength and ferocity" (233). They had succeeded in lifting themselves "out of mere brutality" before they were finally massacred, and therefore the mesa where they built their Cliff City "is a sacred spot" that deserves our respect and even "reverence" (234). Religion and art, it seems, are kin because both can give meaning and order to everyday life. Moral laws are one expression of this order, ceremonies are another, and the architectural design linking the buildings in Cliff City is another. Morality in Cather's fiction is not a matter of adherence to abstract principles but rather of loyalty to traditions. Not all traditions, of course, deserve to be obeyed; a novel like *O Pioneers!* distinguishes carefully between those that enrich life and those that are merely repetitions of the brutality that threatens all cultures, not merely that of Cliff City. If art and religion find their highest purpose in ennobling everyday life, then art denigrates that life

Religion and art, it seems, are kin because both can give meaning and order to everyday life. Moral laws are one expression of this order, ceremonies are another, and the architectural design linking the buildings in Cliff City is another. The fiction of Willa Cather does not preach, but it does dramatize the ways in which everyday life can achieve significance and even beauty. Beauty, in Cather's fiction, is often a token of the good. Anton Rosicky has lived a good life, has been a good husband and father and neighbor, but when Doctor Ed Burleigh passes by his grave, he does not say to himself that Rosicky had been a good man but instead muses that Rosicky's life had been "complete and beautiful."[11]

Mid-West Virtue

The everyday world that Willa Cather knew was the Middle West in which she grew up. She found herself as a writer when, after years of successful editing and writing, she finally turned in *O Pioneers!* to a "story concerned entirely with heavy farming people, with cornfields and pasture lands and pig yards."[12] In her earlier work, in stories like *The Sculptor's Funeral* and *A Wagner Matinée*, "the Middle West was a cultural desert, a region that anybody with sensitivity or artistic feeling would escape from as soon as possible." The Sand City of *The Sculptor's Funeral* is summed up by one of its own citizens, Jim Laird, as a "borderland between ruffianism and civilization," a "bitter, dead little Western town."[13] In *A Wagner Matinée*, Boston is a place where one can hear great music throughout the year, while awaiting Aunt Georgiana at her Nebraska homestead are only "the gaunt, moulting turkeys picking up refuse about the kitchen door."[14]

In *O Pioneers!* Alexandra Bergson has scarcely any more opportunities to hear a symphony than does Aunt Georgiana. Now, however, Willa Cather is ready to do more than simply exploit the obvious differences between the frontier life of Nebraska and the wealthy, cultured world of Boston and New York. Alexandra Bergson is an unusual protagonist for a novel, not merely because she is Swedish and lives on a farm in Nebraska, but because her life contains no great adventures; she commits no great crimes and experiences no intoxicating passions. She works hard, minds her own business and finally becomes the owner of "one of the richest farms on the Divide" (178).

One of the great achievements of the novel is its success in convincing the reader that writing (and reading) a novel about such a life is worth one's while. For most of the twentieth century, both bestsellers and literary masterpieces have united in condemning conventional middle-class life as inherently shallow, hypocritical and mean. Apparently supported by the most enlightened doctrines of the age, including Marxism and psychoanalysis, this sweeping condemnation has encour-aged a feeling of moral superiority to ordinary people which, at best, leads to complacency and at worst to a willingness to support wars and violent revolutions involving millions of deaths—after all, if people are living "inauthentic" lives, then nothing morally significant can happen to them anyway.

Some of the most influential modern novels suggest that spiritual depth can be gained only by rebelling against middle-class conformity, preferably by becoming an artist. In *O Pioneers!* Carl Linstrum leaves Nebraska to become a kind of artist, an engraver, while Alexandra Bergson stays home to mind the family farm. Alexandra regrets Carl's leaving but believes that an artistic career offers him the opportunity to fulfill himself. She tells Carl that now he will have the chance to "'find the work you were meant to do'" (163). When he returns for a visit, however, he discovers that Alexandra has made farming itself into an art. He tells her "'I've been away engraving other men's pictures, and you've stayed at home and made your own'" (194). Her farm has its own "order and fine arrangement," with its "symmetrical pasture ponds" and its "white row of beehives" (178). Meanwhile, Carl's attempt to become an artist-engraver has ended in failure, as he admits to Alexandra: "'Everything's cheap metal work nowadays, touching up miserable photographs, forcing up poor drawings, and spoiling good ones. I'm absolutely sick of it all.'" Carl exclaims to Alexandra that "'I couldn't buy even one of your cornfields'" (197) and, indeed, Alexandra does own "one of the richest farms on the Divide" (178), while Carl has little more than the clothes on his back.

More importantly, however, it is Alexandra who has found personal fulfillment. She had persisted in holding onto the land during "three years of drought and failure" (161), when her brothers were eager to sell out, and now she is reaping the reward. She has succeeded because she has been willing to put all her intellectual and moral energy into carrying out the responsibility her father had conferred on her on his deathbed, when he told his two sons "'I want you to keep the land together and to be guided by your sister . . . I want no quarrels among my children, and so long as there is one house there must be one head. . . . She will do the best she can'" (150).

She has discovered that farming is a task that requires the best energies of her mind and spirit, and she has responded with her whole self. The narrator comments that "it was because she had so much personality to put into her enterprises and succeeded in putting it into them so completely, that her affairs prospered better than those of her neighbors" (237).

The peace of the Nebraska farming country is broken by Frank Shabata's killing of his wife Marie and Emil Bergson, Alexandra's youngest brother, when he finds them sleeping together in the Shabata's orchard. The novel suggests that the source of this tragedy is not so much the sexual passion shared by Marie and Emil as it is a delusive romanticism that affects Marie and Emil and, most strikingly, Frank Shabata. This romanticism is delusive because it leads all three to believe that they are superior people, different from their neighbors in some fundamental way. Marie and Emil come to this feeling only for a moment, while Frank Shabata harbors it for years.

Frank Shabata wants to believe that he is in some mysterious way better than his farm and social position would seem to indicate. Alexandra warns Carl Linstrum that

"Frank's not a bad neighbor, but to get on with him you've got to make a fuss over him and act as if you thought he was a very important person all the time, and different from other people." (196)

Frank Shabata's jealousy of his wife has been fueled by her willingness to accept those around her as equals, interesting people in their own right. Frank himself wanted his wife to resent that he was wasting his best years among these stupid and unappreciative people; but she has seemed to find the people quite good enough (270).

As a young man, Frank Shabata's Byronic pose, signaled by his "slightly disdainful expression" and "the interesting discontent in his blue eyes" had made him excitingly attractive to "every Bohemian girl he met," including Marie Tovesky (208). For a married man farming on the Nebraska Divide, however, there are few opportunities to strike a pose. One way Frank vents his discontent and feeds his sense of superiority is by striking a pose of political and social radicalism. He enjoys "feeling outraged" about the "crimes and follies" of the rich he reads about in the Sunday newspapers, who, he claims to believe, "bribed the courts and shot down their butlers with impunity whenever they chose." With Alexandra's brother Lou, Frank is one of the "political agitators of the county" (210). When politics do not suffice, Frank takes out his anger on Marie, whom he accuses of always siding with the neighbors against him: "They all know it. Anybody here feels free to borrow the mower and break it, or turn their hogs in on me. They know you won't care" (207)! Frank Shabata kills Marie and Emil not because he chooses consciously to do so, but because "it gratified him to feel like a desperate man" whose desperation is the token of his superiority (267).

Marie Tovesky Shabata and Emil Bergson do not, like Frank Shabata, spend their lives nursing a sense of superiority to those around them. After they have died, Carl Linstrum tells Alexandra that the two "were both the best you had here" (288), but Marie and Emil themselves never bothered to make such a judgment. Neither attempted to justify their illicit love on the grounds of the depth or authenticity of their passions. Both, indeed, were determined to avoid surrendering to their feelings. When they do finally meet under the mulberry tree, it is because they have convinced themselves that they have somehow transcended ordinary human nature. Planning to leave Nebraska and Marie behind, Emil discovers within himself "a kind of rapture in which he could love forever without faltering and without sin" (264). This "rapture," Emil imagines, allows him to love Marie without wronging her husband. It is a feeling beyond ordinary emotions and certainly beyond Marie's husband: "The rapture was for those who could feel it; for people who could not; it was non-existent. . . . Frank Shabata had never found it; would never find it if he lived beside it a thousand years; would have destroyed it if he had found it." Wrongly assuming the uniqueness of his situation, "it did not occur to Emil that any one had ever reasoned thus before," (264), and thus he feels himself free to ignore the ordinary taboos and visit Marie alone. Marie, meanwhile, has convinced herself that "Emil once away, she could let everything else go and live a new life of perfect love" (260). She has already started to live this life when Emil finds her alone under the mulberry tree:

> Marie was lying on her side under the white mulberry tree, her face half hidden in the grass, her eyes closed, her hands lying limply where they had happened to fall. She had lived a day of her new life of perfect love, and it had left her like this. (266)

Emil and Marie become lovers despite their determination to withstand temptation because the two have convinced themselves that they are beyond temptation, that they have entered a state of being beyond ordinary human nature.

Middle-Class Ethics

If *O Pioneers!* warns against the kind of romanticism that encourages contempt for ordinary human emotions, it also dramatizes the intensity and depth of feeling that may occur at seemingly unimportant moments of everyday life. After the death of her father, Alexandra must decide whether to keep the farm on the Divide, despite a run of poor harvests, or sell the land and buy another farm in the river country. After a five day visit "down among the river farms" she decides to remain on the Divide. As she and Emil travel along "the first long swells of the Divide" on the way home, Alexandra suddenly feels a new closeness to the land to which she has decided to commit herself and the family fortunes. Nothing happens, except that Emil notices that she looks "so happy" and her face "was so radiant." Alexandra has already decided not to sell the farm, so her sudden emotion has no apparent consequences even for herself. This moment, unnoticed by anybody else and virtually forgotten by Alexandra herself, is presented by the narrator as an occasion of historic significance:

> For the first time, perhaps, since that land emerged from the waters of geologic ages, a human face was set toward it with love and yearning. It seemed beautiful to her, rich and strong and glorious. Her eyes drank in the breadth of it, until her tears blinded her. The Genius of the Divide, the great, free spirit which breathes across it, must have bent lower than it ever bent to a human will before. The history of every country begins in the heart of a man or a woman. (170)

When Alexandra mentions this experience to Carl Linstrum in explaining why she wants to stay, her own words have nothing of the lyrical eloquence of the narrator:

> "When I was on the train this morning, and we got near Hanover, I felt something like I did when I drove back with Emil from the river that time, in the dry year. I was glad to come back to it." (289)

Alexandra's very lack of histrionics testifies to the reality of the experience, while the closing sentence of the novel again affirms the larger significance of Alexandra's life, despite its lack of romantic adventure:

> Fortunate country, that is one day to receive hearts like Alexandra's into its bosom, to give them out again in the yellow wheat, in the rustling corn, in the shining eyes of youth! (290)

O Pioneers! is not a morality tale in which virtue triumphs and evil is punished. Both Alexandra Bergson and Carl Linstrum, the most sympathetic, intelligent characters in the novel, find it difficult to derive a moral from the deaths of Marie and Emil. Reconciling Marie's fate with her character is not easy: "Was there, then, something wrong in being warm-hearted and impulsive like that? Alexandra hated to think so" (283). Carl Linstrum likewise is unable to condemn Marie: "There are women who spread ruin around them through no fault of theirs, just by being too beautiful, too full of life and love. They can't help it. People come to them as people go to a warm fire in winter" (288).

Alexandra does not blame the lovers—after seeing their bodies together on the ground she only wonders "how they could have helped loving each other," nor does she blame Frank Shabata—"Being what he was, she felt, Frank could not have acted otherwise" (278).

If *O Pioneers!* avoids easy moralizing, it nevertheless demonstrates persuasively that life on a Nebraska farm in a middle-class community can possess depth and significance. The novel also suggests that the sort of romanticism whose allure is based on an apparent transcendence of everyday life is probably delusory. In a century in which the many of the most admired works seem to tell us that life is trivial without "authenticity," and the token of authenticity is rebellion against family, community and country, *O Pioneers!* becomes, perhaps against its own intentions, an affirmation of such prosaic virtues of everyday life as neighborliness, hard work, and prudence. It is not that Alexandra is made to seem a paragon of virtue. Cather has accomplished a more difficult task, that of making her way of life seem not only good but also a source of aesthetic pleasure. What "Doctor Ed" felt about Anton Rosicky seems true of Alexandra Bergson; her life as it appears in *O Pioneers!* is "complete and beautiful." If the book points to no simple political moral, it at least urges us not to be in such a hurry, that, while trying to bring about a "better world," we fail to leave room for a way of life like hers.

Notes

1. Marilee Lindemann observes that in the last twenty years Cather's critics "have combed the novels and short stories for signs of how sexuality is translated into textuality, for evidence of lesbianism masked in order to evade detection and censure" (*Willa Cather: Queering America* [New York: Columbia UP, 1999], 9. All quotations in this note are from this source.). Lindemann herself carries on the same project despite her awareness that its "trendiness cannot mask its significant limitations and liabilities" (2). Her reading of *O Pioneers!*, a reading that, in her words, sees the novel in "phobic, terroristic terms" (121) finds the novel marked by both "'corporeal utopianism'" and "a pronounced corporeal dystopianism—a tendency toward erotophobia, homophobia, and general ambivalence toward the condition of embodiment" (39). Such interpretations, it would seem, could occur only to critics unwilling to enter the imaginative world of the novel's characters. Lindemann, objecting with some reason to those feminist critics who "read female characters as if they were real women," boasts that "Alexandra interests me not because she is an exceptional girl . . . but because she is a semiotic field where important cultural work occurs" (46).

2. Aristotle, *Aristotle's Politics*, trans. Benjamin Jowett (New York: Random House, 1943), 191 [Book IV, Ch. 11].

3. Ralph Waldo Emerson, *The American Scholar, Ralph Waldo Emerson: Essays and Lectures* (New York: Literary Classics of the United States, 1983), 71.

4. Alexis de Tocqueville, *Democracy in America*, trans. George Lawrence, ed. J. P. Mayer and Max Lerner (New York: Harper & Row, 1966). Other quotations from this text are cited in the body of the essay by the page number enclosed in parentheses.

5. Thomas Mann, *Lübeck as a Way of Life and Thought, Buddenbrooks*, trans. H. T. Lowe-Porter (New York: Alfred A. Knopf, 1964), xvi. Other quotations from this text are cited in the body of the essay by the page number enclosed in parentheses.

6. Willa Cather, *Escapism*, in *Willa Cather: Stories, Poems, and Other Writings* (New York: Literary Classics of the United States, 1992), 969.

7. Willa Cather, "Miss Jewett," *Not Under Forty*, in *Willa Cather: Stories, Poems, and Other Writings* (New York: Literary Classics of the United States, 1992), 850.

8. Willa Cather, "The Novel Démeublé," in *Not Under Forty*, in *Willa Cather: Stories, Poems, and Other Writings* (New York: Literary Classics of the United States, 1992), 837.

9. Willa Cather, *O Pioneers!*, in *Willa Cather: Early Novels and Stories* (New York: Literary Classics, 1987), 196. Other quotations from this text are cited in the body of the essay by the page number enclosed in parentheses.

10. Willa Cather, *The Professor's House*, in *Willa Cather: Later Novels* (New York: Literary Classics of the United States, 1990), 137. Other quotations from this text are cited in the body of the essay by the page number enclosed in parentheses.

11. Willa Cather, "Neighbour Rosicky," *Obscure Destinies*, in *Willa Cather: Stories, Poems, and Other Writings* (New York: Literary Classics of the United States, 1992), 618.

12. Willa Cather, *My First Novels (There Were Two)*, in *Willa Cather: Stories, Poems, and Other Writings* (New York: Literary Classics of the United States, 1992), 964.

13. Willa Cather, "A Sculptor's Funeral," in *Youth and the Bright Medusa* in *Willa Cather: Stories, Poems, and Other Writings* (New York: Literary Classics of the United States, 1992), 509-510.

14. Willa Cather, "A Wagner Matinée," in *Youth and Bright Medusa* in *Willa Cather: Stories, Poems, and Other Writings* (New York: Literary Classics of the United States, 1992), 496.

Chapter 15

Robert Penn Warren's *Brother to Dragons:*
Complicity and the Beginning of Innocence

Judith Lee Kissell

> *"The recognition of complicity*
> *Is the beginning of innocence"*
> —Brother to Dragons

The Nature of the Political Self and *Brother to Dragons*

The emphasis in philosophy—particularly in ethics—on imagination and discernment, on story and narrative, and on interpretation and hermeneutics enjoys much current popularity. But while this "new philosophy" appears to be innovative and fresh, it is simply a rebirth of an ancient tradition. If the Greeks did not invent this approach to reflecting on how we might live together better, they were, thanks to Homer, surely no strangers to it. The call upon the creative imagination and upon story is not only very old; it recurs constantly throughout the history of political and ethical thought.

These imaginative stories relate to the way in which we view the self vis-à-vis society. They are "political," in the broad sense in which Aristotle uses the concept to include both social and governing structure, as well as living well together—ethics. They are "stories" in that the philosopher calls upon our creative imagination to conceive some idealistic or prophetic vision and in light of that vision to acquire greater moral discernment. Take for instance, Plato's *Republic* where "once-upon-a-time," he as much as tells us, "there was a city." In this city, he continues, we live in the midst of, and are fundamentally dependent upon, others. Later political philosophers have spurred our imaginations as well. Thomas Hobbes, in his *Leviathan*,[1] suggests that "once-upon-a-time," men (literally) got together and decided to establish a contract for living in society. John Locke, in his *Two Treatises of Government*,[2] not only embellishes Hobbes' ideas, but placing the contract in context, tells us that "once-upon-a-time," human beings lived in a "state of nature," having "perfect freedom."[3]

John Rawls, one of the most important of our American, contemporary political philosophers, in his *Theory of Justice*,[4] acknowledges the debt he owes to these early philosophers' "once-upon-a-times" for inspiring him to portray his profound insights about justice in so accessible a way. According to Rawls, rational beings in their "original position" as inventors of society, totally "ignorant" of their social, gender, racial and economic status, create the rules of justice that underlie political structure. In conceding this debt to his predecessors, Rawls' book, with its "veil of ignorance" and "original position," reminds us that some ideas are so vast and so difficult to grasp that we require myth or stories to contain them. One of these unwieldy ideas is that of the human, political self.

Because these are *stories*, however, they demand interpretation. Modern individuals are so indoctrinated by the myths of the social contract and the state of nature—blessed and rugged independence and individualism—that they accept them as fact, as literal truths, rather than as imperfect bearers of profound truths. They are mere *attempts* to articulate our political insights and aspirations. Stories and myths express truths too powerful to be contained in simple statements of fact; for example, the stories of Plato, Hobbes, Locke and Rawls contain multiple layers of meaning.

Like Plato, Hobbes and Locke before him and Rawls after him, Jefferson also creates a "once-upon-a-time" about the meaning of the political self, about human beings, created as equals, born with inalienable rights, governed only with their consent. The history of the United States has been a process of unraveling, in a practical way, the meaning of this profound statement about humanity.

The title of Robert Penn Warren's Pulitzer prize-winning book-length poem, *Brother to Dragons*,[5] is taken from the Book of Job in which Job claims: "I was the brother of dragons, and companion to owls."[6] Warren uses the "brother to dragons" metaphor to reflect Jefferson's disenchantment with his vision—his illusion—about the exalted status of the individual that he immortalizes in the Declaration of Independence. Not only are we animals, he seems to tell us, but as dragons, we are the very mythic beasts that epitomize human evil and misery. We are some strange combination of the rational and the animal, the spiritual and the material, the transcendent and the base.

The poem opens with Jefferson's autobiographical "triple boast," the epitaph carved on his monument at Monticello in Albermarle County, Virginia: Jefferson first lists his authorship of the Declaration of Independence, followed by his writing of the Virginia Statute of Religious Freedom; and finally, his founding of the University of Virginia. In Jefferson's view, foremost among his accomplishments—and at the heart of the poem's drama and tension—lies his exalted definition of humanity. The poem's central event is the narration of how Lilburn, Jefferson's nephew, takes an ax to a slave, George, kills him, and then orders him buried by the other slaves.[7] This chapter focuses upon this section. The main characters besides Jefferson, are R. P. W. (Robert Penn Warren), the narrator;

Lucy Lewis, Jefferson's beloved sister; and Lucy's sons and Jefferson's nephews, Lilburn and Isham Lewis.

Throughout the narrative, we see Jefferson's dream of rugged individualism fail as a moral ideal. Warren uses this story to raise profoundly important questions about the definition of the human being, the nature of society, the ways we should and do relate to one another, the importance of moral responsibility and the meaning of human flourishing. Two hundred years have not dulled the urgency of the play's message.

Warren means for us to recognize as our own, the very definition—one is tempted to write "Definition"—of humankind that plays the role of antagonist in this drama, as it alternately exalts and humbles Jefferson throughout the poem. The author intends that, just as Jefferson discovered this truth, we also should come to the realization that the nature of our political selves is based on a paradox. The convictions that each of us is equal to every other, that each possesses a dignity and rights from which we cannot be alienated, that no one has the right to govern us unless we consent, are fundamental elements of the American dream and self-image. Indeed, the Enlightenment pronouncement of these beliefs forms a lofty chapter in political history.

Jefferson's definition of man is fueled by a dynamic of internal tension—simultaneously its grandeur and its flaw—that Jefferson comes to recognize in increasingly greater depth throughout the course of the drama. Like Jefferson, we are led to see the irony at the core of the Declaration of Independence that clarifies, in more than one way, who we are and explains the dissentions and contradictions of our own times. "Madness is but the cancer of truth, the arrogance of truth gone wild and swollen in the blood" (12).

The glory of Jefferson's definition is confounded by a further two-pronged, and darker, implication: first, Jefferson finds that his earlier conviction has been wrongheaded. The "Enlightened" vision carries with it the belief that if these ideas can be realized through political life, they carry with them a redemption of humankind and of nature, a state frequently referred to in the poem as "innocence." If society acknowledges the dignity and natural goodness of human beings, the Enlightenment thinker would claim, "innocence" will prevail in their relationships with one another, with the world and within their own hearts. But Jefferson, in Warren's poem, comes to think otherwise:

"And [I] was a man once too, and know
that all earth's monsters are but innocent.
But one, that master-monster—ah, but once
I did not think so. For I thought him innocent too." (35)

Second, the dignity of the individual that establishes her rights and prerogatives also isolates and polarizes her from the community toward which she *need* feel no responsibility nor mutuality. Promulgated chiefly by Locke, but defended by such contemporary social thinkers as Robert Novak and John Rawls, the Enlightenment ideal portrays the atomistic individual orbiting in her world, centered on her own interests, essentially unconnected to anyone else. In this new political vision, citizens *elect* to form community—or they elect not to. It is un-like Plato's city, in which inhabitants have an essential connectedness; and, it is unlike a family, in which members are inextricably bound to one another. But Lucy challenges this idea:

> "We had hoped to escape
> complicity,
> You and I, dear Brother. But we have seen the unfolding
> Of Time and complicity . . .
> . . . You must take his [Lilburn's] hand and recognize, at last
> That his face is only a mirror of your possibilities . . ." (189f)

Rugged individualism becomes our undoing.

The quandary of the paradox is not that Jefferson's definition of human beings is wrong and can, or should be, rejected. His definition, from which we receive our dignity, loses none of its glory. The crux of the matter is that individualism and self-indulgence flow from the same source as dignity. This paradox, then, becomes the genesis of conflict that energizes the drama. It is a conflict between human beings and nature, between person and person; and, it is a conflict within the hearts of Jefferson, of Lucy, of Lilburn and of Isham.

Lucy discovers, moreover—and attempts to convince Jefferson—that the paradox must be lived out and embraced. The Enlightenment thinkers seek innocence for humankind, and they believe that a rational approach to society can achieve it. But Lucy realizes that this state is more difficult to come by. It is not the state of nature, with each individual sovereign and detached in the citadel of her mind, heart and property, but the coming together in the city—in compassion, love and mutual responsibility—that finally achieves authentic innocence. Lucy discerns that to deny our radical isolation as moral beings and to concede our responsibility for the acts of, and the harms caused by others is the only way we can redeem ourselves.[8] She tells her brother: "But what I mean to say, / if you would assume the burden of innocence, / If you would begin now your innocence, you must take His [Lilburn's] hand" (190-91). It is this notion of complicity, mutuality and personal responsibility that underlies Warren's narrative.

> "The recognition of complicity
> Is the beginning of innocence." (190)

Jefferson and the Definition of Man

The Enlightenment idea that reason can loose the shackles that have divided ordinary persons between kings and commoners inspired and animated Jefferson. The notions that all human beings were created equal and endowed with inalienable rights, that the ordinary man and woman were equal in dignity to the king and the queen, that political sovereignty could only be justified by the consent of the governed, gave hope to Jefferson as it had to other Enlightenment thinkers. The rationality that grounds human dignity and makes all men and women equal also gave Jefferson cause to believe that he was founding father of a nation of great-souled and moral beings. He exulted in the part he played in establishing a government founded on these principles:

"The boast— it was the boast
That split my heart, the boast which I, in my late
Last year, made, while my heart still hugged some hope
That life had spoken and I'd heard it speak.
It was that boast that split my heart. It split it
As the vernal[9] enlargement of life's green germ will split
The dry acorn . . .
But I digress. If the boast did split my heart,
It was not in pain. But in pride. No, not pride —
. . . Or if in pride, then a pride past pride,
In my identity with the definition of man." (5f)

Jefferson's euphoria begins with the meeting of the signers of the Declaration of Independence in Philadelphia. These men who change the world and the meaning of political life are ordinary men.

"To Philadelphia we came, delegates by accident, in essence men:
Marmosets in mantles, beasts in boots, parrots in pantaloons.
That is to say, men. Like other men.
No worse, no better." (6f)

This remarkable meeting, the results of which have so changed world history, is comprised of ordinary men, reasoning animals who are no better, but no worse, than any one of us. But when these ordinary men meet together to decide their fate as a society and as a political entity, they bring along their "own lusts and languours." Each is "lost, in some blind lobby, hall, enclave, rank cul-de-sac, couloir,[10] or corridor of Time. Of Time. Or self " (7).

While Locke most clearly articulated the ideas of rights, equality and the social contract, America's founding fathers had the task of making this Enlightenment a lived reality. Warren describes how Jefferson and the other visionaries of the Declaration of Independence conceptualize the human being, their vision filtered through the ideas of their Enlightenment forebearers. "'But I, a man, Suddenly saw in every face, face after face. . . . And my heart cried out, "Oh, this is Man!"'"(8)

Against the privilege and the lack of privilege that formed the backdrop of Philadelphia and all that it symbolizes in the poem, and against the privilege and the lack thereof that we see in our own century, Jefferson exulted (as so should we). For we might well revel in the ideal of the equality of human beings—whether black, white or brown, male or female—wherever we find it. Jefferson's insight was no mean revelation.

In Philadelphia, the divine right of kings becomes transformed into the God-given and inalienable rights of the common man and woman. What happened in Philadelphia bore, for Jefferson, the hallowed mark of divine inspiration:

"So seized the pen, and in the upper room
With the excited consciousness that I was somehow

Purged, rectified, and annealed . . .
Time came, we signed the document, went home." (9)

Philadelphia becomes the "upper room," reminiscent of the descent of the Holy Spirit upon the Apostles from the Christian Testament of the Bible. But in this case, divine inspiration must share the room with Reason. Unlike the doctrine of divine kingly prerogative, matter of privileged faith, the concept of equality and inalienable rights—accessible to reason—thrilled Jefferson and his compatriots. Where the English kings had for years considered their favored and divinely established position to be unassailable, the men in the "upper room" of Philadelphia behold divine glory reflected in "every face, face after face, the bleared, the puffed, the lank, the lean, all . . . and witness to a holy sanction on their mission (8)."

But Jefferson and the others failed to see—or adequately articulate—the importance of the common good, of sacrificing one's welfare for the advantage of the whole society, and the notion that our destinies are intrinsically linked together. They failed to see that the creation of government means each of us must abnegate our own preferences so that the larger whole can function. But the "once upon a times" of Locke, Rawls, and others like them, makes it clear: the motivation behind such cooperation is "enlightened self-interest" that by its nature precludes any intrinsic solidarity.[11] To be sure, a person may *prefer* to cooperate and to be community-minded, but such an attitude is to be respected no more than the radical individualism that others might favor.

What Jefferson comes to see is that his noble definition is but an ideal. And the evolution of this ideal led him through contradictions and a certain schizophrenia about concepts such as "all men" and "equal," that seem even now to confuse us. The poem takes us through events in our early history during which the principles of the Declaration itself seem to have given us *carte blanche* to be destructively selfish. The bootstrap mentality of self-sufficiency, independence, individuality and ambition seemed then, as they do today, to possess clear moral superiority. The story of Lilburn and George, occurring at the birth of the country, portrays an ugliness currently reflected in attitudes toward welfare, immigration, sexism, racism and the destruction of the earth. The implication then, that whoever had the power to take—took—is reflected in today's attitude that those of us who are white, male, native-born citizens, English-speaking, well-employed, and insured are not only fortunate but virtuous. This same Declaration seemed to permit our predecessors then, even as it does us at the present time, to cast our national spirit as something less than mutual concern.

This attitude has, as often as not, been articulated through the contract metaphor,[12] raising profound questions about who we are. Are we as a society defined chiefly by our rights as individuals or by our responsibilities as citizens? And what does *community* mean? Do we belong to society only because we *choose* to do so, or are we radically embedded in communities of value and concern? Can our communities make demands upon us and upon our resources or do we owe only what we opt to contribute? If indeed we are contractors, in what sense are we equal bargainers in the contract? Do women and men, blacks, browns and whites, come to the table with the same degree of power? And who negotiates for the powerless, the very young, the very old, and the mentally debilitated?

Our intoxication with our freedom, and thus our glory, can cause us to overlook the idea that the human beings might better be portrayed as a Minotaur, as Jefferson acknowledges.[13]

> "And thus my minotaur. There at the blind
> Blank labyrinthine turn of my personal time,
> I met the beast. (9)

The paradox recurs in these lines in which Jefferson introduces the chimera or hybrid imagery of the human, flesh-eating Minotaur to represent our schizoid view of human beings as at once beastly and divine—a nature simultaneously elevated and destructive.

Historians debate whether Jefferson espoused the Enlightenment ideal of extreme individualism to the exclusion of the Renaissance notion of civic republicanism. That debate itself perfectly frames the struggle in Jefferson's soul when he realizes the erroneousness of his exalted vision of humankind. The grand isolation that characterizes Locke's and Jefferson's perfect freedom allows them to ignore the deeper realities about human beings—that basic flaw in us manifest in our attempts to subjugate and to prey upon one another through racism, sexism, slavery, genocide or economic exploitation. Locke and Jefferson ignore our mutual obligation and responsibility for each other, incumbent upon us as members of the same society.

Still, those men in Philadelphia produced a document that both defines human beings and lays out a blueprint for living together that revolutionized our ideas of humanity and of government for centuries to come and throughout the world. Warren perceives that out of the commerce of ordinary beings, beset by their own self-interest and weakness, and the "corridors of Time or self" that bespoke their narrowness and personal preoccupations, grew the Declaration of Independence with its undeniably lofty legacy.

Never again can we consider any person, from Siberia to East Timor, from Ghana to Montreal, without raising questions about whether each, black or white, male or female, has rights and entitlements to dignity, to freedom from oppression, to food, to jobs, to reproductive freedom. Never again can we ponder governance without raising questions about the right of an individual to choose their form of government.

Complicity and the Beginning of Innocence

Throughout the poem, Warren uses a metaphorical chiascuro. He contrasts Jefferson's sister Lucy—whose name means "light," and whose presence symbolizes warmth, family and connectedness—with the dark of Lilburn's degeneracy and isolation. Lilburn's lonely dark act flows from an utter lack of human gentleness and concern—the human alienation and aloneness connoted by the wild and untamed West, the polar opposite of all that Lucy characterizes.

In Lucy's conversation with R.P.W., we get a glimpse of how this theme of light and dark pervades the poem. The dark, Lucy explains, is partially a result of the family's having moved from the civilization of Virginia, her beloved home, westward to the frontier of Kentucky, where she dies—in her mind deserting Lilburn to his demons:

"I saw the dark land creep into my house.
I saw the dark night creep into my bed.
I saw the river-dark swim in my cup. (22)

For Lucy the darkness that invaded the Lewis household portrayed the evil of the human condition as Lilburn loses his love for and sensitivity toward his wife and brother and his decency toward his slaves. But the darkness also symbolizes the isolation in which Lilburn, and Jefferson too, become imprisoned. This estrangement at once explains Lilburn's sickly deeds and Jefferson's shrinking from responsibility for his fellow beings—the twin evils of individualism.

Jefferson's view of the individual enables him to consider himself an innocent bystander: just as the life of a sovereign individual belongs to himself alone, so do his sins. This tradition allows Jefferson to say to Lucy about Lilburn that you may "blame yourself. / You bred him and you loved him." But as for Jefferson himself he will "have no part, no matter / What responsibility you yourself wish" (188). Jefferson's grand definition emphasizes the rights, protections and prerogatives of the atomistic human being, responsible only for those harms that he himself causes. Similarly, this tradition allows Jefferson to deny that he has any part in his nephew's horrendous deed.

While this liberal tradition of blameworthiness plays an indispensable role within conventional morality, complicity itself outstrips this tradition's ability to explain our common obligations. This narrow tradition, as Warren realizes, fails to satisfy our moral intuitions, and it leaves unfulfilled our moral aspirations as we strive for a different sense of self, of personal accountability, and of responsibility. The very traits that make this tradition efficient and effective also cramp our conceptualization of self and community and of mutual responsibility for wrongdoing.

Lucy urges Jefferson to see that, not only do we have need for one another and one another's support (as Lilburn shows in his apparent urgency for his mother to check his demons) but our natural state is not one of perfect freedom and autonomy as her brother would claim. We are not born as loners who only eventually choose to belong to society. Rather we are born into a family, a race, a gender, an ethnicity, and a nation—all of which determine who we are and that enmesh us in certain commitments. The view of grand solitude and independence has the further implication that because it is Jefferson's ideal, he allows himself to disavow any complicity, not only for his nephew, but for other human evils as well.

By posing questions of personal accountability and mutual involvement to Jefferson, Warren wants to raise these same questions for us who follow in Jefferson's footsteps. Where are the limits of my responsibility for the evils of my society? Am I culpable for those evils that others commit but that I merely tolerate? How blameworthy was the German on the street during the Nazi era? the Serb for the rapes of Albanian women? the Russian for the gulags of the Communist regime? the American for the violence on her streets? the Brazilian for the destruction of the rainforest? This denial of complicity is the error that Lucy helps her brother to admit, for Jefferson multiplies guilt by refusing to accept any responsibility for the heinous deed.

Jefferson: ...If there's responsibility, it's yours,
And if it's yours—

Lucy: But now I say that what he would have defended
Was but himself against the darkness that was his.

Lucy: Compound the crime? Why that's what you have done.
And do, for in your rejection you repeat the crime.
Over and over, and more monstrous still,
For what poor Lilburn did in exaltation of madness
You do in vanity—(189)
No, worse, you do in fear—
Your fear began, the fear you had always denied, the fear
That you—even you—were capable of all.

And so in that consanguinity,[14] still to deny
The possibilities of self.

Morality, Narrative and Exhortation

The narrative tradition of complicity, of which *Brother to Dragons* is a part, is much more than a mere collection of morality tales about wrongdoing. Rather, such stories point to the interpretive potential of narrative as a source of moral wisdom. They go far past the idea of blaming their characters for evil acts and focus instead upon *exhorting* the rest of us who are their listeners and their readers. They disclose censure for, and exhortation about, wrongdoing in its historicity, through which we stand within a recounting that allows the past to reveal to us our own possibilities for our future.

Narrative and stories seek to broaden our moral involvement beyond the perfect freedom of Locke and the inalienable rights of Jefferson. Paul Ricoeur claims that "[to understand stories] is to receive an enlarged self from the apprehension of proposed worlds that are the genuine object of interpretation."[15] Stories help the agent to understand issues that she has yet to experience, that are larger and more challenging than the ones she faces within her private self.

If we imagine the purpose of Warren's narrative to be mere blame, his censuring of Jefferson or Lilburn would be myopic. Mere blame implies "making right" past injury, or "restoring wholeness" to victims (or even offenders) through reparation, retaliation, punishment or even pardon. But in the context of exhortation, fairness is not the issue, for redress is not the point. Rather, the story exists, not to blame, but rather for showing the *listener* how *he* or *she* might be a morally responsible person.

We might protest that we with our twenty-twenty hindsight have no entitlement to judge Thomas Jefferson. But such an outcry reflects misunderstanding of narrative's role as an interpretive and hermeneutic device. The purpose of the narrative, while framed *within* history, is not a lesson *about* history. The idea is that we must allow the story to tell its story, to teach us and to focus us in a forward-looking and hopeful direction—toward a more appropriate response to evil in the future. Exhortation is a striving toward moral flourishing. It tells us, as listeners of narrative, what to anticipate from the morally enriched persons that we hope to become.

For the poet, Jefferson represents Everyman. And in the poet's vision, Jefferson stumbles toward the light to see that indeed, we are marmosets in mantles and beasts in boots. Reason redeems us in our striving to take each other's hands, to bring order out of chaos and light out of darkness.

Jefferson (to George): My son, we have been lost in the dark.
And I was lost, who had dreamed there was a light.

. . . we must create the possibility
Of reason, and we can create it only
From the circumstances of our most evil despair. (194-5f)

Notes

1. Thomas Hobbes, *Leviathan*, Introduction by A. D. Lindsay (New York: Dutton, 1950). See Chapter 14.

2. John Locke, *Two Treatises of Government* (Cambridge, England: University Press, 1960).

3. John Locke, *Two Treatises of Government*, Book II, Chapter 2.

4. John Rawls, *Theory of Justice* (Cambridge, Mass.: Harvard University Press, 1971).

5. While the second version of *Brother to Dragons* actually won the Pulitzer Prize in 1979, I prefer, and use, the original version of the poem, first published in 1953. That version too won much acclaim and was widely considered to be among Warren's best works.

6. Job 30:29.

7. See *Robert Penn Warren's Brother to Dragons: A Discussion*, James A. Grimshaw, Jr., ed. (Baton Rouge: Louisiana State University Press, 1983). Lilburn actually nearly beheaded George and then forced another slave to chop up and burn the body. Lilburn and Isham have been purported to be mentally ill. See Boynton Merrill, *Jefferson's Nephews: a Frontier Tragedy* (Princeton, N.J.: Princeton University Press, 1976).

8. The definition used by Sanford H. Kadish in his authoritative "Complicity, Cause and Blame: a Study in the Interpretation of Doctrine," *California Law Review* 73 (March 1985) 323-410.

9. Pertaining to spring.

10. Gorge or gully.

11. See Michael Sandel's excellent *Liberalism and the Limits of Justice* (Cambridge: Cambridge University Press, 1982).

12. See Warren, *Brother to Dragons*, p. 181.

13. The Minotaur, the son of Pasiphaë, wife of Minos king of Crete, and a bull, had the body of a man and a bull's head. He was committed to the Cretan labyrinth where he was fed with human flesh.

14. To be related by blood as opposed to marriage.

15. Paul Ricoeur, *Hermeneutics and the Human Sciences*, John B. Thompson, ed. and trans. (London: Cambridge University Press, 1981), 182f.

Chapter 16

Fatherhood and Friendship in the Modern Regime: Jean Dutourd's *The Springtime of Life*

Will Morrisey

> *"One sees every day that it is easier to have intellect,*
> *wit and philosophy than heart, or, if you prefer it soul."*
> —*Jean Dutourd,* The Man of Sensibility

Civic Fortitude and *The Springtime of Life*

The Springtime of Life is a novel about fatherhood, love, and friendship in a modern political regime—France in the 1930s, during the last years of the Third Republic. Charles de Gaulle, who knew that terrain well, never stopped asking, How can *this* modern commercial republic defend itself? Given the kind of people who rule in such a regime, how can they, and their fellow citizens, be protected from the consequences of their own worst vices? How can they be encouraged in their virtues? Further, how can those men and women who are by nature not *of* the commercial republic nonetheless be brought to defend it against the much worse tyrannical regimes that seek to exploit the weaknesses of commercial republics?

De Gaulle caused several writers to think about these questions. The most celebrated of them was Andre Malraux. Malraux writes in the tradition—the "regime," the "succession," in Diogenes Laertius' sense—of Victor Hugo, the tradition of the grand gesture, the noble crescendo. Jean Dutourd, a man of very different sensibility, writes in the tradition of Flaubert and Proust—the tradition of meticulous literary craftsmanship and ironic subtlety. This makes him in one sense more interesting than Malraux. A writer in the Hugo tradition might well respond easily to Gaullist statesmanship: *la grandeur, la France, le Tricolore*. A writer in the Flaubert tradition will always hesitate before the grand gesture. How grand is it, really? Where does it point? A Flaubertian artist will apply a properly mixed acidic solution to the surface of Gaullism—treat it with a clarifying irony.

In *The Springtime of Life*, Dutourd presents Jacques de Boissy, a man in his twenties with two friends: Jean Pousselet, the friend of his childhood, and Captain

Lacassagne, a new friend, a few years older. Jean is the most intelligent of the three—or, at least, the most "intellectual." He dislikes his last name, which suggests something like "pushiness," bourgeois vulgarity. He is ill at ease with his family name, with his father's name, with "his own." He believes that he stands in awe of writers, and believes, fashionably, in "the goodness of the world, in justice and loyalty."[1] He gives no thought to the political conditions of writing, to say nothing of the political conditions of goodness and justice. He "believes in" loyalty, but will not practice it, in friendship or in love.

His mother is a silly, self-pitying war widow. The Great War stripped France of fathers, leaving a generation of "feminized," that is, submissive, sons who imagine that good grace consists of intelligence yielding to stupidity, especially if stupidity is vehement. Living in a "feminine universe," young men "readily believe in the fragility of women" (33); deference to Mme. Pousselet's insistent inanities has habituated Jean to a slightly guilty resentment in retreat. By inspiring in her only son "the conviction . . . that he had been created more to be loved than to love" (43), Mme. Pousselet has left him morally and intellectually flaccid, anorectic. Her idea of motherhood is requiring her little boy to eat all the food on his plate, "hungry or not" (43), substituting annoying, pointless duty for natural desire and pleasure.

A feminized world (in this sense) is a privatized world. "[F]rom 1920 to 1940, the child was the Frenchmen's alibi; he made it possible for them to abdicate with untroubled conscience their duties and their rights as citizens, to disregard the future of all under the pretext that they were occupied with the future of one, to think no longer about that pressing matter, demanding such tiresome vigilance, that is called liberty" (44).

Jean marries badly, of course. His wife is exactly like his mother, only more so. His mother's founding moral instruction—eat everything on your plate—deprives him of the strength to push away from the table when young Nadine puts herself on his plate, despite Mother's disapproval of the offering. An only child, habituated only to be loved and not to love, his soul is the prey of the stronger woman, the one who loves him more insistently. His mother had denatured him in order to attach him firmly to herself, failing to see that a soul with no real desires, no firmness, is incapable of firmness of attachment. Jean predictably resents Jacques's new friend, the "solid, patient, indefatigable, unshakable," and above all gentlemanly, Captain Lacassagne. Lacassagne hasn't "read any of the works of Andre Gide" (22). Surely, had he lived thirty years ago, a soldier like this would have plotted against Dreyfus! Dragooned (so to speak) into an excursion to Les Invalides with Jacques and the captain, Jean complains about the boring reminiscences of war veterans, and gives thanks that men like Napoleon "are no longer interested in France" (84). Pious about *litterateurs*, contemptuous of military officers; sure enough, Jean will enjoy a successful career in journalism.

Jacques de Boissy, by contrast, is no "intellectual." He is a young man of not exactly aristocratic pedigree: the "de" was shrewdly separated from the "Boissy" only a century back—but he has some of the cultivation of an aristocrat without having lost the aggressiveness of the bourgeois. The de Boissys are *new* aristocrats.

In childhood he dominates Jean because he has a ready-made attitude "for every circumstance of life" and acts forthrightly thereon (11). When he meets Jean's unfortunate mother, he acts as a sort of social statesman—taking her as she is, leaving her pleased and perhaps a touch better. (As a reader, she likes a good storyteller. Ah, you must try *Les Thibaults*. Humor? Do you know that very funny English writer, P. G. Wodehouse?) Jacques has the good breeding to be a hard man to embarrass, but never leaves others embarrassed.

Above all, Jacques is a man with a father. De Boissy *pere* is "a bit of a shark," a tough businessman. From him, Jacques learns—contra Jean's humanitarian illusions—that society is not at all "benevolent," and "it is a good thing to be on one's guard" (13). He learns to retaliate when insulted, but to take correction from his superiors—and therefore to recognize that superiority really exists. De Boissy *pere* is no paragon of political correctness, but he has kept his eyes open. After the Great War, he observes, women and horses disappeared:

> When the style of short hair appeared some ten years ago, I had an idea, and it may seem backward to you: I said to myself that we were witnessing Samson's revenge, that Delilah had gone mad and in cutting off her curls she had given up her powers. A sort of symbolic surrender, if you like. But notice this: my experience has taught me that people do not give up except in the last extremity, when they see that all is lost, that the situation is untenable, that there is no longer any way of holding their ground. This sort of thing must have happened with women. They felt that they had no place in the world as women . . . that it was necessary to be like men. (55-56)

As for men—according to M. de Boissy—it is really quite simple: justice consists of helping one's friends and harming one's enemies (117). As for his son, he says, with irony, "I am a modern father" (14), considering it "his duty to help his son's personality to 'expand,'" a modern attitude the novelist entertains with some suspicion, and to which M. de Boissy himself sets firm limits (14).

Unlike Jean, Jacques views literary life with cynicism, Captain Lacassagne with respect. In France, Jacques says, the government no longer governs. The police and the financiers govern, but those who wield "the real power today in a country that is no longer serious, a country that prefers words to events, or, if you like, the newspaper serial to history" (23) are women and men of letters. They constitute the real French *politeuma*, that is, the genuine ruling body of France. Women and men of letters always rule when the government and the military are weak. Proust is "the greatest contemporary novelist" because "he alone has understood this and has made it the essence of his work" (24). Ergo, Jacques announces that he shall use literature as "a means to success"; "in 1935, for Julien Sorel, the red and the black are the colors of ink" (35). Jean is shocked. His superficial literary idealism is offended. Jean is superficially an idealist, at core not so much a cynic—that would take strength—but without character. In Jacques, the cynicism is what is superficial. Jacques reads good books seriously and prefers not to discuss them with people who are not serious, mentioning the names of the great novelists Stendhal and Balzac "with a sort of affectionate mockery, emphasizing their eccentricities as though he had known them or as though they were still alive" (48).

While reading an author, he becomes the author—a Christian with Bloy, an atheist with Diderot (79). He treats greatness as a *living* thing without admitting to his friend Jean what Jean will never truly perceive: that greatness is a permanent possibility. In a calculatedly offhand way, he does his best to incorporate greatness in himself. He uses a sinecure at the War Ministry to write his first novel, which would indeed have been a success (his father judges), had he chosen to publish it. It is not long before he begins a serious one, with the support of his father, who senses the change and respects it.

A homely young woman falls in love with Jacques, who does his best to repel her, once he realizes her sentiments (thanks to another young woman, who tells him). But Anne-Marie is a woman who senses how to make the conquest, despite her disadvantage. She is not in the least literary, or intellectual. She scarcely understands the manuscript he reads to her. But what she does understand, well before Jacques understands it, is the significance of the fact that he *is* reading it *to her*. So she praises his work and (she really does love him) learns how to type. Like men in love with literature, women in love with men are chameleons, "instantly assum[ing] the color of the man at whom they have taken aim" (161-162; compare Jacques, p. 79). They become exactly like military men in war; love brings out their intelligence. They discard pettiness—in Anne-Marie's case, their fashionable bohemianism. A real woman is very much like a real aristocrat, the representative man "of the *ancien regime*" (162), tough, ardent and discriminating, kindly conscious of his superiority. Anne-Marie, "ugly at twenty-six, would be beautiful at fifty," thanks to the transformation, the crystallization, of soul that her love will effect. Eventually, and to his credit, "Jacques vaguely fores[ees] this distant metamorphosis" (175), and will marry her.

Jacques' Political Education

Captain Lacassagne tactfully gives Jacques the political education he needs to go with the sentimental education he has been receiving. First lesson: France, and the modern world, though automated and unhorsed, are not "automatic." They need tending. Without tending, they will perish. The Great War very nearly saw the destruction of France. Its aftermath—fatherless sons and daughters—threatens France still. The second lesson is for Jacques to understand that modern France is bourgeois, but bourgeois souls can't defend it. Going along and getting along won't work for a country located beside Germany. France won the Battle of the Marne because General Joffre "did not have the soul of one vanquished." He "made a stand" (96) and showed the courage of an aristocrat, thereby making a modern army of barbers and shopkeepers who were not aristocratic, of course, but stubborn enough to win, to defend that piece of soil that is France. Without soil, where will the soldier, the barber, the shopkeeper—the writer—stand and work? Without France, the French language will become as extinct as Latin—living on as a component of foreign languages, but no more than that. A writer has to write in a language, his own language. Lacassagne shows a novelist why 'his own' matters to him, how literary life depends upon your own country, your own family, your own friends.

Captain Lacassagne's third lesson is this: France should be fighting in Spain, on the republican side with the Communists, against Franco and his fascist allies. This has nothing to do with ideology. Lacassagne has met lieutenant colonel Charles de Gaulle, who observed that Soviet Russia is far away, but Nazi German and Fascist Italy border France. A Francoist Spain would mean "France encircled" (204). Concrete geopolitical circumstance means more than the ideology *du jour*. That a Popular Front government, of all things, could not see this represents the triumph of pacifism over proletarianism—a silly idea trumped by a sillier. Go to Spain, de Gaulle told Lacassagne; "reconnoiter the future enemy" (206). (Jacques offers to go with him, but although Dutourd is a Gaullist he is no Malrauvian, attempting to combine a life of writing with a life of political and military action: the man of letters belongs at his desk, not on the battlefield (207). It is enough that he respect those who go to the battlefield.)

Finally, Lacassagne teaches Jacques that there really are superior men, by nature and not only by social convention. Lacassagne admits that he had allowed himself to become a "bourgeoisified" soldier, a bureaucratic functionary in the War Ministry, "someone who was accommodating himself without reflection to the cowardly mediocrity into which the country had fallen" (200). De Gaulle made him recollect; he *re-minded* Lacassagne. De Gaulle caused Lacassagne to reflect upon what the French army is for, what France is for, why "there was every reason to die" for France (198). Lacassagne wants Jacques to be the kind of man who writes, living on French soil, who makes that soil worth defending. He wants him to be part of the succession of French writers. Lacassagne's attempt at political education succeeds. He changes neither Jacques's ideas nor his passions, but "taught him that there is a certain noble and romantic though realistic way of looking at the world" (211). The reconciliation of nobility and realism is the alliance of the spirited part of the soul with practical reason. In Greek terms, it is the alliance of *thumos*, or spiritedness, and *phronesis*, or prudence. In Dutourd's terms, it is "heart." In his book on Stendhal, *The Man of Sensibility*, Dutourd defines "heart" as "not only courage" but also "a desire to try one's strength, a nobility of character, a horror of what is base or vulgar . . . a passion for honor—in short, soul. And soul precisely as Alain defines it. Heart is what refuses the body."[2]

Intellect should ally itself with soul: "How many cowards there are for one Socrates who dies a hero, and how often our intellectual masters give us opportunities to despise them in their lives! One sees every day that it is easier to have intellect, wit and philosophy than heart, or, if you prefer it soul. Wars have at least this much good, that they permit us to see the souls of those we admire. Danger brings out the soul as rain brings out snails."[3] This alliance constitutes the character of the statesman. To enter the succession of French writers, a writer needs to understand this alliance, to think about how it might be perpetuated in new circumstances. Such an alliance is not "modern." Lacassagne leads Jacques to reflect that the modern world is not mere uprootedness, as Maurice Barres had said and Simone Weil would say, but a *systematized* uprootedness—cars in place of horses, shorthaired, streamlined women in place of long-haired, alluring ones. Politically, the modern world consists of "dictatorships by blackguards" and "republics of the petits bourgeois and the workers" (213), not constitutional monarchies or republics of citizen-soldiers. The Lacassagnian, or Gaullist, political education gives Jacques precisely what a writer needs: a theme worthy not only of his talent, but of his character, his sensibility, a theme that will develop that character and sensibility. Dutourd's reply to Malraux is: a political novel should not be directly political. A novel of manners is the novelistic way of writing about politics, because politics—the answer to the question, Who rules?—shapes manners, giving friendships and love affairs tensions unknown in other regimes. (Malraux's response: Don't write a novel, write an epic in prose. And in reply to Proust: Don't write a memoir, write an anti-memoir.)

Jean resents Jacques's new novel. "Up to that time, Jacques and he had been equals"; Jacques's superior wealth and family connections could be dismissed as mere accidents (231). But now, "without the aid of his family or his money, the individual Jacques had accomplished something of which the individual Jean had not been capable" (231). Jean, the bourgeois democrat, confronts the dilemma bourgeois democracy poses for its representative man. In the old regime, Jean would have been shielded from resentment by the realities of class. Not for a bourgeois Pousselot to concern himself with the accomplishments of a de Boissy! But now, "the unhappy fellow lived in miniature the drama of democracies where social life is insupportable because it is founded on merit, that is to say, you are exposed constantly to seeing someone who was your equal become your superior, and where consequently friendship is no longer possible" (231). Such weak social bonds make a bourgeois democracy susceptible to faction despite nominal equality, and therefore more likely to be heedless to foreign threats.

And so Jean fumes. He tries to discourage Jacques, scribbles a thousand corrections on the margins of the novel manuscript. How can a novelist be so insensitive? Jean complains. How can a novelist fail to wring his hands, feel somehow guilty about the suffering masses, Nazism, Communism, "the war in Spain, the lack of paid vacations, the housing problem, the armaments race" (239)? Jacques ignores the corrections. When Jean sees the uncorrected published version, the friendship is irretrievable. Jacques's father dies not long before the French prime minister Daladier announces the supposed settlement of the crisis in Czechoslovakia. Jacques realizes that Lacassagne is now his best friend, and therefore "suffered less from his father's death together with the feeling of not being unfaithful to his father" (282). *The Springtime of Life* is a story about finding a friend worthy of your father. You will need one. The modern regime needs some men and women of the *ancien regime* within it. They will both be braver than the demi-men and demi-women of the modern regimes, and also, sufficiently gracious not to resent their marginal status in a regime nominally ruled by the persons— hardly to be called citizens—such a regime produces.

Conclusion: France and "Greatness of Soul"

Jean was mistaken when he claimed that France no longer interested men like Napoleon. In Dutourd's view, one such man remained, Charles de Gaulle. Franklin Roosevelt suspected de Gaulle of Bonapartism in the worst sense, claiming to worry that de Gaulle would destroy republicanism, given the chance. In the event, he saved it, twice, and left it on a firmer foundation than he had found it. But it is not regime politics that Dutourd thinks of when he thinks of Napoleon. He thinks instead of greatness of soul. "The phrase 'great soul' turns up over and over again in Stendhal's life of Napoleon," he writes in his 1957 book *The Taxis of the Marne*.[4] "What historian other than Stendhal has perceived the greatness of Napoleon's soul? Yet there lies the whole key to his character" (17). Stendhal writes, "This man's whole life is a paean in praise of greatness of soul," by which he means something like what the American founders meant by fame, joined by courage and firmness of judgment, and exhibited in Napoleon's calmness in exile.[5] Napoleon was a natural aristocrat formed by an aristocratic civilization. He never understood representative government, and so his soul struggled between "the genius of tyranny and the profound reasoning powers that had made a great man of him."[6]

De Gaulle too was "a great soul," one that languished in the last, mediocre decades of the Third Republic, "tied down in the promotion roster of the army," "condemned to vegetate in garrison towns, with an occasional minor command to relieve the boredom. It needed nothing less than the disintegration of the nation to liberate this great soul from his bonds.[7] In his *Conversation with De Gaulle*, Dutourd admits that he had often worried that de Gaulle might turn tyrant. What he found was that de Gaulle reminded him of Flaubert even more than he resembled Napoleon—an even more surprising comparison. Like Flaubert, de Gaulle was a great anti-bourgeois, understanding France not as "a house of commerce" but as "a work of art, a cathedral upon which one has worked for a thousand years."[8] France had been feminized—its government in the Fourth Republic an indulgent mother, its people "one gigantic Madame Bovary, an enormous ninny in the arms of Bohemia."[9] A bohemianized bourgeoisie will no longer have the discipline to maintain something so modest as prosperity; what had hitherto been supposed to be the "low but solid ground" will turn muddy. France needed fatherliness in order to save its republicanism. It found de Gaulle, and de Gaulle re-founded it.

For de Gaulle (Dutourd found in conversing with him), France "had a character and a destiny, like a living creature, which one did not model at will."[10] This seems flatly to contradict the image of France as a work of art, a cathedral, until one reflects on the way Jacques de Boissy reads the literary artists of the past, treating them as living presences. De Gaulle was more than such a reader, he was such a 'writer.' Like Flaubert, in "his Herculean efforts to make one sentence with the balance of those of Montesquieu," de Gaulle strove to perfect a *living* work of art, France.[11] Thus we understand the "strange kinship" of de Gaulle and Flaubert: it is in "their pride of solitaries, their austere love of glory, their disdain for honors and money," their "humble placing of themselves in a French line" of succession—for

Flaubert, the succession of masters of the French language, for de Gaulle, the succession of those who made France "the most astonishing nation in History."[12] "Politics and literature proceeded from an identical patriotism."[13] The patriotism of literature and the patriotism of politics proceeds from a certain nature, from greatness of soul, from the soul-forming love and friendship that the great-souled have for one another. In a commercial republic, or worse, a "bohemianized" democracy, greatness of soul will find its rightful place not in the tyranny of Napoleon and not exactly in Napoleon's grace in exile, but in the political man's patient vigilance and preparedness. The literary man, for his part, must display a readiness to recognize and honor such a man when, if, he sees him.

Notes

1. Jean Dutourd, *The Springtime of Life*, Denver and Helen Lindley translation (Garden City: Doubleday and Company, 1974), 13. Subsequent page references in parentheses in the text. I am grateful to Dr. Michael Platt for drawing my attention to Dutourd and for encouraging me to write on this novel.

2. Jean Dutourd, *The Man of Sensibility*, Robin Chancellor translation (New York: Simon and Schuster, 1961), 218.

3. Dutourd, *The Man of Sensibility*, 219.

4. Jean Dutourd, *The Taxis of the Marne*, Harold King translation (New York: Simon and Schuster, 1957), 17. Subsequent references in parentheses in the text.

On the American founders and their idea of fame see Douglass Adair, *Fame and the Founding Fathers* (New York: W. W. Norton & Company), 1974. "The concept of *honor*," Adair writes, "like the concept of glory, is both the goal of character formation and an instrument of social control, building into the heart and mind of an individual a powerful personal sense of socially expected conduct, a pattern of behavior calculated to win praise from his contemporaries who are his social equals or superiors. For a particular person in a particular culture a sense of honor—a sense of due self-esteem, of proper pride, of dignity appropriate to his station—acts like conscience for a practicing Christian" (10). Adair associates honor with competition, combat, and the struggle for eminence and distinction; he regards it as "traditionally antithetical to the Christian demands for self-abnegation, humility, and altruism. Although this can be true, it need not be. The Fifth Commandment, "honor thy father and thy mother," does not preclude the ambition to act in a manner worthy of honor, as a father or a mother. Alexander Hamilton, who called the love of fame the ruling passion of the noblest minds, ended his life a Christian, without recanting his opinion of fame.

5. Stendhal, *A Life of Napoleon*, Roland Gant translation (London: The Rodale Press, 1956), 28, 184.

6. Stendhal, *Life*, 181-182.

7. Dutourd, *Taxis*, 18.

8. Jean Dutourd, *Conversation avec le general* (Paris: Flammarion, 1990), 31.

9. Dutourd, *Taxis*, 241.

10. Dutourd, *Conversation*, 40.

11. Dutourd, *Conversation*, 40.

12. *Conversation*, 40-41.
13. Ibid, 41.

Chapter 17

Mark Twain on Democratic Statesmanship: *A Connecticut Yankee in King Arthur's Court*

Robert M. Schaefer

> *I am a Yankee of the Yankees.*
> —*Hank Morgan in* A Connecticut Yankee

What is remarkable about Mark Twain's *A Connecticut Yankee* is that it reminds one of the pressing issues addressed by the American founders—the creation and preservation of democracy. The founders agreed that healthy democracies are remarkably difficult to beget and almost impossible to preserve. It is with this in mind that Twain turns his attention to the American regime and, quite consciously, offers a commentary about who we are as a people. This novel, perhaps best described as a work of political philosophy, is ingenious. A modern democrat discovers himself, by means of an accident-induced dream, in a sixth-century aristocratic society and by his presence there illustrates two very different worlds.

Many commentators have noted that Twain is known for his "American" style of writing: his open train of thought, his lack of pretentiousness, and his very straightforward style; he is *the* American writer. Nonetheless, he chooses to set this particular novel in the medieval era, and by so doing exposes the reader to two distinct ways of life.

This delightful story opens with a peculiar preface that first speaks to the "ungentle laws and customs" in which the book finds its context. Although Twain invents the ensuing tale, he asserts that the chaotic social condition described therein is universal, extending throughout time. Human beings are always subject to troubles that are generally of their own making. In the enigmatic preface, Twain also addresses the subject of the divine right of kings and by doing so forces the perplexed reader to wonder if such a thing may legitimately exist. Twain does not clearly offer an answer, but he asserts that the "executive head of a nation should be a person of lofty character and extraordinary ability," and only God is capable of making such a selection.[1] Although leaving the reader without a satisfactory answer to the question of rule by divine right, this brief preface does suggest, as the book confirms, that statesmanship and the common good are the primary themes of *A Connecticut Yankee*. For Twain, it seems that statesmanship means, before all else, that a leader necessarily must understand the people's propensity to vice and their potential for virtue. He needs to embody knowledge requisite to rule. He must understand, as well, the degree to which people can—and should—put aside flawed but inherited traditions in the name of progress and modernization. But by the end of the tale, Twain will again leave the reader slightly perplexed, this time asking the question, "Is statesmanship itself possible?"

Aristocracy versus Democracy

Hank Morgan, superintendent in a Connecticut arms factory, is hit upon the head with a crowbar by a disgruntled employee and awakes in Camelot, land of "old monkish superstitions." Possessing the knowledge of "modern" America, he immediately recognizes the superstitions and backwardness of a bygone era; he awakens a stranger in a strange land—in the year 528 A.D., to be exact.

Hank soon encounters the knight, Sir Kay, and he begins to discover all that the aristocracy really represents—in contrast to his boyhood tales of knights and chivalry. The Knights, unemployed and impractical, wander the countryside looking for adventure and they spend their evenings exaggerating their exploits. Disgusted at their artificiality, Hank is especially distressed when Sir Kay arbitrarily sentences him to death.

Amused with Sir Kay's story about capturing Hank, a "man-devouring ogre," the other nobles are indifferent to Hank's death sentence. Hank begins to learn the reality of medieval life; one different than that pictured in popular stories. The "ladies and gentleman" of the chivalrous past possess a vocabulary and morality that would "embarrass a tramp." Twain elucidates, in delightfully comic fashion, the true nature of this ancient time. The nobility are coarse and superficial, live in filth, and lack any concern for the peasants. The reader is startled to see that poets have rewritten and glamorized history; Twain, for his part, intends to set the reader straight.

Hank observes that human beings, seemingly rational, nevertheless hold closely to their inherited traditions. No matter how obviously wrong or misguided their opinions, they adhere to that which is theirs. Hank arrives from a century where merit is based on talent, but finds himself in a world where title and pedigree take precedence. He compares himself to an elephant in a zoo; a grand animal viewed with awe by those around him; nonetheless, even the lowliest medieval "tramp" does not truly respect Hank, for he is not one of them—they consider him mere "dirt." He sets out to clean up this mess—literally. He cleverly persuades a few of the nobles ("missionaries") to seize unsuspecting knights and wash them with soap.

Hank's disdain for the sixth-century English is summed up with the assertion that he is "a giant among pigmies, a man among children, a master intelligence among intellectual moles: by all rational measurement the one and only actually great man in that whole British world" (40). Fortunately, his knowledge of astronomical history saves him: he remembers that on the twenty-first of June, 528—his date of execution—a total eclipse of the sun had occurred. He then is able to "create" an eclipse of the sun moments before he is to be burned at the stake, cow his captors, and thereby escape execution. The ignorant nobility succumb to his trickery and he instantly assumes the role of a powerful official of the King and second only to the King himself.

In his new role, Hank attempts to enlighten the people to the evils of the Church, to the corruption of the monarchy, and to the virtues of democracy and science. Schools are opened, newspapers published, and scientific knowledge disseminated. He elaborates upon the principles underlying his pedagogical methodology:

> We speak of nature; it is folly; there is no such thing as nature; what we call by that misleading name is merely heredity and training. . . . We have no thoughts of our own. . . . All that is original in us, and therefore fairly creditable or discreditable to us, can be covered up and hidden by the point of a cambric needle, all the rest being atoms contributed by, and inherited from, a procession of ancestors that stretches back a billion years to the Adam-clan or grasshopper or monkey from whom our race has been so tediously and ostentatiously and unprofitably developed. (91)

Hank is optimistic in his ambitious plan to reeducate the masses—he sincerely believes that it can be done. But he must first battle two great enemies, the nobility and the Church.

Beginnings of Civilization

Twain's antipathy toward monarchy and the Church is well documented.[2] He believes that monarchy is a superficial and self-serving institution, doing nothing more than continuously tormenting those whom it should lead. According to Louis Budd, Twain rages about "monarchy as the 'grotesquest of all swindles ever invented by man'" (126). This is sharply indicated when Twain has King Arthur dress like a commoner to see the true condition of his people. In changing his apparel, Twain is dressing the King down, so to speak, and in this way helping the monarch to see the true condition of the peasants, a condition for which he is responsible.

One sees, then, the defining difficulty inherent in the text: good government requires someone with "extraordinary" abilities; if these are lacking, then government is unstable and unjust. What, though, of a republic? Is it inherently good and stable? The protagonist of Twain's tale unabashedly believes that republicanism can prevail against the brutal laws of the privileged classes. It is only *custom* that legitimizes corrupt monarchies and prevents self-government. If popular opinion, however, supports the people's right to rule, "self-appointed specialists" are not needed to rule society (143-44).

Hank believes that English custom should be altered and replaced with yankee common sense. He is the truest of yankees: self-reliant, clever, undaunted.

He describes himself as a practical American concerned with business matters, and disdains more aesthetic matters, such as poetry, art, and music. Set against this is an era in which great poetry and images abound, a time when the fanciful is more real than reality. Hank sees through the artificiality, for he is a reasonable man: he reports that he is "nearly barren of sentiment . . . or poetry" (Twain, 4).

However, to avoid being burned at the stake, Hank is inspired to declare that he is a magician, the Supreme Grand High-yu-Muckamuck. He promises to outsmart the Knights of the Round Table, whose salient characteristic is "manliness," and whose primary "claim to fame" is their alleged ability to overcome unseen monsters and giants. Such stories abound in Camelot. Our hero dryly notes that pride animates the denizens of the sixth century. It is attractive, even lovable, but

> [t]here did not seem to be brains enough in the entire nursery, so to speak, to bait a fishhook with; but you didn't seem to mind that, after a little, because you soon saw that brains were not needed in a society like that, and, indeed would have marred it, hindered it, spoiled its symmetry—perhaps rendered its existence impossible. (14)

Why, though, is poetry or imagination so prevalent in this novel? Obviously, Americans are not enamored of great poetry. Shakespeare and Homer are required in liberal arts colleges, but the everyday American ignores such works. The likes of Anne Rice and John Grisham have replaced Plutarch. Great deeds and the heroic are no longer the concern of contemporary Americans.

Yet, poetry is helpful for it teaches us about nature, limits native restlessness, and makes better citizens.[3] Twain demands that we look more closely at the relationship between poetry and society. A peculiar shift has occurred over the centuries. In the modern world, there is no higher frame of reference by which to judge one's actions. By contrast, classical literature examines man's place in the universe—a prerequisite for ethics—and suggests a course of action as to how we ought to live. Yet, such literature is not simply moralistic. Authors of great works attempt to comprehend the nature of the cosmos, to determine what is wrong in a particular person or society, and they try to prevent future error. Twain's *A Connecticut Yankee* is a good example of such literature, notwithstanding its simple American style. The book does not merely attempt to describe the truth about the sixth century; rather, the reader is expected to reflect upon the modern psyche as it unfolds through Hank's confrontation with his medieval allies and antagonists.

What is curious about the novel and perplexing to many commentators is its inability to be labeled as a comedy or a tragedy. Traditionally, tragedy is a story about the fall of a great person, normally due to *hubris* or pride. Comedy, following the classical pattern, begins with a disordered community or family, and the resolution occurs when things are properly reordered and justice prevails. *A Connecticut Yankee* does not easily fit into any category. It clearly is burlesque; for example, a knight rides the countryside sporting an advertisement for a new toothbrush, "Try Noyoudont." Conversely, the ending of the novel is tragic. Mixing the two genres gives Twain the opportunity to describe man's propensity for error while simultaneously celebrating his achievements.

Louise Cowan succinctly notes that "The knowledge provided by literary works of art frees us from our own limited experience to give us something like 'a second life.'"[4] She also suggests that the function of art is *analogical* in nature. Hence, good literature puts us in different shoes, so to speak, requiring us to examine ourselves. Analogical literature is quite useful, for it causes us to reflect in a different sort of way. Of course, Hank did not really physically incur a "transposition" back to the sixth century. On the other hand, Twain's imagination allows the reader to transmigrate and begin to learn about "a knowledge of the reality of what we nowadays call our 'values' . . . or, classically . . . 'virtues.'"[5] In the novel, American virtues—fairness and decency—are contrasted with those of the medieval era as Twain's protagonist sojourns in a land where the brutal English law demands the death of a mother who steals to feed her starving child.

Dismayed at such cruelty, Hank attempts to foster republican principles of liberty and equality by thrusting England into the future via a form of vulgar "poetry": a newspaper. The "Camelot *Hosannah and Literary Volcano*," a highly irreverent and flippant tabloid ("Arkansas journalism"), pokes subtle fun at the prevailing customs, laws, and vices. Hank's belief in democratic practices, including a free press, is so strong that he claims, "I was no shadow of the king; I was the substances; the king himself was the shadow" (37). Hank's power would be overwhelming were it not for his mortal enemy, the Roman Catholic Church. In Hank's view, the Church and the aristocracy—both artificial entities—must be emasculated. Hank despises both: "The most of King Arthur's British nation were slaves, pure and simple, and bore that name, and wore the iron collar on their necks. . . . The truth was, the nation as a body was in the world for one object, and one only: to grovel before king and Church and noble" (38).

Hank's animosity is driven by his belief that the Church undermines men's freedom and replaces it with a kind of psychological servitude. Using the Beatitudes as a pretext, the priests replace manliness with humility and obedience. Hank's wrath is not necessarily against Christianity per se, but the Church, for she "converted a nation of men to a nation of worms" (39). Churchmen, even with the best of intentions, are dangerous because humans are not perfect and easily become misguided and despotic.

The Protestant/American resolution to the problem of religion is ingenious. Hank suggests, echoing Alexis de Tocqueville, that religion is the "first of [our] political institutions."[6] Christianity appeals to mankind because of its promise of immortality. Hence, human beings are naturally inclined to believe and follow biblical teachings, thereby making good citizens. Corruption tends to filter in when religion is institutionalized. And it is this corruption that Hank rails against.

Tocqueville believes that America prevails because religion is found in public and private forums, but the clergy and churches instinctively adhere to the

notion of separated church and state. Simply put, the clergy do not align themselves with political parties, although they surely attempt to influence them.
When clerics become overtly political and associate with political parties, their
power and influence diminish. Hank understands the secret to the First Amend-
ment: America is healthier when religion is not on center stage. It can be everywhere, but not directly leading day-to-day political affairs.

Hank's solution is Protestant in nature: being faithful is imperative, but the
corrupting power of the institution ought to be limited. Under his tutelage, "Protestant congregations" are spread everywhere, and anyone "could be any kind of
Christian he wanted to" (47). His fear of the Church is irremediable. It is corrupt,
but Hank, so he claims, is not. He attempts to usurp the Church's authority and,
temporarily, rule over England, and he assures the reader that "Unlimited power
is the ideal thing when it is in safe hands" (47).

Equality and Progress

According to Tocqueville, what guides and directs the American soul is a belief in an immortal hereafter, with attendant moral rules in this lifetime. But as
Hank teaches, what also animates Americans, contrary to the Russians or English, is our faith in progress. We do not appreciate "great" literature, or nobility
or intellectual virtue. We appreciate work. Common sense suggests that work
protects us, literally, from the exigencies of nature. The world is difficult and
cruel. Hard work overcomes nature.

Tocqueville states that "It is not that aristocratic peoples absolutely deny
man's capacity to improve himself, but they do not think it unlimited. They think
in terms of amelioration, not change."[7] When classes disappear—and equality
reigns in the hearts of men—then the "human mind imagines the possibility of an
ideal but always fugitive perfection"[8] Tocqueville asserts that modern democrats
believe that anything is possible. This is good in most cases, but not all.

Tocqueville indicates that a people always live according to some conception
of honor or pride and that "every time men come together to form a particular
society, a conception of honor is immediately established among them."[9] In the
Middle Ages, honor is based on martial valor, courage, and on specific individual deeds. One needs to appear self-sufficient and above the everyday needs of
the commoner, including his need to work. Even poor aristocrats disdain work,
to avoid the dishonor of their fellow nobles. Tocqueville concludes by noting

> Humanity and gentleness were no part of [feudal] law, but it praised generosity;
> it set more store by liberality than benevolence; it allowed men to enrich them-
> selves by gambling or by war, but not by work. It preferred great crimes to small
> earnings.[10]

A desire for divine self-sufficiency and freedom from necessity animates
aristocrats. These old conceptions of honor are like a forgotten religion in which
no one now believes; the new religion is progress. Although the modern definition of progress is not clearly articulated by Hank nor by Tocqueville, it seems

that honor is bestowed to those who work unceasingly to achieve greater production. Many people consider work an end itself. Others, such as Hank, succumb to the belief that perfection of society is possible. Twain rejects the notion of indefinite perfection, especially witnessed in futuristic novels. The desire for perfection is dangerous, leading to immoderate expectations. The future is uncertain, but an examination of the past shows our limitations.

Most of us see the world through democratic eyes and naturally do not understand the attraction of aristocracy. Democrats regard aristocrats as their equals—for surely they cannot be fundamentally different. We are all equal! Aristocrats are incapable of looking upon commoners as anything other than their inferiors—commodities to be disposed of at their whim. Their lives, and deaths, mean nothing. The aristocratic propensity is not toward progress, but greatness. What animates Hank is the belief in equality and the possibility of "perfection" of the English commoners. The greatness of the church, the nobility, and the heroic feats of the knights impress most denizens. No matter how unbelievable the yarn, all believe. The only true followers of Hank's project are quite young, for their souls have yet to be influenced by aristocratic notions and propaganda.

In Plato's *Republic*, all those over the age of ten are exiled from the city. Those remaining are properly "educated" to be good citizens. But Plato's republic is only a city in speech, not a blueprint for an actual society. Hank, however, genuinely attempts to transform England. He realizes that this can only be done with a bloody war and, in his zeal for progress, he embraces it. Lacking statesmanship, Twain's protagonist tries to supply the lack by force of arms. If statesmanship is indispensable for political peace and prosperity, Twain prods the reader into asking whether one can "learn" statesmanship or if it only occurs by chance? If the latter, then all societies are subject to the whims of fortune.

The Failed Republic

A Connecticut Yankee prompts the reader to adopt a new perspective. By so doing, he gains a clearer insight in the mysterious machinations of the human soul. Hank, decent, sincere, and well-intentioned, presumes that with the aid of science he will overthrow the ancient regime and institute a republic. He "hankers," of course, to be its first president, but he does not fully appreciate the difficulty of the enterprise and in pursuit of it becomes as despotic as the nobility. Hank proclaims freedom of the press and allows Sir Dinadan the Humorist to publish a book of humor. Hank nonchalantly notes that one of the jokes aggravates him, so the book is suppressed and the author hanged.

The Church then imposes an "Interdict" to stop the budding tyrant at which point he meets the challenge by waging war upon "civilization." He issues his own proclamation:

> The monarchy has lapsed, it no longer exists. By consequence, all political power has reverted to its original source, the people of the nation . . . all men are become exactly equal . . . *A Republic is hereby proclaimed.* (259)

The "republic" consists of fifty-two lads, well trained in modern warfare. Urged to destroy their homeland, the handful of boys apprehensively respond: "These people are our people, they are bone of our bone, flesh of our flesh, we love them—do not ask us to destroy our nation!" (262). Hank rebuts that they are warring *only* against 30,000 knights, not civilians. Hank appeals to the boys' honor by asking if they are afraid of the knights. Naturally their pride overwhelms them and "they went gaily to their posts."

Hank's inclination toward despotism becomes clearer during a subtle and unsettling conversation with a young assistant, Clarence. The war against chivalry is underway and the two plan their defense. Following a discussion about educating the "superstition" out of the English, they invent another "miracle." By arranging electrical wires outside of the cave in which they are hiding, the enemy will be electrocuted when they advance. In a calm and rational fashion, the two give great thought to the most efficient means of killing everyone. Under Hank's tutelage, Clarence learns that if the wires are ungrounded, they will not use any power until touched. Clarence declares "Of course! I don't know how I overlooked that. It's not only cheaper, but it's more effectual than the other way"(258).

Progress is good yet dangerous, for it misleads individuals into thinking that any course of action can be taken without danger. In Twain's Camelot, twenty-five thousand "friends" are about to die, which fact induces the reader to conclude that Hank's science is both immoral and aimless. Even Clarence begins to recognize the problem and chastises him by pointing out that the adult commoners "were born in an atmosphere of superstition and reared in it. It is in their blood and bones. We imagined we had educated it out of them" (256).

This classic novel is helpful for it brings to light the inherent and eternal problems with democracy and illustrates the challenges for those who wish to preserve and perpetuate it. Tocqueville, again, serves as a thoughtful guide in the modern world. He teaches that "in democracies individual interests and those of the state demand that education for most people should be scientific, commercial, and industrial rather than literary."[11] Too much classical literature—of the great exploits of the Greeks, Romans, or Medieval Knights—causes people to become unrealistic in their expectations and "always make them want things which their education had not taught them how to earn."[12] They become dangerous citizens or rulers. Too little classical education unleashes individualism and a lack of understanding of the limits of politics. A balance between the two is required. To achieve this, however, is difficult. The attempt to do so is the mark of statesmanship.

The two worlds—of knight errantry and modern democracy—cannot live together and the protagonist cannot make one conform to the other, despite all the advantages of progress at his disposal. Unable to transform the world of chivalry, Hank ultimately chooses to wage war against it. He admits that he is "drunk with glory" about defeating his opponent and is filled with the desire for greatness and becomes that which he scorns. The Church, knights, and Hank all battle for earthly glory.

Hank himself does not invent the marvels of the modern world, but he appears to be the creator. As such, the people are awed by his achievements and he drinks in the astonishment and praise over his deeds. He is "drunk with enjoyment" that surpasses any deeds of "king, conqueror, or poet" (159). He desires to become king, conqueror *and* poet; and he is willing to wage "a final struggle for supremacy." Overcome by his own pride, Hank utilizes technology to ensure destruction. Although he possesses a modicum of common sense and the ability to live as a free citizen, he is no statesman. Twain notes "this Yankee of mine . . . is a perfect ignoramus; he is boss of a machine shop; he can build a locomotive or a Colt's revolver, he can put up and run a telegraph line, but he's an ignoramus, nevertheless."[13] Hank, a self-appointed specialist, blames his eventual failure on fortune, but it is actually due to a lack of prudence. He does not possess deliberative knowledge, the ability to comprehend that rulers cannot simply remake society—they must rule in light of tradition and circumstance.

Return to Camelot

The most peculiar part of the story is the ending. The thousands of rotting corpses lying nearby have poisoned the air, slowly killing the inhabitants within the cave. Hank's science has backfired, causing Clarence to utter "We had conquered; in turn we were conquered" (271-72). Meanwhile, Merlin sneaks into the cave where the rebels are hiding and sentences the boys to death. Throughout the novel, Hank ridicules Merlin's powers by demonstrating that nineteenth-century rationalism is superior to absurd spells. But, magically, Merlin's powers are very effective, and he curses Hank to fall asleep for thirteen centuries. Awaking in the nineteenth century, Hank lives out his days in modern England, alone. The postscript by Twain describes the eventual death of the Yankee. Hank greets his final moments with "pleasure, gratitude, gladness, and welcome," for in his delirious state of mind he returns to the sixth century. Happy to be back, he cries out about the terrifying nightmares he dreamt. He cannot believe that the nobility is gone, the king is dead, nor that a revolution occurred destroying the "chivalry of England" (274). Frightened by the prospect of again returning to the nineteenth century, Hank moans:

> *don't* let me go out of my mind again; death is nothing, let it come, but not with those dreams, not with the torture of those hideous dreams—I cannot endure *that* again. (274)

Delirious on his deathbed, he imagines the return of King Arthur. The glory of the king and his court comforts the dying man by inspiring him with its elegance and nobility. The king's presence embodies that which "could make life worth the living," and a kind of aristocratic honor swells his soul, granting meaning to his life one last time (274). Hank sees a greater good in non-scientific chivalry and thereby is transformed into that which he sought to overturn. "We had conquered; in turn we were conquered," his friend Clarence ruefully writes in the "Postscript."

The dark ending reflects Twain's doubt that the masses can truly learn to rule themselves or that statesmen are present in sufficient numbers to assist them. Budd notes that "Like Voltaire, in hating superstition [Twain] often despised the masses for holding on to it. In his novels most of the mob that the self-reliant thinker tries to enlighten are dull and unwilling pupils."[14] Individuals can learn about being independent and self-reliant, however, these democratic virtues do not suffice for a stable society. Statesmanship requires a deeper understanding of custom and law. Hank lacks this knowledge, however, and believes that the American regime is a "machine" that, once founded, would regulate itself in a rational and businesslike manner. His pathetic demise suggests that although humans are capable of being reasonable, they are still very human. Their pride, sentiment, self-interest and religious inclinations cannot be willed away.

Hank's tragic failure brings to light the limits of what leaders may expect of a people: they are incapable of godlike, rational perfection and, in many instances, are animated by illusions of grandeur. Reflecting upon Hank's ironic metamorphosis enables one to appreciate the intricacies of the human soul and the difficulty of founding and perpetuating a good society.

Notes

1. Mark Twain, *A Connecticut Yankee in King Arthur's Court* (New York: Bantam Books, 1989), vii. All parenthetical references in the text refer to this edition. In addition to other works cited, the following texts are recommended: Harold Bloom, ed., *Mark Twain* (New York: Chelsea House Publishers, 1986); James M. Cox, *Mark Twain: The Fate of Humor* (Princeton: Princeton University Press, 1966); Bernard DeVoto, *Mark Twain's America* (New York: Houghton Mifflin Company, 1960); Forrest G. Robinson, ed., *The Cambridge Companion to Mark Twain* (United Kingdom: Cambridge University Press, 1998). A charming edition of *A Connecticut Yankee*, including reproductions of the 1889 first-edition illustrations by Daniel Carter Beard, is now part of the Mark Twain Library, Bernard L. Stein, ed., (Berkeley: University of California Press, 1979).

2. Louis J. Budd, *Mark Twain: Social Philosopher* (Bloomington: Indiana University Press, 1962), 111-127.

3. Cf. Alexis de Tocqueville, *Democracy in America*, ed. J.P. Mayer trans. George Lawrence (New York: HarperPerennial, 1988), 484.

4. Donald and Louise Cowan, eds., *Classic Texts and the Nature of Authority* (Dallas: The Dallas Institute Publications, 1993), 16.

5. Cowan, *Classic Texts*, 18.

6. Tocqueville, *Democracy*, 292.

7. Tocqueville, *Democracy*, 453.

8. Tocqueville, *Democracy*, 453.

9. Tocqueville, *Democracy*, 620.

10. Tocqueville, *Democracy*, 618.

11. Tocqueville, *Democracy*, 476-77.

12. Tocqueville, *Democracy*, 476.

13. Albert Bigelow Paine, *A Biography* (New York: no publisher given, n.d.), Vol. II, 887-88, quoted in James M. Cox, *Mark Twain*, 206.

14. Budd, *Mark Twain*, 137-38.

Chapter 18

Pagan Virtue and Christian Charity: Flannery O'Connor on the Moral Contradictions of Western Culture

Gregory R. Johnson

> *My subject in fiction is the action of grace
> in territory held largely by the devil.*
> —*Flannery O'Connor*

Flannery O'Connor's short story "Revelation" vividly dramatizes the tension in Western political thought between the ideal of equality and the necessity of hierarchy or class structure and social distinction. The idea of the equal dignity of all men derives from the Christian teaching that God is infinitely distant from creation and thus equally distant from all created beings. Measured by the standard of God, all created beings, whether masters or slaves, kings or commoners, appear to be equal. On the other hand, the politically realistic acceptance of social hierarchy derives from pagan Greek thought, which operates only within the mundane horizon of natural differences and hierarchies. The conflict between equality and hierarchy in the city is present in the soul of the individual political actor as the conflict between the virtues of charity and magnanimity.

The conflict between the two ethical ideals and their corresponding worldviews is more acute today than in previous decades and centuries. Western society is no longer a monolithic Judeo-Christian environment since pagan virtue, made respectable by the ascendance of modern secularism, offers an apparently viable alternative to Judeo-Christianity. Thus, the Christian businessman or public official living out the precarious charge to be "in the world but not of it," and the secular government striving to accommodate evenhandedly men and women of faith, are both in need of O'Connor's resolution.

Magnanimity versus Charity

For pagan philosophy, the highest virtue is magnanimity (*megalopsychia*, greatness of soul). For Christianity, the highest virtue is charity (*agape*). Magnanimity and charity often resemble one another: both virtues lead to generosity, forbearance, and forgiveness in dealing with human failings. Both virtues reject small-minded calculations of selfish advantage. But fundamental metaphysical and moral differences lie behind these virtues.

For the Greeks, magnanimity is a kind of pride or self-esteem. In common parlance, it is the pride of those in "high society"—the people on the upper rungs of the social ladder. For Aristotle, however, conventional social status is not the highest thing to take pride in. Instead, one should take greater pride in one's moral character. Thus for Aristotle, magnanimity is the well-justified pride of the highly virtuous, and it is opposed to two related vices, smallness of soul, in which one underestimates one's virtues, and boastfulness, in which one overestimates them. The greatest good for the magnanimous man is his own character, the perfection of his own soul. The greatest external good for the magnanimous man is the recognition and honoring of his virtue by his peers. Thus magnanimity inevitably involves self-love and self-gratification. Aristotle defends the love of one's own moral self-perfection as entirely praiseworthy. Magnanimity, moreover, involves an awareness of moral and social differences and hierarchies, which fit perfectly into the hierarchical cosmos of the pagan philosophers.

Charity, however, does not involve self-love or self-gratification. The concept of charity arises from the metaphysics of creation *ex nihilo*. If one holds that God is goodness himself, that God can exist undiminished even if the world does not exist, and that God nevertheless chose to create the world, then it is difficult to understand the motive of creation. Since God can exist without the world, he did not create it because he needed it. Since God is goodness itself, creation produces no net increase in existing goodness, for the goodness of creation is merely borrowed from God. Creation, therefore, cannot be understood in terms of egoistic motives. There is simply nothing in it for God. It can only be understood as an act of love or generosity, a love or generosity that does not, and indeed cannot, aim at any recompense.

The name of this gift-love is charity. God creates the world out of charity, enters the world as Jesus out of charity, dies for the redemption of mankind out of charity, and Christians must imitate his example. Of the three theological virtues, faith, hope, and charity, charity is the highest, because God himself practices it.

Flannery O'Connor's "Revelation" explores the conflict between the virtues of charity and magnanimity in the soul of a single woman, and in doing so illuminates the conflicts in the soul of our entire civilization.[1] O'Connor's treatment of this conflict is particularly interesting, for although she was deeply committed to the Christian vision, she also recognized the genuine moral intelligence of the pagan viewpoint and was not, therefore, quick to dismiss it. Indeed, it is likely that she herself saw a potential resolution to the conflict, a synthesis that can and should embrace both charity and magnanimity

The Plot of "Revelation"

The plot of "Revelation" is quite simple. The story begins in a doctor's waiting room. The protagonist, Ruby Turpin, is accompanying her husband Claud, who is visiting the doctor because of an ulcer on his leg. In economic terms, Mrs. Turpin belongs to the upper middle class. Morally and socially, she regards herself as a member of the Southern upper class. She is also a pious Christian, apparently a Baptist, for she seems to believe that her acceptance of Christ has assured her redemption once and for all.

As she waits, Mrs. Turpin carefully sizes up the people in the room in terms of their social class and their moral character. She then strikes up a conversation with another lady of her class, a conversation that eventually involves other people in the waiting room. The conversation abundantly displays Mrs. Turpin's prejudices, her snobbery, and her complacent conviction of her own salvation.

This enrages the upper-class lady's college-age daughter, the surly and unattractive Mary Grace, an alienated secular egalitarian seething with resentment against her own mother and her social class and its prejudices. Mary Grace hurls her *Human Development* textbook at Mrs. Turpin, striking her on the head, then tries to strangle her before she is pulled off. Mary Grace's parting shot to Mrs. Turpin is, "Go back to hell where you came from, you old wart hog" (207).

The remainder of the story is set on the Turpin farm. Mary Grace's words have struck home, setting in motion a process of moral reflection in Mrs. Turpin, forcing her to question her moral complacency, particularly her conviction that she has been saved, and to confront the conflict between her class-obsessed snobbery and her Christian commitment to charity. Mrs. Turpin's reflections open her soul to receive a revelation: a vision of souls ascending into heaven as the hierarchies of her world, and even the virtues of her class, are burned away by God's chastening love.

The Pagan Virtues of Ruby Turpin

Ruby Turpin is typical of O'Connor's female protagonists. She is a strong and capable white Southern woman who runs a farm. She dominates her husband and all around her. But she seems an unlikely person to whom one would ascribe classical magnanimity. Indeed, she seems more characterized by smallness of mind rather than greatness of soul. Mrs. Turpin, after all, is obsessed with ranking people in terms of social class. The opening paragraph is thick with terms denoting size. When Mrs. Turpin enters the waiting room, it is described as "small" and she is described as "very large" (191). But she is large in body. Her eyes, the windows of her soul, are described as "little bright black." They immediately "take in" and "size up" the room and its occupants, honing in on such small details as the smallness of the room, the limpness of the magazines, and the overflowing ashtray (which would have been emptied if she had been running things), and taking special note of people's shoes, hair styles, clothes, posture, deportment, and cleanliness, from which she could determine their income levels and social class. A constant refrain throughout the story is Mrs. Turpin's thankfulness that she and her husband have "a little of everything" (198, 199, 203, 205, 218).

At night, Mrs. Turpin lies awake thinking about social class. If given the choice between being "a nigger or white-trash," she decides that she would prefer to be a "neat, clean, respectable Negro woman, herself but black" (195). Other times, she occupies herself naming and ranking the classes of people. On the bottom are "most colored people" and "the white-trash." Above them are homeowners. Above them are home- and landowners, like her and Claud. And above them are people with bigger homes and more land. At this point, however, the hierarchy becomes somewhat confused, for there are colored people who own homes and land, trashy people who owned more than she did, and fallen upper-class people who owned neither homes nor land. "Usually by the time she had fallen asleep all the classes of people were moiling and roiling around in her head, and she would dream they were all crammed together in a box car being ridden off to be put in a gas oven" (196).

At a certain point in the conversation, Mrs. Turpin mentally dismisses the opinion of a white-trash woman, noting to herself that, "you had to *have* certain things before you could *know* certain things" (199). She discounts the woman's look of disapproval because of "where it came from" (201).

Magnanimity is a kind of pride, and although her social standing and virtues are modest by Aristotle's standards, Ruby Turpin is a very proud lady. She is not particularly proud of her appearance. She weighs 180 pounds and is incapable of dieting (203, 193). Even the name "Turpin" brings to mind the squat, earthy, ungainly turnip. Mrs. Turpin does, however, take pride in the fact that at age 47, "there was not a wrinkle in her face except around her eyes from laughing too much" (194). This last physical flaw is, apparently, merely the price she pays for the spiritual virtue of a sense of humor.

Mrs. Turpin puts a much higher premium on the spiritual virtues. She regards a good inner disposition as more important than external appearances. She has a high opinion of her disposition, and she is thankful for it:

> If Jesus had said, "You can be high society and have all the money you want and be thin and svelte-like, but you can't be a good woman with it," she would have to say, "Well, don't make me that then. Make me a good woman and it doesn't matter what else, how fat or how ugly or how poor!" Her heart rose. He had not made her a nigger or white-trash or ugly! He had made her herself and given her a little of everything. Jesus, thank you! she said. Thank you thank you thank you! Whenever she counted her blessings she felt as buoyant as if she weighted one hundred and twenty-five pounds instead of one hundred and eighty. (203)

Later, the last straw that precipitates the attack by Mary Grace is when Mrs. Turpin voices these sentiments aloud:

"If it is one thing I am," said Mrs. Turpin with feeling, "it's grateful. When I think who all I could have been besides myself and what all I got, a little of everything, and a good disposition besides, I just feel like shouting, 'Thank you, Jesus, for making everything the way it is!' It could have been different! For one thing, somebody else could have got Claud." At the thought of this, she was flooded with gratitude and a terrible pang of joy ran through her. "Oh thank you, Jesus, Jesus thank you!" she cried aloud. (206)

But Mrs. Turpin's meticulous attention to details, her obsession with class, and her pride, although extreme, are not necessarily signs of small-mindedness, particularly in the classical pagan sense. Indeed, the classical idea of greatness of soul presupposes both the existence and awareness of a hierarchical social order, even though it also encourages an inner detachment from it. Furthermore, for Aristotle, a person with the vice of small-mindedness (*micropsychia* or *pusillanimity*) falls short of his moral potential because he has an insufficiently high estimation of his moral worth and potential; a pusillanimous man lacks pride and therefore sets low standards for himself and lives down to them. He concerns himself with trifles that are beneath him. Mrs. Turpin, however, has very high moral standards and is quite satisfied that she lives up to them; indeed, she is certain that she has assured her own redemption.

Furthermore, Mrs. Turpin exemplifies another characteristic of classical magnanimity: irony. Irony in the classical sense is a form of reserved dissimulation through which a superior person does not display his superiority in front of his inferiors. Mrs. Turpin does display her snobbery, but never to the objects of her disdain. She is even careful not to be noticed when she examines people's shoes (194). In the waiting room, she mentally registers her disdain for the white trash present, yet although she does not wish to converse with them, she does not speak frankly and does not treat them rudely. O'Connor constantly illustrates her reserve by contrasting what Mrs. Turpin says and what she thinks. She tells the white trash woman how she keeps her pigs clean, while she thinks to herself that they are cleaner than the white trash woman's child (198). When the woman says that she would never hose off a hog, Mrs. Turpin thinks to herself that the woman would never own a hog in the first place (198, cf. 199, 203). She does speak negatively of some blacks, but never in their presence. Indeed, one of the things she talks about is the necessity of "buttering up niggers," but "you got to love them if you want them to work for you" (199). When a black delivery boy enters the waiting room, she helps him, albeit somewhat patronizingly, by showing him the buzzer to summon the nurse, further demonstrating her practical mastery and attention to detail.

Another characteristic of classical magnanimity Mrs. Turpin displays is a sense of the superior importance of the internal goods of character compared to the external goods of fortune. It is this feature, in particular, that demonstrates her breadth of soul. When she contemplates the choice of being made a respectable black woman or white trash, she chooses being a respectable black woman, clearly showing that inner decency is worth more to her than social status (195).[2] When she inventories the different classes of people, she clearly understands that class is different than money, for she notes that there are trashy people with lots of money and respectable people with none, and she clearly regards the latter as superior (196). Looking at Mary Grace, she notes that "it was one thing to be ugly and another to act ugly," clearly regarding the latter as worse (196). Mrs. Turpin immediately sees past the outward resemblance between Mary Grace and her mother to the radically different temperaments beneath (196). This attitude is shared by Mary Grace's mother, who points out that as long as Mrs. Turpin has a "good disposition it does not matter that she is overweight" (193).

The Intelligence of Mrs. Turpin's Snobbery

Most readers of "Revelation" find Mrs. Turpin thoroughly repulsive. Gilbert Muller characterizes her as, "a negative moral agent, unaware of her own absurdity because she is so attached to an inauthentic existence" and as "unrelieved by any redeeming qualities."[3] Dorothy Walters castigates her as "smug" and close-minded.[4] Carol Shloss regards Mrs. Turpin's self-esteem as "ill-founded."[5] O'Connor's letters, however, make it clear that she does not entirely share these judgments: "If the story is taken to be one designed to make fun of Ruby, then it's worse than venal."[6] In another letter, O'Connor vows to revise an early draft of the story to make clear that, "Ruby is not just an evil Glad Annie."[7] Finally, she states: "I like Mrs. Turpin as well as Mary Grace. You got to be a very big woman to shout at the Lord across a hogpen. She's a country female Jacob."[8]

These sentiments are evident to a careful reading of the story. Unlike Jane Austen, who invariably takes wicked pleasure in portraying snobbery as a form of stupidity, O'Connor quietly underlines the intelligence of Mrs. Turpin's snobbery. First of all, Mrs. Turpin is shown to be a master of reading and decoding the meaning of people's clothes, hair, posture, cleanliness, etc. Second, Mrs. Turpin's ability to read people allows her to make accurate predictions about their behavior.

As soon as she enters the waiting room, she notices a small blond child, taking up enough room for two people in an otherwise full room. She notes that his clothes are dirty, his posture slumped, his arms idle, his gaze blank, and his nose snotty. She pegs him immediately as white trash and correctly infers that the child will not make room for her, nor will he be told to by his family (191-2).

Mrs. Turpin spotted the child's family instantly. Sitting next to him was his grandmother, "a thin leathery old woman in a cotton print dress"; she recognized the pattern: it was the same as the pattern on the chicken feed sacks in her pump house. She knew that the woman and child belonged together because of the way they sat, "kind of vacant and white-trashy, as if they would sit there until Doomsday if nobody . . . told them to get up" (194). Mrs. Turpin correctly guessed that the child's mother was a "lank faced" woman sitting separately from them. She had dirty clothes, dirty hair, and her lips were stained with snuff. She was wearing a pair of bedroom slippers and had not bothered to remove the cast from one of her eyes.

Mrs. Turpin has a rather elaborate set of prejudices against white trash: "There was nothing you could tell her about people like them that she didn't know already" (203). But O'Connor does not mock or undermine these prejudices. Instead, she shows them to be well-founded. For instance, Mrs. Turpin pegged the mother as the kind of person who would try to monopolize the conversation, and her prediction was immediately and amply confirmed (197, 204). Mrs. Turpin also knew, from personal experience, that such people could not be helped, for they had no pride. Whatever was given them would be filthy or destroyed within two weeks. This particular family turned out to be especially nasty. The mother complained that the child was vicious and mean from birth. He only became manageable when he became sick with an ulcer. The mother preferred that her son stay sick, and was at the doctor for her own maladies (204). Finally, the mother turned out to be a typical lower-class racist. She hated all blacks and wished them forcibly deported to Africa, whereas Mrs. Turpin and the upper-class lady were careful to distinguish between good and bad black people, and professed themselves unable to do without good black friends (200-1).

When Mrs. Turpin notices the only man in the room besides Claud, she notes that he is "a lean, stringy old fellow with a rusty [read: dirty] hand spread out on each knee." She immediately pegs him as white trash, which disposes her to give a suspicious interpretation to the fact that his eyes were closed "as if he were asleep or dead or pretending to be so as not to get up and offer her a seat" (192). Her suspicion is soon confirmed when the man, evidently awake, laughs at Claud's joke (202).

Other signs of lower-class standing Mrs. Turpin notes are the nurse's high stack of yellow hair and graceless way the woman in the chair next to Claud's, "hoisted herself up . . . pulled her dress free from her legs and lumbered through the door." (193). Mrs. Turpin also appraised a "red-headed youngish woman, reading one of the magazines and working a piece of chewing gum, hell for leather" as "not white trash, just common." (195)

Mrs. Turpin is also correct in her estimation of the upper-class lady. She immediately notes that she is well-dressed, in a red and grey dress with matching suede shoes. The dress and shoes harmonize with her grey hair (192, 194). Mrs. Turpin regards her appearance as "pleasant" (192) and "stylish" (193). Her outward appearance coheres well with her character. Her sense of propriety was immediately evident. Her eyes met Mrs. Turpin's and there was an immediate mutual understanding. Mrs. Turpin read her expression as saying: "if that child belonged to me, he would have some manners and move over" (192). This impression was immediately confirmed when the woman suggested, in vain, that the little boy move. The woman shows polite interest in Claud's malady, magnanimously denies that Mrs. Turpin is fat, and praises the superiority of inner dispositions to external appearances (192-3). She blushes at her daughter's rudeness (204) and is mortified by her violence (208).

In sum, O'Connor does not show a single one of Mrs. Turpin's snobbish prejudices to be false or foolish. Instead, she characterizes Mrs. Turpin's prejudices as both well-founded in past experience and useful for predicting future behavior.

Mrs. Turpin's Christian Conscience

For all of her pagan attitudes, Ruby Turpin is by conscious conviction a Protestant Christian. Mrs. Turpin's complacent assurance of her own salvation is evident from the line she supplies to complete the half-audible gospel tune playing in the waiting room: "And wona these days I know I'll we-ear a crown" (194). Later, another half-audible gospel song leads her to reflect on her charitable activities: "Mrs. Turpin didn't catch every word but she caught enough to agree with the spirit of the song and it turned her thoughts sober. To help anybody out that needed it was her philosophy of life" (202). Furthermore, Mrs. Turpin's commitment to charity transcends all distinctions of race and class: "She never spared herself when she found somebody in need, whether they were white or black, trash or decent. And of all she had to be thankful for, she was most thankful that this was so" (202-3). When dealing with white trash, Mrs. Turpin's commitment to charity even trumps her knowledge that all such help is futile: "if you gave them everything, in two weeks it would all be broken or filthy or they would have chopped it up for lightwood. She knew all this from her own experience. Help them you must, but help them you couldn't" (203).

But O'Connor uses two ironic devices to indicate that for all of her conscious convictions, Mrs. Turpin is only half a Christian. First, the half-heard gospel music is a sign that Mrs. Turpin has only half-heard the Gospel. Second, when Mrs. Turpin complains about the necessity of "buttering up niggers" to get them to work for her, the pleasant lady responds, "'Like you read out of the same book'"—showing she understood perfectly—to which Mrs. Turpin responds, "'Child, yes.'" (199). Mrs. Turpin never pauses to consider that she and her black workers do read from the same book, the Bible, and what this might imply.

Mrs. Turpin's Moment of Grace

Like Pascal, O'Connor thinks that God is hidden in the modern world, by the modern world. Like Pascal, O'Connor is in search of "traces of a hidden God." For O'Connor, God's grace is manifested in miraculous transformations of the settled order of things. But God no longer works spectacular miracles, but tiny, unobtrusive miracles. In O'Connor's stories, God's grace is primarily manifest in subtle transformations of character. Even in "Revelation," Mrs. Turpin's spectacular vision can only be received because of a prior, internal transformation of character.

The miraculous nature of these transformations of character consists in two things: their departure from settled patterns and their being occasioned by shocking acts of violence. As O'Connor writes, "in my own stories I have found that violence is strangely capable of returning my characters to reality and preparing them to accept their moment of grace. Their heads are so hard that almost nothing else will do the work."[9]

In "Revelation," the agent of God's grace is the appropriately named Mary Grace. She shares her first name with the female closest to God and Jesus; her last name needs no comment. In spite of her role in the story, Mary Grace's name seems unfit for her character, for there seems nothing holy or gracious about her person and demeanor. She is introduced as "a fat girl of eighteen or nineteen, scowling into a thick blue book . . . entitled *Human Development*" (193-4). The *Human Development* book epitomizes the secular, naturalistic approach to human nature that O'Connor found seductive in college and which she sought to combat in all her writings. Not only is Mary Grace fat and ugly, her face is "blue with acne" (194), "seared" (196), "raw complexioned" (201), "almost purple" with anger and embarrassment" (205), and "raw" (207)—features which indicate not only intense inner anger but also a hyper-sensitivity to the world, for her inner anger has burned and scraped away her "skin," her protection against the world. She is visibly, then demonstratively, then stridently irritated by the talking of others, scowling, slamming her book shut, making hideous faces, and snapping her teeth together. She seems deeply hostile to religion, for her assault is prompted by Mrs. Turpin's exclamation, "Oh thank you, Jesus, Jesus, thank you!" (206). She even defies good taste by wearing "Girl Scout shoes and heavy socks" (194-5).

The most strikingly underlined characteristic of Mary Grace, however, is her eyes. Even before she assaults Mrs. Turpin, her eyes "appeared alternately to smolder and to blaze" (196); "She looked straight in front of her, directly through Mrs. Turpin and on through the yellow curtain and the plate glass window. . . . The girl's eyes seemed lit all of a sudden with a peculiar light, an unnatural light like night road signs give" (197); "the ugly girl's eyes were fixed on Mrs. Turpin as if she had some very special reason for disliking her" (197); "every time Mrs. Turpin exchanged a look with the lady, she was aware that the ugly girl's peculiar eyes were still on her, and she had trouble bringing her attention back to the conversation" (199); "She was looking at [Mrs. Turpin] as if she had known and disliked her all her life—all of Mrs. Turpin's life, it seemed too, not just all the girl's life" (201); "All at once the ugly girl turned her lips inside out again. Her eyes were fixed like two drills on Mrs. Turpin. This time there was no mistaking that there was something urgent behind them" (203). This last incident prompts Mrs. Turpin to speak to the girl, who "continued to stare and pointedly did not answer" (204). When her mother breaks in, "the girl looked as if she would like to hurl them all through the plate glass window" (204). After Mary Grace attacks Mrs. Turpin and is subdued and sedated, her eyes become especially prominent:

> [Mrs. Turpin's] gaze was drawn slowly down to the churning face on the floor, which she could see over the doctor's shoulder.
> The girl's eyes stopped rolling and focused on her. They seemed a much lighter blue than before, as if a door that had been tightly closed behind them was now open to admit light and air.

Mrs. Turpin's head cleared and her power of motion returned. She leaned forward until she was looking directly into the fierce brilliant eyes. There was no doubt in her mind that the girl did know her, knew her in some intense and personal way, beyond time and place and condition. "What you got to say to me?" she asked hoarsely and held her breath, waiting, as for a revelation.

The girl raised her head. Her gaze locked with Mrs. Turpin's. "Go back to hell where you came from, you old wart hog," she whispered. Her voice was low but clear. Her eyes burned for a moment as if she saw with pleasure that her message has struck its target.

Mrs. Turpin sank back in her chair.

After a moment, the girl's eyes closed and she turned her head wearily to the side. (207-8)

Any other writer would attribute such behavior to a victim of demonic possession, not an instrument of divine grace. O'Connor's correspondence indicates that she saw the demonic quality of Mary Grace's actions, but that she did not conceive of her as a vehicle for the Devil: "I wasn't thinking of Mary Grace as the Devil but then the whole story just sort of happened."[10] In another letter, O'Connor indicates a genuine affection for Mary Grace. She wrote to a friend, "Maryat [Lee]'s niece asked her why I had made Mary Grace so ugly. 'Because Flannery Loves her,' said Maryat. Very perceptive girl."[11]

There is, furthermore, an element of self-portraiture in Mary Grace: "Mary Grace I found in my head, doubtless as a result of reading too much theology."[12] Mary Grace, like O'Connor's other portraits of alienated, resentful secular intellectuals, is rendered with such psychological acuity that O'Connor could only be drawing upon her own inner experience of the psychological forces that lead to such a worldview, even though she herself did not embrace it.

Finally, O'Connor's description of Mary Grace's eyes is actually more consistent with divine rather than demonic influences: "The girl's eyes stopped rolling and focused on her. They seemed a much lighter blue than before, as if a door that had been tightly closed behind them was now open to admit light and air." Light, air, and light blue are associated not with hell, but with heaven.[13] Mary Grace's mind, which was closed to the divine, was opened up to it through her righteous, violent anger. Just as Mary Grace serves as a conduit of grace for Mrs. Turpin, Mrs. Turpin serves as a conduit of grace for Mary Grace.[14]

Mrs. Turpin's reaction to Mary Grace's eyes also indicates the presence of divine rather than demonic forces. "Looking directly into the fierce brilliant eyes," Mrs. Turpin sees that "the girl did know her, knew her in some intense and personal way, beyond time and place and condition." But to know someone "beyond time and place and condition" is not possible for a mere mortal. What Mrs. Turpin glimpses through the eyes of Mary Grace is the mind of God, and she reacts appropriately, asking "What you got to say to me?" and then she "held her breath, waiting, as for a revelation."

The Revelation

Mary Grace's attack has set in motion a process of moral reflection, undermining Mrs. Turpin's smug conviction of her own salvation and her obsession with distinctions of class, opening her soul to a revelation. This transformation takes place on a number of levels.

First, the attack heightens Mrs. Turpin's sense of her own vulnerability to suffering and death. Suffering and death, however, are no respecters of persons. They tend to erase all distinctions of class. This theme appears early in the story. When Mrs. Turpin lays in bed at night, categorizing and ranking people, she finds that her neat classificatory system is strained by certain exceptions. The system collapses, however, when she contemplates the great equalizer, death: "Usually by the time she had fallen asleep all the classes of people were moiling and roiling around in her head, and she would dream they were all crammed together in a box car being ridden off to be put in a gas oven" (196).

This heightened sense of vulnerability is apparent when the Turpins return home after the attack. Mrs. Turpin "gripped the window ledge and looked out suspiciously" at their very proper and well-maintained house: "their small yellow frame house, with its little flower beds spread our around it like a fancy apron, sat primly in its accustomed place between two giant hickory trees. She would not have been startled to see a burnt wound between two blackened chimneys" (209). That evening, she had the same experience as she watched Claud driving the black workers home: "A tiny truck, Claud's, appeared on the highway, heading rapidly out of sight. Its gears scraped thinly. It looked like a child's toy. At any moment a bigger truck might smash into it and scatter Claud's and the niggers' brains all over the road" (217).

Second, Mrs. Turpin's need to discuss the attack forces her to confront the limitations on frank communication imposed by the Southern class structure. When Mrs. Turpin takes water to the black women employed to pick her cotton, one of them asks "in a solicitous voice" about the bruise over her eye where she was struck by the book (211). Under normal circumstances, Mrs. Turpin would feel socially constrained from talking frankly to her black workers, but her desire to work through her traumatic experience and maybe to reassure herself of her position in the world leads her to cross this boundary. Looking around to make sure that her husband is gone, Mrs. Turpin reported the assault and what Mary Grace had said. But her attempt at frankness was not responded to in kind. Instead, she received only inane flattery, and "Mrs. Turpin knew just exactly how much Negro flattery was worth and it added to her rage" (213). Mrs. Turpin is angered when her social inferiors repay her magnanimous condescension with insincere and patronizing flattery. Magnanimous irony preserves the boundaries between people by papering them over with insincerity and good manners. It is only the spirit of charity that allows people to communicate with open-hearted frankness across the divisions of race and class.

Third, Mrs. Turpin is driven to an angry confrontation with God himself because of the contradiction between two propositions she believes to be true: that she is Ruby Turpin, a respectable, church-going woman whose salvation is assured, and that she is an old wart hog from hell:

> "I am not," she said tearfully, "a wart hog. From hell." But the denial had no force. The girl's eyes and her words, even the tone of her voice, low but clear, directed only to her, brooked no repudiation. She had been singled out for the message, though there was trash in the room to whom it might justly have been applied. . . . The message had been given to Ruby Turpin, a respectable, hardworking, church-going woman. The tears dried. Her eyes began to burn instead with wrath. (210)

Later that evening, again after furtively determining that Claud has gone, she stands before setting sun, hosing off pigs in her pig parlor, and vents her wrath at God himself: "'What do you send me a message like that for?' she said in a low fierce voice, barely above a whisper but with the force of a shout in its concentrated fury. 'How am I a hog and me both? How am I saved and from hell too?'" (215). As Mrs. Turpin speaks, she uses her hose to torment her pigs. Once, when she shakes her fist at God, Satan surges up momentarily as "a watery snake . . . in the air" (216).

God's half of the dialogue is represented by the descending sun; it is his own face, his own eye: "The sun was behind the wood, very red, looking over the paling of trees like a farmer inspecting his own hogs"—and tormenting one of them, Ruby Turpin herself (215). After each verbal assault by Mrs. Turpin, the sun moves and the landscape changes its aspect, as if in dialogue with her. These passages contain some of O'Connor's best writing. No summary can do them justice.

> In the deepening light everything was taking on a mysterious hue. The pasture was growing a peculiar glassy green and the streak of highway had turned lavender. She braced herself for the final assault and this time her voice rolled out over the pasture. "Come on," she yelled, "call me a hog! Call me a hog again. From hell. Call me a wart hog from hell. Put that bottom rail on top. There'll still be a top and a bottom!"
>
> A garbled echo returned to her.
>
> A final surge of fury shook her and she roared, "Who do you think you are?"
>
> The color of everything, field and crimson sky, burned for a moment with a transparent intensity. The question carried over the pasture and across the highway and the cotton field and returned to her clearly like an answer from beyond the wood.
>
> She opened her mouth, but no sound came out of it. (216-17)

The drama here is rich. Mrs. Turpin defends her obsession with class and status with the old Southern analogy of the split rail fence. One can switch the position of the rails, but by the very nature of the fence there will still be a top and bottom. Likewise, one can switch the positions of the social classes, but by the very nature of society there will still be a hierarchy. She addresses this challenge to God, across the pasture in the direction of the setting sun. And, as if it were God's reply, a garbled echo comes rolling back over the pasture. Perhaps goaded by this reply, Mrs. Turpin hurls her final challenge to God: "Who do you think you are?" Who is God to overturn the neat, orderly, smug, complacent life of Ruby Turpin? Who is God to challenge the social mores of the American South? This time the echo comes back clearly, the question returned to its sender: "Who do you think you are?" Was it God or the Southern gentry who laid the foundations of the world? Mrs. Turpin opens her mouth, but for once she has nothing to say, for she sees that no answer is possible.

Mrs. Turpin's mind has finally been opened to a revelation. But before it arrives, O'Connor narrates a small and touching detail. Mrs. Turpin pauses in her struggle with God long enough to make sure that Claud returns safely after driving their black workers home. Then she takes on an attitude of prayer and acquiescence to the will of God, whose life-giving charity is refracted toward her from the lowly piglets, whom she had seen as "idiot children" and tormented with the watery snakes from her hose. She was

> like a monumental statue coming to life, she bent her head slowly and gazed, as if through the very heart of mystery, down into the pig parlor at the hogs. They had settled all in one corner around the old sow who was grunting softly. A red glow suffused them. They appeared to pant with a secret life.
>
> Until the sun slipped finally behind the tree line, Mrs. Turpin remained there with her gaze bent to them as if she were absorbing some abysmal life-giving knowledge. At last she lifted her head. There was only a purple streak in the sky, cutting through a field of crimson and leading, like an extension of the highway, into the descending dusk. She raised her hands from the side of the pen in a gesture hieratic and profound. A visionary light settled in her eyes. She saw the streak as a vast swinging bridge extending upward from the earth through a field of living fire. Upon it a vast horde of souls were rumbling toward heaven. There were whole companies of white-trash, clean for the first time in their lives, and bands of black niggers in white robes, and battalions of freaks and lunatics shouting and clapping and leaping like frogs. And bringing up the end of the procession was a tribe of people whom she recognized at once as those who, like herself and Claud, had always had a little of everything and the God-given wit to use it right. She leaned forward to observe them closer. They were marching behind the others with great dignity, accountable as they had always been for good order and common sense and respectable behavior. They alone were on key. Yet she could see by their shocked and altered faces that even their virtues were being burned away. She lowered her hands and gripped the rail of the hog pen, her eyes small but fixed unblinkingly on what lay ahead. (217-18)

In a letter, O'Connor describes this vision as "purgatorial."[15] Whatever its provenance, its meaning is clear: from the point of view of God, all of the distinctions of race and class Mrs. Turpin clings to are flattened out. It is only by seeing herself and human affairs from this point of view that she can open herself to the action of charity, God's melting, transgressive, all-penetrating love.

The Moral of the Story

Is there a moral to "Revelation," over and above showing the conflict between charity and magnanimity in the mind of Ruby Turpin and in Western culture as a whole? O'Connor does show sympathy toward both charity and magnanimity. Thus, one might wonder if O'Connor thinks that they are necessarily in conflict. In closing, let us consider a case for the thesis that O'Connor thought that charity and magnanimity, equal human dignity and social hierarchy, could ultimately exist in harmony.

Flannery O'Connor was a Christian, an orthodox Catholic who accepted the philosophical theology of St. Thomas Aquinas; yet, O'Connor arrived at Thomism by a different path than did Aquinas. Aquinas begins the *Summa Contra Gentiles*, his apologetic work against the gentiles of his time, with epistemological arguments about faith and reason and natural theological proofs of the existence of God. O'Connor too wrote with an apologetic intent, but she begins her apologia against the gentiles of our time with an account of the miseries and mysteries of the human condition that lead us to look above and beyond it for meaning and salvation. O'Connor's account of the human condition draws upon such Christian humanists as Augustine and Pascal and upon modern existentialism. This fusion of Thomism and Christian existentialism can, moreover, be glimpsed in her stories, but only if one reads between the lines.

O'Connor frequently generates the conflicts that drive her stories from the deformations of consciousness that arise from a fundamental misunderstanding of the human condition. As a Christian humanist, O'Connor believes that man occupies a middle position in the cosmos. Neither beast nor god, neither wholly material nor wholly spiritual, neither fully immanent nor fully transcendent, neither entirely ignorant of salvation nor entirely certain of it, man is instead stretched between these poles and participates in both extremes. The human condition defies the logical either-ors of traditional metaphysical dualism and can only be captured in the paradoxical language of "both-and."

To own up to his paradoxical and unstable condition, man must be a tightrope walker on a quavering strand between two poles. He must maintain his balance and master the anxieties that might lead him to retreat to one pole or another. When man retreats to the pole of transcendence, he pretends to certitude about divine things and proclaims himself a prophet, an angel, or even a god, thus falling into the ancient temptation and heresy of Gnosticism. When man retreats to the pole of immanence, he feigns a skeptical indifference to divine matters and proclaims himself merely a clever animal, a hunk of matter or of meat who needs a dose of therapy or social engineering to overcome his delusions of transcendence, thus falling into the error of naturalism and atheism.

Since neither gnosticism nor atheism is true, neither can be fully satisfying to a human being. After a while, each position begins to chafe, leading sensitive souls to question it and eventually to abandon it. But, so long as truth about man's middling position is unknown, there will be a tendency to bounce back and forth between gnosticism and naturalism. These two extremes are often represented today, on the one hand, by uncompromising religious enthusiasts advancing theocratic agendas, and, on the other hand, by zealous secularists, determined to expurgate all traces of public—and if possible, private—faith and to force man into a procrustean "harmony" with nonhuman, indeed subhuman, nature.

This pattern is present in O'Connor's best novel, *Wise Blood*, in which Hazel Motes swings from a worldly, atheistic naturalism, which is based upon the evidence of his own two eyes, to an anti-worldly, spiritualistic gnosticism, in which he blinds himself to this world in order to open his mind to something higher. In O'Connor's most famous short story, "A Good Man is Hard to Find," the Misfit is also trapped in the "either-or" of naturalism versus gnosticism. The Misfit thinks that the Bible presents man with a choice: Either give up one's Earthly life to follow Jesus, or embrace Earthly life, which is bereft of morality and full of "nothing but meanness." The absent middle is the possibility that Earthly life itself can be sanctified. The Misfit decides on his life of meanness because he thinks that we either know the truth of Christianity or we don't. We know it with certitude, based on the evidence of the senses. And if we do not have the evidence of the senses, then we are certain that we do not know it. The Misfit, because he did not witness the death and resurrection of Jesus, is an atheist. What he leaves out, however, is the possibility of a middle state between certitude and ignorance: faith.

In "Revelation," the gnostic pole is represented by the secular egalitarianism of Mary Grace, who wishes to burn away the hierarchies of the world in the fires of resentment and violence. This gnosticism is false, because it denies the differentiation and hierarchy of natural kinds found in all created beings. Mrs. Turpin's vision cannot be called gnostic, for it does not deny hierarchy as such, but merely denies its ultimate importance from the point of view of divine grace.

The closest thing to purely naturalistic perspective on hierarchy is represented by the white trash mother, with her crude and violent barnyard racism, unmitigated by either charity or magnanimity.[16] This naturalism is false, because it denies the possibility of seeing beyond the differentiation and hierarchy of natural kinds by imagining the created world as seen by God.

In short, in "Revelation" the gnostic pole is represented by grace without hierarchy. The naturalist pole is represented by hierarchy without grace. The absent middle, therefore, would be hierarchy infused with grace. And this is precisely the position of Aquinas, the position one would expect O'Connor to embrace. In the Questions on Charity in his *Summa Theologica* (IIa IIae, QQ 23-46), Aquinas makes clear that he regards certain hierarchies and preferences as entirely natural, such as social hierarchies and the preferences we have for friends and family over strangers, fellow countrymen over foreigners, etc. Aquinas also makes clear that the operation of charity does not erase these natural hierarchies and preferences, but instead flows through them, placing such distinctions in their proper, i.e., subordinate metaphysical and moral position. As Robert Sokolowski writes:

although Christian belief may emphasize the common dignity of all men as created and loved by God, it does not reduce to insignificance the many differences
that exist among them, nor does it imply that all people should be treated exactly
alike: there remain differences between the good and the bad, the talented and the
untalented, the strong and the weak, leaders and followers, and friends and
strangers, and such differences must be taken into account when we act, even
though they are seen against as setting in which the common humanity of all men
is made more vivid. Christian belief does not diminish, for example, the public
honor due to virtue, and it obviously does not imply that public responsibility
should be given to the ignorant or the incompetent instead of to those who are
suited for it. Such discriminations are not to be eliminated when Christians emphasize the common dignity of all men before God.[17]

This Thomistic perspective encompasses both the pagan ethic of magnanimity and the Christian ethic of charity, without reducing one to the other or eliminating the vital tension between them. It allows one to appreciate the genuine
moral intelligence of paganism's proud pursuit of virtue and its sense of the conventional and natural hierarchies that divide men, yet it places these within the
ultimate context of the order of grace. It preserves both man's rootedness in nature and his openness to the divine.

Notes

1. Flannery O'Connor, "Revelation," in her *Everything that Rises Must Converge*
(New York: Farrar, Straus, and Giroux, 1964), page numbers cited parenthetically in text.
2. Even though Mrs. Turpin places blacks and white trash on the same social level,
she regards some blacks as good but all white trash as bad; nonetheless, she cannot be
unaware that being white is a social advantage even for white trash.
3. Gilbert H. Muller, *Nightmares and Visions: Flannery O'Connor and the Catholic
Grotesque* (Athens: University of Georgia Press, 1972), 47.
4. Dorothy Walters, *Flannery O'Connor* (Boston: Twayne, 1973), 108-9.
5. Carol Shloss, *Flannery O'Connor's Dark Comedies: The Limits of Inference* (Baton Rouge: Louisiana State University Press, 1980), 112-13.
6. Flannery O'Connor, *The Habit of Being: Letters*, ed. Sally Fitzgerald (New York:
Farrar, Straus, and Giroux, 1979), 552.
7. O'Connor, *The Habit of Being*, 554.
8. O'Connor, *The Habit of Being*, 577.
9. O'Connor, "On Her Own Work," in *Mystery and Manners: Occasional Prose*, ed.
Sally and Robert Fitzgerald (New York: Farrar, Straus and Giroux, 1969), 112.
10. O'Connor, *The Habit of Being*, 552.
11. O'Connor, *The Habit of Being*, 578.
12. O'Connor, *The Habit of Being*, 579.
13. In *Wise Blood*, the patrolman who deprives Hazel Motes of his car (which represents Haze's deluded desire to make the human condition absolute and self-contained) is
also an agent of divine grace. He is described as having "eyes the color of clear fresh ice"
(Flannery O'Connor, *Wise Blood* [New York: Harcourt, Brace, 1952], 208).
14. The same relationship holds between the grandmother and the Misfit in
O'Connor's "A Good Man is Hard to Find," in *A Good Man is Hard to Find and Other*

Stories (New York: Harcourt, Brace, 1955). See O'Connor's "On Her Own Work," *Mystery and Manners*, 111-13.

15. O'Connor, *The Habit of Being*, 577.

16. It would seem, then, that even pagan magnanimity is something more than natural; perhaps it is elevated by its orientation toward superlative virtue.

17. Robert Sokolowski, *The God of Faith and Reason: Foundations of Christian Theology* (Washington, D.C.: The Catholic University of America Press, 1995), 84.

Index

About the Authors

J. Patrick Dobel is professor and associate dean of the Daniel J. Evans School of Public Affairs at the University of Washington, as well as Adjunct Professor of Political Science. He has written numerous articles on public ethics along with the books, *Compromise and Political Action: Political Morality in Liberal and Democratic Life* and *Public Integrity*. The National Academy of Management recently awarded him a prize for best article on public management. He has trained and consulted with numerous public and nonprofit institutions on issues of management, leadership, and ethics. He has chaired several public committees, helped write numerous ethics codes, and, most recently, chaired the King County Washington Board of Ethics.

Henry T. Edmondson III is professor of political science and public administration at Georgia College & State University where he is also Director of the European Government and Culture Study Abroad Program. He writes in the areas of administrative ethics, ethics and literature, and educational philosophy. His articles have appeared in the *Political Science Reviewer*, *Public Integrity*, *PS: Political Science*, and other journals and books.

Gregory R. Johnson is a phiiosopher in "private practice" in Atlanta. In addition to consulting with individuals and institutions, he runs The Invisible College, a private adult education organization that teaches courses on topics in philosophy, psychology, and literature. He is the author of articles on such thinkers as Aristotle, Rousseau, Kant, Swedenborg, Heidegger, Gadamer, Hayek, Isaiah Berlin, and Ayn Rand, as well as topics in moral and political philosophy. He can be reached at *gregoryrjohnson@mindspring.com*.

Peter Kalkavage is a tutor at St. John's College in Annapolis, Maryland. He has taught in the all-required liberal arts program of St. John's since 1977 and is the author of various essays and articles on Plato, Dante and Hegel. He is the co-translator (with Eva Brann and Eric Salem) of Plato's *Sophist* and *Phaedo* for Focus Philosophical Library and has recently translated the *Timaeus*, also for Focus Press. His other essays on Dante are *Dante and Ulysses: A Reading of Inferno 26* and *Peter of the Vine: The Perversion of Faith in Inferno 13* (both published in the *St. John's Review*).

Judith Lee Kissell lectures both nationally and internationally on issues in medical ethics and has published broadly in that field. She has taught medical ethics at Georgetown University Medical School, where she served as Clinical

Scholar at the Center for Clinical Bioethics. She is currently assistant professor, Center for Health Policy and Ethics, Creighton University, Omaha, Nebraska.

Peter Augustine Lawler is professor of government and Director of the Honors Program at Berry College. Among his many and diverse publications is *Postmodernism Rightly Understood: The Return to Realism in American Thought.*

Alan Levine is assistant professor in the Department of Government in the School of Public Affairs at American University. He edited *Early Modern Skepticism and the Origins of Toleration* (Lexington Books, 1999) and has written on Montaigne and Achebe.

Daniel J. Mahoney is associate professor of political science at Assumption College. He is the author of *The Liberal Political Science of Raymond Aron* (1992) and *De Gaulle: Statesmanship, Grandeur, and Modern Democracy* (1996) and the editor of *Modern Liberty and its Discontents by Pierre Manent* (1998). He is presently completing a book on Aleksandr Solzhenitsyn. His writings have appeared in *The National Interest, First Things, The New Criterion,* and *Perspectives on Political Science,* among other journals.

Will Morrisey is Executive Director of the Monmouth County Historical Commission and a longtime assistant editor of *Interpretation: A Journal of Political Philosophy.* He has published five books: *Reflections on De Gaulle: Political Founding in Modernity (1983); Reflections on Malraux: Cultural Founding in Modernity* (1984); *Our Culture "Left" or "Right": Litterateurs Confront Nihilism* (1992); *Culture in the Commercial Republic* (1996); and *A Political Approach to Pacifism* (1996). He has written for *The New York Times, The Jerusalem Post,* and *The Washington Times.* His scholarly articles and book reviews have appeared in *The American Political Science Review, Philosophy and Literature, Book Forum, The Political Science Reviewer, This World,* and *The St. John's Review.*

Pádraig Ó Gormaile is professor of French and head of the French Department at the National University of Ireland, Galway. A graduate of Maynooth College, he has published on literature and Christian spirituality and in the area of Quebec Studies. His Ph.D. (University of Toulouse, France) was the first doctoral thesis on the work of the French writer of Christian inspiration, Jean Sulivan (1913-1980), and he is co-editor of *Litterature et sources spirituelles: l'oeuvre de Jean Sulivan* (Association des amis de Jean Sulivan, Paris, 1999). He has taught annual courses on Rabelais and Pascal since 1988. He has been Visiting Professor of French and Comparative Literature at the Universite catholique de Louvain (Belgium) since 1994.

Paul Peterson is a professor in the Department of Politics at Coastal Carolina University, where he teaches courses in American government and political philosophy. He has written numerous essays, reviews, and professional papers on American politics and American political thought. He has published articles and reviews in such journals as *Publius: The Journal of Federalism, The Review of Politics, The Political Science Reviewer,* and *The American Political Science Review.*

Michael Platt has taught literature, political science, and philosophy in the United States at Dartmouth and the University of Dallas, where he directed the literature part of the Philosophic Institute, and abroad, at the University of Heidelberg. His *Rome and Romans According to Shakespeare* first appeared in 1976 (second edition: University Press of America, 1982) and his *Seven Wonders of Shakespeare* will appear as part of Rowman & Littlefield's Lexington series in 2000. He has also written for the *Journal of Value Inquiry*, *Nietzsche Studien*, and *Interpretation: Journal of Political Philosophy*. Other essays may be found on the Claremont Institute for Statesmanship website http://www.claremont.org. Dr. Platt teaches regularly at George Wythe College and in the Spring of 2000 lectured on the American Founding at the International Theological Institute in Gaming, Austria.

Robert M. Schaefer is chairman of the Department of Social and Behavioral Sciences and associate professor of political science, at the University of Mobile. He is coeditor of three books, including *American Political Rhetoric* (third edition: Rowman & Littlefield Publishers, Inc).

James Seaton is a professor in the Department of English at Michigan State University, where he teaches courses in American culture and criticism, the history of criticism, and comparative literature. His most recent book is *Cultural Conservatism, Political Liberalism* (Ann Arbor: University of Michigan Press, 1996). His essays and reviews have appeared in *The Hudson Review*, *The American Scholar*, *First Things*, *New Oxford Review*, *Yale Journal of Law and the Humanities*, *Academic Questions*, *Humanitas*, *The Journal of the History of Ideas*, *The Wall Street Journal*, and many other publications. He is married to the playwright Sandra Seaton.

Juan José Sendín Vinagre is professor of Spanish literature at the University of San Pablo, C.E.U., Spain. He teaches in the area of, and has published articles and reviews on, the Golden Age of Spanish literature. He was a member of the Spanish team of scholars at the University of Valladolid, Spain, that produced the CD-ROM, *El ingenioso hidalgo don Quijote de la Mancha* (1996), the prodigious compilation of commentary and scholarship on Cervantes' novel *Don Quixote*.